THE FIRST LINCOLN CAMPAIGN

The
First Lincoln Campaign

By

REINHARD H. LUTHIN
Columbia University

GLOUCESTER, MASS.
PETER SMITH
1964

E
440
.L85
1964

57801

To the Memory of My Mother
MARGARET COLLINS LUTHIN

Preface

IT IS DIFFICULT, perhaps impossible, to conceive of the origins of the American Civil War without immediately bringing to mind the national victory of the Republican party in 1860. Whether South Carolina led the southern states out of the Union because of Abraham Lincoln's election to the presidency or whether the Great Emancipator's triumph gave the cotton states the pretext for leaving a Union which they wanted to forsake in any event, will probably remain a controversy among historians. Nevertheless many students of the period are agreed that without Lincoln's victory in November 1860 war between the sections would not have been precipitated in the following April, if indeed this greatest of American tragedies (which still has its repercussions to-day) would have occurred at all. Several scholars of the ante-bellum period have even become highly critical of Lincoln's policy toward the "border slave" states during the critical weeks preceding the firing on Fort Sumter. Others have suggested that slavery, because of its unprofitableness and the unsuitability of the soil in the West to unsalaried Negro labor, would have expired by the very economic unsoundness of the slave-plantation system—that slavery became a cause of bloody strife because it was made a pawn on the national political chessboard by both northern and southern extremists. Accordingly, Lincoln's election to the presidency—a direct cause of the war between the states—assumes more significance than perhaps any American national election; the fight for the White House in 1860 was no mere political contest. It is with this campaign, as seen through the focus of the Republican leaders and their organization and culminating in Lincoln's victory, that this volume is concerned.

The present author is above all under obligation to Dean Harry J. Carman and Professor Allan Nevins, of Columbia University, under whose joint direction this study has been prepared. To Dean Carman and Professor Nevins must go much of the credit for whatever merit that this volume might contain.

Professor Charles C. Tansill, of Georgetown University, and Professor Ollinger Crenshaw, of Washington and Lee University, have given freely of their profound knowledge of historiography. My colleague, Dr. George D. Crothers of Columbia University, has been of great aid in improving the literary style. The author wishes also to thank certain friends and colleagues in the Department of History of Columbia University for their active interest in the work: Professor J. Bartlet Brebner, Professor Henry Steele Commager, Professor John Allen Krout, Professor Jacques Barzun, Professor Dwight C. Miner, Dr. Cornwell B. Rogers, Dr. Eugene O. Golob, and Dr. Paul H. Beik. Access to source material was made possible by those distinguished Lincoln scholars: Professor James G. Randall of the University of Illinois, Dr. Harry E. Pratt of Ball State Teachers College, Dr. Paul M. Angle of the Illinois State Historical Library, and Dr. Louis A. Warren of the Lincoln National Life Foundation, Fort Wayne, Indiana. Miss Margaret Carscadden, Miss Mary A. Reilly, Miss Carolyn Robinson, Miss Clotilde Luthin, Miss Hildegard Luthin, and Mr. Hugh Harvey have performed noble service in preparing the manuscript for the press.

R. H. L.

Columbia University
June, 1944.

Contents

I   The Rise of a New Political Power   3

II   Chieftain of the Anti-Slavery Whigs   23

III   Champion of the Free Democracy   36

IV   A Pillar of Conservatism   51

V   An Anti-Nebraska Whig of the Prairies   69

VI   A Conservative Protectionist   92

VII   Other Hopefuls   106

VIII   Democratic Dissension   120

IX   The Triumph of Availability   136

X   Organizing for Victory   168

XI   The Safe States   178

XII   The Doubtful States   193

XIII   New York—and the Decision   210

XIV   Summing Up   220

Notes   229

Bibliography   287

Index   309

THE FIRST LINCOLN CAMPAIGN

CHAPTER ONE

The Rise of a New Political Power

THE AMERICAN POLITICAL SCENE at the beginning of the year 1856 was changing and confused. Veteran leaders were passing from the stage; old combinations were declining; and new leaders, armed with new phrases and catchwords, were elbowing their way to the fore. The Whig party had largely disappeared. The American party (Know-Nothings) were at the height of their ephemeral power. And a presidential election was approaching. At this moment, the new Republican party, having recently appeared from the wings, assumed the rôle of a protagonist and pushed to the center of the stage.

On February 22, 1856, Republican leaders—comprising a curious agglomeration of political malcontents, Abolitionists, Free Soilers, disgruntled Democrats, Whigs, German-Americans, and Know-Nothings—met at Pittsburgh and planned a national nominating convention for June.[1] On that same day, Washington's Birthday, the American party, convening in Philadelphia, split on the slavery issue. Some of the nativistic delegates bolted and sent word to the Republicans in Pittsburgh: "The American party is no longer a unit. The national council has gone to pieces. Raise the Republican banner. The North Americans are with you." [2]

The Republicans had yet to win wide popular support. Their anti-slavery program was anathema to many in the North. The Republican leaders undertook to mould the public mind. A propaganda machine was developed. Pamphlets poured from the press. Congressmen and Senators franked literally thousands of printed speeches and campaign leaflets.[3] Newspapers were enlisted in the cause.[4]

Know-Nothings, under the spell of the anti-slavery crusade, forgot their anti-Catholic, anti-immigrant creed and now decided to "take care of the Dutch and Irish after the nigger question is settled." [5]

Before the Republican convention met in June there ocurred two events which party strategists used to exacerbate the hatred of slavocracy in the North. The Kansas imbroglio reached a new crisis, and the South Carolina Congressman, Preston S. Brooks, assaulted Massachusetts' anti-slavery Senator Charles Sumner. One Republican leader observed: "The attack upon Mr. Sumner and the news from Kansas has engrossed the public mind to the exclusion of almost every other subject." [6] The Republican press was glutted with graphic tales of both subjects. The Republican party could hardly have grown so rapidly had it not been for Kansas and Brooks.[7]

In the midst of this agitation the Republican national convention met in Philadelphia on June 17, 1856. Veteran anti-slavery leaders were passed over and the colorful explorer, Colonel John C. Frémont, was nominated Republican candidate for President. The party platform opposed the extension of slavery in the territories. The Democrats nominated James Buchanan of Pennsylvania; and the American party named ex-President Millard Fillmore as their standard-bearer on a conservative, anti-sectional platform.

In the elections, Buchanan triumphed. But Frémont carried the entire North except Pennsylvania, New Jersey, Indiana, Illinois, and California. The Republicans, although defeated, were jubilant.[8] One leader exulted: "The Republicans are settling on the conviction that they have suffered a victorious defeat. They have not got a President but they have what is better, a North." [9] Another was overjoyed at the "immensity" of the Republican showing over a disciplined Democratic party with the federal patronage at its disposal.[10]

The sectional passions aroused by the campaign were a deep concern to President-elect Buchanan, who felt that the Republicans were doing the nation irreparable harm by agitating the slavery question.[11] He looked to a decision from the Supreme Court that would settle the status of slavery in the territories.[12] While Buchanan prepared for his inauguration, the case of Dred Scott, which had begun in the Missouri courts, lay on the Supreme Court docket. A majority of the Court had agreed to dispose of the litigation without raising the delicate questions of the lower court's jurisdiction, of the Negro's citizenship, or of the Missouri Compromise. Justices McLean and Curtis, however, anxious to demonstrate their anti-slavery views for personal and political reasons, declared their intention of filing dissenting opinions. Their insistence on reviewing the status of slaves in the territories forced the other judges to review the whole question of the constitutionality of the Missouri Compromise.

Meanwhile Buchanan, anxious for a decision that would settle the controversy in the territories, wrote to one of the judges, Catron, to ascertain whether a decision on the Dred Scott case might be expected before March 4. The President-elect emphasized the need for strong language (without, of course, advising what the decision should be). In his inaugural speech of March 4, Buchanan referred to the forthcoming decision and expressed his intention to submit to the Court's ruling, "whatever this may be." Two days later, Chief Justice Roger B. Taney delivered the majority opinion of the Court: that a Negro was not a citizen, and that the Missouri Compromise was unconstitutional.[13]

The Republicans made good propaganda of Taney's opinion.[14] The Court's effort to transform the problem of slavery in the territories into a question of cold jurisprudence was a failure. Republicans, Free-Soil Democrats, Abolitionists, and southern hotspurs had made it a burning issue too long.

The most vindictive attack made on the Dred Scott decision, and on the integrity of the Court itself, was made by William H. Seward of New York, Republican leader in the Senate. Whether or not Seward knew of Buchanan's correspondence with Justice Catron is uncertain; but he seized on the passage in Buchanan's inaugural message to charge the President with conspiring with the Supreme Court to render a pro-slavery decision.[15] Thus the story that the Court was hand-in-glove with the Slavocracy entered history. Buchanan, while guilty of a breach of propriety in communicating with Catron on the Dred Scott matter, was not guilty of conspiring with them to render a pro-slavery opinion.[16] But Buchanan had given the opposition party much ammunition. Ohio's Republican governor, Salmon P. Chase, wrote: "Mr. Buchanan's administration thus far has done a good deal for us. The decision in the Dred Scott case was one of its first fruits." [17]

Although Kansas and the Dred Scott decision were strong moral issues for the Republicans, the sectionalism upon which the Republican party rested would not have been so intense had not the North and South differed over legislation of a material nature to be secured from the Federal Government. There arose questions of transportation, communication, trade, land, and foreign relations that drove the wedge deeper between the two sections.

The subsidy awarded by Congress to Cyrus W. Field's project for a trans-Atlantic telegraph cable, for example, was a force that brewed animosity between North and South. The British Parliament had offered an annual subsidy of £14,000, provided the United States Government did the same and in December 1856 Field had enlisted the aid of Congress in his enterprise.[18] The influential Chamber of Commerce of the State of New York supported him.[19] Field enlisted lobbyists.[20]

In January, 1857, Seward sponsored a bill in the Senate providing for an annual grant of $70,000 and the use of a naval vessel in laying the cable, on condition that the British do the same. Seward's bill also provided that the government was to enjoy the privilege of sending telegraph messages over the cable. Southerners, such as Senator Robert Toombs, of Georgia, assailed the proposal because such legislation favored New York and Northern speculators.[21] The South's hostility was revealed in the Senate's vote on the bill, which passed. Of the 29 "ayes," 20 were from Northern states and only 9 from slave states. Of these 9 "ayes" from below the Mason and Dixon line, 7 came from seacoast slave states whose oceanic trade with Europe or Latin America would be benefited by the cable. Of the 18 "nays," all except three came from slave states. Every Republican present, save one, cast an affirmative vote.[22] The House returned the bill to the Senate with minor amendments, and slave-state Senators seized the opportunity to launch a new attack.[23] Despite southern opposition, the subsidy for the Atlantic telegraph passed both houses of Congress and was signed by President Franklin Pierce.[24]

The controversy over the tariff also played its part in provoking sectionalism between North and South. Southern advocates of secession, portraying the protective tariff as an iniquitous system which benefited the North and impoverished the South, found in it their most potent propaganda, especially in South Carolina.[25]

Most southerners, motivated by the belief that a protective tariff would benefit northern manufacturing interests alone, upheld a low tariff.[26] When the Democratic administration of President James K. Polk, a Tennesseean, came into office, Congress superseded the protective tariff of 1842 with the low "Walker" act of 1846. This tariff provided for only a 30 per cent duty on foreign iron and wool.[27]

From 1846 to 1859 the protectionists were usually at the mercy of the low-tariff and free-trade men. The Democrats in power kept the rates down.

In 1857 the Democratic-dominated House of Representatives passed a bill reducing duties on certain commodities and placing others on the "free" list. When it reached the Senate, Robert M. T. Hunter, Democrat of Virginia, sponsored a substitute measure, which became the basis of the Tariff of 1857, making a general *reduction* of *all* duties contained in the Walker act.[28] The fight against Hunter's proposal was led by Republicans.[29] The Republican fight was futile, for the southern Senators were supported by northern Democrats. The Senate approved Hunter's proposal. Not a single slave-state Senator joined the Republicans in voting against it.[30]

No sooner had the new tariff passed Congress than the panic of 1857 came.[31] Manufacturing interests in Pennsylvania and other northern states, inspired by Republican politicians, found it convenient to lay the nation's economic ills at the door of the low tariff.[32] Demands for higher rates were heard. Thus the Republican party (which had lost the Presidential election of 1856 by failure to carry Pennsylvania) was provided with a magnificent issue. In August, 1859, one anti-Democratic leader wrote to Vermont's Republican Congressman Justin S. Morrill: "We *must pass* a bill in the H. R. & force the Senate to accept or defeat it. It is sound policy—a necessity—nay more—honesty. . . . Pass it in one shape or another it ought to be." [33] In May, 1860, Morrill sponsored a tariff bill in the House that raised the rates to the old Walker levels. The free states gave only fourteen votes against Morrill's bill, the slave states but eight in favor of it.

The Morrill measure was sponsored by the Republicans primarily to attract votes in Pennsylvania, New Jersey and other regions with protectionist leanings. The wool rates were intended to be raised in order to lure the West. Western Republicans, realizing that Pennsylvania must be carried in 1860 if victory were to crown their party, were willing to accept a protective-tariff. In addition, there were isolated sections in the West whose economy, based partly on minerals and agricultural products, would be benefited by the exclusion of incoming European products.[34] Western Republicans began "selling" protectionism to their section: In March (1860) the Republican candidate for Lieutenant-Governor of agrarian Indiana, Oliver P. Morton, impressed upon his followers that a high tariff would "afford just encouragement and protection to the agricultural and manufacturing interests." [35] The widely read Chicago *Press & Tribune* preached the same message; [36] this journal was confident that the coming National Convention would adopt a tariff plank that would be "satisfactory alike to Pennsylvania and Illinois, to Massachusetts and Minnesota." [37] The latest research establishes that the Republicans adopted protectionism primarily to cater to Pennsylvania. [38]

The breach between the sections was further widened when the Republican party, aware of the importance of the western vote, [39] embraced the old Whig program for internal improvements. The West had consistently championed this program and the national Democratic party had always opposed it. [40] The Democrats' opposition to rivers-and-harbors appropriations had inspired the Republicans to advocate the cause; moreover, the Whigs in the Republican party were only too happy to resurrect their ancient doctrine. Consequently, the Republican national platform of 1856 declared in favor of federal subsidies for improving rivers and harbors. [41] Republican orators preached that, with Frémont as President, rivers would be made more navigable, harbors better developed, and the needless loss of life from shipwrecks on Lake Michigan ended. Republicans asserted that their party stood for "free harbors" as well as "free soil, free labor, and Frémont." [42]

The Great Lakes country was particularly anxious for federal aid to improve transportation on the inland seas. Congressmen John Wentworth of Chicago, Schuyler Colfax of South Bend, and Senator Zachariah Chandler, from the Great Lake port of Detroit, were the most militant crusaders for the cause in Congress. [43] In 1856 the issue of improvements aided in electing Republican Congressmen from the northern counties of Illinois, where lake shipping was a vital interest. Indeed, the Illinois Republican platform of 1858 "demanded" internal improvements. [44]

The campaign of 1856 had hardly closed when the issue was raised again. In December, George Pugh, senator from Ohio, introduced a bill appropriating $70,000 for a survey of the Ohio River and its principal tributaries. When the Senate considered the matter, a motion to table Pugh's proposal was lost 18 to 24, all but one of the 18 votes coming from the slaveholding states. Senator Stephen Adams of Mississippi ironically proposed to extend the provisions of the bill to include the Alabama and Tombigbee rivers. [45] The

Republicans had definitely adopted as their own the principle of internal improvements.

In the first session of the Thirty-fifth Congress, Senator Chandler, Republican of Michigan, endeavored to secure an appropriation for deepening the channel at St. Clair Flats, near Detroit. But he was defeated by southern hostility to internal improvements and southern alarm at the growth of the Northwest. Chandler's threats during the debate are revealing. "I want to have the yeas and nays upon it," he said. "I want to see who is friendly to the great North-West and who is not; for we are about to make our last prayer here. The time is not far distant when, instead of coming here and begging for our rights, we shall extend our great hands and take the blessing. After 1860, we shall not be here as beggars." [46]

A specific internal-improvement measure that reacted to the Republicans' advantage, especially in Illinois, was one which passed the Senate in May, 1858, providing an appropriation of over $87,000 to repair works at the harbor of Chicago. Southern senators, chiefly C. C. Clay of Alabama, tried to defeat it. The Republicans, led by Benjamin F. Wade of Ohio, pressed for its adoption, and the Senate passed the bill, 26 to 17. All but two of the 17 "nays" came from slave-state Senators. [47] The Democrats, however, now offended Chicago interests and gave the Republicans an opportunity for criticism by spending only a portion of the appropriation on the Chicago harbor. The Secretary of the Treasury, under whose jurisdiction harbor-improvement came, was Howell Cobb, a Georgian. Several years previous Cobb had written: "On the subject of internal improvements, and more particularly the improvement of rivers and harbors, I have been uniformly opposed to the whole system, and regard it as the most fruitful source of profligacy and corruption that our federal system is liable to." [48] He had not changed his mind, and the Republican press in 1860 denounced the "dodge by which the Democratic Secretary of the Treasury avoids the expenditure of the appropriation . . . for the improvement of Chicago Harbor." [49] The Chicago *Press & Tribune*, under the headline "Chicago to Be Cheated Out of Her Harbor Appropriation by the Democracy," appealed to "commercial men who are inclined to Douglasism . . . to ask themselves if their interests ought not now to be looked at. Have they not served the nigger-drivers long enough?" [50] This journalistic attack was continued against Cobb and other Democrats. Senator Lyman Trumbull, Republican of Illinois, introduced a resolution in the Senate requiring Cobb to give an accounting of the funds appropriated for Chicago harbor. Although nothing came of this, the Republicans continued their attacks.[51]

Sectional rivalry was provoked also by the West's demands for federal aid in support of railway building—more particularly for a railway to California. The competition for land grants to railway promoters was evident as early as 1850 when Senator Stephen A. Douglas fought for a land bounty for the Illinois Central Railroad. Southern interests were now determined to oppose such grants to northern groups unless they, too, were given the same help.[52]

Sectional controversy raged over the route which the proposed Pacific railroad was to traverse. Those below the Potomac wanted a southern route. Leaders in the North and certain border states, however, feared that such a southerly route might result in the political and economic extension of the slave system to California. Congress was flooded with projects, all agreeing that the government should subsidize the Pacific railroad, but each differing as to route and termini.[53] The Republicans inserted in their 1856 platform a plank favoring a Pacific railway, with an eye particularly on the California vote. The Democrats, meanwhile, were forced to accept the stigma of having been in power when nothing was accomplished.[54]

Closely linked with the West's demand for internal improvements and a Pacific railroad was the issue of the regular communication across the continent, such as telegraph and mail facilities to California. These, too, had strongly sectional aspects.

During the fifties, Congress gave little consideration to a transcontinental telegraph. But in 1860 Hiram Sibley, president of the Western Union Telegraph Company, lobbied through Congress a bill for a $40,000 annual subsidy for ten years for such a line.[55] The Senate vote on the subsidy revealed 28 votes favoring a grant to the northern telegraph promoters, 15 of which were Republicans, 5 northern Democrats and 8 southern Democrats. Of the 15 votes against the bill, 13 came from southern Democrats and 2 from Republicans. Thus the Senate approved the Pacific telegraph bill by a strongly sectional vote which, incidentally, revealed the Republicans as allies of northern business enterprise.[56]

Another communications issue involving conflict between North and South was the route over which the overland mail would travel.[57] In February, 1857, the Senate passed an act providing for a subsidy to a private company to carry the mails in stagecoaches from the Mississippi River to California; the grant was not to exceed $600,000 annually for semi-monthly service. Since the so-called South Pass—the more northerly—route was believed to be that over which the mail could best go, northern and northwestern Senators supported the amendment ardently.[58] Of the 24 Senators supporting the overland-mail subsidy, 17 came from the "free" states and only 7 from the slave states; all of the 10 dissenting votes came from the South.[59]

Since a provision of the act gave the Postmaster General authority to award the contracts, the latter could indirectly designate the route over which the mail was to be carried. Buchanan's Postmaster General, Aaron V. Brown, a Tennesseean, awarded the contract to John Butterfield, with the specific provision that the coaches carrying the mails to California travel over a southern route—from St. Louis to Arkansas, where it was to meet a branch route from Memphis, thence on through Texas to California. Northern interests immediately charged the Postmaster General with pro-southern bias in favor of his section.[60] Even before Butterfield started his horse-drawn Concord coaches from St. Louis and Memphis to San Francisco in September 1858, the sponsors of the route were obliged to defend themselves in Congress.

The friends of the central route (from St. Joseph, Missouri, to Placerville, California) resented what they considered the partiality shown by the Postmaster General in choosing the southern route, and Brown found it necessary to make contracts for carrying the mail over this central path too.

Still the sectional conflict over the overland mail continued. The northern-controlled House of Representatives passed a resolution directing the Postmaster General to order an increase of speed on the St. Joseph-Placerville mail run from thirty-eight to thirty days, with a pro-rata increase of compensation to the contractors. This also passed the Senate. David C. Broderick, of California, a critic of Buchanan and a recent convert to anti-slavery, sponsored the measure in the Senate. Southern senators led the opposition to an increased appropriation.[61] Broderick denounced the "pro-slavery" Brown.[62] Lyman Trumbull, of Illinois, came to Broderick's aid.[63] The poll on the proposal to aid the St. Joseph-Placerville, or central route resulted in 29 ayes and 17 nays. Twenty-four of the ayes came from "free" states; 15 of the negative votes were cast by slave-state Senators.[64] The measure was vetoed by Buchanan, and northern opinion assailed the Chief Executive's "pro-slavery" action. The San Francisco *Bulletin* commented: "It is quite evident . . . that the President is guided by the filibuster faction who will support no other but the extreme Southern route." [65] The California Republican state platform of 1859 demanded concessions for the central route.[66]

Undaunted by Buchanan's rebuke, northern interests were determined to show the superiority of a central route over a southern route. Thus early in 1860 the Pony Express was established by private parties.[67] Northern interests continued to seek aid from Congress. Following the Republicans' great victory of 1860, East and Northwest (now a solid political unit under the Republican banner) were to combat the South in Congress over the selection of a new daily-mail route.[68]

The Republicans made political capital out of the overland-mail controversy. In 1859 the Republican Association of Washington, publicity adjunct of the national party, devoted its fifth tract to the overland mail, accusing the Buchanan administration of undue partiality to southern interests.[69] In the Presidential campaign of 1860 the Republicans made the daily overland-mail issue a test for votes.[70]

Yet another source of discord between North and South which the Republican party turned to advantage was that perplexing problem of western lands.[71] Certain eastern groups, wishing to develop the Northwest into a great market for eastern goods, joined in advocating free land for actual settlers. Easterners had also invested heavily in northwestern railways and Republican leaders saw the advantage of a political tie-up with the Northwest. The deep South, on the other hand, was by 1854 almost unanimously opposed to homestead legislation because it would attract native- and German-born citizens to the Northwest rather than the South; moreover, the more enterprising, non-slaveholding southern whites would be attracted to free land and migrate to the Northwest.[72] Southern journals criticized the "free-land" proposal as "the most flagrant act of depredation on the public domain that has ever been attempted." [73]

From December, 1854, to July, 1858, a combination of slave-conscious southerners, land-warrant interests and railroad speculators agitating for generous land grants, prevented passage of a home-stead law. In opposition to these groups the national Republican party adopted free land as a cardinal doctrine. Early in 1859 Representative Galusha A. Grow, Republican of Pennsylvania and the party's floor leader, maneuvered a homestead bill through the House of Representatives by a vote of 120–76. The vote showed a clear North-South division. Grow's bill received 83 Republican votes and 37 Democratic votes (most of the latter from Northerners); against it were 62 Democrats (almost every one a Southerner), 13 southern Know-Nothings and only one Republican.[74] An Indiana Republican leader remarked: "Grow's speech and the vote in the House on the 'Homestead Bill' strengthens us." [75] The measure then went to the Senate, where it met the furious opposition of southern Senators.[76] Mason of Virginia led the southern attack.[77] When the Senate voted a measure to postpone consideration of Grow's bill, there was a 28–28 tie. Vice-President John C. Breckinridge, a Kentuckian, then cast his vote for postponement, and all hope of passing a home-stead act failed for the time being.[78]

The Republicans capitalized on Democratic and southern hostility to free land. By press and circular they told the West that only a Republican President could make homesteading a reality.[79] The Republican Association of Washington issued a tract, "Land for the Landless." [80] This campaign leaflet listed the affirmative votes on homestead by Republicans and negative votes by Democrats in both Senate and House.[81]

When Congress convened in December, 1859, the Republicans took up the homestead issue again. United States Senator James Harlan, Republican of Iowa, asked to be excused from his duties as a member of the Senate Committee on Pensions so that he could devote more time to his work on the Committee on Public Lands.[82] Harlan regarded the land question as inseparably bound up with the anti-slavery movement.[83] In March, 1860, a modified homestead bill finally passed both houses of Congress. Buchanan played directly into the Republicans' hands by vetoing the measure. In June, 1860, the Republicans failed to pass the bill over the President's veto, the slave-state Senators upholding Buchanan. Thus the Republicans were able to go before the West in the campaign of 1860 with the distinct advantage of being the staunchest supporters of the homestead program.[84]

Another land issue that stimulated friction between North and

South was the proposal to grant federal land to states for the establishment of agricultural and technical colleges. The embittered southerners argued that such legislation would favor not only agriculture but also navigation, commerce, and manufacturing, which were already overshadowing the slave-plantation system.[85] Northern agricultural and industrial interests persisted in their demands. In December, 1857, Representative Morrill (of tariff fame) sponsored a measure in the House, to provide a grant of 6,340,000 acres of federal land to the states, each state to share in it proportionately according to population; the proceeds from sale of this land to be used to erect agricultural and mechanical colleges. In April, 1858, after much effective lobbying by northern groups, Morrill's bill passed the House in amended form and went to the Senate, where the sectional division on the bill was most apparent.[86]

Most southerners in the Senate would have none of the Morrill bill. Aside from fear that it would aid northern industry, there was the question of free popular education odious to slave-plantation interests.[87] Senator Benjamin Fitzpatrick, of Alabama, demanded a postponement, and on a vote taken to consider this, a sectional tie resulted, which was broken in favor of the South by the vote of Vice-President Breckinridge, a Kentuckian.[88] A week later the bill came up again, and once more southern Senators blocked its consideration.[89] Not until February (1859) was Morrill's land-grant bill debated for a final vote. This time it passed the Senate, 25 to 22. The poll is most instructive. Of the 25 "ayes," only 4 came from the slave states; while of the 22 "nays," only 4 were cast by the "free" states.[90]

Morrill's bill now went to Buchanan. Horace Greeley, editor of the New York *Tribune*, most widely-circulated Republican journal, wrote to a friend in Congress: "If Old Buck vetoes the College bill and the Senate kills the Homestead, we can make our expenses out of them in the next canvass. That's the only good thing you have done this winter; and if we can hold them right there till 1860, we shall worry them [the Democrats] badly in the West." [91] Buchanan, as usual, unwittingly accommodated the Republicans. He vetoed the Morrill Land-Grant Bill, at the insistence of southern Senators, particularly John Slidell, of Louisiana.[92]

To the sectional cleavage caused by the conflict over tariffs, internal improvements, communications, free land, and free schools, southern ambitions for expansion in Cuba and Mexico added another disruptive force. In pressing for the addition of more territory to the Union, out of which slave states could be carved, an influential southerner wrote Senator Hunter, of Virginia: "You have I repeat no alternative. The North has more states and more territory than the South. It has the immigration of Europe to aid it." [93]

The desire of certain southerners to annex Cuba, the efforts of American and British abolitionists to end Negro slavery there, and fear of American diplomatists that the island might fall into the hands of Britain or France had already made Cuba an explosive issue in American politics. Between 1849 and 1851 the Venezuelan "General" Narciso Lopez and his followers had undertaken three unsuccessful filibustering expeditions to seize Cuba from Spain. And the fact that these adventurers were generously supported by some American slaveholders had caused ill feeling between North and South. In 1854 the Pierce administration, elected on an expansionist program, plunged into the Cuban question by appointing as minister to Spain Pierre Soulé of Louisiana, who had been the most militant of all senators in agitating for Cuban annexation. In Madrid Soulé received instructions from President Pierce to meet in a conference with James Buchanan (then minister to England) and John Y. Mason (then minister to France) to formulate plans for purchasing Cuba. The result of the meeting of the three ministers at Ostend, Belgium, in October, 1854, was their historic "Ostend Manifesto." This document, in the form of a report to Secretary of State William L. Marcy, had as its most startling novelty the threat that, under certain conditions, "we shall be justified in wresting it [Cuba] from Spain if we possess the power." By November 4 word of this leaked out. In February (1855) the House of Representatives called on the State Department for the Ostend correspondence.[94] Northern Whigs, many of whom were about to enter the newly formed Republican party, made political capital: they flayed the Pierce administration for its part in the Ostend Conference.[95]

The Cuban imbroglio, with its violently sectional aspects, became even more acute when Buchanan, one of the authors of the famed Manifesto, was nominated for President by the Democrats in 1856. The Republicans, in their national convention of that year, seized on the saber-rattling phrasing of the Ostend Manifesto to accuse the Democrats of shameful and dishonorable conduct.[96] On the stump Senator Seward stirred up the northern masses and the South alike when he charged that President Pierce had offered

Spain $200,000,000 for Cuba so that two new slave states might be brought into the Union, and that Pierce had threatened other European powers with war if they should interfere with such American plans.[97]

Certain southerners expected much from Buchanan. Following the latter's election a Virginia leader wrote Senator Hunter: [98]

If we can succeed in Kansas, keep down the Tariff, shake off our commercial dependence on the North, and add a little more slave territory, we may yet live free men under the Stars and Stripes. Mr. Buchanan, if not committed to the 'balance idea,' is to the acquisition of more southern territory.

Buchanan, an expansionist at heart, inaugurated plans to acquire Cuba. In December, 1858, he asked Congress for money with which to buy Cuba.[99] When in the following month Senator Slidell, of Louisiana, Buchanan's trusted adviser, introduced into the Senate a bill appropriating $30,000,000 for the purchase of Cuba, the Republicans rose in opposition.[100] By obstructionist tactics the Republican Senators prevented action on Slidell's Cuba bill until the Democrats finally abandoned hope for it. This was a major victory for the new party. Although the Republicans numbered less than one-third of the Senate, they had, by adroit and united maneuvering, blocked their opponents.[101]

Southern longing for the acquisition of Mexico created almost as much bickering between Northerners and Southerners as Cuba. When the Gadsden treaty was before the Senate in 1854, northern Senators opposed it lest the purchase of this small strip of land should give the South a transcontinental railway route and set a precedent for the acquisition of more Mexican territory.[102]

When Buchanan entered the White House certain southerners, including railroad speculators, expected the new President to bring into the Union huge tracts of Mexican land. "I had a very long and satisfactory interview with Buchanan about our Mexican policy, in which I was happy to find that he generally concurred," Senator Toombs, of Georgia, confided to an associate. Toombs added: [103]

If we can . . . get a charter from the Rio Grande to Tiberon from Mexico *before* we buy Sonora and secure the Tehuantepec route, we shall do pretty well for years. The charter, etc. must be gotten before we buy, to get rid of grants for the Northern and Central Pacific routes which the North will insist on before they would give us a charter.

In 1859 Robert M. McLane, of Maryland, minister to Mexico, negotiated a treaty of "transit and commerce" with the Latin-American republic, which in effect gave the United States in perpetuity the right of way across the Isthmus of Tehuantepec and also the right to transport American troops over the region. This treaty further provided that, in case of imminent danger to the lives and property of American citizens, the United States Government might act with military force even without Mexico's consent. Such a treaty, if ratified by both governments, might well have led in time to the absorption of most of Mexico into the United States. But the Republicans in the Senate, fearing more slave states and wanting to strike a blow at Buchanan, blocked it with the aid of insurgent northern Democrats.[104]

McLane's treaty was utilized by Republican leaders as another instrument in their attack upon Buchanan and the Democratic "slavocracy." At Cooper Institute, in January, 1860, Congressman Frank P. Blair, Jr., Republican of Missouri, denounced the Mexican treaty:[105]

Mr. Buchanan has leagued himself with the Indian Juarez [President of Mexico], in this war of religion and caste . . . The treaty which has been negotiated by our President proposes to furnish four millions of money to Juarez, to prosecute this war against the Catholic Church and the white men of Mexico . . . [in order] to prosecute further conquests in the South for the extension of slavery.

Had it not been for the sectional contests over economic policies —Field's Atlantic cable, protective tariff, internal improvements, Pacific railroad, transcontinental telegraph, overland-mail routes, homestead, endowments for agricultural-mechanical colleges, and the proposed acquisition of Cuba and parts of Mexico—it may well be concluded that the sectionalism on which the Republican party rested would not have been so profound, and the emotional rantings of anti-slavery and pro-slavery extremists would not have been so intense.

During the 1858 and 1859 campaigns the Democratic party split wide open over personalities, policies and patronage,[106] but the Republican party, under the skilful leadership of Governor Edwin D. Morgan of New York, Chairman of the Republican National Committee, increased its unity and strength. Circulars were issued to the state committees, agents were sent to watch developments in Kansas, and advice was tendered to Republicans in Congress.

Morgan was ably assisted by Gideon Welles, of Connecticut, a member of the Committee whom Lincoln later rewarded by appointing him to his Cabinet.[107] Republican editors from Maine to Minnesota featured the Democrats' hostility to "free land." Homestead was made a national party issue, and Republican conventions in every northern state, with the addition of Missouri and Kentucky, adopted "land for the landless" planks.[108]

Coöperating with the Republican National Committee was the self-styled Republican Association of Washington, a small group of editors and politicians who circulated tracts based on the votes of southern members of Congress. In the summer of 1859 the party press exhorted the faithful to do more field work along this line, appealing to them to purchase such documents "at the cheap rate of seventy cents per hundred" for distribution.[109] Copies of such tracts issued by the Republican Association are still preserved.[110]

The Republican party's most noted campaign document of 1859–1860 was Hinton Rowan Helper's *The Impending Crisis of the South: How to Meet It*. A native North Carolinian, Helper had become imbued with the determination to lead his own class, the nonslaveholding whites of the South, in an onslaught against slavery. He was convinced that slavery was the cause of the South's degradation and economic inertia. He accordingly assembled statistics from the census of 1850 and other sources and utilized them in such a way as to prove his thesis—that the South was inferior to the North because of slavery, and was doomed if that institution were not abolished. In his book Helper threatened the slaveholders with dire consequences if they did not emancipate their blacks. Just as Harriet Beecher Stowe's *Uncle Tom's Cabin* appealed to emotions and the heart, so did Helper's work appeal to reason and the head. The possibilities of such a scorching indictment of slavery by a southerner, backed by statistics and logic, drew the attention of Republican leaders. William M. Chace, of Rhode Island, Treasurer of the Republican National Committee, suggested that money be spent on a new printing of *The Impending Crisis*.[111] Early in 1859 the Republicans published a "Compendium"—a condensed version of Helper's book—and distributed it by the thousands. Chapter VIII of this campaign version, entitled "Testimony of Living Witnesses," quoted Seward, Cassius M. Clay, Gerrit Smith, Wendell Phillips, William Lloyd Garrison and other anti-slavery zealots.

Helper's volume gained special prominence when in the closing days of 1859 Democratic members of Congress brought it into the fierce sectional debate over the election of a Speaker of the House of Representatives. Representative John Sherman of Ohio, the Republican choice for Speaker, had endorsed Helper's work. A Missouri Democrat sponsored a resolution "that no person who has endorsed and recommended Helper's book, or the compendium of it, is fit to be Speaker of the House." When in late January 1860 Sherman was forced to withdraw from the speakership contest, the volume had been given a new significance. Not only did more northerners read it, but the southerners became more inflamed than ever against those who supported what they considered to be an insidious political organization—the Republican party.[112]

Even more effective than Helper's volume in stimulating southern hostility toward the North was John Brown's raid—although most northerners discountenanced such a bloody act. In October, 1859, the abolitionist Brown—son of a family reputed to have no less than eight insane people in it—led his historic raid on the arsenal at Harpers Ferry, Virginia, in order to free the slaves; some of the combatants were killed or wounded. Brown paid with his life on the gallows, but the affair did not end there.[113]

The fact that most Republican leaders regretted Brown's unfortunate exploit did not prevent northern Democrats as well as southerners from using the act as campaign material in 1859. With the November elections pending, Democrats charged that Republicans were implicated in Brown's conspiracy; the Democratic press alleged that Seward and other noted Republican leaders had met Brown at the abolitionist Gerrit Smith's house before the raid. The Democrats also maintained that Brown had simply made a practical application of Seward's extreme anti-slavery doctrines. The New York *Herald*, particularly violent, printed Seward's most radical speech beside the tragic news from Harpers Ferry.[114] In 1858 one Hugh Forbes, a European adventurer in the employ of Brown, had applied to Seward for assistance in financing a slave uprising in Missouri—a request which Seward promptly refused.[115] The story of Forbes's visit to Seward was resurrected and twisted by the Democratic and conservative press to prove that the New York senator knew beforehand of Brown's plans at Harpers Ferry. Mayor Fernando Wood, of New York City, was typical of many northern Democrats who asserted to Governor Henry A. Wise, of Virginia, that the Republican leaders, not John Brown, were the real instigators of the bloody affair at Harpers Ferry—all of which inflamed the South more.[116] Virginia's Governor continued to exploit the affair.[117] "Gov. Wise has made entirely too much 'fuss and feathers' in regard to Harpers Ferry revolutionists," a fellow Democrat observed. "He has acted like the whole North sanctioned and knew of it when perhaps not 500 men in all the Free States knew of Brown's designs and not one man in 5,000 sanctions his bold but wicked designs." [118] Northern sentiment overwhelmingly disapproved of the Harpers Ferry raid. Abraham Lincoln assured his audience at Cooper Institute that "John Brown was no Republican," and that the Democrats had "failed to implicate a single Republican in his Harper's Ferry enterprise." [119]

John Brown's grim adventure stirred Congress, where Democrats and southerners vented their vials of wrath upon the Republicans. Stephen A. Douglas led the northern Democratic assault. Brown found his inspiration, the Illinois Senator charged, in the extreme teachings and doctrines of the Republican party press, pamphlets, and books, and "especially in the speeches of their leaders." [120] In the South, the belief that Brown's raid was sanctioned by the North and particularly by the Republican party caused such hostility to northerners, that the last feeble efforts to resurrect the nationally minded Whig party in the border states failed. Henceforth extreme southern sectionalists for the most part were in the saddle below the Potomac.[121]

Certain regions of the deep South were already veering toward secession. Senator Jefferson Davis had recently declared to his Mississippi constituents that, in event of the election of a Republican President in 1860 on a decidedly anti-slavery platform, "let the Union be dissolved." The future President of the Confederacy added: "As did the great and good Calhoun, from whom is drawn that expression of value, I love and venerate the union of these States—but I love liberty and Mississippi more." [122]

In such an atmosphere charged with explosive sectionalism the Republican National Committee convened at the Astor House, in New York City, on December 21, 1859, in order to plan their national convention. Among the national committeemen present, in addition to National Chairman Morgan of New York, were: Gideon Welles, of Connecticut; Cassius M. Clay, of Kentucky; Zachariah Chandler, of Michigan; Carl Schurz, of Wisconsin; Frank P. Blair, Jr., of Missouri; and, significant in view of later events, Norman

B. Judd, of Illinois. The proceedings were conducted behind doors and newspaper reporters were not allowed to be present. The committeemen talked, agreed, disagreed, and then agreed "all day." [123] Judd pleaded for Chicago as the convention city, while other members wanted St. Louis, Cleveland, Wheeling, and a host of other places. Chicago was considered neutral ground since few, except Judd and his Illinois junta, then regarded Lincoln seriously as a presidential candidate. It was largely due to Judd's zeal that Chicago was chosen by a majority of one vote over St. Louis as the site for the convention.[124]

The wording of the summons to the Chicago convention, at which candidates for President and Vice-President would be nominated, created intense wrangling at the Astor House meeting. In conservative Pennsylvania the opposition to the Democracy was united in the "People's party," while in equally conservative New Jersey it was organized in the so-called "Opposition party." While these state organizations were opposed to the Buchanan administration, especially because of the Democrats' low-tariff policy and a sentimental attachment to defunct Whiggery,[125] they were not anxious to adopt the Republican label. On the other hand, the extreme Republicans at the Astor House conference hesitated to compromise principle. Practical politics ultimately prevailed, and an arrangement was reached whereby the Pennsylvania People's party and the New Jersey Opposition party, as well as the Republicans, were all mentioned by name in the invitation to Chicago. The crusaders' demand for singular emphasis upon the slavery issue was soft-pedaled, and the committee chose to stress the idea of "opposition" to the administration which was more palatable to the Pennsylvania, New Jersey, and other anti-Buchanan elements.[126]

Both Thomas Williams, Republican National Committeeman from Pennsylvania, and Senator James R. Doolittle, of Wisconsin, have claimed credit for drafting the summons to the national convention at Chicago.[127] Whoever the author, the invitation appeared in the press two days after the Astor House meeting.[128]

The year 1859 closed. The prospect of Republican success in 1860, now enlarged by the ever-widening split in the Democratic ranks,[129] presented opportunities for the ambitious, and Republican aspirants for the White House began to prepare for the battle at Chicago. They hoped to lead a new party comprising a perplexing variety of men—former anti-slavery Whigs, erstwhile Old Line

Whigs, die-hard Whigs, former Free-Soil Democrats, disgruntled organization Democrats, Know-Nothings, abolitionists, protective-tariff devotees, "free land" reformers (now called "homesteaders"), sponsors of a Pacific railroad, internal improvement champions, naturalized Germans, and others who for some reason hated Franklin Pierce, James Buchanan, or Stephen A. Douglas.

In spite of the new party's heterogeneity, it was bound together by a common hostility to the Democrats. Republican leaders were optimistic. The sanguine view of Alexander H. Bullock, a future governor of Massachusetts, was typical. "Made up of somewhat diverse antecedent fellowships and association," he observed, "we can nevertheless move on harmoniously in solid column." [130]

CHAPTER TWO

Chieftain of the Anti-Slavery Whigs

FEW POLITICAL LEADERS of the ante-bellum decade were more familiar to the American public or were the center of greater controversy than William H. Seward. The anxiety to hear him in the Senate was equaled only by the impatient desire to read that which he had uttered. Newspapers of every shade of opinion published the speeches of the talented United States senator from New York. Throughout the North hundreds of thousands considered Seward the premier Republican; they revered him as the symbol of the new party and believed that justice required his selection as the Republican standard-bearer in 1860.[1]

Born in Orange County, New York, in 1801, Seward was graduated from Union College. Finally settling in Auburn, in upstate central New York, he entered politics as an internal-improvement enthusiast and a follower of De Witt Clinton. He was soon intimate with Thurlow Weed, described as the "most astute, skillful, and indefatigable political manager ever known."[2] A warm friendship sprang up between the two men. Weed, having organized the anti-Jackson forces into the "Anti-Masonic" party, helped to send Seward to the state senate.

During the 1830's both Seward and Weed joined the new Whig party. The New York state Whig organization, captained by Weed and with Seward as its first statesman, successfully merged the heterogeneous groups opposed to President Andrew Jackson. The Whig campaign chests were filled by New York city merchants. Weed's Albany *Evening Journal* and Horace Greeley's New York *Tribune* were the party's principal mouthpieces. In 1838, with Weed's support, Seward was elected Governor of New York. Following two terms as New York's chief executive, he retired to practice law, then found the magnetic attraction of politics irresistible. In the election of 1848, by virtue of a Democratic split, the Whigs captured control of the New York legislature. Weed was able to send Seward to the United States Senate.[3]

In the Senate Seward became leader of the anti-slavery forces along with Salmon P. Chase of Ohio, Charles Sumner of Massachusetts, and Benjamin F. Wade of Ohio. In 1850 he favored the admission of California as a free state, declaring in an historic speech that there was a "higher law" than the Constitution.

A schism developed in the national Whig party when President Zachary Taylor died in 1850 and Seward's arch-foe in New York Whig politics, Vice-President Millard Fillmore, became Chief Executive. Seward was leader of the anti-slavery Whigs and Fillmore of the conservative Whigs. Fillmore, a favorite of the South because of his rigid enforcement of the Fugitive-Slave Law, began a "purge" of pro-Seward federal officeholders in New York. Fillmore aspired to succeed himself as President for a full term, but the Seward-Weed wing of the party adopted General Winfield Scott. The Sewardites controlled the National Convention in 1852 and captured the presidential nomination for Scott, who was decisively defeated in the general election by Franklin Pierce, the Democratic standard-bearer. The Whigs were definitely handicapped by the Seward-Fillmore feud.[4]

During 1853 Seward refrained from anti-slavery agitation. Neither he nor Weed knew where to go following the Whig decline. Greeley and his New York *Tribune* turned their attention to the temperance movement.[5] Weed declared: "We are content to be mere 'lookers on' till the services of Whigs are needed. The call to arms, however, is likely to be earlier and more emphatic than friend and foe anticipate."[6]

The "call to arms" came when Stephen A. Douglas introduced the Kansas-Nebraska Bill in the Senate in January 1854. Seward deemed the occasion auspicious. On January 8, after a conference with the venerable Thomas Hart Benton, he wrote to Weed:[7]

I have just had a long conversation with Col. Benton. He says we can save ourselves from Douglas's bill if the Northern states will remonstrate in public meetings and Legislative resolutions, and he desires that such proceedings shall be made. I submit it for your consideration.

Weed needed no urging. When, two weeks later, Senator Douglas agreed to include in his bill a specific repeal of the Missouri Compromise, the Seward-Weed forces acted. The legislature at Albany instructed the New York state delegation in Congress to oppose the bill.[8] Greeley's *Tribune* and Henry J. Raymond's *Times* in New York City fulminated against the pending legislation and promoted monster "anti-Nebraska" meetings in the metropolis.[9] To one of these demonstrations Seward sent a message of greetings.[10]

On February 17 Seward took the Senate floor against the Kansas-Nebraska bill. He touched the heart of much of his personal opposition to slavery extension. "The slaveholding states . . . stretch their dominion now from the banks of Delaware, quite around bay, headland, and promontory, to the Rio Grande. They will not stop." He cautioned his northern colleagues: "If we of the non-slaveholding States surrender to them now the eastern slope of the Rocky Mountains, and the very sources of the Mississippi, what territory will be secure, what territory can be secured hereafter, for the creation and organization of free States?" [11] Seward's speech created a deep impression.[12] Letters and resolutions against the Nebraska bill poured into Washington from all over New York State. Seward and his colleague, Senator Hamilton Fish, kept the attack moving by presenting numerous "anti-Nebraska" resolutions to the Senate.[13]

Nevertheless the Kansas-Nebraska bill became law in May, 1854. To the crumbling Whig party in the North, "Americanism" (Know-Nothingism) and temperance seemed the only remaining issues left to champion. For Seward, however, nativism was out of the question. His own gubernatorial message back in 1840, recommending that public money be voted for parochial schools, had precipitated the early anti-Catholic, anti-immigrant Native American movement in the Empire state. Ever since then Seward has been *persona non grata* to the Know-Nothing elements; many of his own party disapproved of his attempts to wean the Catholics and foreign-born citizens from the Democrats. The Know-Nothing party, when finally formed in 1854, held no door open to him.[14]

The Republican party assumed embryonic form in most northern states by August, 1854. Seward, as leader of the anti-slavery Whigs and senator from the Empire state, was the hope of many who desired a new anti-slavery party. He was easily the logical leader to raise the Republican standard in the East. Strenuous efforts were accordingly made to lure him into the Republican ranks. But he hesitated. Various national anti-slavery leaders had approached him with the offer of a vice-presidential nomination for 1856 on a ticket with Thomas Hart Benton, with the understanding that he (Seward) would be the presidential candidate in 1860. To this Seward, with characteristic caution, turned a deaf ear. He wrote to Weed: "The Free Soilers here are engaged in schemes for nominating Col. Benton, and dissolving the Whig Party . . . I hope to get through without doing or saying any indiscreet thing." [15] Weed took the cue, and in his Albany *Evening Journal* he argued against the absorption of the Whigs into a new party.[16]

In this same year 1854 Seward rejected another invitation to cooperate in forming a single anti-slavery party. Theodore Parker wanted him to aid in calling a national gathering of all anti-slavery groups at Buffalo. To him Seward explained: [17]

We are not yet ready for a great national convention at Buffalo, or elsewhere . . . The *States* are the places for activity, just now. . . . Let us make our power respected, *as we can*, through the elections in the States, and then bring the States into general council.

Both Seward and Weed were conspicuous by their absence from the great Anti-Nebraska convention held at Saratoga in August, 1854, to consider the organization of a Republican party in New York.[18] Weed contracted a diplomatic illness for the occasion.[19] In the New York state elections that fall the Seward-Weed candidate for governor, Myron H. Clark, was elected as a Whig with the aid of the prohibitionists and the nativists.[20] The close of 1854 found Seward still clinging to the moribund Whig party.

Early in 1855 Seward, with the backing of Weed, was reëlected to the Senate over the protests of the Know-Nothings. Nevertheless, the Whig party was disintegrating, and Weed had been compelled to exert his ingenuity as never before.[21] Seward was grateful, and amazed at the adroitness with which Weed had guided the "shattered bark" of the Whig party and "saved us all from so imminent a wreck." [22]

As the year 1855 wore on, the inflammable issues of Nebraska and slavery gradually destroyed the remnants of the national Whig party. In the fall of the year Seward severed his ties with the Whigs to bind himself to the new Republican party, cautioning his followers: [23]

Now there is neither Whig party nor Whig south of the Potomac. Let, then, the Whig Party pass. . . . The Republican organization has laid a new, sound, and liberal platform. Its principles are equal and exact justice; its speech open, decided, and frank. Its banner is untorn in former battles, and unsullied by past errors. That is the party for us.

Thus did Seward lead his anti-slavery followers into a union with other heterogeneous groups to give vigor to the new Republican organization.

Seward's tardy entry into the Republican ranks revealed him as a practical politician. One of the last great anti-Democratic chieftains to leave the party of Clay and Webster, he did not join the Republicans until the Whig party had virtually ceased to exist.[24]

In December, 1855, two months after Seward's formal entry into the Republican party, Congress assembled. Washington became a hive of political intrigue. Francis P. Blair, Sr., veteran Democrat who had cast his lot with the Republicans, entertained anti-Democratic leaders at his home. The guests included Salmon P. Chase, recently elected governor of Ohio.[25] On this occasion Seward revealed his characteristic caution. He was invited to Blair's gathering, but declined. He wrote Weed: [26]

On Friday afternoon Mr. Blair sent me a note inviting me to meet some friends at his country seat the next day at dinner, to take measures for an organization of the Anti-Nebraska forces for the Presidential election. . . . On Saturday I wrote to Mr. Blair approving of his activity but declining his invitation . . .

Today Preston King desired to speak with me about the organization of the party, because he had promised Mr. Blair he would. He added that means were in progress to have a convention called from Ohio to meet at Pittsburgh or Cincinnati simultaneously with the Administration [Democratic] Convention & to nominate a ticket . . .

I answered Mr. King that I took no part & no responsibility in Conventions or organizations. That I desired not to be committed and I should give no advice nor should I speak or attempt to speak for the Republicans of New York. I referred him to you. I said in reply . . . [that] if my position was asked I must distinctly protest against any combination with Know-Nothings.

Seward realized that the "Americans" would not accept him. But he believed that the nativists would soon expire as a political factor.[27]

Blair, Chase and their friends were instrumental in organizing the Republican party on a national basis at Pittsburgh, February 22, 1856. Neither Seward nor Weed attended the Pittsburgh meeting, although Henry J. Raymond, their associate and editor of the New York *Times*, was active there.[28] Seward remained in Washington to make a campaign issue of Kansas and fulminate against the extension of slavery.

Ever since the passage of the Kansas-Nebraska bill in 1854 there had been a race between slavery and anti-slavery advocates to fill the new territories, especially Kansas, with sympathizers. Southerners from neighboring Missouri gained control of the territorial legislature, but in 1855 the anti-slavery settlers along the Kansas River met at Topeka and drew up a free-soil constitution. In 1856 it was not certain whether the slavery advocates had a majority in the territory or not. They were favored by proximity, and it appeared that with time they could defeat the North in the contest for settlers.[29]

In March, 1856, Senator Douglas introduced a bill in the Senate providing that Kansas Territory might not acquire statehood until it contained a population of 9,420. Republicans feared that slavery advocates would fill the territory with southerners in the additional time thus provided and that Kansas would ultimately be admitted as a slave state. Seward therefore promptly introduced a substitute measure in the Senate favoring the immediate admission of Kansas under the Topeka, or anti-slavery, constitution.[30]

Republican strategy had a twofold aim: to compel the Democrats to accept or reject Seward's bill and thus admit Kansas free or go on record as favoring the cause of slavery extension; and to create an issue which would arouse the public. Seward and his lieutenants in the House wrote to Weed asking for strong editorials, public meetings and petitions demanding the "immediate admission of Kansas." [31]

Seward took the Senate floor in support of his bill on April 9. After a dramatic introduction, he accused President Pierce of collusion in the invasion of Kansas by pro-slavery Missourians. In language saturated with anti-slavery idealism and Republican partisanship, he spoke for the people of Kansas: "Holding in my hand the arraignment of George III, by the Congress of 1776, I impeach—in the words of that immortal text—the President of the United States." [32] Seward's speech was a great success; the New York *Tribune* sent out 162,000 copies.[33]

When the Republican national convention met in June, however, Seward was not nominated. Weed, the Blairs and other party chieftains favored the more "available" John C. Frémont.[34] Weed's decision not to press for his nomination hurt Seward and troubled him for several years thereafter.[35] Nevertheless, he took the stump for Frémont.[36] Although Frémont lost the Presidency to Buchanan, New York went Republican. John A. King became the state's first Republican governor, and the Republicans carried the Assembly. Weed had been a skillful manager.[37]

Control of the New York Assembly gave Weed the opportunity to reward the free-soil Democrats in the Republican party and to give Seward a more militantly anti-slavery Senatorial colleague than Hamilton Fish, whose term was about to expire. Fish was a representative of declining Whig conservatism—a moderate free-soiler at best, who contributed little to Seward's war on the "Slave Power." [38]

Weed had promised to support as Fish's successor Preston King, leader of New York's Free-Soil Democrats, who had gone over to the Republican party.[39] Weed did not forget King's help.[40] King put his fate in Weed's hands [41] and succeeded Fish in the Senate. Fish bitterly ascribed his "shelving" to the desire for King's help in making Seward President in 1860.[42]

During 1857 and 1858 Weed continued to organize the party, while Seward served the cause in the Senate and on the hustings. In the latter year Seward delivered his tirade on the Dred Scott decision.[43] In the fall he made one of the most historic speeches of his career, the famous "Irrepressible Conflict" address at Rochester— a fierce indictment of the Democrats and the proponents of slavery extension. Early in his oration Seward had proclaimed that the two existing systems of labor—the "slave" and the "free"—were incompatible.[44] This point later inspired several historians to give an almost purely economic interpretation to the causes of the War between the States, and to declare that a conflict between the two systems was inevitable. Although Seward had preached the same theme before,[45] the words "irrepressible conflict" summed up the antipathy between the two sections. The phrase was accepted as a challenge to the South, and soon rang from ocean to ocean.

The New York state election of 1858, of which Seward's Rochester speech was the highlight, sent the Republicans into ecstasy. The Republican gubernatorial candidate's plurality over his Democratic opponent was more than 17,000.[46] Moreover, glad tidings came from Pennsylvania: the "People's Party"—composed of Republicans, Know-Nothings, disgruntled Democrats, protective-

tariff advocates and other anti-Democratic groups—had won a magnificent victory.[47]

Republican success in the two largest states, plus victories elsewhere throughout the North in the elections of 1858, made the ambitious hopeful. With the national convention only one year and
a half off, Republican contenders for the Presidency began preparations for 1860. The stars pointed to Seward. His home state commanded the largest convention and electoral vote; he enjoyed en-
viable prestige nationally as an exponent of the Republican opposition to extension of slavery, and he had the backing of an efficient
political organization piloted by the most skilled of tacticians.
Before the year 1858 ended those in the inner party councils knew
that Weed was determined to support his friend for the Republican
nomination.[48]

Seward's course in the Senate during 1859 was a bid for support
from Pennsylvania and the Northwest. The Keystone state was enthusiastic for a protective tariff.[49] The Northwest, of course, wanted
free land and a railroad to the Pacific. When, in 1859, the homestead bill was given preference over the Administration's proposal
to purchase Cuba, Seward was on his feet: "The Homestead Bill
is a question of homes, of land for the landless free men of the
United States; the Cuba bill is a question of slaves for the slaveholders." He also denounced Buchanan for being opposed to a
protective tariff.[50]

The Seward forces courted Pennsylvania assiduously. The large
number of "Americans" and other conservatives in Pennsylvania,
however, were an embarrassment to Seward. His chief Rochester
lieutenant, E. Peshine Smith, corresponded with Henry C. Carey,
of Philadelphia.[51] Smith sought to prove that, despite the thousands
of nativists in New York state, Seward was unbeatable; that Seward
was the only Republican who could carry New York in 1860
and that he had not need of nativist support.[52] He wrote Carey:
"We don't want the Americans inside of the Republican party in
New York. . . . We can carry this state for Seward in 1860. . . .
Let them join the Democrats and it is all we ask of them for they
will repel more votes than they bring."[53] Smith maintained that
all elements opposed to the Democrats *"must* vote with us, whether
we invite them or not."[54] Smith further contended that the German-
born citizens who were flocking to the Republican party were
worth twice as much as the "Americans."[55]

The most prominent Republican of Pennsylvania was not Carey, however, but United States Senator Simon Cameron. Following adjournment of Congress in March, 1859, Seward visited Cameron at his home near Harrisburg.[56] Seward reported to Weed: [57]

Speaking of Cameron, I promised him when he left Washington to spend a day with him on my way home. He took me to his home, told me all was right. He was for me, and Pa. would be. It might want to cast a first ballot for him or might not. He brought the whole legislature of both parties to see me. . . . They were in the main so free, so generous as to embarrass me. Among them were the American representatives from Philadelphia. I was not a candidate—but left all things to them.

Pennsylvania Republicans who witnessed Seward's grand reception by Cameron undertsood that a "deal" had been arranged between the two Senators: The Pennsylvania delegation at Chicago was to cast a "favorite-son" vote for Cameron on the first ballot before switching to Seward.[58]

Following his visit to Cameron, Seward departed for Europe. He told his well-wishers that he went abroad to acquire "the knowledge derived from the sufferings and strivings of humanity in foreign countries—to teach me how to improve and elevate the condition of my own countrymen." [59] He and Weed, however, had decided that he should absent himself from the country and feign disinterest in the pre-convention presidential canvass. Horace Greeley had been acting coolly of late regarding Seward's bid for the presidency, but Weed assured his distinguished protegé that the temperamental *Tribune* editor was reconciled.[60] Important and unimportant followers of the Seward-Weed organization in New York City collected to bid godspeed to "Governor William H. Seward, the next President of the United States." Senator King assured the assembled throng that his colleague would be the next chief executive.[61]

Seward returned to the United States in December, 1859. As he was conveyed from the New York pier to the Astor House, fireworks were set off by the Republican Central Committee. The Mayor and Common Council welcomed him, amid hysterical shouts, as "the next President." [62] On his journey to Auburn, even Democrats joined in paying homage to him.[63]

The Republican National Convention was several months off

when, in January, 1860, Seward resumed his Senate seat. He found himself the target of both southerners and conservative northerners.[64] The southerners were incensed by the Democratic charge that Seward was hand in glove with John Brown in the Harpers Ferry raid.[65] Moreover, the southerners remembered all too well that he had endorsed Helper's *The Impending Crisis.* Weed had contributed funds for the circulation of the compendium of the Helper volume. Now, however, with an eye on the coming National Convention, Seward endeavored to throw off the yoke of radicalism. Before the Committee of Congress investigating Brown's raid he denied that he had anything to do with that bloody affair.[66] In the edition of *The Impending Crisis* printed in January, 1860, Seward's endorsement was deleted.[67] Moreover, Seward's close friend, ex-Mayor Benjamin F. Hall of Auburn, journeyed to St. Louis to consult with the conservative leader, Judge Edward Bates, for the purpose of persuading Bates that Seward was no radical.[69]

Seward continued his efforts to placate the conservatives. In late February (1860) he saw the urgency of reassuring the South and moderate Northerners. On the other hand, the New York senator could not go to such conservative extremes, since the Republican party had to retain its ultra anti-slavery supporters. In late February, 1860, he spoke in the Senate upon a bill for the admission of Kansas. His speech avoided the "higher law" and "irrepressible conflict" doctrines. He did not demand, as formerly, that the Supreme Court rescind its Dred Scott decision. He declared against John Brown's raid. His erstwhile provocative anti-slavery convictions were subordinated to a determination not to quarrel: [70]

Differences of opinion, even on the subject of slavery, are with us political, not social or personal differences. There is not one disunionist or disloyalist among us all. We are altogether unconscious of any process of dissolution going on among us or around us. We have never been more patient, and never loved the representatives of other sections more than now.

This did not sound like the "irrepressible conflict" portrayed at Rochester. One Democrat commented: "It is as smooth as oil, but in other respects it is unlike Seward." [71]

The ultra anti-slavery men were furious at the New York senator.[72] Nevertheless, to conservative Republicans he became less obnoxious.[73] Seward had made the speech of a practical politician.

The oration undoubtedly left him practically where he had always been—admired by the advanced anti-slavery men, distrusted by the moderates.

Weed watched Seward's progress closely. All-important was the selection of a pro-Seward delegation to the Chicago convention from New York. Weed gave this matter personal attention, controlling the state Republican convention in Syracuse on April 18. A resolution was unanimously adopted, declaring "that the Republican electors of the State of New York, represented in this convention, present the name of Wm. H. Seward to the Chicago Convention, for the office of President." Applause and hysterical cheering followed. The four delegates-at-large selected had been trusted Seward men for years. The other ("regular") delegates were also chosen on the basis of their loyalty to Seward. One untoward incident marred the Weed-controlled harmony: David Dudley Field, slated as a delegate to Chicago, was accused of being anti-Seward (which he subsequently proved to be)—but he was quickly dropped, his place being given to James W. Nye, a tried Seward follower. Thus Seward was certain of New York's 70 votes, the largest block in the National Convention.[74]

Seward's weakness lay in Pennsylvania, where Senator Cameron held great power. Seward and Weed had over-confidence in Cameron's loyalty. Seward had let it be known that Pennsylvania would be for him in the National Convention.[75] And so apparently Weed believed. But signs were multiplying which indicated Cameron's unreliability: Weed's Washington scouts reported that Cameron was secretly playing for delegates for himself, that Cameron was working for his own interests. Suggestions were made that Weed counteract this by intervention in the Keystone state;[78] that Seward be given a public reception in Philadelphia.[79] Pleas for funds came to Weed from Pennsylvania.[80]

If Weed distrusted Cameron, he believed that it was best to maintain a hands-off policy in Pennsylvania lest he offend Cameron and lose all chance of getting his state's support for Seward at Chicago. Weed realized that the Pennsylvania senator was playing his own game but believed that he would cut no figure at Chicago and in the end would throw his support to Seward. Thus Weed made no move to attract Keystone state delegates directly, trusting Cameron to support Seward when the time came. Weed sat idly by while Cameron had himself endorsed by the Pennsylvania People's (Republican)

party at Harrisburg on February 22, 1860. There seemed justification for Weed's policy: Congressman Spaulding of Buffalo wrote
to Weed: "At Washington . . . it seems to be settled that he
[Seward] will be nominated at Chicago. Mr. Cameron seems to be
acting well." [81] And as National Convention time approached,
Seward himself let it be known in Washington that Cameron was for
him.[82]

All the while Cameron, probably intentionally, avoided meeting
Weed. Seward wrote the latter on April 5 that the Pennsylvania
senator wished to consult with him,[83] but when Weed made the
effort to see him, Cameron was never in the same place at the
same time as Weed. "When our Legislature adjourns I will see
you at Washington," the Albany editor wrote to Cameron on
April 8, "or ask you to meet me in Philadelphia." [84] The meeting
never occurred. The Republican state chairman of Pennsylvania,
Alexander K. McClure, reminded Cameron that Weed wished to
see him.[85] In late April Weed sent word to Cameron: "Will you
be in Philadelphia any day next week? Or if not, shall I find you
in Washington?" [86] May 7 arrived—only one week before the
Chicago convention—and still Weed and Cameron had not met.
On this day Weed appealed to Cameron: [87]

I cannot go to Washington and must, therefore, forego the opportunity of conferring with you.
I hope that you and Seward will put your heads together and let
me know the result of your deliberations; or at any rate, that you
will have a *confidential* friend at Chicago with whom I can com-
municate.

Thus, before leaving for Chicago to capture the party's presidential nomination for Seward, Weed did not confer with the
Pennsylvania senator, who controlled the largest bloc of delegates
outside of New York.[88]

Despite the strange conduct of Cameron, Seward felt confident
that he would become the Republican standard-bearer. Various
Senate colleagues agreed that nothing could stop him.[89] The incipient
boom in New York for Governor Chase, of Ohio, soon collapsed
and Seward was thus assured of unanimous support from his own
state.[90] Parts of New England were overtaken by Seward influence.
Maine Republicans had selected a pro-Seward delegation to Chicago.[91] The Republicans of Massachusetts chose delegates favorable

to Seward.[92] With the exception of Indiana and Ohio, much of the great Northwest favored Seward.[93] The Minnesota Republican delegation agreed to cast its solid vote for the New York senator,[94] and Wisconsin Republicans adopted a resolution declaring Seward to be their first choice.[95] In May Michigan Republicans instructed their delegates to the National Convention to vote as a unit for Seward.[96] Three-quarters of the Iowa delegates were said to be favorable to him.[97] Even Illinois, pledged to Abraham Lincoln, had some Seward men on its delegation.[98] Kansas, still a territory, resolved to support him.[99] The Republicans of California instructed their delegates to the Chicago convention to vote for him for President.[100]

Several days before the assembling of the Republican National Convention in May, Thurlow Weed, although not a delegate, led the New York delegation to Chicago, intent on capturing the prize for his friend. Seward remained in his Auburn home confidently awaiting word of his nomination. On the day that the balloting began at Chicago, friends set a cannon upon the lawn of Seward's home, to be fired as soon as the good news should come from Chicago.[101]

CHAPTER THREE

Champion of the Free Democracy

A NOTHER AMBITIOUS anti-slavery leader was Salmon Portland Chase, Ohio's first Republican governor. Cold, dignified and reserved, Chase commanded respect if he did not inspire love.

Born in New Hampshire in 1808, Chase was graduated from Dartmouth College. In 1830 he removed to Cincinnati, where in that anti-slavery atmosphere he became converted to the cause of freedom. In 1841 he forsook the Whigs and joined James G. Birney's struggling Liberty Party.[1]

Chase brought to the idealistic program of his new party a definitely pragmatic approach. He urged Liberty men to merge with practical politicians. At the great inter-party convention at Buffalo in 1848, Chase and his Ohio Liberty party contingent joined with insurgent New York Democrats, anti-slavery Whigs and postal reformers to nominate Martin Van Buren for President on a "Free Soil" ticket.[2] The Biblical and religious basis of Birney's party was shortly overshadowed by a practical and extensive political program. The party's leader was no longer the visionary Birney but the grizzled politician Van Buren.[3]

Chase campaigned for Van Buren in 1848, but the Free Soilers in Ohio did not make a formidable showing.[4] In the state legislature, however, they possessed strength wholly out of proportion to their small numbers because they held the balance of power between the Whigs and the Democrats. Chase's handful of Free Soil supporters adroitly exploited a deadlock between the two major parties and persuaded the Democrats to elect Chase to the United States Senate.[5]

When the new senator reached Washington in December, 1849, he hoped to create a "free" Democracy. As Calhoun led the pro-slavery Democrats, he, Chase, would lead the anti-slavery Democrats. His great ambition, futile as it now seems, was to compel the Democratic party, even with its strong southern attachments, to abjure slavery, embrace Free Soil, and become a part of the "Free Democracy." [6] Although Chase considered himself a Democrat, his party colleagues in the Senate did not welcome him. He was not even given a Senate committee post at the Democratic party's disposal; neither was he invited to the Democratic caucuses.[7] Chase allied himself with the modest anti-slavery group led by Seward, John P. Hale of New Hampshire, Benjamin F. Wade of Ohio, and Charles Sumner of Massachusetts. In 1852 Chase voted for Sumner's motion to repeal the Fugitive-Slave Law.[8] In spite of his isolation, however, he continued to urge fusion between Democrats and Free Soilers.

Suddenly, in 1851, Chase joined the regular Democratic party.[9] One Ohio historian ascribes Chase's action to his "concern for his political future rather than regard for his past principles. Chase as a Democrat stood a better chance for re-election than Chase as a Free Soiler." [10]

The year 1853 marked the beginning of a great transitional period in Ohio politics. General Winfield Scott's severe defeat the year previous produced a disastrous effect on the Whigs in Ohio and elsewhere. The "Free Soil Democrats," led by Chase, started a movement to unite with the disheartened Whigs on the prohibition issue for the state elections of 1853. This fusion of anti-slavery and temperance forces cut across both Whig and Democratic lines. The regular Democratic candidate for governor was elected, but the Free-Democratic-Anti-slavery-temperance coalition attracted so many Whigs that the regular Whig candidate polled the smallest number of votes of any gubernatorial nominee of his party since the Whigs were organized. The Whigs were desperate.[11]

Party ties were loose in the Northwest, but the main reason for this merger of Whigs and Free Soilers was that the Whigs had been losing ground for years, and by 1854 their name attracted few adherents.[12] This new anti-Democratic coalition in Ohio, however, needed an issue. Temperance was too weak a reed on which to lean. And the issue came to them in January, 1854, when Senator Douglas reported to the Senate his Kansas-Nebraska bill, which repealed the Missouri Compromise of 1820 and would thus legally open up parts of the Northwest to Negro slavery.[13]

On January 24 (1854) Douglas asked that the Senate consider

the bill. Here was Chase's chance to merge Free Soilers and Whigs on a common anti-slavery program. He requested that Douglas agree to a week's postponement of consideration of the bill. Chase's Free Soil friend, Sumner, supported Chase, and Douglas agreed. Consideration of the Kansas-Nebraska bill was put off until the week following.[14]

Chase and his group had urged postponement upon Douglas so that they might have time in which to arouse an opposition. On the very afternoon that they requested postponement, the abolitionist Washington *National Era* published an "Appeal of the Independent Democrats to the People of the United States." This manifesto was signed by Chase, Sumner, Joshua R. Giddings and other Free-Soil congressmen, and called for a united opposition to the proposed repeal of the Missouri Compromise. The burden of the argument was that the Nebraska bill, should it become law, would open all Federal territories to slavery, that it would settle the blight of slavery upon the whole land, and that it was a "gross violation of a sacred pledge." People were implored to protest in the name of the Christian religion. It was implied that Douglas was simply courting southern favor to promote his own presidential ambitions.[15] Chase and Sumner recognized the political usefulness of emotional hysteria.[16] Chase drafted the "Appeal";[17] he referred to it as "the *most valuable* of my works."[18]

Douglas was outraged at the action of Chase and Sumner in persuading him to postpone debate on the Kansas-Nebraska bill in order to give anti-slavery newspapers time to publicize the "Appeal."[19] The Illinois senator refused to be calmed, and denounced Chase in the Senate.[20] Chase answered Douglas[21] with a blistering philippic, and even the Whig Cincinnati *Gazette* praised his efforts. The *Gazette's* endorsement indicated that most Ohio Whigs were ready to unite with Free-Soil Democrats on a common anti-slavery program. The "Appeal" put wavering Whigs on the defensive,[22] and an influential Whig editor of Columbus admitted: "That address of Chase, Sumner, Giddings and Company, issued on the introduction of the Nebraska bill, came near swamping us altogether."[23]

Chase was prepared to exploit the anti-Nebraska sentiment in Ohio. "I am entirely ready," he wrote on May 10, "to unite with all my heart in a new political organization embracing the names of the existing Whig Party and the liberal Democrats."[24] The Whigs, with little to lose, were even more ready than Chase to participate in such a new movement.[25] In the hope of establishing an "anti-Nebraska" common front against the regular Democrats, Chase held conferences with at least two Whig congressmen from Ohio, Giddings and Lewis D. Campbell. Then he wrote William Schouler, editor of the Cincinnati *Gazette:* [26]

A call for a Convention of the People of Ohio has been agreed on here by us & Messrs. Campbell & Giddings & which will be believed be acceptable to all the opponents of the Nebraska outrage for a convention at Columbus, on the 13th of July. The plan is to have the Convention called by the people themselves, who, we believe, are prepared to do it. With this view the call will be forthwith sent into every county in the State for signers, with requests to forward them to Judge J. R. Swan, Mr. J. W. Andrews or Dr. J. H. Coulter, one of each of the existing political parties, who are requested to act as a Committee by the 12th of June to be published forthwith in every paper of the State willing to record the movement. We want the Call signed by at least ten thousand good & true men.

The object of this note is to apprize you of what is being done that there may be concert. A copy of the Call will be sent you to-morrow and perhaps it will be well for you, *without publishing it at present* to say that you are advised that such a Call is in circulation and will soon make its appearance.

The Cincinnati *Gazette* accordingly called for a state Anti-Nebraska convention, and other leading Whig organs in Ohio supported the move. The Free Democratic forces under Chase were more than willing to coöperate with the Whigs. On July 13, as agreed by Chase, Giddings, and Campbell at Washington, the fusion convention met at Columbus. Various German elements, fearful lest the Kansas-Nebraska Act would open the territories to Negro slavery and interfere with "free land" for actual white settlers, also participated. Chase was not present but all knew that he had inspired the meeting. Judge Swan, a Van Buren Democrat of 1848, and Jacob Blickensderfer, a Whig, were nominated for state offices. One resolution adopted pledged the party to render "inoperative and void" the *repeal* of the Missouri Compromise. The day after the adjournment of the convention the Columbus *Ohio State Journal*, now the principal organ of fusion, placed the words "Republican Nominations" over the names of Swan and Blickensderfer. This was the term used in Michigan and Vermont. But as yet there was really no Republican party in Ohio—merely a loose union of all forces opposed to the regular Democracy.[27]

The election of 1854, which resulted in an overwhelming "fusion" victory, turned on several factors. The fusionists had Know-Nothing support. Paradoxically, many Germans also supported the fusion ticket out of opposition to the Democratic application of popular sovereignty in Kansas and Nebraska. Furthermore, the Democrats had aroused hostility in northwestern Ohio by their defeat of the homestead act in Congress, and they had irritated conservative Cincinnati business interests by their radical taxation and currency policies. In addition, Chase himself, a powerful figure and persuasive speaker, had toured the state for weeks. Undoubtedly it was principally opposition to the Kansas-Nebraska Act which brought together in a common cause so many diverse groups ordinarily having little in common with each other.[28]

Obviously Stephen A. Douglas and the Pope had few friends in Ohio. But to whom did the triumph of 1854 belong? The Anti-Nebraskans or the Know-Nothings? The anti-slavery men or the nativists?

Following their success in 1854 the fusion forces—comprising dissatisfied Whigs, conservative Whigs, Free Soil Democrats, Know-Nothings, naturalized Germans and homesteaders—resolved itself into two contending groups: the Whig-Know-Nothing, or conservative element; and the Democratic-Free Soil, or radical anti-slavery element. The first believed in a moderate anti-slavery policy, opposing the Missouri Compromise repeal chiefly because it would result in a renewal of slavery agitation and in danger to the Union. This element would accept the restoration of the 36° 30' line and desired an end of militant anti-slavery agitation. It was willing to organize a new political party on a national, rather than a sectional basis and adopt anti-Catholicism as a substitute for abolition. The second element of the Ohio "fusion" movement was Chase's Democratic-Free Soil group. It was ardently opposed to further slavery extension; and it was hostile to nativism because it wanted the German vote,[29] which was becoming an increasingly important factor in Ohio elections.[30]

Chase, who had courted the German vote since 1850,[31] was firmly convinced that the main "fusion" issue must be anti-slavery, not nativism. A new party organized against the pro-slavery influence, he confided in a letter, "will unite all the Independent

Democrats, the Liberal Whigs & the Liberals among the old Democrats & especially the Germans." [32] Besides, he wrote another, "Know-Nothingism, will, I think, gracefully give itself up to die." [33] He continued to inform the Germans that he was their champion.[34] In the Senate Chase fought for the right of the foreign-born, along with native-born Americans, to have ownership of 160 acres of free land if they settled on it.[35] The fight against the regular Democrats, he felt, should be fought on an anti-slavery issue which would bring with it the German vote.

At the close of the 1854 campaign Chase decided: "I have not the smallest doubt that parties must now reorganize themselves; nor have I any doubt whether Slavery must be the controlling element of the new organization. Other ideas may have more or less permanent importance, but there is no question of the depth, breadth & permanence of the Slavery question." [36]

In his aspirations for Republican leadership Chase was opposed by most of the Whig-Know-Nothings, who disliked him because of his friendliness to the Teutonic element and because of his abolitionist proclivities. Furthermore, these Whig-Know-Nothings would not forget the intrigue of 1849 that had secured him the United States senatorship. In these circumstances, the shrewd minority of radical anti-slavery men who backed Chase undertook to smash Ohio Know-Nothingism in a manner that enhanced Chase's personal fortunes and to a great extent guaranteed the growth of the Republican party.[37]

In the East Know-Nothingism generally tended to operate as a separate political party in 1854–1855, but in Ohio, where the Anti-Nebraska movement had swept all before it, the anti-foreign and anti-Catholic elements did not comprise a separate party. The rise of nativism alarmed the Anti-Nebraska forces who feared that the secret order might seize control of the fusion movement. Thus they set out to counteract the growing nativist menace and secure for Chase the fusion nomination for governor. Adopting a "rule-or-ruin" policy,[38] they openly denounced Know-Nothingism and threatened to place an independent Chase ticket in the field if the fusion convention, called for July 13 (1855), turned down their favorite. The Chase men won. They weakened the Know-Nothing resistance to anti-slavery demands. The "fusion" convention was controlled by Chase men and formally organized the Republican party in Ohio. A platform was adopted devoted to the slavery issue. Chase was nominated for governor.[39] Although every nominee except Chase was a Know-Nothing, the real victors were the anti-slavery men; they had forced a Know-Nothing majority to accept Chase. Opposition to slavery and the desire for office had triumphed over anti-foreign and anti-Catholic principles.[40]

In his gubernatorial campaign of 1855 Chase was obliged to appeal to the Germans while heading a ticket of Know-Nothings, and yet offend neither. The troubles in Kansas, however, proved a safe theme. Chase was elected Governor by a plurality of nearly 16,000. A three-cornered race gave him victory without a majority of the vote. "I had a hard canvass," Chase admitted, "I spoke at fifty-seven places in forty-nine different counties." [41] It is questionable if Chase, an extremist, represented his state correctly on the slavery issue: his nomination had been forced on the Republican state convention by a minority of anti-slavery radicals, and only the fear of wrecking a united opposition to the Democratic party induced many conservatives to vote for him. Moreover, in southern Ohio the support of Know-Nothings, many of them not anti-slavery men, contributed powerfully to his success. His election, however, insured the permanence of the Republican party in Ohio (third among the states of the Union in population) and heartened Republicans all over the North.

Chase emerged as a leader with prestige in the new Republican party.[42] His burning ambition now was to be President of the United States. For long his party colleagues had suspected him of such lofty ambitions.[43] His election as Governor convinced him that the Republican party owed him the nomination in 1856. Immediately following his election as Governor of Ohio, he assured one leader: "I will not deny that it *seems* to me that I have as much right if not more of the right kind of strength than any other of the gentlemen named. The elements required for a Presidential election have been harmonized in my election in Ohio." [44] His admirers encouraged him.[45]

Committees of correspondence were formed among Chase's friends, who started a campaign the nation over to harmonize the various elements opposed to President Pierce's Democratic administration under an anti-slavery banner; they sounded northern leaders on the prospect of calling a national Republican Convention for 1856. Chase himself visited New England and upper New

York State. The Ohio governor coöperated with the Blairs, who were said to favor him for president.[46] Several weeks before the first Republican National Convention met at Philadelphia in June 1856, Chase appealed to his friend, Senator Sumner: "What about Presidential matters? Before we departed a year ago, you expressed a preference for me. . . . Our people here in Ohio appear at present to be in my favor." [47]

Chase was soon eliminated from the race, however. Friends had helped to fire his ambition, but he was not considered "available." He had scant following among the party's influential leaders. Even the Blairs, with whom he had worked closely, adopted the picturesque Frémont.[48] Chase was left without experienced managers and without backstage support; he had no workers in the East who could secure delegates or make combinations for him. Worse still, he could not even secure solid support from his own Ohio. The Know-Nothing element of Republicans, who had supported him for governor, suspected his friendship for the Germans; many Germans, on the other hand, frowned on him because of his support by the Know-Nothings. The Whig element opposed him, for they still resented the "bargain" by which he secured the United States senatorship in 1849. Conservative business interests feared that his radical opinions on slavery would offend and alienate southerners, with whom they traded.[49] Moreover, United States Supreme Court Justice John McLean, another Ohioan, was also an aspirant for the Republican nomination. By convention time Chase's candidacy had collapsed.[50]

The Republicans' selection of Frémont for the Presidency was galling to Chase, particularly since Frémont had not labored long in the anti-slavery vineyard. The Republican party, Chase concluded bitterly, had "committed an act of positive injustice . . . in failing to take as their nominees men who truly personified the great real issue before the country." [51] But confidently he looked to 1860 to achieve his burning ambition.

As Chase pondered the question of renomination for governor in 1857, his personal advisers urged him not to risk his reputation in another gubernatorial campaign. However, the embezzlement of public funds by one of his administration compelled him to stand for reëlection to vindicate himself and his party. Under a withering fire of Democratic assaults, Chase emerged victor in the campaign to succeed himself. But it was an uncomfortably narrow victory; out of some 325,000 votes cast, he polled a plurality of only 1500 over his Democratic and Know-Nothing opponents—a result which did not bolster his presidential stock.[52] An almost solid German vote saved him from defeat.[53] "It was a fierce one," [54] he remarked of the campaign.

Chase's close escape from defeat did not dampen his ambition. During 1858 he made known to Giddings [55] and Sumner [56] that he was in the field for nomination in 1860.

During the winter of 1859–1860 Chase worked to line up delegates to the Chicago convention. Supporters in Michigan informed him that he might be successful in their state.[57]

During 1854 the Michigan Free Soil Democrats united with Whigs and prohibitionists to form a "Republican" party. Veteran leaders of the older parties, desirous of a share in the patronage, joined them, and in the fall they succeeded in carrying the state elections. Michigan Republicans also attracted the internal-improvements advocates. In a state where there are 1600 miles of coastline on four Great Lakes, the Democrats were almost ruined by their party's opposition to harbor bills. Republican journals printed such articles as "Slavery and Sailors," contending that the federal government under Democratic rule had given little aid for the improvement of rivers and harbors because of Democratic and southern opposition. The Republicans kept the issue alive until well into the Buchanan administration.[58]

The large number of Free Soil Democrats in the Republican party in Michigan and the radical character of Republicanism there should have made Chase a favorite in that state. But he was not, largely because Seward had the inside track. Seward spoke the language of Michigan more accurately than Chase. The New York senator had been an old Whig—which made him particularly acceptable to the internal-improvements people. Moreover, one-fourth of the people of Michigan had been born in New York and might naturally prefer Seward.[59] The New Yorker, too, had the support of Austin Blair, leader of the Michigan Republicans. Seward and Blair, both alumni of Union College and both former Whigs, were close personal friends. With Blair in command of the Michigan Republican party, Chase did not stand a chance. When the Republicans met in state convention in May, 1860, they instructed their delegation to the Chicago convention to support Seward—and Blair, soon to become governor of Michigan, was chosen chairman of the delegation.[60]

The preponderant Seward strength in Michigan did not dampen Chase's spirits. He turned his eyes toward Wisconsin.

Since the late 1840's the small Free Soil party had been active throughout Wisconsin—exercising a balance of power between Whigs and Democrats.[61] In the presidential election of 1852 the Wisconsin Whigs were dealt a stunning blow by the defeat of General Winfield Scott. In the following year, the state election was dominated not by the slavery or "Free Soil" issue, but by temperance. The candidates for governor were a Democratic, an old-line Whig, and one supported by Free Soilers and reforming Whigs. All the Free Soil candidates were avowed temperance men, while Barstow, the Democrat, was not. As a result, the Germans turned out to vote for Barstow, who was elected. The Free Soilers and discontented Whigs stood second, while the old-line Whigs mustered less than 3400. This campaign marked the end of Wisconsin Whiggery. The stage was set for a realignment of parties when in January, 1854, Douglas sponsored his Kansas-Nebraska bill.[62]

As in Ohio, Michigan and other northern states, the Republican party in Wisconsin was composed of many groups: Free Soilers, Whigs, Prohibitionists, dissatisfied Democrats, Know-Nothings, German-Americans and homesteaders. Frémont's huge vote in 1856 convinced practical politicians that the Republican party was the coming one.[63] Realistic leaders now took over the Republican organization in the Badger state and, in a move to attract the German vote, abandoned the "extreme Yankee attitude on the liquor question."[64] The Teutonic vote was indeed a major factor in Wisconsin.[65]

Of incalculable aid in attracting the German element to Republicanism in Wisconsin was the German-born Carl Schurz, who had been Republican candidate for lieutenant-governor in 1857, but had been defeated by a mere 107 votes, largely because the Know-Nothing element within the party would not support him. He redoubled his efforts to win recruits for Republicanism among the naturalized Germans. A revival of Know-Nothingism in Massachusetts brought the passage of a "Two Year Amendment," requiring naturalized citizens to pass a two-year probationary period before being permitted to vote. This threatened to drive Germans back into the arms of the Democrats, and Schurz became alarmed.[66]

Chase's endeavors to secure Wisconsin support consisted of efforts to cajole Schurz. The Ohio governor sought to have friends in Cincinnati induce Schurz to speak there.[67] On March 17 (1860) Schurz arrived in Columbus to deliver an address. Chase entertained him at his home and introduced him to his audience in highly complimentary terms.[68] The German leader has left an account of his stay with Chase on this occasion: [69]

He [Chase] avowed to me with a frankness which astonished but at the same time greatly fascinated me, his ardent desire to be President of the United States. . . . He said that I would undoubtedly be sent by the Republicans of Wisconsin as a delegate to that convention, and that he wished very much to know what I thought of his candidacy. . . . I had formed a general judgment of the situation, which I expressed in this wise: "If the Republican Convention at Chicago have courage enough to nominate an advanced anti-slavery man, they will nominate Seward; if not, they will not nominate you." The Governor was silent for a moment, as if he had heard something unexpected. . . . The Governor carried on the conversation in the best of temper, although I had evidently disappointed him, and he remained as cordial in his demeanor as before. Still I thought I observed a note of sadness in his tone.

Chase was disappointed indeed—but by no means discouraged. He communicated with his Cincinnati followers the day after Schurz's visit to Columbus. "Carl Schurz gave us a capital lecture last night. . . . He has the opinion that if Seward must be set aside as unavailable at Chicago Chase must be also," he wrote to Robert Hosea. "Perhaps he has seen some reason to change it while here; but it will be desirable to have him brought in contact with our best men and made to understand our arguments." [70] Chase instructed Hosea: "Please see Mitchell, Dickson & others & if possible get them to meet Mr. Schurz at your house [in Cincinnati] & Mitchell's after the lecture and get Hassaurek [Frederick Hassaurek, German Republican leader of Cincinnati] & Elliott and some others with them to talk with him." Chase cautioned further: "This is important. Mr. S. will reach Cincinnati by the 2:40 P.M. If one of our friends could meet him at the depot & take him home it would be well. I think Hassaurek knows him." [71]

Schurz was correct. Chase was not Wisconsin's favorite. As in Michigan, Seward was the hero—and for substantially the same reasons. The New York senator had more influential friends than Chase. Most ardent of pro-Seward leaders in Wisconsin was Rufus

King, whom Seward as governor of New York had appointed state adjutant general in 1839 but who had moved to Milwaukee. Now, in 1860, King threw the support of his paper, the Milwaukee *Sentinel*, behind Seward's presidential candidacy.[72] The large number of ex-New Yorkers in Wisconsin was another factor that favored Seward. Out of the state's 775,000 inhabitants in 1860, over 180,000 had come from New York State and less than 25,000 from Ohio.[73] Chase's hopes were dashed when in March the Wisconsin Republicans selected a pro-Seward delegation to the Chicago Convention, with Schurz as chairman and delegate-at-large.[74]

Chase concentrated his personal campaign for delegates in Pennsylvania, New Jersey and Illinois, all of which had been carried by Buchanan over Frémont in 1856. A supporter informed him: "The Republican nomination lies between you & Gov. Seward. The great point to determine the choice of the convention is to secure the voices of Penna., New Jersey & Illinois in the Convention—in my opinion the man who shall be the choice of these three States will be the nominee." [75] Thus the Ohio Governor made efforts in these three pivotal states.[76]

In Pennsylvania the dominant issue was the tariff, and throughout his career Chase had expressed free-trade sentiments.[77] Accordingly he now labored to create the impression that, despite his Democratic leanings, he was no free-trader.[78] The tariff was also an issue in New Jersey.[79] James A. Briggs, an Ohioan resident in New York, invaded New Jersey to raise the protectionist standard for Chase. At New Brunswick he assured a gathering: "I believe with Gov. Chase of Ohio that a Tariff for Revenue should be so adjusted as to . . . afford adequate encouragement to all departments of American Industry." [80] Briggs reported to Chase: "The people shouted. This is a good Tariff plank. . . . I am going to other meetings, & shall not fail to refer to that plank." [81]

Chase's supporters exerted strong pressure on him, to declare himself on the tariff, lest he lose all chance of attracting Pennsylvania support.[82] Accordingly, in January (1860) he released his views on this vexsome question, in a public letter: [83]

I am a practical man, and wish to take practical views of this tariff . . . No man in my judgment deserves the name of an American states-man who would not so shape American legislation and administration as to protect American industry and guard impartially all American rights and industry.

Chase's pretension of protectionist sentiments availed him little, however. His record and his leanings toward the low tariff haunted him. He was assailed by that portion of the Republican press which had hitherto been Whig.[84] Pennsylvania Republicans were not impressed either; no sudden conversion to the protectionist cause could overcome Chase's Democratic, free-trade past. By April (1860) one of his Pennsylvania workers reported: "I find that the Penn. men are not for you generally. They all admit that you would make the best President of any of the candidates, but say your tariff views are not those of the people of their State." [85] Moreover, Senator Cameron was developing some strength as the Keystone state's "favorite son." [86] Neither was New Jersey convinced by Chase's tariff pretensions and was too conservative on the slavery issue to be satisfied with the Ohio governor.[87] In addition, the New Jersey Republicans had their own candidate in William L. Dayton.

In Illinois, another pivotal state, Chase pursued a vigorous campaign for support. Again he was coolly received, for another "favorite son," Abraham Lincoln, had captured this state's imagination. In February Chase's erstwhile follower, Governor William H. Bissell, of Illinois, reported: [88]

You have not a few friends in this state, among whom I count myself, who would be very glad to have you nominated at Chicago as our Presidential candidate; but our folks have recently taken a notion to talk up Lincoln for that place. Of course, while that is so, it would be ungracious and impolitic to start anybody as his seeming rival.

An attempt was finally made to attract support from the Germans, whom Chase had courted so ardently. He had fought for homestead legislation and for immigrant rights in the Senate and had disapproved of the anti-immigrant "Two Year Amendment" in Massachusetts.[89] From one of his workers the Ohio governor received word: "I have written to Mr. Mitchel in Cincinnati and urged him to have Hassaurek [German leader of Cincinnati] open a correspondence with the Germans everywhere—especially in *Texas*—Wheeling—Baltimore—Delaware. Sending them printed Circulars." [90] The Chase boom found little response among the Teutonic element, however. In Texas, no Republican party could be organized; in Virginia they were inclined toward Seward; as for Maryland

and Delaware, Republican organizations there were controlled by the Blair family, who were pushing Judge Edward Bates, of Missouri, as their candidate for the Republican nomination.[91]

In late February (1860) the influential *Ohio State Journal*, of Columbus, came out in favor of Chase for President—but it added that, if he did not receive the prize at Chicago, Buckeye Republicans would "cheerfully support any nominee who truly represents their principles." [92] In March the Ohio Republican convention at Columbus adopted a resolution declaring "that while the Republicans of Ohio will give their united and earnest support to the nominee of the Chicago Convention, they would indicate as their first choice, and recommend to said Convention the name of Salmon P. Chase." [93] But this resolution—which bound only the four delegates-at-large, and not the regular delegates who were to be chosen at county conventions—was not even passed unanimously.[94] Even the Republican organization in his own Hamilton county (Cincinnati) was lukewarm to Chase. One Cincinnati lieutenant wrote him: "The result is very different from what your warm friends had hoped. Mr. Hassaurek is the only reliable friend you have on the delegation [from Hamilton county]. . . . They all probably have sufficient friendship for you to vote for you on a complimentary ballot, but none of them desire your nomination." [95]

Shortly before national convention time the anti-Chase forces started a movement to present Senator Benjamin F. Wade as Ohio's "favorite son." The possibility of nominating "Honest Ben" for President led several of the party leaders to his standard because of their aspirations to succeed him in the Senate.[96] To further divide the Ohio delegation to Chicago, the aged Supreme Court Justice John McLean was again being pressed for the nomination, principally by the older, more conservative Republicans.[97]

These discouragements—the lack of enthusiasm for him in other states, the inability to attract strong German support, division of opinion regarding him even in his own Ohio delegation, the rival Ohio presidential candidacies of Wade and McLean—all would have convinced any other man that he would cut no large figure at Chicago. Not so Chase. In April he journeyed to Washington to work among the Pennsylvania and New Jersey members of Congress and to persuade Wade to withdraw his candidacy.[98] Chase found: "Mr. Seward naturally is most spoken of." [99] But he consoled himself by adding: "Nobody can tell what sentiment will be uppermost to-morrow." [100]

Some of Chase's friends were frank enough to inform him that his chances were not promising.[101] But he listened more to those who told him what he wanted to hear, and he optimistically continued his canvass for delegates. When his personal friend, Dr. Gamaliel Bailey,[102] advised him that, in the interests of party success, he should withdraw from the race in favor of Seward,[103] Chase heatedly replied that he expected much more from a friend. He accused Bailey of conspiring with Thurlow Weed to promote Seward's candidacy, adding:[104]

I cannot change my position. I have no right to do so. A very large body of the people—embracing not a few who would hardly vote for any man other than myself as a Republican nominee—seem to desire that I shall be a candidate in 1860. No effort of mine, and so far as I know none of my immediate personal friends has produced this feeling. It seems to be of spontaneous growth. Under these circumstances those to whose judgment I am bound to defer say that I must suffer my name in the roll of those from whom the selection is to be made.

With three entries from Ohio in the Republican presidential race and with scant support elsewhere, Chase had little chance of capturing the prize. An Ohio delegate to Chicago observed: "Chase will get the majority vote of our delegates from Ohio, but the vote will be merely complimentary, as most of those who will vote for him will do so because he is of Ohio." [105] With not even his own state behind him, Chase remained confident. "As to the Chicago nomination, I possess my soul in patience," he wrote to one in quest of support. "That I shall have some friends outside of Ohio who prefer me to all others, I know; that many more prefer me as a second choice is plain enough." [106] And this remained his belief as the Ohio delegation entrained for Chicago in mid-May, 1860.

CHAPTER FOUR

A Pillar of Conservatism

IN ST. LOUIS, MISSOURI, there was a third candidate for leadership of the Republican party in 1860. He was Edward Bates, an aging, white-bearded jurist still devoted to the conservative Whig tradition, and the antithesis of Seward or Chase.

The Whig party was a religion for Judge Bates. In a frontier atmosphere of aggressive Jacksonian democracy, he had nevertheless risen high in Missouri politics as an avowed Whig and follower of Henry Clay. He was not a talented politician nor an able statesman, but he was widely revered for his integrity and respectability.

Born in Virginia in 1793, Bates had migrated to St. Louis as a young man. There he had read law, entered politics, held several state offices, and served one term in Congress. Political leadership, however, soon passed to those who spoke the language of the frontiersman, and Bates, who had no sympathy for "dangerous" Jacksonian doctrines, returned to the law, intermittently sitting on the Missouri bench. In 1847 he achieved some modest national fame as president of the great Rivers and Harbors convention in Chicago.[1] Subsequent efforts to induce him to re-enter public life were without avail, and in 1850, he declined President Millard Fillmore's proffer of a cabinet post.[2] A decade later his patriotic concern over the issues of 1860 caused him to return to active politics.

Bates derived his strength as a presidential candidate from among the conservative opponents to radical anti-slavery agitation. He had always scorned the extreme "higher law" doctrine of Seward and the pro-slavery, states' rights teachings of Calhoun.[3] "Slavery is not the real question," he maintained. "The question is only a struggle among politicians for sectional supremacy, and slavery is drawn into the contest only because it is a very exciting topic about which sensible people are more easily led to play the fool, than on any other subject."[4] Bates was ready to ignore slavery and concentrate on other issues.[5]

Missouri politics in the 1850's were extremely confused. Sec
tional interests of North, South, and West converged here t
create a political whirlpool that resulted in kaleidoscopic change
of scene, alliances, and personalities. Slavery, abolition, internal im
provements, railways, currency, "Americanism," and expansio
were local as well as national problems, and both leaders and partie
found it impossible to form more than temporary alliances whic
might vanish the moment a new issue came to be considered.

Through all this complexity, Judge Bates maintained a consisten
course of conservatism between extremes, in support of all trend
toward preservation of the Union and the avoidance of sectiona
ism.[6] In 1854 he endorsed the incipient "American" party in Mis
souri, primarily because, in the border states, Know-Nothingism wa
at least national and non-sectional.[7] In the campaign year of 185
Bates, who was alarmed by the sectional candidacies of bot
Frémont and Buchanan, served as the chairman of the last nationa
Whig convention which endorsed the "American" candidate, ex
President Fillmore.[8] In Missouri, meanwhile, Bates and other Whig
left without a party, transferred their allegiance to Americanism

The Democrats, on the other hand, were split into two opposin
factions over currency, the constitution, states' rights, and the pe
sonality of United States Senator Thomas Hart Benton. This Demo
cratic schism was a Missouri extension of the conflict between tw
dead leaders, Andrew Jackson and John C. Calhoun. Benton ha
been Old Hickory's staunch supporter. By 1851 Benton's opponen
within the party sided with the Whigs to prevent his reëlectio
to the Senate and to send a Whig Senator to Washington. Th
feud between Bentonites and anti-Bentonites became more bitte
when they took opposite positions on the Compromise of 185
Then Benton, shortly elected to the lower house of Congress, wid
ened the breach by opposing the Kansas-Nebraska bill becaus
it was a sectional proposal. In 1856 he ran for Governor of Mi
souri and was badly defeated.[9]

Benton's antipathy to the rising sectionalism made him equall
distrusted by the northern anti-slavery zealots, and in 1856 he op
posed Frémont, his own son-in-law.[10] Benton died in 1858, but h
bequeathed to his followers the principle that the preservation o
the Union was all important and that extremism both North an
South should be shunned, a principle, incidentally, which now in
spired Bates and Benton's other Whig opponents.[11]

The political confusion in Missouri and the emptiness of part abels had been obvious in the 1856 presidential election. Benton indeed supported Buchanan the Democrat. But Bates the Whig supported Fillmore the "American." And Francis P. Blair, Jr., a former Democrat and erstwhile Benton lieutenant, supported the Republican Frémont. One veteran leader commented: "I am absolutely bewildered, men are acting so entirely contrary to the course of their whole past lives as to confound me." [12]

Nevertheless, it is possible to see some order in this confusion. With the split in the Democratic party ever widening, there were three main contending groups in Missouri politics by 1858. First there were the conservatives: old Whigs, "Americans," and others anxious to suppress sectionalism and to preserve the Union. Second there were the northern-minded Democrats with mild Free-Soil leanings, led by Blair and his cousin B. Gratz Brown, editor of the St. Louis *Democrat*. Third there were the southern-minded Democrats championing slavery and states' rights. A fourth possible group, the abolitionists, hardly existed in Missouri except perhaps among the Germans near St. Louis.[13]

By 1859 Edward Bates was drifting from conservative Whiggery and "Americanism" toward the northern-minded former Democrats. He agreed to lend himself to a possible "national" coalition of former Whigs, "Americans," northern Democrats and mild Free Soilers which would defend the Union. This hope formed the background of Bates's presidential candidacy in 1860.

Bates's presidential campaign received much of its motive power from the Blair family.[14] Francis P. Blair, Sr., had once been Andrew Jackson's "right arm." He and his son, Montgomery Blair, lived in Silver Spring, Maryland, not far from Washington. Francis P. Blair, Jr.,—otherwise known as "Frank"—had settled in St. Louis, where he became a leader of the Benton, or anti-administration wing of the Democratic party and inherited the late Benton's mantle.[15]

Frank Blair's ally was his talented cousin, B. Gratz Brown, editor of the St. Louis *Missouri Democrat*, which Blair himself owned in part. The *Democrat* had been started by Frank Blair as a Benton paper in 1853 but in 1856 it had become the Blairs' organ in the Republican party. The *Democrat* advocated the Blair scheme of colonizing emancipated Negroes in Latin America, for the freed Negro was a serious labor and disciplinary problem in Missouri; the *Democrat's* attitude was: "White men for Missouri and Missouri for white men." [16] Late in 1858 the *Democrat* announced the free-soil program for the next presidential election: "Today the campaign of 1860 begins. . . . Missouri belongs to her free white citizens—there is no room in it for slaves." [17]

In the following spring (1859) Blair began organizing against the "administration" Democrats, with whom he and his family had long been at odds. Blair foresaw that the "Americans" were an ephemeral political group and that nativism offered no strong issue against the Democrats.[18] Moreover, he believed in supremacy of "free" white labor and in Negro colonization in tropical America as a solution to the race problem.[19] At the same time his own Jacksonian-Bentonian antecedents were strong. Thus he was of opinion that the campaign against the "administration" Democrats in power must be waged on a mild anti-slavery basis and organized as the "Free Democracy." In 1859 Blair's Free Democracy, which became substantially the nucleus of the Republican party of Missouri, was concentrated mainly in and around St. Louis. Its main element was the German population, who were dissatisfied with any truckling to slavery and with the Democrats' hostility to "free land." Other groups in the Free Democracy were advocates of Negro colonization, champions of internal improvements and those who wanted a Pacific railroad built from St. Louis to California with government aid.[20]

In 1859 the "Opposition"—the term applied collectively to all groups opposed to the administration Democrats—was divided into at least three separate factions. Besides the Free Democracy, there were the remnants of the American party, whose members knew not where to go following the decline of the anti-immigrant issue. Third there were the Old Line Whigs who still refused to concede that the Whig party was dead. The "Americans" and the Old Line Whigs, in contrast to the Free Democracy, were ultra-conservative on the slavery question, believing with Bates that further agitation or even heated discussion could bring only a dissolution of the Union.[21]

Blair and Brown believed that if the three Opposition elements —their Free Democracy, the "Americans," and the Old Line Whigs —could be united, a victorious fight could be waged against the Democrats in Missouri. The one man who could bring these groups together in a successful Presidential election was Edward Bates. Blair desired to promote his own candidacy for Governor.[22]

In April, 1859, Blair and Congressman Schuyler Colfax, of Indiana, met Bates in a private conference. Bates recorded:[23]

The object of Messrs. Blair and Colfax, no doubt, was . . . to pproximate the terms upon which the Republican party might dopt me as its candidate for the Presidency. . . .

Both these gentlemen are influential leaders of their party, and oth declare that I am their first choice. They both say that Mr. Seward cannot get the nomination of his party. . . . Mr. Colax is very anxious to consolidate the whole N. W. [Northwest] o as to ensure what he considers the main point for which, as he inderstands it, his party contends—i.e., that the U. S. shall not exend slavery into any country where they do not find it already stablished.

To that I have no objection.

Mr. C. is also a warm friend of Mr. Blair and is anxious to conolidate in Missouri, so as to put Mr. B. on a good footing with a najority in the State.

And, working for that end, Mr. Blair is eager to form a combinaion within the State, upon the precise question of slavery or no lavery in Missouri. This, undoubtedly, would be a good policy for Mr. Blair personally, because it would strengthen the local free soil arty (of which he is the acknowledged local head) with all the 'orces that I and my friends could influence.

Finding Bates sympathetic toward his plans, Blair undertook to mite all forces of the opposition behind Bates for President. The Old Line Whigs never quite trusted Blair who had been a Demo-crat, but it was hoped they would support Bates. The *Democrat* iccordingly appealed to the Old Line Whigs to forget Clay: "Let he bones of the 'Ashland martyr' be suffered to lie in the mauso-eum. . . . Let the dead sleep. Edward Bates is a live man, sus-ained by a live party. His opinions on the [slavery] question [are] dentical with those of Clay." [24] And the *Democrat* continued in his vein: [25]

We are fully alive to the policy, nay the duty, of rallying all the livisions of the Opposition against the profligate and imbecile rule of the National [Buchanan] Democracy.

The desired union can be effected by nominating a man for whom Republican, Whig, American, and honest Democrat will vote. Such a man, we believe, is Edward Bates.

A week after the dinner conference at Blair's home, there ap-peared in newspapers throughout the nation a letter addressed by Bates to the self-styled "Whig General Committee of New York," in which Bates gave his views on national topics. He disapproved of anti-slavery agitation, which "was a dangerous vortex into which good men are drawn unawares." He could attribute slavery agitation pro or con, to "no higher motive than personal ambition or sectional prejudice." [26] As to foreign policy, he avowed himself "not much of a progressive"; he was "content to leave it where Washington placed it," without entangling alliances. He had no sympathy for greedy acquisition of foreign territory. He indicted Buchanan's administration, denouncing it for concentration of power into the Executive's hands and for extravagance. Much money was spent by the Democrats yet the Army and Navy were neglected, improvement of rivers and harbors was abandoned, and the Pacific railroad was not even begun. [27]

Bates's letter was essentially the platform of the older conservatives in the anti-Democratic camp who were opposed to making slavery a dominant issue and who wished to emphasize other problems—corruption, extravagance, internal improvements, and the Pacific railroad. Bates's views were received favorably by the more moderate Republicans, who hoped for a coalition with conservatives in the border slave states, by "Americans" who believed slavery to be no main issue, and by those optimistic Old Line Whigs who still believed that the Whig skeleton might be reinvigorated with flesh and blood.

In the border slave states Bates hoped to attract what was termed the "Opposition"—a conglomeration of Old Line Whigs, "Americans," dissatisfied Democrats, and conservatives in general; their only common aims were hostility to the Democrats in both local and national affairs and a demand for a cessation of the "eternal wrangling and spouting of abolitionism." It was soon proposed that this Opposition might be united with the more conciliatory Republicans of the North to form a national conservative party opposed to both northern abolitionists and southern pro-slavery extremists. [28]

The hope for such a grand coalition was recognized by Bates himself. In June (1859) he wrote: [29]

Many suggestions, in various parts of the country, to take me up as the Opposition candidate for the Presidency. . . . A large section of the Republican party, who think that Mr. Seward's nomination would ensure defeat, are anxious to take me up, thinking that I could carry the Whigs and Americans generally, and thus ensure the Northern States and have a strong party in the border slave states, consisting of Whigs and Americans.

The formation of any such national conservative party, however, would require a cessation of anti-slavery activity in the North and secession activity in the South. Bates and his Missouri backers hoped that many southerners opposed to the extremism of the newer Democratic leaders would coöperate with conservative Republicans in the North. Bates wanted an "Opposition" party, he declared, composed of "the good men of other parties—Democrats, Whigs, Americans, Republicans." [30] He muffled the slavery issue.[31]

Bates's views met the full approval of Blair and Brown, who now portrayed the Republicans as the conservative, Union-saving party, since the Democrats had sectionalized the nation by propagating slavery.[32] Blair and Brown disparaged violent anti-slavery doctrines and condemned John Brown's Harpers Ferry raid.[33] They persisted in believing that gradual emancipation and colonization of the slaves in Central America constituted the only solution to the race problem. Instead of pressing the slavery issue Blair and Brown demanded concessions for the West, homestead legislation, a Pacific railroad, internal improvements, and an adequate overland mail.

In the summer of 1859 Blair and Brown began organizing their Free Democratic forces in St. Louis—sometimes they were referred to as "Republicans"—for a "clean" ticket in the forthcoming municipal elections. The preliminary work was done in the office of the *Democrat*. Editorially the paper emphasized that the county election was tied up with the presidential battle of 1860, and with Bates's candidacy in particular.[34] In July the Free Democracy nominated a county ticket composed of Republicans, "Americans," and Whigs. It was politically balanced, economically and racially, and was expected to satisfy the manufacturing interests, farmers, "Americans," Germans, and Creoles.[35] During this municipal campaign the *Democrat* blasted the "corrupt" Democratic "County Court" junta because of high taxes and hurled editorial projectiles at President Buchanan. Slavery was rarely mentioned.[36] Clearly the *Democrat* was anticipating 1860.[37]

The "county reform ticket," sponsored by Blair and Brown, achieved only moderate success, since the "Americans" and Whigs placed their own separate candidates in the field.[38] But they were not discouraged. If they could not induce most Old Line Whigs and "Americans" to enter into concert with Free Democrats and Republicans to promote Bates's candidacy, they could have the Whigs endorse Bates separately.

At the Whig convention of Lafayette County in Lexington on October 17, Bates's friend, Charles Gibson, working in close cooperation with Blair, was instrumental in having Bates endorsed for the presidency. The convention also provided for a state "Whig" convention to be held at Jefferson City, on December 28, 1859. Only "conservatives" would be welcome at the proposed convention.[39]

The fact that only "conservatives" were invited to the Jefferson City conclave did not dampen the spirits of Blair and Brown;[40] they were quite willing to fawn upon the Whigs in order to defeat the regular Democracy in 1860. Blair and Brown now issued a call for a "Republican" state convention at the same place and on the same day as the Whig convention![41] The Whigs, however, resented this maneuver and accordingly postponed their own convention at Jefferson City until February 22 (1860)[42]—only to learn that the Republicans were arranging a similar postponement![43] The Whigs were furious. They were determined to "repudiate the action of any State Convention of which F. P. Blair, Jr. should be a member."[44] The *Democrat* bemoaned that "the Free Democracy and Republicans of Missouri . . . differ from the Whigs and Americans on the slavery question."[45]

In January (1860) Bates decided:[46]

My nomination for the Presidency, which at first struck me with mere wonder, has become familiar, and now I begin to think my prospects very fair. . . . There is now great probability that the Opposition of all classes will unite upon me. And that will be equivalent to election.

The great Opposition convention met, not on February 22, but on February 29 at Jefferson City. An erstwhile Whig, James O. Broadhead, who believed in coöperation with the Republicans, called the meeting to order. Colonel William L. Switzler, "American" leader and editor of the *Missouri Statesman*, was conspicuous there, as was the German leader, Arnold Krekel. The convention, after denouncing the Democrats for promoting "disunion," endorsed Bates for President. The only mention of slavery was a declaration against reopening the African slave trade.[47]

Discord arose, however, when the Convention debated whether to send delegates to the Republican National Convention at Chicago or to the Constitutional Union (Whig conservative) National Convention at Baltimore.[48] No decision was reached. Furthermore, the platform adopted, although essentially conservative, was too radical for certain Old Line Whigs and "Americans" who, despite their endorsement of Bates for President, met later and formed a state central committee, preparatory to sending delegates to the Constitutional Union National Convention. Indeed, many of the Old Line Whigs and "Americans" were by now looking upon Bates with suspicion.[49] In this they were justified, for Bates was indeed straying farther away from his old Whig moorings.[50]

The inability of the Jefferson City convention to agree on whether to send delegates to Chicago or to Baltimore left Blair, Brown and the St. Louis *Democrat* junta no other alternative than to meet in a "Republican" state convention to select pro-Bates delegates to Chicago. This they did on March 10 in St. Louis, where fireworks started—precipitated this time not by Whigs or "Americans," but by the Germans.[51]

For years the German immigrants, who had trekked westward to till the soil, had agitated for free land. When the Democrats consistently refused to hear their pleas and when the Kansas-Nebraska Act was passed and the Republican party was launched, the Germans, fearful lest the extension of slavery and the southern landed aristocracy would close the West to settlement by free whites, flocked to the Republican party.[52] By 1860 the Germans were the dominant foreign-born element in Missouri [53] and constituted the largest single group in the state Republican party.[54] For years Blair had carefully cultivated them.[55] The Republican vote, it was observed, was "composed mostly of Germans, a few anti-slavery men from New England . . . and the personal following of Francis P. Blair, Jr., Edward Bates, and B. Gratz Brown." [56]

In early 1860, however, the German element was in a rebellious mood. The revival of Americanism, illustrated by the "Two Year Amendment" in Massachusetts in 1859, had aroused Germans everywhere.[57] Germans of Iowa, for instance, had only recently assembled in convention and opposed the nomination of Bates for President because he was a former Know-Nothing (who had supported Fillmore on the "American" ticket in 1856) and because he was favorable to enforcement of the Fugitive Slave Law. The Iowa resolutions were forwarded to German leaders in Missouri.[58] The reaction of the Missouri Germans was reflected in the comment of Car Daenzer, editor of the St. Louis *Westliche Post*, who declared that Bates was being sponsored by "the finest models of Missouri fire-eaters—rabid pro-slavery men,—old Know-Nothings—Whigs, and office-hunting ex-Republicans." [59]

On March 10 the Republican convention, under Brown's chairmanship, met in St. Louis. Resolutions were read which called for colonizing the freed Negroes, for a homestead act, a Pacific railroad by the central route, for "equal rights of citizens of all nativities," for opposition to any change in the naturalization laws, and for the nomination of Bates for President. At once the Germans opposed the endorsement of Bates for President. Moritz Pinner, Jewish editor of a Kansas City German-language paper, and Carl Daenzer were on their feet. Confusion followed. Pinner offered the resolution: "*Resolved*, That the delegates of the Republican party of Missouri have no preferred candidate for President of the United States, and that our delegates to Chicago shall not cast their votes for any candidate who does not stand fairly and square upon the Philadelphia [National Republican] platform of 1856." This, of course, would eliminate Bates. Cries of "Dry up!" "Simmer down!" and "Switch off!" were hurled at Pinner amid the stamping of feet and the banging of the Chairman's gavel. Pinner's efforts were fruitless, and the resolution endorsing Bates was approved. A number of Germans marched out of the hall. Daenzer remained. A Bates supporter demanded to know if Daenzer would support Bates if he were nominated, and the *Westliche Post* editor replied: "No!" Bates was endorsed, but it was obvious that most Germans would have no part of his candidacy.[60] The Missouri delegation to Chicago, among whom were Blair and Brown, stood twelve for Bates and six against him.[61]

Although the Germans did not block a Missouri endorsement of Bates, their opposition compelled him to commit himself compromisingly on the issues of the day. A series of questions were put to him. To the first question, "Are you opposed to the extension of slavery?" Bates answered that "within the States it exists by local law, and the Federal Government has no control over it there. . . . The National Government has the Power to permit or forbid slavery within [the territories]. . . . I am opposed to the extension of slavery." To the second question, "Does the Constitution carry slavery into the Territories?" Bates said: "I answer no." The third question concerned colonization of freed Negroes, and Bates replied that he was in favor of it. The fourth, aimed at pacifying the German vote, related to equality of rights of natives and foreign-born. Bates rejoined: "I recognize no distinction among Americans." The fifth and sixth queries related to the construction of a Pacific railroad under Government auspices and to a homestead act, and Bates replied that he favored both proposals. The seventh question concerned the admission of Kansas as a free state, and Bates replied: "I think that Kansas ought to be admitted without delay, leaving her like all other states, the sole judge of her own constitution." [62]

Bates's letter, designed to conciliate the Germans and other advanced Republicans, weakened him considerably because it made him unacceptable to many Whigs and "Americans." [63] Colonel William F. Switzler, editor of the *Missouri Statesman* and leader of the "Americans," stated that Bates's acceptance of the Republican doctrine of Congressional inhibition of slavery in the territories made him unacceptable to the Whigs and "Americans." [64] In other border states, too, Bates became *persona non grata* to such groups. In Kentucky the influential Louisville *Journal* commented: [65]

He has deliberately and formally subscribed to every article in the Republican creed. . . . It settles the position of Mr. Bates decisively. He is just as good or bad a Republican as Seward, Chase or Lincoln is. As such, of course, the constitutional Union [conservative Whig] men of the South will scorn to touch him. He has by a single blow severed every tie of confidence or sympathy which connected him with the Southern Conservatives.

Thus was doomed Blair's and Brown's plans for a united "Opposition" that would support Bates for the presidency. Bates had offended the conservative Whigs and "Americans" without winning the Germans to their cause.

Perhaps it was natural that the Blair-Brown-Bates plan of a conservative anti-Democratic union crumbled. The radicalism of the early Republican movement, no matter how Blair might portray the Republicanism of 1860 as the essence of conservatism, could not so suddenly be effaced. The anti-southern record of such extreme Republicans as Seward, Chase, and Sumner had made an indelible impression. Republicanism had become identified with these leaders, not with such moderates as Edward Bates and Frank Blair.

Many continued to consider the words "Republican" and "Abolition-ist" as synonymous.[66]

In addition to Frank Blair and his conservative Missouri group, another force backing Bates was the radical Horace Greeley, who had become interested in Bates. The New York *Tribune* editor had seen the Missouri jurist in 1859 and was impressed.[67] Greeley had withdrawn from the political firm of "Seward, Weed & Greeley" when his suppressed ambition for public office was ignored.[68] Bates's views on internal improvements in particular pleased Greeley, who informed his vast *Tribune* reading public that Bates was a con-servative who could draw the Old Line Whig and "American" vote.[69] Greeley, a veteran anti-slavery agitator, had become fright-ened over the danger of disunion. Moreover, he also wanted to be a "king-maker." [70]

Greeley wrote to his friend, Schuyler Colfax, about Bates and asked Colfax to consult Frank Blair.[71] Colfax, a founder of the In-diana Republican party and former New Yorker, had been elected to Congress on an anti-Nebraska, temperance, and "American" ticket in 1854. Like Bates, he opposed northern and southern sectionalism, and favored internal improvements.[72] Adopting Greeley's suggestion, Colfax supported Bates in his South Bend *St. Joseph Valley Register* and consulted with Frank Blair. Colfax wrote: "Blair says he [Bates] can carry Missouri, if brought out right, and Illinois, of course, he being quite strong in Southern Illinois, where our cause is weak. And Winter Davis says he can carry Maryland and Dela-ware, if we do not repel them by too strong a platform." [73]

Colfax undoubtedly represented Indiana sentiment correctly in backing the conservative Bates. The Hoosier state had never been rabid against slavery; in the lower counties, settled by southerners, anti-slavery work was discouraging.[74] The Kansas-Nebraska Act caused relatively little excitement in Indiana, and the anti-Demo-cratic forces there in 1854 were able to unite only on a platform of "Freedom, Temperance, and our *Native* Land"; [75] Democrats dis-missed their opponents as "the Abolition Free-Soil Maine-Law Native-American Anti-Catholic Anti-Nebraska Party of Indiana." [76] In 1856 Indiana refused to support the anti-slavery Republican Fré-mont.[77] By 1859 public opinion in Indiana had not changed. The people were indifferent toward slavery, and the Democrats mo-nopolized state politics.[78]

Nevertheless, Indiana was a political prize, ranking third among the northwestern states in convention and electoral votes. Like Pennsylvania and Illinois, it was considered indispensable for the success of either party in 1860. The Bates forces worked particularly hard in Indiana. Many Hoosier leaders, wanting none of Seward, threw their support to Bates.[79]

Unfortunately for Bates, the anti-Democratic forces in Indiana were still divided into three main groups—the Republicans, the "Americans," and the Whig remnants. Coöperation between them was especially difficult because the large German element in the Republican party disliked the "Americans," and the old Whigs feared Republican radicalism. One factor, however, was in their favor: a growing schism in the ranks of the Democrats, who, surfeited with success, had begun to quarrel among themselves. Some Democrats were disappointed over meager spoils, and some were angry at the party autocrat, United States Senator Jesse D. Bright, and others were grieved because their party neglected internal improvements and homestead legislation.[80] Therefore Colfax and others felt that, given the proper candidate and a moderate platform, a union of Republicans and "Americans" might attract the old Whigs and even a few disgruntled Democrats. The proper conditions, however, were difficult of achievement.

In 1860 the "American" leaders of Indiana gave to the Republicans their terms for coöperation: that Republicans, "Americans" and Whigs participate on equal terms in a state convention; that no radically anti-slavery presidential candidate be given Indiana's support at the Chicago convention and that the state's delegation be instructed to vote for Bates, or some other conservative; that the platform adopted at Chicago be national and not sectional. The Republicans agreed, and a "Mass Convention of the people of Indiana opposed to the policy of the present Administration of the General Government" was called to meet at Indianapolis on February 22; the name "Republican" was adroitly avoided.[81] One Bates manager in Missouri, watching these Indiana developments studiously, suggested: "I hope a good delegation will go over from St. Louis; now is the time to *strengthen* Mr. Bates."[82]

When the "Mass" convention met at Indianapolis, the Missouri Bates men, headed by Peter L. Foy, of the St. Louis *Democrat*, were present and urged their favorite's claims to Indiana support. Foy held a levee at his hotel, and displayed a letter written by Bates to Colfax, which was an exposition of the more moderate brand of

Republicanism, such as would be palatable to Indianans. An article from Greeley's New York *Tribune*, favoring Bates for President, was distributed in pamphlet form. The Bates men were working hard to secure the Hoosier delegation to Chicago.[83] Their plans, however, were disrupted by the radical, nativist-hating Germans, led by Theodore Hielscher, editor of the Indianapolis *Freie Presse*, who wanted no conservative or Know-Nothing nominated at Chicago.[85] As for mollifying the South, Hielscher said: "Let the chivalry go; the sooner, the better. . . . Let those that will, secede." Hielscher offered a resolution to instruct Indiana's delegates at Chicago to vote for no candidate "who was not a good Republican in 1856."[86] Although his proposal was laid on the table, there were no pro-Bates instructions given to the delegates then selected.[87] Majority sentiment among the Hoosiers was for Bates, but the Germans obstructed selection of a unanimous delegation.[88]

Bates, in St. Louis, found encouragement in the Indiana situation. He confided to his diary: "Gibson and other friends have returned from the *Indiana* Rep. Convention, and report favorably. A large majority of the delegates appointed to the Chicago Convention is made up of 'Bates men'—20 to 6 or 22 to 4."[89]

The Bates movement made some headway in Illinois, too, particularly in the lower counties where the influence of the Old South was strong. The most active Bates supporter in the Prairie state was Orville Hickman Browning, an old-time Clay Whig, who had travelled to St. Louis in September, 1859, to see Bates about the coming presidential campaign. Both men agreed in nearly all their opinions including the tariff and slavery. Browning concluded that Bates was "the best man the Republicans can support."[90] At this conference, incidentally, it was agreed that Bates should make his political views public in an open letter to be published in the press.[91] Browning's reasons for supporting Bates were, he said, "to strengthen our organization in the South, and remove apprehension in the South of any hostile purpose on the part of Republicans to the institutions of the South . . . to bring to our support the old whigs in the free states . . . and to give some check to the ultra tendencies of the Republican party."[92]

When Browning returned home he sought out Norman B. Judd, Republican state chairman of Illinois, and urged Bates's claims for the Presidency. Judd was not sympathetic unless Bates "would put himself on Republican ground."[93] Then, in early February,

1860, Browning visited Springfield and talked with Abraham Lincoln, who was at this time a Republican presidential contender himself. Of his interview with Lincoln, Browning wrote: [94]

Feby 8. . . . At night Lincoln came to my room and we had a free talk about the Presidency. He thinks I may be right in supposing Mr. Bates to be the strongest and the best man we can run —that he can get votes even in this County [Sangamon] that he cannot get—and that there is a large class of voters in all the free states that would go for Mr. Bates, and for no other man. He says it is not improbable that by the time the National convention meets in Chicago he may be of opinion that the very best thing that can be done will be to nominate Mr. Bates.

Browning was not discouraged by Lincoln's non-committal attitude, and he continued his activity.[95]

While Frank Blair, B. Gratz Brown, Colfax, and Browning were laboring for Bates in the West, the other Blairs in Maryland boosted Bates in the East.

Maryland, with commercial as well as agricultural interests, was a traditional Whig state.[96] Conservative and nationally minded, it had maintained a consistent opposition alike to both secession and abolition. When the Whig party declined in 1854–1855 most Marylanders gave their support to the new American party which, in addition to combating German and Irish influences, also opposed sectionalism and preached the necessity of muffling the seemingly everlasting Negro question. In 1856 Maryland voted for the conservative Fillmore. In this same year a few Republicans attempted to hold a meeting in Baltimore, but a mob finally broke up the gathering. In 1857 Maryland, although its governor was Democratic, had a Know-Nothing, Whig-tainted legislature and by 1858 Baltimore was completely in the nativists' hands.[97]

Henry Winter Davis, Know-Nothing candidate for re-election to Congress from Baltimore, championed a union of the "Americans" and Republicans for 1860: "I feel sure the opposition could carry both [North Carolina and Tennessee] in 1860 for either Bell or *Bates* of Mo. In my judgment the opposition are fools if they do not take the latter: it will give us the Govt. for 12 years at least, & in the next six years every seat on the Supreme Court Bench will be vacated by the hand of time." [98] Davis believed that the "Americans" and Republicans should not be kept "asunder at the next presidential election"; that Maryland's interests were with the North, rather than the South.[99] In Congress Davis coöperated with the Republicans, casting the deciding vote for William Pennington, New Jersey Republican, for Speaker of the House.[100] In return for this vote the Republicans gave to a Davis follower the position of sergeant-at-arms.[101] When he was censured by the Maryland legislature for supporting a "Black Republican," [102] Davis maintained that he was simply opposing the "disunion" or secession-minded Democrats, emphasizing that Pennington was "sound on the protection of American industry and on river and harbor improvements," and in favor of ending the internecine strife of sections." [103] Davis's wing of the American party, favoring coalition with the Republicans, was supported by the Baltimore *Patriot*,[104] which in January 1860 came out for Bates for President.[105] The Republican movement, thus started from conservative, semi-nativist origins, soon attracted the radical Germans of Baltimore.[106]

Republican leadership in Maryland, however, was not seized by Davis or German leaders, but by the Blairs. The two Maryland Blairs—Montgomery Blair and Francis P. Blair, Sr.—believed that if the South were assured that the Republicans did not advocate white and Negro equality, many southern states would support them. The Blairs therefore advocated solving the slavery question by colonizing Negroes. In 1859 Montgomery Blair wrote another Republican chieftain: [107]

It [colonization] would do more than ten thousand speeches to define accurately our objects and disabuse the minds of the great body of the Southern people of the issue South that the Republicans wish to set negroes free among them to be their equals and consequently their rulers when they are numerous. This is the only point needing elucidation and comprehension by the Southern people to make us as strong at the South as at the North. If we can commit our party distinctly to this I will undertake for Maryland in 1860.

On the basis of this program the Blairs hoped to have slaveholding Maryland represented in the Republican National Convention at Chicago.[108] The Maryland Republican party, one Republican wrote, was "a concealed one, its sentiments felt by those who held them as sentiments not safely or wisely to be avowed." [109] In late April, amidst the threats of mobs, the Blairs called a Republican state convention at Baltimore, with Montgomery Blair as chairman: The elder Blair was selected as delegate-at-large to Chicago; George E. Wiss, a German-American leader, was chosen as a regular delegate. A typical Blair plank advocating Negro colonization was approved. Essentially a Blair project, this sparsely attended Republican convention assured Maryland votes for Bates at Chicago.[110]

The situation in neighboring Delaware was somewhat similar to that of Maryland. Here conservative, anti-Democratic forces organized themselves into the "People's party," [111] which was willing to accept Bates and send delegates to Chicago. This sentiment was given expression in the Wilmington *Delaware Republican*.[112]

Much of the strength of the People's party lay in the support of Delaware manufacturing interests who were dissatisfied with the low tariff and wanted protection; the Opposition was primarily an anti-Democratic, Unionist and protectionist movement.[113] The *Delaware Republican* insisted that the Republican party was not radical, and that border-state conservatives could consistently support such a candidate as Edward Bates on a protective-tariff platform.[114] In February, 1860, this paper began advocating Bates for President [115] and declared that, since no third party to combat the Democrats was practicable, the Delaware People's party should send delegates to Chicago.[116] Accordingly, the *Republican* sponsored a state convention, to be held at Dover May 1.[117] It was explained: "There is no Republican organization in this State, and there is no intention to form one. The voters who are in favor of holding the convention at Dover . . . intend to act with the People's party, particularly in the nomination of candidates, and to use their best and most earnest efforts to defeat the Locofocos [Democrats]." [118] The all-important aim was to defeat the Democrats.[119]

The Opposition convention met as planned. The main speaker was the veteran Whig, "Tom" Corwin of Ohio, who nurtured ideas of transforming the Republicans into a great conservative party such as the Whigs had been. He glossed over the repulsive features of *bona fide* Republicanism.[120] In his speech Corwin advocated a higher tariff and explained that Republicans should not be considered abolitionists just because abolitionists voted with Republicans. The convention appointed pro-Bates delegates and adopted resolutions which took the anti-slavery sting from Republicanism by advocating a protective tariff and a homestead bill.[121] Bates was assured of Delaware support at Chicago.[122]

The two Maryland Blairs, in their search for Bates delegates, also courted the Kentucky delegation. They invited to their home Cassius M. Clay, leader of the Kentucky Republicans. Clay later wrote: [123]

The Blairs were for Edward Bates, a respectable old Whig of Missouri. They invited me to their residence at Silver Springs, in Maryland; and without ceremony, said, if I would go for Bates, I should be made Secretary of War. . . . But I knew nothing of Bates' principles; and I frankly declined to support him. For this I lost favor with the Blairs.

Clay's story about the Blairs' tender of the War portfolio cannot be taken too seriously. There was, however, a potent reason why Clay was not interested in supporting Bates: he planned to present himself as a candidate for the Republican nomination and soon wrote to various Republican leaders offering himself as party standard-bearer.[124]

Despite Bates's inability to conciliate the die-hard Whigs, the Germans, and the more radical Republicans, he regarded his chances as reasonably satisfactory. He confided to his diary: [125]

The signs indicating my nomination are growing, in numbers and strength every day. Several State conventions . . . have appointed "Bates" Delegates to the Chicago Convention . . . and a vast number of newspapers, from Massachusetts to Oregon, have placed my name at the head of their columns. . . .

But knowing the fickleness of popular favor, and on what small things great events depend, I shall take care not so to set my heart upon the glittering bauble, as to be mortified or made at all unhappy by a failure.

On the eve of the Chicago convention—with the greater part of delegations from Missouri, Indiana, Maryland, and Delaware apparently assured him and with a possibility that he would be second choice in other states—Bates appeared to be Seward's most formidable rival.

CHAPTER FIVE

An Anti-Nebraska Whig of the Prairies

W HILE THE MANAGERS of Seward, Chase, and Bates mapped their strategy, Abraham Lincoln rose to national prominence. To most people he was not a presidential contender but an Illinois lawyer who had made a brilliant showing against the mighty Stephen A. Douglas in the senatorial campaign of 1858.

Lincoln was Illinois' leading Republican next to United States Senator Lyman Trumbull. When not practicing law he fraternized with fellow-townsmen and denounced the Democrats. He corresponded with plain voters and prominent Republicans. He plodded on with his legal practice, social obligations, and political activity, unaware of the immortal distinction that the future held for him.[1]

Born in a log cabin in what was then Hardin (now Larue) County, Kentucky, in 1809, Lincoln moved with his parents to Spencer County, Indiana. After several years of migration the Lincoln family eventually settled in Macon County, Illinois. Lincoln was successively clerk in a store, manager of a mill, odd-jobs man, village postmaster, and deputy surveyor. All the while he read law and interested himself in politics. In 1834 he was elected to the state legislature in an era when personality was a major factor in politics. He served four successive terms, until 1841. Five years later he was elected to Congress, where he was the lone Whig representative from Illinois.[2]

Lincoln was attracted to the Whig party by admiration for Henry Clay and his "American System." He supported Clay for President in 1844; but four years later he threw his support to General Zachary Taylor.[3] When Taylor became President, Lincoln demanded a share of the federal patronage for Illinois.[4] He sought for himself the lucrative job of Commissioner of the General Land Office, but that went to another, and Lincoln was disheartened.[5] When offered the Governorship of Oregon Territory, he declined it.[6] In 1850 he wrote of his "fidelity to the great Whig cause," but insisted that he "would not now accept the Land Office, if it were offered" to him.[7] In 1852 Lincoln emerged from his law books to speak for General Winfield Scott, the Whig presidential candidate—but it was a half-hearted oration.[8]

Meanwhile, politics in Illinois, as in other regions of the North, underwent a drastic transition which comprised not only the decline of the Whig party but also the split in the long-dominant Democratic party.

By the end of 1853 the Democracy in the upper Mississippi Valley was subjected to many disintegrating influences.[9] The successive national Democratic administrations had ignored internal improvements and homestead legislation which the West viewed as essential. Moreover, in Illinois factions developed within the Democratic ranks over patronage and leadership. Furthermore, temperance, free soil, and Know-Nothingism disrupted party solidarity. And early in 1854 Illinois' own Senator Stephen A. Douglas presented the mightiest of all issues by incorporating into his Kansas-Nebraska bill the repeal of the Missouri Compromise.[10]

The Kansas-Nebraska bill aroused all the latent opposition forces in Illinois to action. Democrats dissatisfied with the Little Giant's leadership, German-Americans, Whigs, homestead advocates, internal-improvement enthusiasts, abolitionists and other groups seized upon the issue thus presented to attack the Democratic party and Douglas personally.[11]

By the fall of 1854 Whigs were prepared to enter the state elections on an "Anti-Nebraska" plank, in coöperation with abolitionists and "Anti-Nebraska" Democrats. An orthodox Democratic leader commented on this maneuver: "It is amazingly surprising how these Whigs, Free Soilers & Abolitionists have hoodwinked the Democrats on the Nebraska question. The infamous Whigs to resuscitate their dying party—I may say their almost defunct party—have combined with these miserable factions to annihilate the old Democracy." [12] The entire Whig party, of course, did not enter the Anti-Nebraska ranks: "Some of its members went into the Know-Nothing lodges; some enlisted under the Abolition flag, and the others drifted about." [13]

Lincoln did not combine with the Know-Nothings; nor did he enter the "abolition" Republican ranks in 1854. He remained in his party as an Anti-Nebraska Whig, in the hope that this was the most likely guarantee of his cherished ambition—to enter the United States Senate. Not until May, 1856—when the Whig party had all but disappeared and the Republican party was in the hands of moderate groups—did he become a member of the party which he was destined to lead.[14] Lincoln was, in the words of his law-partner, William H. Herndon, "not a speculative-minded man; was, like Washington, severely practical; he never ran in advance of his age." [15] The central and lower regions of Illinois, settled largely by southerners, were opposed to extreme Republicanism.[16] In this same year (1856) Lincoln supported the aging, conservative, Whig-minded Supreme Court Justice John McLean for the Republican presidential nomination.[17] When Frémont was nominated, Lincoln took the stump for him.[18] Frémont lost Illinois, incidentally, largely because the conservative Fillmore polled a huge anti-Democratic vote.[19] Mrs. Lincoln wrote: "Although Mr. Lincoln is, or was a Fremont man, you must not include him with so many of those who belong to that party,—an abolitionist." [20]

Following Frémont's defeat, Lincoln avoided anti-slavery radicalism. Maintaining his interest in politics, he attended almost every Republican meeting that he could reach, speaking frequently, managing details of party machinery and carrying on an extensive correspondence. He was soon Illinois' leading Republican, Senator Lyman Trumbull excepted.[21] His desire to reach the United States Senate was undiminished.

In 1858 Lincoln secured the Republican nomination for Senator.[22] His campaign against Douglas was remarkable for the gravity of the issues involved. The joint debates gave Lincoln a degree of national renown. Henceforth he was regarded as the man who had bearded the Little Giant.[23] A majority of the state legislature elected in 1858 supported Douglas, but an analysis of the vote revealed that the pro-Lincoln members of the new assembly represented a population larger than did the pro-Douglas members. An antiquated apportionment law had discriminated against the northern counties, where Republican strength lay.[24] Lincoln kept up his spirits, declaring that "the fight must go on" and he predicted "another 'blow up' in the democracy." [25] The legislature formally elected Douglas for another term in January 1859.

Although disappointed over his defeat,[26] Lincoln kept up his spirits. To Senator Trumbull he predicted that "we shall be far better organized for 1860 than ever before. We shall get no just apportionment; and the best we can do (if we can even do that), is to prevent one being made worse than the present." [27] He also assured Trumbull that he had no intention of running against him at the next senatorial election.[28] Soon he was back on the stump. In March (1859) he journeyed to Chicago where, on the occasion of that city's municipal elections, he made his first political speech since his campaign against Douglas.[29] On March 14 he joined with twelve other Republicans (including Herndon), in calling a Republican city convention to be held shortly in Springfield.[30] It was clearly evident that Lincoln had not put politics behind.

Perhaps Lincoln was inspired by reports and rumors mentioning his name for the presidency or vice-presidency of the United States! His brilliant showing against Douglas had induced a few Illinois editors—and some outside the state—to adorn their editorial columns with the words "Lincoln for President." [31] Other sheets proposed that Lincoln be given the Republican nomination for Vice-President on a ticket headed by Seward.[32] During 1859 Lincoln spoke in Kansas, Iowa, Ohio, Indiana, and Wisconsin but his goal was still to vanquish Douglas for the senatorship.[33]

Throughout the spring and summer of 1859, Lincoln did not take his chances for first place in 1860 too seriously. "I must in candor say I do not think myself fit for the presidency," he wrote one admirer in April. "I certainly am flattered and gratified that some partial friends think of me in that connection; but I really think it best for our cause that no concentrated effort, such as you suggest, should be made." [34] To another in July he admitted that he "may not be the most suitable as a candidate for the presidency," adding: "I must say I do not think myself fit for the presidency." [35]

Lincoln was distrustful of anti-slavery radicalism and maintained a moderate attitude throughout 1859. He had been born in Kentucky, and had married into one of the prominent Kentucky families. His first political idol was Clay, a Kentucky slaveholder; and he numbered many Kentuckians among his intimate friends. As late as 1856 Lincoln referred to Kentucky as "my State." [36] In 1858 he had written: [37]

I will say I do not understand the Republican party to be committed to the proposition "No more slave States"—I think they are not so committed—most certainly they prefer there should be no more; but I know there are many of them who think we are under obligation to admit slave states from Texas, if such shall be presented for admission; but I think the party as such is not committed either way.

Lincoln became convinced that radicalism would jeopardize the Republican chances in 1860.[38] On one occasion he declared: "For my single self I would be willing to risk some Southern man without a platform; but I am satisfied that is not the case with the Republican party generally." [39] In July he warned Schuyler Colfax against the tendency of local Republicans to advocate measures which might harm the cause elsewhere. "In a word, in every locality," he advised, "we should look beyond our noses; and at least say nothing on points where it is probable we shall disagree." [40] Two months later he repeated his preference for a southerner on the presidential ticket in 1860, this time to an audience in Cincinnati; he insisted that the Republicans were friends of the Union.[41]

Lincoln's conservatism ultimately stood him in good stead, for it made him "available" in the crucial states of Pennsylvania, New Jersey, Indiana and, Illinois—all of which Frémont had lost to Buchanan in 1856. The importance of these conservative states was obvious. One important Republican journal confessed: "Now we would be almost willing to let the delegates from these four states nominate the candidate." [42] And in Chicago, Joseph Medill's widely read Republican *Press & Tribune* remarked in October (1859) that the problem was to carry those states.[43]

Medill, who was born in Ohio, personally favored his friend, Governor Chase. But he concluded that Chase could not carry the four pivotal states, and he began to reappraise the candidacy of Lincoln. When Pennsylvania supporters of Senator Simon Cameron or Judge John M. Read suggested Lincoln as a Vice-presidential candidate to balance the national ticket geographically, Medill wrote another Republican editor on October 30: [44]

The Pennsylvanians will press the names of Cameron and Judge Reed [sic] the former may have a maj. of the Pa. delegates. The friends of each desire to have Lincoln of Illinois run with them as Vice P. But the friends of the gallant old Abe will never consent to put the tallest end of the ticket behind. If the doubtful states of Pa. Ind. and Ill. are to name the candidate the west will settle down upon the tall son of this State. He can carry the entire Northwest— Ind. included. He is a Kentuckian by birth, lived 10 years in Indiana —stumped it for Henry Clay in 44,—and 25 [sic] in Illinois, was an old Clay Whig, is right on the tariff and he is exactly right on all other issues. Is there any man who could suit Pennsylvania better [?] The West is entitled to the president and he lives in the very heart of it. How does the matter strike you [?] On the hypothesis that the four states lost by Fremont should name the candidate, has not Old Abe more available points than any man yet named [?] Personally I prefer Gov. Chase to any man—believing that he possesses the best executive ability but if he is not considered available is not Old Abe the man to win with [?]

There was logic in Medill's reasoning about Lincoln's "availability." Lincoln was a westerner. He was sound on the tariff and would be strong in Pennsylvania and New Jersey, where protection was a live issue.[45] Moreover, Lincoln had lived in Indiana during his youth.

There was still another ground on which Lincoln would be "available." A Republican victory seemed to require a candidate not tinged with anti-slavery radicalism, since most people of the Northwest disliked the Negro although they did not favor slavery. Many regions of Illinois, Indiana, and Iowa were conservative. The great churches of the Northwest were alarmed by radicalism. Douglas and "squatter sovereignty" seemed even stronger than in 1858. Moreover, John Brown's raid had frightened western people who had no taste for Negro uprisings.[46] Medill realized all this.[47] He and other Republican leaders in Illinois, therefore, decided to put forward Lincoln as a candidate on grounds that he was a conservative—a "Henry Clay Whig."

Lincoln was aware of this conservative sentiment. To Chase he objected to the Ohio Republicans' demand for repeal of the Fugitive-Slave Law and wrote: "I assure you the cause of Republicanism is hopeless in Illinois, if it be in any way made responsible for that plank. I hope you can, and will, contribute something to relieve us from it."[48]

In October (1859) a relative by marriage, Dr. Edward Wallace, commissioned by the Cameron forces who wanted Lincoln for Vice-President, sounded Lincoln on his tariff views. Lincoln wrote in reply:[49]

I was an old Henry-Clay Tariff Whig. In old times I made more speeches on that subject than on any other.

I have not since changed my views. I believe yet, if we could have a moderate, carefully adjusted, protective tariff, so far acquiesced in as not to be a perpetual subject of political strife, squabbles, changes, and uncertain ties, it would be better for us. Still, it is my opinion, that, just now, the revival of that question will not *advance the cause itself, or the man who revives it.*

Lincoln's desire to avoid inexpedient issues and to pursue a moderate policy while fighting under the banner of "Republicanism," was manifest again in November, when he spoke at Mechanicsburg, Illinois. He charged the Democratic party with responsibility for the wrangling over slavery. Lincoln hoped that Douglas, "the prime mover in the conspiracy," would be rebuked in his home state.[50] Several weeks later in a speech at Elwood, Kansas, Lincoln condemned John Brown's raid.[51]

Regarding overtures of Senator Cameron's supporters of Pennsylvania for second place on a Cameron ticket for 1860, Lincoln refused to commit himself. On November 1, 1859, he answered the query of a Cameron lieutenant: [52]

Yours of the 24th ult. was forwarded to me from Chicago. It certainly is important to secure Pennsylvania for the Republicans in the next presidential contest, and not unimportant to also secure Illinois. As to the ticket you name, I shall be heartily for it after it shall have been fairly nominated by a Republican national convention; and I cannot be committed to it before. For my single self, I have enlisted for the permanent success of the Republican cause; and for this object I shall labor faithfully in the ranks, unless, as I think not probable, the judgment of the party shall assign me a different position. If the Republicans of the great state of Pennsylvania shall present Mr. Cameron as their candidate for the Presidency, such an endorsement for his fitness for the place could scarcely be deemed insufficient. Still, as I would not like the public to know, so I would not like myself to know, I had entered a combination with any man to the prejudice of all others whose friends respectively may consider them preferable.

This letter indicated that Lincoln vaguely sensed that he might be one of the nominees at Chicago. At least he avoided at this date making special commitments to particular candidates which would prejudice his popularity elsewhere. His disclaimer of particular interest in Cameron certainly did not mean that he had no interest in Pennsylvania, as his correspondence with Jesse W. Fell proves.

Fell was a Pennsylvania-born journalist in Illinois. He had known Lincoln since the 1830's and had been a staunch Whig. Later he became secretary of the Republican State Central Committee. While in the East in 1858, Fell noticed an interest in the Illinois lawyer who was then so effectively debating with Douglas and on his return to Illinois he suggested Lincoln as a possible Republican presidential candidate. He proposed that Lincoln prepare a sketch of his life to be printed in a Pennsylvania newspaper. On December 20, 1859, Lincoln furnished Fell a short autobiography. Fell sent it to his friend, Joseph J. Lewis, of West Chester, Pennsylvania.[53]

Lewis, a local political leader of eastern Pennsylvania, informed himself rather minutely concerning Lincoln before he prepared, from Fell's material, an article for the *Chester County Times*.[54] But he wanted to know more and wrote to Fell on January 30, 1860: [55]

The facts in Mr. L's statement are exceeding meagre and few. I want more. I want to know when he first began to speak. What was the success of his first efforts. . . . Whether he is a good shot with the rifle—a good horseman—fond of the hunt—geneal [sic] in manners, entertaining in conversation. . . .
Mr. Lincoln is popular in Chester Co and would make a fine poll with our people.

Lewis expanded the autobiografical material into two columns in the *Chester County Times* on February 11, 1860. It was later reprinted in the Illinois newspapers. Lewis selected from the material at hand those elements which would count for most in the Keystone state. Lincoln was "certainly not of the first families," Lewis said. His ancestors were Friends who had gone from Berks County, Pennsylvania (which was true); but in Illinois no one traced the Lincoln family back of its Virginia ancestors. Descendants of the same stock, Lewis continued, still lived in eastern Pennsylvania. Lewis wrote that Lincoln had been a strong Whig leader, a friend of Henry Clay, and master of "the principles of political economy that underlie the tariff. . . . Mr. Lincoln has been a consistent and earnest tariff man from the first hour of his entering public life." [56]

Lincoln was interested in Fell's ideas. On January 15, 1860, he wrote a Chicago friend: "Our Republican friend, J. W. Fell, of Bloomington, Illinois, can furnish you material for a brief sketch of my history, if it be desired. I shall be happy to receive a letter from you at any time." [57]

Meanwhile Joseph Medill, growing cooler toward Chase's candidacy, filled his Chicago *Press & Tribune* with accounts of Lincoln: mention of Lincoln's speech in Beloit, Wisconsin; [58] extracts from Lincoln's speeches in the debates with Douglas in 1858; [59] accounts of Lincoln's response to Republicans of Springfield who came to exchange congratulations on the fall victories in Pennsylvania, Ohio, Iowa, and Minnesota.[60] And an extract from a Norwich, Connecticut, newspaper which "speaks of a strong feeling in that section in favor of Hon. Abraham Lincoln, of Illinois, for the Presidency or Vice Presidency." [61] On December 9, 1859, Medill printed a lengthy communication, signed "A Union Lover," protesting against Seward's radicalism.[62] Throughout January, 1860, Medill kept Lincoln's name before his readers.[63] A reprint from a Milwaukee journal characterized both Seward and Chase as more "unavailable" than "Old Abe." [64] Medill himself went to Washington and talked Lincoln to Republican congressmen "chiefly upon the ground of availability in the close and doubtful states." [65] Finally, on February 16 the *Press & Tribune* editor came out for Lincoln in an editorial entitled "The Presidency—Abraham Lincoln." [66]

Newspaper favor avails a candidate little if practical politicians are not convinced of the candidate's strength. Indeed, the weakness of Governor Chase in 1856 and again in 1860 was partly owing to his lack of support by able tacticians—men who worked in county conventions and party caucuses. Seward had Thurlow Weed. Bates had the Blairs. Lincoln had Norman B. Judd, of Chicago.

Judd was by 1859 chairman of the Republican State Central Committee and Illinois member on the Republican National Committee.[67] At this time he was a contender for the nomination for governor.[68] Although an adroit political strategist, he had enemies within the party, particularly among certain former Whigs who accused him of being untrue to Lincoln when he voted for Trumbull, then an Anti-Nebraska Democrat, for United States Senator in 1855. Lincoln was asked categorically whether Judd had shown "unfairness" toward him in 1854–1855 and whether Judd had done his duty as a Republican during Lincoln's campaign against Douglas in 1858. In his search for party harmony Lincoln wrote first to Judd and then to Judd's critics exonerating Judd and commending Trumbull's election in 1855 as sound party strategy. To Judd he wrote: "You know I am pledged to not enter a struggle with him [Trumbull] for the seat in the Senate now occupied by him; and yet I would rather have a full term in the Senate than in the presidency." [69] To the critics he wrote: "During the canvass of 1858 for the Senatorship my belief was, and still is, that I had no more sincere and faithful friend than Mr. Judd." [70] Lincoln added, incidentally: "I have been and still am, very anxious to take no part between the many friends, all good and true, who are mentioned as candidates for a Republican gubernatorial nomination." [71] This was tactful, for Judd's two rivals for the nomination for governor were Richard Yates and Leonard Swett, both former Whigs and both friendly to Lincoln.

In December Judd left for New York to attend the meeting of the Republican National Committee which was to plan for the national convention. Lincoln was much interested in the choice of the Illinois delegates to the national convention and wrote to his friend, Jackson Grimshaw, about it: [72]

Judd has started East to attend the sitting of the National Committee at N. Y. the 21st. Previous to going he wrote that soon after his return he would call the State Committee together; and he wished me to see some of the members, including yourself, upon a matter which I can tell you better when I see you, than I can write about it—in a general way I may say it was relative to whether Delegates to the National Convention shall be appointed, by general convention, or by districts—Perhaps it would be as well to make no committal on this, till we have a conference.

In New York City, Judd persuaded the National Committee to hold the nominating convention in Chicago, a decision which was most encouraging to Lincoln's friends. [73]

Sometime between December, 1859, and January, 1860, Ward H. Lamon, Lincoln's friend and one-time law partner, and others met Lincoln in the State House. Judd was present at this meeting after which Lincoln authorized his friends to consider him as a candidate for the presidency and work for him if they pleased. [74]

Lincoln's letter to Judd exonerating him of treachery in 1855 was made public at the end of January, 1860. [75] On February 9 Lincoln wrote to Judd again, appealing for an Illinois delegation to Chicago instructed to vote for him: [76]

I am not in a position where it would hurt much for me not to be nominated on the national ticket; but I am where it would hurt some for me not to get the Illinois delegates. What I expected when

I wrote the letter to Messrs. Dole and others is now happening. Your discomfited assailants are more bitter against me, and they will, for revenge upon me, lay to the Bates egg in the South and the Seward egg in the North, and go far towards squeezing me out in the middle with nothing. Can you not help in your end of the vine-yard? (I mean this to be private.)

Lincoln had referred to the embarrassing position in which he was placed because he had defended Judd from the attacks of his former Whig associates and Judd, apparently, was grateful, or he wanted Lincoln's support in his gubernatorial ambitions—or both. Soon Judd was moved to vigorous activity in Lincoln's behalf.[77] On February 10, the day following Lincoln's written appeal to him, Judd addressed the "Cameron and Lincoln Club" in Chicago.[78] Judd continued his work for Lincoln and in April he was writing to Senator Trumbull: [79]

Cannot a quiet combination between the delegates from New Jersey, Indiana and Illinois be brought about—including Pennsylvania. United action by those delegates will probably control the convention. Nothing but a positive position will prevent Seward's nomination. The movement for Lincoln has neutralized to some extent the Bates movement in our State. It will not do to make a fight for delegates distinctly Lincoln. But state pride will carry a resolution of instruction through our state convention. This suggestion has been made to Mr. L.

Meanwhile, events in New York City had a major effect on Lincoln's fortunes.

In the fall of 1859 James A. Briggs, who was working for Chase and coöperating with the anti-Seward forces in New York City, [80] invited Lincoln to speak at the Reverend Dr. Henry Ward Beecher's Plymouth Church in Brooklyn. Lincoln consulted with Herndon about accepting the invitation.[81] According to Herndon: "I advised Lincoln to go by all means and to lecture on politics. . . . Thought it was a move against Seward, thought Greeley had something to do with it, think so yet." [82] Lincoln accordingly answered Briggs on November 13: "I shall be on hand, and in due time will notify you of the exact day. I believe, after all, I will make a political speech of it. You have no objection?" [83] Briggs was fearful about the financial success of the venture.[84] The sponsorship of Lincoln's address finally was undertaken by the "Young Men's Republican

Union," which had been formed in 1856 as the "Young Men's Frémont and Dayton Central Union." It now occupied rooms at Stuyvesant Institute, 659 Broadway.[85] The "Advisory Board of the Young Men's Republican Union" consisted of, among others, 65-year-old William Cullen Bryant, 49-year-old Horace Greeley, 51-year-old Hamilton Fish, 54-year-old William Curtis Noyes and the aging Hiram Barney—all staunch anti-Seward Republicans.[86] Bryant, Noyes, and Barney were working for Governor Chase's nomination.[87] The "Young Men's Republican Union" was bringing Lincoln to New York to bolster the opposition to Seward. On February 9 Charles C. Nott, an officer of the "Union," invited Lincoln to speak "about the middle of March." [88]

Lincoln settled on February 27 as the date for his address in New York. He set to work digging into diverse sources for his speech. On February 23 he left Springfield for New York, and the local Democratic newspaper sarcastically reported his departure: [89]

Significant: The Hon. Abraham Lincoln departs today for Brooklyn under an engagement to deliver a lecture before the Young Men's Association in that city in Beecher's church. Subject: not known. Consideration: $200 and expenses. Object: presidential capital. Effect: disappointment.

It was still thought that Lincoln would speak at the Reverend Dr. Beecher's church in Brooklyn.

Passing through Philadelphia on his way to New York Lincoln just missed seeing Senator Cameron. On reaching New York he wrote to Cameron (who was still working for himself): [90]

I write this to say the card of yourself and Hon. D. Wilmot was handed to me yesterday at Philadelphia just as I was leaving for this city. I barely had time to step over to the Girard, when I learned that you and he were not in your rooms. I regret that being so near, we did not meet. . . .

Evidently Cameron and Wilmot were planning to enlist Lincoln's support for Cameron at Chicago.

Upon reaching New York Lincoln discovered that he would speak at Cooper Institute, not at Beecher's church—and on February 27 he delivered a most celebrated address. He maintained that the Republicans were a conservative party; he condemned John Brown's raid. He did not repeat his "House Divided" theory, but instead declared: "Wrong as we think slavery is, we can yet afford to let it alone where it is, because that much is due to the necessity arising from its actual presence in the nation."

Lincoln's Cooper Institute speech was conservative.[91] It received wide circulation in the Republican press. Greeley's New York *Tribune* probably had the original manuscript from which the address was set in type by Amos J. Cummings, who stated that Lincoln came to the *Tribune* office after the speech to read proof. The *Tribune's* copy was made available to other papers and served as the master galley proof. The speech was immediately put in pamphlet form by Medill in Chicago.[92] The mass distribution of Lincoln's speech, according to Dr. Louis A. Warren, "was one of the most important contributions to his candidacy for the Presidency." [93]

Lincoln had captivated his New York audience and he was besieged with requests to speak in New England.[94] He might have declined such invitations had he not wanted to see his eldest son, Robert, a student at Phillips Exeter Academy in New Hampshire.[95] Lincoln decided to invade New England.

On February 28 Lincoln spoke at Providence, Rhode Island,[96] and then proceeded to New Hampshire, where he made four addresses at Concord, Manchester, Dover, and Exeter. Returning south via Connecticut, he spoke at Hartford, New Haven, and Meriden. Entering Rhode Island again, he delivered "one of his most powerful addresses" at Woonsocket on March 8. The following day he was in Norwich, Connecticut, where he "made a manly vindication of the principles of the Republican party, urging the necessity of the union of all elements to free our country from its present rule." On March 10 Lincoln made his last New England address at Bridgeport. Then he entrained for New York and then on to Springfield.[97] On March 14 he arrived home—"in excellent health and in his usual spirits." [98]

Almost immediately Lincoln set about publicizing himself. On his arrival home he made arrangements with the editors of the *Illinois Journal* to have his Cooper Institute speech printed locally,[99] and he soon wrote an associate: [100]

Pamphlet copies of my late speech at Cooper Institute, N. Y. can be had at the office of the New York Tribune; at the Republican Club Room at Washington, and at the Illinois Journal at this place. At which place they are cheapest, I do not certainly know.

As a result of his eastern trip Lincoln's name became known in New England, particularly in conservative Connecticut and Rhode Island—states which, unlike Massachusetts and Maine, would not support the radical Seward. Lincoln kept in touch with at least one leader in Connecticut.[101] When the Republican Governor William A. Buckingham was having an uphill fight for reëlection, Lincoln appealed on March 26 to Senator Trumbull, who had been born in Connecticut: [102]

They are having a desperate struggle in Connecticut; and it would both please, and help our friends there, if you could be with them in the last days of the fight—Having been there, I know they are proud of you as a son of their soil, and would be moved to greater exertion by your presence among them—
Can you not go? Telegraph them, and go right along—The fiendish attempt now being made upon Connecticut, must not be allowed to succeed.

Buckingham was re-elected by a majority of less than 600 votes.[103] In Rhode Island, however, the Republican candidate for governor —Seth Padelford, an advanced anti-slavery man—was defeated.[104] Lincoln recognized that such election returns would not help Seward. "You know I was in New England," he wrote one friend on April 14. "Some of the acquaintances I made while there, write me since the elections that the close votes in Conn. and the quasi defeat in R. I. are a drawback upon the prospects of Gov. Seward; and Trumbull writes Dubois to the same effect. Do not mention this as coming from me. Both those states are safe enough for us in the fall." [105]

Within Illinois Lincoln's trip strengthened him. To many Illinoisans filled with state pride, he was a native son who had carried all before him in the East. Lesser Illinois papers joined the Lincoln column.[106] Medill went to work for Lincoln harder than ever. His Chicago *Press & Tribune* reprinted eulogies of Lincoln's Cooper Institute address from New York journals,[107] and an account of the ovations given Lincoln in New England.[108] Medill deprecated Seward's strength because of the prevalence of the conservative "American" element in the "doubtful" states of Pennsylvania, New Jersey, Indiana, and Illinois.[109] As for Bates, the Chicago editor maintained that the Missourian was unacceptable to the German and radical elements of the party.[110] According to Medill,

Seward was too radical and Bates was too conservative to satisfy all Republican factions; therefore, Lincoln was the logical man: "Mr. Lincoln excited no hates anywhere; he has made no record to be defended or explained." [111] In short, Illinois' favorite son was "available." [112]

Throughout March and April (1860) the work of organization went on. From Washington Trumbull and other Republican members of Congress "flooded" the lukewarm central and southern counties of Illinois with party documents mailed under their "franks." [113] Internal improvements were endorsed, and the Buchanan administration was denounced for its inept handling of the fund appropriated for the Chicago harbor. [114] The homestead issue was emphasized by calling attention to the Democratic party's hostility to "land for the landless." [115] This issue appealed to the land-hungry Germans, and mass meetings in the German language were held in Chicago and elsewhere. [116] In March, during the Chicago municipal campaign, Carl Schurz was brought from Wisconsin to speak at the Deutsches Haus, Chicago's German fraternal center. [117] The German-born former Lieutenant-Governor Gustave Koerner assembled mailing lists of naturalized Germans and directed the work of distributing party literature to them. [118]

Lincoln was keenly interested in the German vote. For years he had endeavored to draw this element from its traditional loyalty to the Democratic party. [119] He now redoubled his efforts, for western Republican leaders knew that without the German vote the Northwest would be lost to the Democrats. [120] The anti-alien laws enacted by the Republicans of Massachusetts in 1859 seriously handicapped Republicans in the Northwest in their endeavors to attract the Teutonic element. Lincoln was concerned over the situation. "Massachusetts Republicans," he wrote Schuyler Colfax, "should have looked beyond their noses, and then they could not have failed to see that tilting against foreigners would ruin us in the Northwest." [121] In the same month that the Massachusetts voters ratified the anti-alien amendment a German editor in Springfield, Dr. Theodore Canisius, wrote Lincoln asking his views on the measure. On May 17, 1859 Lincoln replied to Canisius: "Massachusetts is a sovereign and independent State; and it is no privilege of mine to scold her for what she does. Still, if from what she has done an inference is sought to be drawn as to what I would do, I may without impropriety speak out. I say, then, that, as I under-

stand the Massachusetts provision, I am against its adoption in Illinois, or in any other place where I have a right to oppose it." [122]
Lincoln's letter to Canisius, given wide publicity in the northwestern Republican press, created a favorable attitude toward
Lincoln among the German elements.[123] At the end of May, 1859,
Lincoln had turned over to Canisius a printing press and German types which he (Lincoln) had purchased, with the object
of having resumed the publication of a German-language newspaper in Springfield. Canisius was to bear all expenses and to
derive all income from the enterprise.[124] Canisius started the paper, and soon Lincoln was soliciting circulation among the German
leaders.[125]

In view of the foregoing, it is easy to understand why Lincoln
became generally acceptable to the German groups within the
Republican party. The first choice of most Germans was the
radical, anti-nativistic Seward. But about two weeks before the
Republican Convention assembled in Chicago, the central organ of
the German Turner Bund of the United States, the Baltimore *Turn
Zeitung*, declared: "If on the score of expediency we pass Mr.
Seward by, then will Mr. Lincoln be the man." [126] This prompted
Medill to declare with eagerness that the *Turn Zeitung* "has declared
in favor of Abraham Lincoln for the Presidency." [127]

In late April Medill concentrated on undermining Seward's
strength in northern Illinois, where anti-slavery feeling was strong.
He reprinted articles from anti-Seward newspapers in New York
which denounced the Weed-controlled legislature at Albany as "the
most corrupt body which ever assembled" in the Empire State.
Medill further quoted William Cullen Bryant's anti-Seward New
York *Evening Post* to the effect that the Seward-pledged New
York delegation, recently selected at Rochester, was packed with
"corrupt" men.[128] Seward, as long as he lived, never forgave Medill
for this.[129]

The campaign for Lincoln conducted by Medill in his *Press &
Tribune* and by Judd, Grimshaw and others in county conventions
and party caucuses, found a ready response among diverse groups
of people. To obscure citizens, "Old Abe" became Illinois' "favorite son." To county leaders he was "available." This was not true
of Seward who could command support only in the northern counties. One county leader observed: "I think Mr. Seward to be the
most deserving of the nomination at Chicago yet I think him not

the most available candidate in our party and hence am not
for his nomination." [130] Another wrote: "The name of Seward on
the ticket would it seems to me place success beyond hope." [131] Still
another reported: "The Republicans would be sanguine of the success of their whole ticket this fall were it not that they expect that
Mr. Seward will be nominated at Chicago. Seward is a great man
but he cant run in Central & Southern Illinois." [132]

When the National Convention was scarcely a month off, the
Republican State Central Committee, under Judd's chairmanship,
issued a "call" for the state convention to be held at Decatur on
May 9. Many on the state committee who signed the "call" were
friends or close associates of Lincoln: besides Judd, there were
Herndon, Jackson Grimshaw, Jesse W. Fell, C. D. Hay, E. L.
Baker (editor of the Illinois State Journal and Lincoln's relative
by marriage), and David L. Phillips. The state convention at
Decatur was well "timed"—May 9, not too far in advance, so that
the National Convention, which would assemble on May 16, would
receive the full impact of the spontaneous Lincoln force.

The Republicans of Lincoln's home county of Sangamon met
at Springfield on April 28 to select delegates to the state convention. Five were chosen; among them was Herndon.[133] An eloquent
resolution, endorsing Lincoln for the presidency, was adopted.[134]

This action of the Sangamon County convention was the signal
for other county conventions in Illinois to endorse Lincoln also.
In the closing days of April the Republican conventions of Stark,
Carroll, Coles, Will, Morgan, and Henry Counties declared for
him; in the opening days of May, Edwards, La Salle, and Marshall
Counties did likewise.[135] Grimshaw and other Lincoln supporters
were operating in these county gatherings. Moreover, Judge David
Davis, with whom Lincoln had ridden the circuit on horseback
from courthouse to courthouse, laid aside his judicial robes and
devoted his time to the Lincoln cause.[136]

Meanwhile, Lincoln was by no means idle. Declining an invitation to lecture on April 7, he wrote: "What time I can spare
from my own business this season I shall be compelled to give to
politics." [137] Lincoln's correspondence in the spring of 1860 displays a very real interest in his own candidacy. His chief rival
in Indiana and Illinois was Justice McLean who, except for age,
was almost as "available" as Lincoln. Toward the end of April,
Lincoln wrote to Trumbull: [138]

As you request, I will be entirely frank—The taste *is* in my mouth a little; and this, no doubt, disqualifies me, to some extent, to form correct opinions. You may confidently rely, however, that by no choice or consent of mine, shall my pretensions be pressed to the point of endangering our common cause—

Now, as to my opinions about the chances of others in Illinois— I think neither Seward nor Bates can carry Illinois if Douglas shall be on the Democratic track; and that either of them can, if he shall not be—I rather think McLean could carry it with D. on or off— in other words, I think McLean is stronger in Illinois, taking all sections of it, than either S. or B.; and I think S. the weakest of the three. I hear no objections to McLean, except his age; but that objection seems to occur to every one; and it is possible it might leave him no stronger than the others—By the way, if we should nominate him, how would we save to ourselves the chance of filling his vacancy in the Court? Have him hold on up to the moment of his inauguration? Would that course be no draw-back upon us in the canvass?

Recurring to Illinois, we want something here quite as much as, and which is harder to get than, the electoral vote—the Legislature —And it is exactly in this point that Seward's nomination would be hard upon us. Suppose he should gain us a thousand votes in Winnebago, it would not compensate for the loss of fifty in Edgar—

A word now for your own special benefit—You better write no letters which can possibly be distorted into opposition, or quasi-opposition to me—There are men on the constant watch for such things out of which to prejudice my peculiar friends against you—

While I have no more suspicion of you than I have of my best friend living, I am kept in a constant struggle against suggestions of this sort—I have hesitated some to write this paragraph, lest you should suspect I do it for my own benefit, and not for yours; but on reflection I conclude you will not suspect me—

Let no eye but your own see this—not that there is anything wrong, or even ungenerous, in it; but it would be misconstrued—

Lincoln also wrote to his Kansas friend, Mark W. Delahay: [189]

As to your kind wishes for myself, allow me to say I can not enter the ring on the money basis—first, because, in the main, it is wrong; and secondly, I have not, and can not get, the money. I say, in the main, the use of money is wrong; but for certain objects, in a political contest, the use of some, is both right and indispensable. With me as with yourself, this long struggle has been one of great pecuniary loss. I now distinctly say this: If you shall be appointed

a delegate to Chicago, I will furnish one hundred dollars to bear
the expenses of the trip.

Present my respects to Gen'l Lane; and say to him, I shall be
pleased to hear from him at any time.

Delahay wanted to be United States Senator from Kansas and
had appealed to Lincoln to use his influence with any Kansas
friends. Lincoln replied that he was not personally acquainted
with a single member of the Kansas legislature [140] but he wrote
Senator Trumbull at Washington: "Our friend Delahay wants to
be one of the Senators from Kansas. He writes me that some of
the members of the Kansas Legislature have written you in a way
that your simple answer might help him—I wish you would consider
whether you can not assist him that far, without impropriety—I
know it is a delicate matter; and I do not wish to press you beyond
your own judgment." [141] Delahay was not elected to the Senate but
Lincoln had proved his fidelity. Lincoln wrote Delahay again: "I
see by the dispatches that since you wrote, Kansas has appointed
Delegates and instructed them for Seward. Don't stir them up to
anger, but come along to the convention, and I will do as I said
about expenses." [142] Delahay was on the scene early at Chicago,
several days before the assembling of the National Convention, and
Lincoln wrote him on the eve of the convention, again urging him
to be discreet and to work with the Iowa and Minnesota delegations. Lincoln arranged for the payment of Delahay's expenses.[143]

Lincoln's quest for support was not confined to the West. On
April 14 he dispatched a message to James F. Babcock in Connecticut. "As to the Presidential nomination," Lincoln wrote, "claiming
no greater exemption from selfishness than is common, I still feel
that my whole aspiration should be, to be placed anywhere, or
nowhere, as may appear most likely to advance our cause." [144]
Nevertheless, Lincoln gave Babcock a long list of friends with whom
the latter might correspond regarding Lincoln's candidacy.[145]

Furthermore, Judd reserved accommodations for the Connecticut
delegation at the Tremont House in Chicago,[146] where, incidentally,
Judge David Davis was to establish Lincoln headquarters during
the convention.[147]

Lincoln also corresponded with Hawkins Taylor, of Iowa, and
Samuel Galloway, of Ohio. To Taylor, an Iowa delegate to the
Chicago convention, Lincoln wrote in April offering to entertain
him and his party should they pass through Springfield on their

way to Chicago.[148] Lincoln had been in touch with Galloway in March. The Ohioan was for Lincoln because he was an "available man of sound principles" upon whom "all elements of the opposition can be more fully united." [149] On March 24 Lincoln thanked Galloway and analyzed his own candidacy:[150]

I am here attending a trial in court. Before leaving home I received your kind letter of the 15th. Of course I am gratified to know I have friends in Ohio who are disposed to give me the highest evidence of their friendship and confidence. Mr. Parrott, of the legislature, had written me to the same effect. If I have any chance it consists mainly in the fact that the whole opposition would vote for me, if nominated. (I don't mean to include the pro-slavery opposition of the South, of course.) My name is new in the field, and I suppose I am not the first choice of a very great many. Our policy, then, is to give no offense to others—leave them in a mood to come to us if they shall be compelled to give up their first love. This, too, is dealing justly with all, and leaving us in a mood to support heartily whoever shall be nominated. I believe I have once before told you that I especially wish to do no ungenerous thing toward Governor Chase, because he gave us his sympathy in 1858 when scarcely any other distinguished man did. Whatever you may do for me, consistently with these suggestions, will be appreciated and gratefully remembered. Please write me again.

Lincoln also wrote to the prominent Cincinnati lawyer, Richard M. Corwine, who was to be an Ohio delegate to the Chicago convention. Corwine had written to Lincoln with the intention of attracting Illinois support to seventy-five-year-old Justice McLean. Lincoln, in a cautious reply, answered: "I think Mr. Seward is the very best candidate we could have for the North of Illinois, and the very worst for the South of it. The estimate of Governor Chase here is neither better nor worse than that of Seward, except that he is a newer man. They are regarded as being almost the same, seniority giving Seward the inside track. Mr. Bates, I think would be the best man for the South of our State, and the worst for the North of it." [151] Then he gave his estimate of McLean's strength: "If Judge McLean was fifteen, or even ten years younger, I think he would be stronger than either, in our state, taken as a whole; but his great age, and the recollection of the deaths of Harrison and Taylor have, so far, prevented his being spoken much of here." [152]

In his next letter to Corwine a month later, Lincoln frankly attempted to enlist delegates from Ohio. He outlined the "lay of the land" much as he did in letters to Trumbull and Galloway, observing that while he was first choice only in Illinois, he was second choice in many other states, that Indiana "might not be difficult to get," and especially that no one appeared to have "any positive objection" to him. Lincoln's availability was, obviously, his main strength. In closing, Lincoln remarked to Corwine that Judge Davis and Jesse K. Dubois, State Auditor of Illinois, would be happy to confer with him upon his arrival in Chicago.[153] The day before Lincoln had written to Cyrus M. Allen, of Vincennes, Indiana, also stating: "Our friend Dubois, and Judge David Davis, of Bloomington, one or both, will meet you at Chicago, on the 12th. If you let Usher and Griswold of Terre-Haute know, I think they will coöperate with you."[154] Allen had much in common with Lincoln —both had been born in Kentucky, both had later migrated to Indiana, both had served as Whigs in their respective state legislatures.[155] Lincoln wrote later that Allen "particularly has been my friend."[156] The "Usher" referred to was John P. Usher, whom in 1861 he appointed Assistant Secretary of the Interior and in 1863 elevated to the Secretaryship of that department.[157]

Lincoln had some justification for believing that "the whole of Indiana might not be difficult to get." He had spent much of his youth in Indiana, the Lincoln-Douglas debates had attracted widespread attention there and Lincoln had been well received in Indianapolis in September, 1859. More significantly, Lincoln, like conservative leaders of the Indiana Republican party, had been a Henry Clay Whig. His views did not antagonize the dominant abolitionist-hating element, who were normally for Bates. Indeed, the Bates men in Indiana could easily support Lincoln, who himself had declared to Orville H. Browning that he might "be right in supposing Mr. Bates as the strongest and best man we can run." All could logically support Illinois' favorite son.[158]

It was not surprising, therefore, that in April Indiana's foremost Republican organ, the Indianapolis *Journal*, encouraged the Lincoln backers: [159]

It may be that we had better suffer defeat with him [Seward] or Chase than achieve victory with McLean or Lincoln, but we can't so see it. . . . We say Judge McLean—and Mr. Lincoln of Illinois stands in very much the same relation—presents a strong claim on the attention of the Republican Convention. . . . Next to Judge McLean, we believe Abram [sic] Lincoln of Illinois presents the best combination of qualities as a candidate and officer.

Lincoln was second choice of Indiana's leading Republican organ! Lincoln people in Illinois put this editorial to good use. On May 11 the Indianapolis *Journal* printed an anonymous letter, apparently written by one of Lincoln's Springfield friends, which assured the *Journal* that its mention of McLean and Lincoln had been well received in Illinois. The letter, adroitly worded, disposed of Bates as unsatisfactory to the Germans and was careful not to offend the McLean supporters.[160]

On May 9 and 10—only a week before the National Convention— the Illinois state Republican convention met at Decatur. Lincoln men were in control. Lincoln himself was outside the convention hall. Inside, Richard Oglesby, his friend and later Governor of Illinois, announced to the convention that "a distinguished citizen of Illinois, and one whom Illinois will ever delight to honor is present; and I wish to move that this body invite him to a seat on the stand." When Oglesby announced the name "Abraham Lincoln" a roar of applause went up. A rush was made for Lincoln.[161] He "was 'troosted,'—lifted up bodily,—and lay for a few seconds sprawling and kicking upon the heads and shoulders of the great throng . . . toward the stand. . . . The cheering was like the roar of the sea. . . . Mr. Lincoln rose, bowed, smiled, blushed." [162] He addressed the convention. Soon Oglesby announced that an "Oldtime Democrat of Macon county" wanted to make a contribution to this Republican state convention. Into the hall marched one John Hanks, carrying two time-stained fence rails, surmounted by a banner with the inscription: "Two Rails, from a Lot Made by Abraham Lincoln and John Hanks, in the Sangamon Bottom, in the Year 1830." After a burst of cheering, Lincoln was called on for a speech. He admitted that he had split rails in Macon County, but whether these were of his manufacture he did not know. At any rate, he had split a great many better ones. Thus Lincoln became the "Rail-Splitter." And as such the convention endorsed him as the Illinois Republicans' first choice for the presidency and Illinois' "favorite son" at the Chicago convention.[163]

Since there was some Seward sentiment in the Decatur convention,[164] the Lincoln men determined that only those unqualifiedly for Lincoln should be selected as delegates to Chicago. According to Lincoln's friend, Isaac N. Arnold, who attended the Decatur gathering, the committee appointed to select delegates to the national convention, along with "other friends of Lincoln, among whom were Judd, David Davis, Swift, Cook, and others, retired from the convention, and, in a grove near by, lay down upon the grass and revised the list of delegates, which they reported to, and which were appointed by, the convention." [165]

Following the adjournment of the Decatur convention the small group of Lincoln leaders commenced their intensive preparations for the Republican National Convention. Judge David Davis was particularly active and shared with Judd the high command of Lincoln's campaign. Davis, who was a delegate-at-large, was in Chicago on May 12—four days before the national gathering assembled.[166] He opened Lincoln headquarters at the Tremont House, finest of the city's forty-two hotels, and was thus installed and ready for action several days before the national convention officially opened on May 16.[167]

CHAPTER SIX

A Conservative Protectionist

DIVIDING HIS TIME between Washington and Harrisburg during the late 1850's was Senator Simon Cameron of Pennsylvania. In 1860 he, like others, hoped to lead the Republicans to their first national victory.

A self-made man by 1845 with a fortune in coal, iron, railroad building, and banking, Cameron aspired to the United States Senate. Although he was a Democrat, his own interests induced him to favor a protective tariff.[1] He accordingly formed an alliance between protectionist Democrats and high-tariff Whigs in the Pennsylvania Legislature and was elected Senator over James Buchanan's picked candidate.[2] Cameron also received "Native American" support, giving the nativists in return a written pledge to tighten the Naturalization Laws.[3] Cameron's victory at Buchanan's expense led to ill feeling between the two men,[4] particularly when Buchanan allied himself with the free-trade Democrats of the South. Soon Buchanan was speaking of "that scamp"[5] while Cameron termed his rival an "old political hack."[6] Cameron's ambition was to block Buchanan's moves to make himself president.[7] Although he achieved small success in this, Cameron managed to increase his own power.[8]

In 1854 Pennsylvania, not strongly anti-slavery, was only mildly excited over the Kansas-Nebraska Act;[9] the state was more concerned over the Catholics and foreign-born. Therefore, the ailing Whigs allied themselves with the Know-Nothings in the gubernatorial campaign of that year and, with the help of the temperance advocates and anti-Nebraska groups, elected their candidate, James Pollock, over the Democratic incumbent.[10]

The Democratic defeat in 1854 convinced Cameron that he must find a new political haven. Although in many parts of the North the opposition to the Kansas-Nebraska Act had precipitated a party styled "Anti-Nebraska" and then "Republican," in Pennsylvania the resistance to the Democracy did not generally take the form of opposition to slavery, except in isolated regions.[11] Republican meetings were sparsely attended.[12] One Pennsylvania Congressman, personally anti-slavery, was asked by his advisers to cease "franking" Republican documents.[13] The sagacious Cameron, jealous for his own advancement, recognized Pennsylvanians' moderation on the slavery issue and did not immediately board the untried Republican bark. He chose rather an expedient course, watching the political gales before permitting his course to be veered leftward toward Republicanism. When he found it no longer desirable to act with the Democrats, Cameron consorted not with the Republicans, but with the Maine-Law men and the Know-Nothings. He spoke kind words to the temperance leaders.[14] To the nativists he was most conciliatory. One critic describes his conversion: "General Cameron had made a speech in favor of Bigler [the Democratic candidate for Governor] in Harrisburg the night before the election but before the Legislature met. When he found that the Know Nothings controlled both branches of the Legislature, he turned up as a full-fledged member of the Order, and became an aggressive candidate for United States Senator." [15]

In February, 1855, the Know-Nothing members of the Pennsylvania legislature adopted Cameron as their candidate for senator. He almost captured the prize; he was not quite able to command a majority in the Legislature, and the election of a senator was postponed.[16]

Throughout 1855 Cameron, now nominally a Know-Nothing, still declined to cast his lot with the Republicans, for anti-slavery progress in conservative Pennsylvania continued slowly.

During the spring of 1855 the Harrisburg *Telegraph*, state organ of Governor Pollock's "Whig-Know-Nothing-Temperance-Anti-Nebraska" Opposition, denounced anti-slavery extremists.[17] Within a few months, however, this same journal saw the futility of division among all the anti-Democratic forces and recommended a meeting of Republicans, Whigs and "Americans" to meet in Harrisburg on August 9 (1855) to nominate a candidate for canal commissioner.[18]

The *Telegraph's* proposal proved abortive. The Whigs demurred and called their own convention at Harrisburg, to meet on September 11.[19] The "Americans" were hesitant about fraternizing with Republicans and were annoyed at the abuse which the Republicans levelled at them.[20] Something tangible was accomplished, however, when the Republicans of ten counties, not caring what the Whigs or the "Americans" did, met at Reading on August 8 and invited "all our fellow citizens of Pennsylvania without former distinctions, to meet in general Mass Convention in the city of Pittsburgh, on Wednesday the fifth day of September, 1855, to organize a Republican Party, whose chief object shall be to place all branches of government actively on the side of liberty." [21]

This convention apparently did not represent strong popular sentiment in Pennsylvania.[22] The convention received letters of congratulation from Republicans throughout the North. Joshua R. Giddings, Ohio anti-slavery Congressman, delivered the main address. The convention boldly emphasized slavery, called for repeal of the Fugitive-Slave Law, and nominated Passmore Williamson, an abolitionist, for Canal Commissioner;[23] Williamson was then in prison for harboring runaway Negro slaves.[24] Senator Cameron, a practical politician, was not present at the Pittsburgh conventions; he did not even send a letter to the delegates.[25]

Williamson's nomination was received coldly.[26] The Pittsburgh convention itself was not solidly behind the selection, since many delegates were "opposed to action which would isolate the Republicans from other anti-administration parties." [27] The Whigs would not accept Williamson, and on September 11 they nominated their own candidate for canal commissioner.[28] The "Americans," too, named their candidate,[29] and appealed to the electorate: [30]

Overthrow the foreign hordes and their native allies, who are banded together to place the land of our birth under the political control of Irish Roman Catholics and German Infidels. Americans! fling your starry banner to the breeze, and charge upon the Foreign foe!

At length the three elements of opposition to the Democrats—Republicans, Whigs, and "Americans"—saw the folly of divided action. On September 27 the state central committees of the Republican, Whig, and American parties met in Harrisburg, and each committee withdrew its candidate for canal commissioner in favor of Thomas Nicholson as the "Union" candidate. Nicholson was defeated.[31] The significant point was that the Whigs and "Americans" had finally accepted the Republicans as equals.

The election convinced the Opposition forces that united action was necessary if victory were to be achieved. Consequently in

February, 1856, Republican, "American," and Whig members of the Pennsylvania legislature called a convention at Harrisburg for March 26, of "all opposed to the destructive policy and principles of the National Administration." It met on the appointed day and nominated "Union" candidates for canal commissioner, auditor-general, and surveyor-general. Cameron did not attend this convention.[32]

Before the "Union" convention met at Harrisburg, Congressman David Wilmot, in pursuance of a resolution adopted at a Republican National Convention at Pittsburg, called a state Republican convention in Philadelphia for June 16.[33] This convention met and selected delegates to the National Convention of Republicans which was to meet the following day.[34]

At the National Convention a majority of the Pennsylvania delegation, realizing their State's mild anti-slavery sentiment, favored the nomination of the conservative Supreme Court Justice John McLean; but they reluctantly acquiesced in the nomination of Frémont.[35] At this gathering, Cameron's name became linked with the Republican party for the first time; he was suggested as candidate for vice-president. The Blair family vetoed such a proposal, however, and William L. Dayton, of New Jersey, was chosen as Frémont's running-mate.

In the three-cornered presidential campaign waged by Frémont, Buchanan, and Fillmore, Cameron proved a valuable addition to the Republican ranks. His nemesis, Buchanan, was the Democratic entry, after all.[36] The Republicans emphasized anti-slavery.[37] But anti-slavery extremism as preached by the Republicans, combined with a united Democratic party with the power of federal patronage and money, and the Old-Line Whigs' and Know-Nothings' determination to vote for the moderate Fillmore, won Pennsylvania, and consequently the presidency, for Cameron's enemy Buchanan.[38]

In the following year, 1857, Cameron finally achieved his ambition. By forming an alliance between Republicans and three disgruntled Democratic members of the legislature, he was returned to the United States Senate.[39] This brought him prestige. Likewise it fed his ambition. Two months after his election, local political chieftains mentioned him for president in 1860.[40]

In the meantime, many among the anti-Democratic opposition emphasized the moral issue of anti-slavery. The preachings of Abolitionists, Quakers and other groups had not converted Pennsylvania to deeply rooted convictions against slavery. Moreover, Philadelphia, the state's metropolis, had strong commercial and cultural ties with the South.[41] Consequently, after the campaign of 1856 the Republicans saw the folly of emphasizing the slavery issue. One Republican leader spoke disdainfully of "the stagnant blood of Pennsylvania," [42] and when the abolitionist William Lloyd Garrison spoke at Harrisburg in 1858 he found only twenty-five people in his audience![43] The protective tariff was the state's dominant concern; affairs in Kansas were of secondary importance.[44]

In 1858, however, one man, Andrew H. Reeder, stimulated Pennsylvania into thinking of "Bleeding" Kansas. After his removal by President Pierce from the governorship of Kansas Territory in 1856 because of his land-speculations and tactless administration,[45] Reeder went to Illinois and issued an appeal for the distressed territory.[46] In public letters he announced his change from Democrat to Republican and his support of Frémont for President.[47] At Easton in June, 1858, Reeder referred to the unhappy conditions in Kansas and the failure of Buchanan's administration to remedy them. He was particularly outspoken in his condemnation of the methods used to force slavery upon Kansas.[48]

Kansas and the tariff were not the only issues that rendered President Buchanan vulnerable to the Opposition within his own state: the patronage was no less important.

The federal patronage proved discomforting to Buchanan.[49] "The number of applicants for office in Pennsylvania has been very great," the President complained in 1858. "The appointment of one is the disappointment of many." [50]

The most serious of the President's patronage troubles concerned the editor, John W. Forney. An erstwhile friend of the President, Forney had labored for Buchanan's election in 1856, expecting in return to secure federal contracts and the editorship of the administration newspaper in Washington. Following his inauguration as President, however, Buchanan informed Forney that he could not keep his promise because of Southern opposition. Forney then wanted the United States senatorship and Buchanan supported him —but Cameron, now a Republican, won that prize. In 1857 Forney, much against Buchanan's wishes, started the Philadelphia *Press*. He expected government printing contracts for the *Press* but they were not forthcoming. To make matters worse, Mrs. Forney requested the President to appoint her husband postmaster general;

but political considerations prevented the President from giving Forney a Cabinet post. The final break came when Buchanan determined to make the support of his Kansas policy a party test. Forney favored Douglas's interpretation of the Democratic national platform of 1856 and Buchanan declined to exempt him from the rule. This meant the loss of the government printing. Forney launched a frontal attack on Buchanan. The Democracy of Pennsylvania was split wide open. In 1858 Forney was elected clerk of the House of Representatives by Republican and pro-Douglas Democratic votes.[51]

The summer of 1858 also witnessed the formal dissolution of the "Americans" as a separate party in Pennsylvania. At a "Union state convention held in Harrisburg in July, composed of Republicans and "Americans," it was deemed advisable to change the name of the Opposition to the "People's party." Thus the foes of the Democracy were fused into a single, united organization. The "Americans" accepted the fact that they alone could not defeat the Democrats; while the Republicans, now the dominant element of the anti-Democratic forces, dropped the name "Republican."[52]

The People's party, embracing doctrines numerous and general enough to attract diverse elements, was accurately described in 1858 as "an organization that combines all the best elements of the opposition," including opponents of the Buchanan administration's Kansas policy, its extravagance, abuse of patronage, corruption, and especially its low tariff stand.[53] Cameron was sound on the tariff, the state's dominant issue. "It is our nigger,"[54] he said of it; and he urged the increase of import duties on coal and iron.[55] One Democratic leader remarked: "His superior strength arises mainly from his long devotion to a protective tariff."[56] There were Republicans, however, who thought it wise for the party to acquire a mild anti-slavery—more particularly, an "anti-Lecompton"—flavor. Cameron had no conspicuous anti-slavery record but he wanted to embarrass Buchanan, who wished to have the Lecompton constitution adopted by Congress. In April (1858) he went on record against slavery extension;[57] he assailed both Buchanan and the Lecompton constitution.[58]

Such a meagre anti-slavery stand in conservative Pennsylvania enabled Cameron to appear in agreement with the People's party's stand.[59] In 1858 the party's state convention at Harrisburg eulogistically mentioned Cameron specifically.[60]

As the issues of the state campaign of 1858 crystallized, it became apparent that Cameron had steered a most expedient course; opposition to the Lecompton constitution, emphasis on the need for a protective tariff, and evasion of advanced anti-slavery doctrines were the cardinal doctrines of the People's party.[61]

During the campaign of 1858 Cameron's name was first put forward for President by the Democratic New York *Herald*, whose editor, James Gordon Bennett, had for years assailed Seward and Thurlow Weed. Eminently conservative, Bennett viewed Seward's anti-slavery extremism with alarm; he feared that Seward would capture the Republican presidential nomination in 1860. Believing that the Buchanan administration would be held responsible for the Panic of 1857 and that an "Opposition" victory would result in 1860, the New York editor sought to promote the presidential candidacy of a conservative man, preferably a former Democrat, who had no violent anti-slavery or sectional record. Accordingly, on June 8 (1858) Bennett inserted in the *Herald* an editorial suggesting Cameron for President.[62]

Bennett's editorial did not escape the notice of Cameron's followers in Pennsylvania. It was reprinted in the Harrisburg *Telegraph*, Cameron's journalistic organ.[63] In Philadelphia Cameron's devoted friend, Alexander Cummings, published it in his Philadelphia *Evening Bulletin*.[64] A Cameron supporter wrote the New York *Herald:*[65]

In the *Herald* you suggested the name of General Simon Cameron, United States Senator from Pennsylvania, as an available candidate for President in 1860. . . . His position on the tariff question is sound, and always has been so, and has recommended him to the admiration of all true Pennsylvanians. . . . His nomination would be the initiative of a glorious triumph, and Pennsylvania would pour out such a vote from her coal and iron districts.

Several days later the *Herald* published a list of forty candidates (in which Abraham Lincoln was not included), and Cameron was classified under the elastic label of "Democratic Know-Nothing Republican Conservative."[66] Two days later the *Herald* published another boost for the Pennsylvanian: "As an available candidate for the opposition forces of all factions and sections we have mentioned General Simon Cameron. . . . His antecedents are democratic, and with a little spicing of Know-Nothingism, he is, withal a republican, though not an ultra republican." [67] Throughout July the *Herald* continued to laud the Pennsylvania senator as a logical Opposition standard-bearer in 1860.[68]

The Harrisburg *Telegraph* began reprinting articles from rural Pennsylvania newspapers which followed the New York *Herald's* lead.[69] Cummings did the same in his Philadelphia *Bulletin*.[70] During July (1858) the Cameronians sponsored picnics, fire-works displays and other popular social functions, exhibiting banners with the slogan "Simon Cameron and the Tariff, 1860." [71]

If thoughts of winning the glittering prize captivated Cameron, he and his advisers preferred to make no public manifestation of it at this time. When the Dauphin county People's convention assembled in early August a resolution "approving of Mr. Cameron for the Presidency," which was presented, was not acted upon.[72]

The state campaign of 1858 gave the People's party a glorious triumph. Hostility to Buchanan because of the Panic of 1857, the President's low-tariff views and "Lecompton" policy in Kansas, plus the split between himself and Forney, were the main factors in the Democrats' defeat.[73] The victory raised Cameron's political stock. The New York *Herald* maintained: "He now stands at the head of the column of the opposition availables for the Presidential battle." [74] Cameron's supporters in Pennsylvania became increasingly hopeful of making him the Republican standard-bearer in 1860,[75] for the People's party victory assured Cameron of the state patronage with which to build a strong organization.[76] The pro-Cameron press proclaimed: "His antecedents upon the protection question have now placed him in the foremost ranks." [77]

However hopeful Cameron might be, the leading Republican presidential contender was Seward, who appreciated Pennsylvania's pivotal position in 1860.[78] Following a visit to Cameron's home, "Lochiel," near Harrisburg, in early April (1859) Seward reported to his manager, Thurlow Weed, that Cameron had given the assurance that Pennsylvania, after a complimentary vote for him (Cameron) on the first ballot, would switch to Seward.[80] The political wiseacres at Harrisburg were certain that the two senators had agreed upon a "deal" whereby Pennsylvania was to cast a "favorite son's" vote for Cameron before turning to Seward at the National Convention.[81]

Two weeks following Seward's visit, Cameron started on a "visit" through the coal and iron regions, along with Henry C. Carey,

"Father of Pennsylvania Protectionism," and others.[82] Cameron and his party appeared at the home of his son-in-law, Judge Burnside, in Bellefonte. Bands serenaded him and he gave a speech to the assembled throng: "Gentlemen, when labor is shielded from unfair competition, and fostered by liberal protection, you protect the whole community, and prosperity must necessarily follow." [83] Judge Burnside's residence was crowded with people, who swarmed about to shake the senator's hand.[84] From Bellefonte Cameron and his party went to Philadelphia, where he toasted Carey at a testimonial dinner given the latter.[85] Several weeks later the "opposition" convention of York county unanimously nominated Cameron for President.[86]

Seward's faith in Cameron was destined to be misplaced, for the presidential bee had indeed bitten the General. In May one Theodore Adams left on an extended tour as far west as Minnesota to sound Cameron sentiment.[87]

Before May, 1859, closed, the Dauphin county People's party, his home district organization, adopted a resolution naming him for President.[88] All doubt of Cameron's candidacy was removed two days following when, on June 1, the Harrisburg *Telegraph* came out for him in an editorial, "Cameron for President." [89] The *Telegraph* now launched an energetic campaign, reprinting extracts from other newspapers, arguing that Cameron was the only one who could carry Pennsylvania against the Democrats; that Seward could not win.[90] Cameron had recently induced an able journalist, Wien Forney, to assume the *Telegraph* editorship.[91] In June the People's party state convention met in Harrisburg, and Cameron invited the delegates to a "strawberry party" at his home; champagne was served.[92] An observer remarked: "Depend upon it, these strawberries of 'Lochiel' will work to the disadvantage of Seward." [93]

One of Cameron's most confidential advisers was Alexander Cummings, editor of the Philadelphia *Evening Bulletin,* who had reprinted the New York *Herald*'s original suggestion of Cameron for President.[94] Cummings publicized the Pennsylvania senator's devotion to high-tariff duties.[95] In June Cummings followed the *Telegraph*'s example and launched a vigorous press campaign in Cameron's behalf.[96]

In mid-July Cameron was in Philadelphia, accompanied by his Harrisburg associates, to "fix things up," [97] as one onlooker expressed it. Cameron's appearance in the Quaker City, along with the state treasurer, the manager of Cameron's home newspaper, and the cashier of a Harrisburg bank, it was reported, revealed that unusual things were afoot. One correspondent observed: [98]

Gen. Cameron is in the field, a candidate for the Presidency . . . The General is trying to curry favor with both sides—with those who dislike Senator Seward, and express fears that they are indirectly helping him when working for Cameron: the General quiets their fears by telling them that whatever chances he had for the nomination he will not yield to any man; and that the next moment when he comes in contact with the admirers of the orator of Rochester [Seward], he lauds him to the skies—neither side are (sic) therefore sure of him.

Thus Cameron went about, using his skill to secure the presidency; or, if that were impossible, to place himself in such a strategic position as would give him a strong voice in the new administration.

By early September 1859 Cameron himself was still protesting: "In regard to what you say of the Presidency, I can assure you, if it comes, it will have to come without any efforts of mine." [99] Cameron's lieutenants, however, were conducting a vigorous undercover campaign throughout the country.

The widespread belief that Cameron was committed to Seward embarrassed the General's managers. Joseph Casey wrote a Cincinnati editor, who had offered Ohio support to Cameron,[100] that Cameron was not committed to Seward. "While Gen. Cameron" he explained, "in common with us all has the highest regard and admiration for the character & ability of Mr. Seward . . . yet we all feel that . . . it would be almost impracticable, if not entirely impossible, to unite the Opposition of this State in his support.[101] Then, while Seward was absent in Europe in October, 1859, Cameron himself spread stories in Washington that "Seward cannot carry Penna." [102]

Cameron's forces outside of Pennsylvania were most active in Illinois, attempting to make a "deal" whereby Cameron would receive Illinois support for the presidential nomination in return for Pennsylvania's support of Abraham Lincoln for the vice-presidency. But "Old Abe" was not interested. By this time the Springfield man was vaguely thinking of first place himself.[103]

Lincoln's coolness did not dampen the enthusiasm of Cameron's supporters in Illinois. "Colonel" Charles Leib, a political adventurer and erstwhile Democrat, became Cameron's chief lieutenant in the

Prairie state.[104] "Leib promises to become a straight Republican and no mistake, if Cameron is the Republican nominee for President in 1860," [105]—so one paper declared sarcastically. When the Lancaster (Pennsylvania) *Examiner* printed an editorial suggesting Cameron for President and Lincoln for Vice-President in October 1859,[106] the article was printed in circular form and distributed throughout Illinois by Leib.[107] In late December (1859) Leib journeyed to Washington, and word reached Chicago: [108]

Col. Leib has arrived at the "National." He is the bearer of dispatches to Gen. Cameron, and will carry back to the West the latest instructions. The Colonel claims to be the General's plenipotentiary for the Northwest, and in the improbable event of the realization of the former's aspirations, nothing less than a seat in the cabinet would be an adequate appreciation of the latter's services —in his own humble opinion.

Leib returned to Illinois and organized a "Cameron and Lincoln" club in Chicago.[109] But it was evident that the Illinois Republicans were determined that Lincoln should have first place. The ardently pro-Lincoln Chicago *Press & Tribune* observed: "We fancy the Republicans of the Northwest will insist upon turning it [the Cameron-Lincoln ticket] end to end, so that it may read Lincoln for President, and Cameron for Vice-President." [110]

Cameron's supporters professed to see Lincoln's state swinging to their favorite. When the Illinois state Republican convention at Decatur adjourned on May 10, a Cameron man informed the Pennsylvania senator that he was the state's second choice.[111] But such a report was wishful thinking. Illinois was first and last for Lincoln.

The workers for Cameron also tried to secure delegates in Indiana. They approached Daniel D. Pratt, delegate-at-large from Indiana. "Governor Seward can not carry Pennsylvania," they explained. "Nor is it certain that our vote can be carried with any other Republican man, except Cameron." [112] Again: "Our only safety is to have Genl Cameron as our candidate for President." [113]

Indiana Republicans, however, were cool toward Cameron. His record was against him, and he was a vulnerable target for the Hoosier Democrats, who sarcastically referred to him as an "immaculate statesman"; one declared: "He is known as the prince of stock and claim jobbers." [114]

Cameron's lieutenants opened a secret correspondence with delegates to the Chicago convention from Massachusetts,[115] Connecticut,[116] and Minnesota.[117] Russell Errett, editor of the Pittsburgh *Gazette* and an original Cameron enthusiast,[118] sent out a form letter, marked "private," to delegates in all the northern states, reminding them that Cameron was the only Republican who could carry pivotal Pennsylvania in 1860. He requested replies. Encouraging but noncommittal answers came from New Jersey, Maine, Indiana, Connecticut, Vermont, Iowa, and Ohio.[119] Of the replies Errett wrote Cameron: "The tone is good, but you will see they carefully abstain from pledges." [120]

Cameron's ability to attract support from other states would depend largely on his strength within his own bailiwick. If Pennsylvania should go to Chicago "as a *unit*" for Cameron, Casey wrote him in January, there was a prospect of attracting the entire Iowa delegation.[121] The Cameronians believed that this was true of other states as well. Their strategy then was to secure a solid pro-Cameron delegation from the Keystone state. One Philadelphia journalist commented in early February: [122]

This [Cameron] regency . . . have for months been secretly corresponding with persons all over the State, to get their agents and friends in the distant parts of the State to force the (state) Convention to appoint the delegates to the National Convention. They have everywhere sought to get the party presses to declare for it. Hungry expectants of Presidential favors have been raising outcries in favor of it.

The People's party state convention met in Harrisburg on February 22, 1860. The Cameronians, after weeks of careful operation, however, encountered two obstacles—Cameron's tarnished past and Andrew G. Curtin.

Cameron's public record was far from spotless. In 1838, as commissioner to settle certain claims of the Winnebago Indians in Wisconsin, he had adjusted these claims by giving the Indians depreciated notes of his own Middleton Bank—all of which brought against him the first of numerous charges of dishonesty and earned for him the derisive sobriquet "The Great Winnebago Chief." [123] Subsequently "Cameron" and "corruption" became synonymous terms.[124] And in 1860 one caustic critic declared that "if Cameron had his deserts, he would be serving out a sentence in the penitentiary instead of serving in the United States Senate." [125]

For long there had been bad blood between Cameron and Curtin.

In 1855 they had opposed each other for United States senator—and Cameron claimed subsequently that Curtin had not fulfilled the terms of an alleged agreement whereby he was to support Cameron for the senatorship in return for which Cameron would use his influence to make Curtin secretary of state for Pennsylvania.[126]

When the Harrisburg convention met, Curtin was the strongest gubernatorial contender. The convention centered about the Cameron-Curtin feud. Cameron, fearing his rival's power should he be nominated and elected governor, threw his support to John Covode. Before any business could be introduced a pro-Cameron delegate from Erie proposed that the convention consider Cameron as Pennsylvania's presidential choice. Curtin's friends were on their feet instantly, but a majority favored Cameron and he received the recommendation for President, 89 to 39. A Cameronian then proposed that the convention elect the district delegates to Chicago and instruct them to vote as a unit. Alexander K. McClure, leading the Curtin forces, proposed that the several Congressional districts of the state should select four delegates in each district; and also that the delegates should support Cameron's candidacy. The partisans of Cameron and Curtin wrangled for an entire day. The outcome was that Cameron became Pennsylvania's choice for President, and Curtin was nominated as candidate for Governor—but many of the delegates to the Chicago Convention were left to be chosen in districts. The resolutions adopted at Harrisburg endorsed the principle of the protective tariff and adopted a most conservative stand on slavery.[127]

Cameron's friends were disappointed. Although they constituted an undoubted majority in the convention, they had been outmaneuvered by the Curtinites. Their original intention had been to elect a full pro-Cameron delegation to Chicago. Not only did they swallow the obnoxious Curtin as gubernatorial candidate but they had agreed to these complicated modifications for electing delegates: That the delegates should be chosen by the representatives present from each Congressional district. Under the operation of this provision only eleven districts nominated their delegates in the convention. That the delegates already chosen in any district should be accepted. Two districts took advantage of this provision. That in case the representatives from any district should decline to nominate delegates to Chicago, the people of such districts should be permitted to choose delegates for themselves. The delegates from twelve districts had declined to appoint delegates. That only the delegates chosen by the convention should be bound by the instructions to vote for Cameron. While the resolutions adopted at Harrisburg instructed the Pennsylvania delegation to vote as a unit and authorized the majority of the delegation to cast the state's entire vote at Chicago, there was the possibility that the National Convention would permit voting by districts. Thus Cameron's friends had been forced to concede much.[128]

Although the contest in Pennsylvania had not closed in Cameron's favor, his friends continued the search for delegates to the National Convention throughout late Winter and early Spring of 1860. On entraining for Chicago in early May they were sanguine. "Our purpose," wrote Casey to Cameron, "is to go there and seek an acquaintance with as many as possible of the different delegations & prominent gentlemen outside from the various states as they arrive," and also "to treat all kindly and respectfully—and especially Mr. Seward and his friends." [129]

CHAPTER SEVEN

Other Hopefuls

WHILE THE PRE-CONVENTION campaigns of Seward, Chase, Bates, Lincoln, and Cameron were being waged, other less formidable contenders also hoped to become the anti-Democratic standard bearer in 1860. Ever working under cover were potential Warwicks—"Kingmakers" who had become convinced of their respective protégé's availability.

Among the "dark horses" who hoped to be trotted out at the opportune time in Chicago was Nathaniel P. Banks, governor of Massachusetts.

During the late 1840's the Boston-dominated aristocratic Whig party of Massachusetts had split on the slavery issue into two hostile camps—the "Cotton" Whigs and the "Conscience" (anti-slavery) Whigs.[1] By virtue of this Whig schism, the humbly-born Democrat, Banks, was elected to the Legislature in 1848 by an ingenious coalition of Democratic and anti-slavery forces. Maintaining a discreet silence on the slavery issue when he was not "see-sawing," the opportunistic Banks was sent to Congress from the Waltham district in 1852. After registering his vote against the Kansas-Nebraska bill in 1854, Banks returned to his constituency to defend his action.[2]

Although the Massachusetts election of 1853 had defeated the "Coalitionists" with whom Banks had worked, this was only a temporary lull in the anti-Whig, anti-Boston and anti-conservative cause. For following the passage of the Kansas-Nebraska bill the Know-Nothings absorbed most of the Coalition elements and continued the war alike against conservative Whiggery and the "immigrant-loving" regular Democratic party. Banks accepted a Know-Nothing nomination for reëlection to Congress and won. He never declared, as did others, that he turned nativist to advance the anti-slavery cause. He simply told an old friend: "I am in politics and

I must go on." His Know-Nothing lodge was Council Number 20 at Waltham.[3] He was reëlected. The "Americans" elected their candidate for governor, Henry J. Gardner, and a huge majority of the legislature.

Massachusetts Know-Nothingism was a blend of three distinct elements: anti-Catholicism, Maine-lawism, and anti-Nebraskaism. The Democratic Irish-Catholic naturalized immigrant, as well as the plutocratic Boston Whig of colonial ancestry, was viewed as an enemy, for the son of Erin was competing with native-born American labor and allegedly filling the poor-houses; was opposing rural puritanical efforts to enact a state prohibition law; and his "Jesuitical" press was supporting the South in defending slavery. In 1855 the Know-Nothing–dominated legislature adopted a policy of "Protestantism, Temperance, and Liberty"; it waged warfare against "Rome, Rum, and Robbery."[4]

In 1856 Banks, by his very inconsistencies, attracted the votes of enough anti-Administration members of Congress to have himself elected Speaker. His triumph was hailed as the "first Republican National Victory." Banks enjoyed tremendous prestige. He used his position to bring northern groups together and to promote his own fortunes. He led the more anti-slavery-minded "Americans" into the Republican party in anticipation of the presidential election of 1856. He aspired to run for President, and actually accepted such a nomination from the anti-slavery (or anti-Fillmore) faction of Know-Nothings. He withdrew from the race to throw his support to Frémont when the Republicans nominated the latter. He took the stump for Frémont but when the Pathfinder lost in November he turned his attention to Massachusetts politics. The governorship beckoned to him. Steering his usual middle course in the gubernatorial race of 1857—he still retained the charm of appealing to both anti-slavery Republicans and nativistic "Americans"—he was elected Massachusetts' chief executive. As one of Banks's opponents said: "He always retires from something good to something better." He could well hope to be his state's "favorite son" in 1860. He had brought the Republicans and anti-slavery "Americans" together, forming an effective state organization that even used his name: the majority in the Legislature caucused not as "Republicans" or "Americans" but as "Banks members"! Soon the party became known as "American-Republican" and later "Republican."[5]

Just as Seward gave leadership to those northern anti-slavery

Whigs who entered the new Republican party, just as Chase served as pioneer to those western Free-Soil Democrats who did the same, just as Bates proved to be an example to those more advanced border-state "Americans" who espoused Republicanism, and just as Lincoln gave approval to those Illinois Anti-Nebraska Whigs who did the same—so, too, did Banks become the main personal force who steered the Massachusetts "Americans" into the Republican party. By 1859 incongruous elements in Massachusetts were organized into a strong Republican organization. The influential Springfield *Republican* declared: [6]

The formation of the republican party in this state, out of such variant elements as cool, conservative, commercial, federalistic but anti-slavery whigs, radical Jeffersonian democrats, and hot, fiery free soilers and liberty-party abolitionists, with such prejudices and hates as the old coalition and the know-nothing experiences introduced into our local politics, scattered freely among them all,— was a very difficult task.

The lack of harmony among the various groups that constituted the Massachusetts Republican party spelled obstacles for Banks in the executive house at Boston. The radical wing, led by Senators Charles Sumner and Henry Wilson, and John A. Andrew—those advanced Republicans who had accepted Banks only because they would get rid of the conservative, nativistic Henry J. Gardner— were intent on transforming the party into an extremist organization. They were only too ready to crush Banks in doing so. Banks was not the one to force a show-down.[7] This antagonism between the two factions revealed itself during the controversy over the so-called "Two Year Amendment"—an issue that was partially to affect the choice of a Republican presidential candidate at Chicago.

To Massachusetts nativistic elements in 1859 Roman Catholicism was still considered alien to American institutions, hostile to the "Maine Law" and allied to slavery. Since Bay State Republicanism drew largely from the rank and file of Know-Nothingism, rather than from conservative Boston Whiggery, a nativistic prejudice continued to exist within the organization. Frémont's defeat had convinced Massachusetts Republican leaders that the naturalization period should be extended if the national Democracy were to be dethroned in 1860.[8] Of 1,231,066 people in Massachusetts by 1860, over 260,000 were foreign-born, 185,434 being natives of Ireland.[9]

Thus in April, 1859, the Republican-dominated legislature adopted for submission to the voters an amendment to the state constitution, providing that foreign-born persons should not have the right of voting until two years after they had become American citizens.[10] "There is a decided evil," wrote Republican State Chairman John Z. Goodrich to Banks, "in the quite too frequent practice of 'putting foreigners through' just before election, which I think such an amendment would cure." [11]

Numerous Republican leaders in the Northwest were most concerned over the action of their Massachusetts brethren in enacting such a proposed amendment.[12] A Chicago party editor warned Banks that such legislation handicapped the northwestern Republicans in courting the German vote.[13] The Chicago German Republican leader, Hermann Kreismann, wrote Banks: "I fear it will lose us votes enough in Wisconsin, Iowa, Illinois, and even Ohio to give these states to the Democrats." [14] Appealing to Banks to use his influence to have the Massachusetts voters reject the "Two Year Amendment," Kreismann promised Banks: "We would of course take good care that the credit of defeating [it], so far as we germans are concerned, should belong to you. . . . I know we cannot elect a man on anti-slavery ground exclusively. We must carry the American or conservative element in the middle states and you can do that. The West with the foreign element will go for you if we can have such an argument, as the defeat of those amendments would furnish." [15]

Banks, by now having hopes of receiving the presidential nomination, believed that the best course would be his usual one of evasion. In May, 1859, when the Massachusetts electorate voted on the amendment—and approved it—Banks was absent from the state. One of his opponents reported to Sumner: "The 2 Yrs. amendment has passed by 5000 majority. . . . Gov. Banks did nothing one way or the other. He went to N. Y. the day or two before the election & did not return till afterwards." [16]

Banks was indeed in New York to confer with the anti-Seward Republican elements of the Empire state, who had settled on him as a likely choice to head off Seward.[17] By July one Republican in the inner councils was noting: "Banks has been to N. Y. several times of late" to confer with Seward's opponents.[18] Throughout the last half of 1859 Banks's friends operated in various regions of the North, consulting with party leaders and editors.[19]

Chief among Banks's boosters were W. O. Bartlett, Anson Burlingame, and Samuel Bowles, editor of the Springfield *Republican*.
Early in 1860 Bowles lauded Seward; but he always insisted that
the New Yorker should be withdrawn if his nomination appeared to
be disastrous to party success.[20] This was the Banks leaders' strategy.
In March Burlingame wrote Banks: "Our old policy of 'running
with the Seward machine' is the true one." [21]

The Banks leaders were also courting the radical anti-Seward men
of New York, among them William Cullen Bryant and David
Dudley Field. In April certain New York City Republicans, headed
by Bryant and Field, invited Banks to be guest of honor at a dinner sponsored by distinguished New Yorkers of New England origin.[22] Bowles advised Banks to accept the invitation: [23]

I am inclined to the New York demonstration. . . . Seward will
claim the nomination, but I think not get it, though there will be
a sharp struggle. And then I should hope for you to lead the column.
. . . Of course there is danger of coming into antagonism with
Seward; but you can manage that.

Bowles was not alone in advising Banks to accept. Bartlett,
in consultation with the intensely anti-Seward James Gordon Bennett, editor of the New York *Herald*,[24] wrote the Massachusetts
governor on April 27: "I talked the matter over with Mr. Bennett
and he semed to think favorably of it. The paragraph in the *Herald*
of Wednesday was the fruit of our consultation." [25] The *Herald*
notice read: [26]

Proposed Dinner to Governor Banks—A large number of the
leading republicans of the several States have invited Governor
Banks, of Massachusetts, to accept the honor of a public dinner,
and it is generally supposed that he will do so. It is the intention
of the republicans to make this a grand and celebrated banquet.
It is well known that Governor Banks has been and is the most
eminent and conservative member of that party since its organization . . . On this occasion he will make one of his great oratorical
efforts, in which he will give expression to his views on the present
confused and unsettled state of the country. According to popular
belief this movement has a great many ramifications throughout the
country, and we shall await the oration of Governor Banks with
some interest.

Banks did not deliver the much-planned oration. His supporters
finally deemed it inexpedient for him to do so, lest he offend

Seward's supporters and thereby lose all chance of attracting the New York delegation when Seward should be forced to drop out at Chicago. Banks's supporters concluded that making a bid in New York City, under anti-Seward Republican sponsorship, was bad policy. Accordingly, Horace Greeley, affiliated with the anti-Seward faction, made apologies for Banks's postponement of his speech: "The Governor's official duties [do] not . . . allow him to be present just at this time." [27]

Samuel Bowles carried on a vigorous Banks campaign in Massachusetts. Until late April, through his Springfield *Republican*, he moved cautiously, since the Massachusetts Republicans had already selected a delegation to Chicago in favor of Seward.[28] On May 1 Bowles assured his public: "Gov. Banks prefers Seward to McLean or Bates. Gov. Banks is also a warm friend of Mr. Lincoln." [29] A week later the *Republican* commented that Seward would encounter more prejudices than any other Republican, and presented Banks as an "available" man. Bowles minimized the nativist issue.[30] On the following day Bowles printed the editorial, "The Republican Candidate—Gov. Banks." [31] On May 10 the *Republican* editor advised: "Nothing will be more stupid than any attempt at Chicago to revive the dead issues of Americanism." [32] The *Republican's* parting shot to the Massachusetts delegation as it entrained for Chicago was: "Mr. Banks . . . is the man of all others in Republican high places to become the accepted leader of those who have left, or have been left, by the Democratic party." [33]

In addition to Governor Banks, there were other Republicans who were being urged for president. Among these were two Ohioans, Supreme Court Justice John McLean and Senator Benjamin F. Wade.

Since the early 1830's McLean had been regarded as a candidate.[34] John Quincy Adams had then observed that McLean thought "of nothing but the Presidency by day and dreamed of nothing else at night." [35] Frémont's nomination over him in 1856 did not dampen McLean's ambition. In 1859 the Supreme Court jurist wrote a friend: "The bargain had been made [in 1856] by the New Yorkers with Frémont, a man not fit to discharge the duties of an auditor. . . I have said to no man that I should consent to the use of my name; but my friends requested me to keep the subject open until the next Congress." [36]

There were certain Republicans who felt that a conservative elder statesman—even one born in 1785—would be the strongest candidate. This bloc rallied behind McLean.[37] Late in 1859 McLean received word from Iowa that he was the prime favorite.[38] An Illinois leader wrote him encouraging words.[39] In April, 1860, a McLean enthusiast, Richard M. Corwine, sounded Lincoln on the prospect of Illinois support for McLean. But "Old Abe," himself a candidate by now, dismissed the suggestion diplomatically: "If Judge McLean was [sic] fifteen, or even ten years younger, I think he would be stronger than either [Seward or Bates], in our state, taken as a whole; but his great age, and the recollection of the deaths of Harrison and Taylor have, so far, prevented his being spoken of much here."[40] The McLean boosters remained confident.[41]

Another Ohio aspirant was Wade, whose entry into the race after Chase and McLean gave the Buckeye State three contenders.

Wade came from Ashtabula, on the strongly anti-slavery Western Reserve. Wrote one contemporary: "The Reserve was for many years seemingly the residence—the home of the various *isms*, the vagaries, *mental ailments*, many called them—of a people, noted throughout the land for this distinctive feature, so that whoever had a hobby elsewhere rejected, rode it straightway to the Reserve, where it was quite certain of hospitable pasturage and shelter."[42]

Although not so anti-slavery as Seward or Chase, Wade was more radical than Bates, Lincoln, Cameron, Banks, or McLean. His candidacy got under way early in 1860. Those erstwhile Chase supporters, despairing of their favorite's chances, turned to Wade. Chase's eastern manager, James A. Briggs, wrote the Ohio senator: "I am under obligations to Mr. Chase. He has been my friend, good & true. . . . But if he cannot be nominated I hope *you* will be. . . . Your name is often mentioned favorably. You must work and wait."[43]

Chief of Wade's campaign was Robert F. Paine, of Cleveland, who communicated with key leaders in Wisconsin, Minnesota and Michigan—strong pro-Seward territory. Moreover, the Wade leaders sounded the anti-Seward New York leader James S. Wadsworth—declared to be "rich and influential"—on the proposal to accept the vice-presidency on Wade's ticket.[44] In March Wade's latest Senate speech was circulated by his managers.[45] Carl Schurz, while confident of Seward's nomination, believed that Wade's and Lincoln's prospects were the next best.[46] And Wade himself became optimistic. To his brother he expressed the belief that his nomination was "not impossible." [47]

Wade's pre-convention campaign irritated Governor Chase, who considered himself Ohio's favorite. Chase, following his endorsement by Ohio Republicans, wrote Wade: [48]

You see what the [Ohio Republican State] Convention here has done. It was altogether spontaneous. Not a letter to my knowledge was written from Columbus to influence the choice of delegates or their action. It was pure people's work. I hope you are satisfied with it, & that you will take hold on our side.

Wade's supporters provoked the Ohio governor by asking him whom his second choice for President would be if he (Chase) could not be nominated. Chase answered acidly that he was Ohio's first and only choice.[49] "The great thorn in your way," Chase's Washington lieutenant reported to his chief, "is the persistent use of Wade's name"; and when this same Chase supporter endeavored to persuade Wade to withdraw and declare for Chase, the Ohio senator declined to do so. "Honest Ben" was determined that he would be entered in the race.[50]

The Ohio delegation entrained for Chicago divided in their loyalties among Chase, McLean, and Wade.

Another Republican presidential contender was William L. Dayton, of New Jersey. Having served in the New Jersey legislature, as state Supreme Court Justice, and in the United States Senate, Dayton had been Frémont's running-mate on the national ticket in 1856. In the following year he had become state attorney-general.[51]

Probably no other northern state was so pro-southern as New Jersey,[52] whose seashore resorts were filled with slaveholding southern families during the summer.[53] The census of 1860 actually listed eighteen slaves in New Jersey.[54] In 1856 the state had given its electoral vote to Buchanan.[55] A Republican organizer reported: The [New Jersey] people are not educated up to a very high anti-slavery standard." [56]

Dayton was thoroughly acceptable to those who controlled the New Jersey anti-Democratic movement. For he was both conservative and sound on the tariff. Next to Pennsylvania, the state was the most enthusiastic champion of protection to American industry.[57] Certain New Jersey politicians, such as Thomas H. Dudley and James T. Sherman, brought out Dayton to stop Seward. They operated in both New Jersey and Pennsylvania since both states contained large conservative "American" elements who would not accept Seward.[58] In November, 1859, Dudley accepted invitations from influential Philadelphians to have Dayton "see and be seen by the leading men" of the Quaker City. And Dudley preached Dayton's availability to his old Philadelphia friend, Henry C. Carey.[59]

When the New Jersey "Opposition" convention—the label "Republican" was not used—met at Trenton in March, 1860, it was plain that Dayton was their favorite son and would have their solid support at Chicago.[60] Then Sherman sounded Gideon Welles, leader of the Connecticut Republicans.[61] In April Sherman corresponded with Iowa leaders, insisting that Dayton could carry New Jersey and Pennsylvania.[62]

Pennsylvania was in the most strategic position. Cameron was working furiously to secure his state's solid backing. Seward was courting Pennsylvania as were Lincoln and Chase. Besides Cameron, Pennsylvania had another possibility for the White House—Judge John M. Read, of the state Supreme Court, whose candidacy, essentially an anti-Cameron move to throw Cameron overboard, had support in scattered regions.[63] Some encouragement was given to Read by Senator Hannibal Hamlin, of Maine, who wanted the Pennsylvania jurist as a stalking-horse for himself.[64]

A Republican leader who engineered his own boom was the tempestuous and fearless Cassius M. Clay, of slaveholding Kentucky.

Kentucky had been a traditional citadel of Whiggery. The Whig party had gradually come to include Kentucky's people of wealth, conservatism, and education. The state was ever loyal to Cassius's more famous relative, Henry Clay.[65] Long after Harry of the West had passed on and the Kansas-Nebraska act had destroyed the Whigs as a national organization, the Kentuckians remained conservative and Union-loving. In 1856 the state had voted for Buchanan for President primarily because he was considered less sectional than Frémont. In this year, Cassius M. Clay had organized a Republican party in Madison County—just at the border between the "blue grass" region and the mountains, where economic conditions were the least favorable to the slave-plantation system.[66]

For years Cassius M. Clay had fought for the anti-slavery cause. Concerned with the economic disaster that slavery was visiting upon the South, his speeches and letters repeatedly revealed his understanding of the "poor whites." He believed that the slave-plantation system was one of waste and impoverishment and was the reason why the North excelled the South in material progress.[67] In 1856 Clay joined the Republicans.[68]

Clay had a comparatively large following among Kentucky Republicans. "So," he wrote, "I was much courted by the aspirants for the presidency." He related how Seward invited him to a dinner; but he had refused to support the distinguished New Yorker. The Blairs, too, dined Clay and solicited his support for Edward Bates, promising him the portfolio of War in Bates's Cabinet. Clay declined this also, he alleged. On January 27, 1860, he wrote a public letter stating his opposition to Bates and exhibiting a leaning toward Seward, whom he described as Slavery's most potent foe. Then, writing later, Clay affirmed that Chase was his choice; but that if the choice narrowed down to Lincoln and Seward, he was for Lincoln. The truth was that he, Clay, was for himself for President! [69]

In February, 1860, Clay spoke at Cooper Institute in New York City. A voice from the audience barked: "All in favor of Mr. Clay being the nominee for the next President say aye," which was followed by a roar of "ayes" throughout the hall. Then Clay journeyed to Hartford, Connecticut, where he delivered a similar address.[70]

Returning home, Clay adopted a certain moderation in his speeches. He now rejected the orthodox Republican stand that Congress had power to prohibit slavery in the territories and adopted views similar to Douglas's "popular sovereignty." [71] It was most singular that the firebrand Clay—who for years had risked bodily injury by preaching straight anti-slavery in Kentucky—should suddenly be converted to moderate Republicanism. Already, at this very time, he had some strength in conservative-minded Indiana; [72] one Hoosier leader reported: "C. M. Clay seems to have about as many friends as any of the candidates for President." [73]

Clay even appealed to radical New England Republicans. On March 3, 1860, he wrote Senator Sumner: [74]

After the old leaders Chase & Seward are voted for it seems to be the idea if one or the other is not at once chosen that a new man may come up. From my position, as taking away the great cry of "sectionalism" it is now generally thought that I am the most likely man to be chosen standard bearer. This is no seeking of my own—

but as a widespread movement is making and will be made in that way; I am desirous of winning if put to it! . . . Write me at once.

Sumner received Clay's offer of himself coldly. Clay apologized to the Massachusetts senator: [75]

So far as my name is connected with the candidacy, I assure you it was not by my seeking. I have absolutely again and again refused to allow myself to be balloted for till Chase and Seward were chosen or defeated—then I was willing to be voted for as against all eleventh hour men, or good men of less service than myself. I have seen so much intrigue since that I almost regret this much—but being put up I naturally feel anxious not in that emergency to be beaten; or not to receive a respectable vote. Hence I have written a few friends like yourself . . . I beg therefore you will not regard me as an office seeker!

When the Kentucky Republicans met in state convention at Covington, Clay addressed the gathering. Resolutions were adopted which took Republican ground, and delegates appointed to represent Kentucky at Chicago.[76] Clay became ever more confident. On May 7 he wrote to a New York leader: [77]

I shall not go to the Convention myself. I am assured that Chase's friends will go for me after him. I have a first strength in Indiana; and Missouri will sustain me after Bates. . . .

> Very truly your friend,
> C. M. Clay.

P.S. In case you don't go to Chicago: our N. Y. friends must send a representative in your place to act for us.

> C.

Our delegation will divide on Seward and Chase.

> C.

Clay was not the only Republican leader who was his own most ardent backer for the presidential nomination. In Minnesota Governor Alexander Ramsey was maneuvering in his own behalf.

Minnesota was more concerned over free land than slavery.[78] The homestead issue became particularly important. In 1859 both Republican and Democratic parties in Minnesota incorporated homestead planks in their platforms. In this state campaign copies of the Republican Congressman Galusha Grow's homestead bill were circulated in German. One southern Congressman denounced the Republicans' support of homestead as an electioneering trick to gain foreign votes.[79] And the Republicans had the best of the argument. Grow stumped Minnesota to appeal to the "land for the landless" sentiment. Carl Schurz was also imported from Wisconsin for the campaign. Ramsey was running for governor. Aided by the homestead issue and questions of local concern, Ramsey was elected.[80]

Ramsey's election instilled in him the obsession that he was presidential timber. He sought to capture control of his state's delegation to Chicago, which was enthusiastically for Seward. Wrote a Minnesota Sewardite to Thurlow Weed: "Our state delegation will, I fear, do a foolish thing, in choosing delegates, to the National Convention, And who for, think you? If you don't already know, I will tell you—*Alexander Ramsey*. D—m foolish idea, of course, but the thing will be done. . . . Ramsey would like to go into the Cabinet if we succeeed in '60 and wants the Delegates from this State as capital to trade on—that is, if he cant be Prest." [81] Ramsey found himself, however, not powerful enough to cut into Seward's strength.[82]

Ramsey was not disheartened. He continued to work under cover.[83] A native Pennsylvanian, the Minnesota governor corresponded regularly with Simon Cameron, who still nursed his own candidacy and was anxious to destroy Seward. Ramsey maintained to Cameron that Seward could not be nominated; that if the Republican standard-bearer should be a Westerner and if Lincoln were not chosen, he (Ramsey) would be an available man.[84] Cameron's purpose was to court Ramsey's support for himself, but the Minnesota governor was out for his own interests. The Ramsey men's plans, before leaving for Chicago, were to bring suddenly forward their man for president or vice-president when the major candidates deadlocked the Convention. The Ramsey movement was kept a dark secret and was known only to a few members of the Minnesota delegation.[85]

Still another possible contender for presidential honors was United States Senator William Pitt Fessenden, of Maine. Unlike Ramsey and others, he seems to have done nothing to encourage his candidacy. Fessenden had been elected to the Senate in 1854 as a Whig from then Democratic-ribbed Maine by virtue of a split in the Democratic party and emergence of the "Maine-law" (or temperance) issue and the Nebraska question.[86] In the Senate the Down-Easter had made an anti-slavery record. Fessenden remained indifferent to the boom set up for him.[87] His "availability" was all but destroyed because he was of a state too small in convention and electoral votes and too far north to attract support in the border regions. One Iowa admirer admitted: "Pitt Fessenden would make a President after my own heart. But, he is too near the 'open Polar sea.' . . . If he lived in Iowa . . . or Indiana, he might come in; but we can't go into the tall timber of Maine. . . . I am for the man who can carry Pennsylvania, New Jersey, and Indiana." [88] Fessenden remained a slight potential factor.

Another minor New England possibility was United States Senator Jacob Collamer, of Vermont. An erstwhile Whig who had served as postmaster general in President Taylor's Cabinet in 1849–1850, Collamer had then served as state judge, finally being elected to the United States Senate as a Republican in 1855.[89] However, Collamer's weaknesses were the same as those of Fessenden: he came from a state too small and too northerly.

In addition to Banks, McLean, Wade, Dayton, Read, Cassius M. Clay, Ramsey, Fessenden, and Collamer, there were other contenders for Republican honors in 1860, among them United States Senator John Bell, of Tennessee. Like Bates, Bell was being suggested by conservative "American" elements.[90] The Tennesseean had steered a middle course in the Senate between North and South. He had often defied the interests of his state to combat sectionalism; he was indeed the only slave-state Whig senator to vote against the Kansas-Nebraska bill. A staunch Union-lover, Bell was instilled with the spirit of compromise—and this quality was his principal handicap. Horace Greeley, an extreme Republican inconsistently supporting the conservative Edward Bates, presented the count against Bell: [91]

Before you say much more about John Bell, will you just take down the volumes of the Congressional Globe for 1853–4 and refresh your recollection of the part he played with regard to the Nebraska bill? Will you look especially at his votes February 6th, on Chase's amendment; February 15th, on Douglas's amendment (the present slavery proviso); March 2d, on Chase's amendment (allowing the people of the Territories to prohibit slavery); March 2d, against Chase again, etc. It does seem to me that you or I must be mad or strangely forgetful about this business. I venture to say that Bell's record is the most tangled and embarrassing to the party which shall run him for President of any man's in America. And as to his wife's owning the slaves—bosh! We know that Bell *has* owned slaves—how did he get rid of them? That's an interesting question. We know how to answer it respecting Bates.

Although Bell was unacceptable to most Republican leaders, he became the standard bearer of a new party in the field—the conservative-minded, Whig-tainted "Constitutional Union" party, which met in Baltimore on May 9th.

Those groups who assembled at the Constitutional Union Convention to nominate Bell for president and Edward Everett for vice-president comprised fragments of "American," Old-Line Whig and other Union-loving elements who had found it morally impossible to cast their lot with either the Republicans or the Democrats. Most of them "respectable" and advanced in years, the Constitutional Unionists had been influential leaders in their heyday. But that time was past. New leaders were in control. For years most of the Constitutional Unionists had watched with alarm the rising tide of sectional wrath, and they were now making a last-hour stand to check it. They combated northern and southern sectionalism alike and considered neither of the major parties Union-minded. Besides nominating Bell and Everett, they adopted a vague and somewhat evasive platform declaring for "the Constitution of the Country, the Union of the States, and the Enforcement of the Laws." [92] Greeley referred to them as "the Old Gentlemen's Party." [93]

As the Constitutional Union Convention at Baltimore disbanded on May 10, and as the Republicans converged on Chicago, it might be well to turn attention to momentous happenings in the Democratic party.

CHAPTER EIGHT

Democratic Dissension

THE REPUBLICAN PARTY became a formidable organization partly by virtue of the Democratic family troubles. As the Republicans are preparing to assemble in national convention, we may profitably summarize some factors that led to the split within the Democracy.

Much Democratic dissension centered in the controversy between President Buchanan and Senator Douglas—a feud of long origin. During the 1850's those closest to Buchanan, particularly Senator John Slidell of Louisiana, were personally antagonistic toward Douglas. At the Democratic National Convention of 1856 Buchanan had defeated Douglas for the Presidential nomination. The Illinois senator supported Buchanan against the Republicans. With Buchanan's elevation to the presidency, differences between the two arose over the formation of the Cabinet.[1]

Douglas went to Washington, expecting to secure Cabinet appointments from the President-elect for two of his northwestern followers, W. A. Richardson and Samuel Treat. But Buchanan's staunch friends, Slidell and Senator Jesse D. Bright of Indiana, blocked this.[2] Douglas, crestfallen, shortly before Buchanan's inaugural, complained to an associate: [3]

The patronage for the Northwest was disposed of before the nomination. Bright is the man who is to control it if they dare to carry out their designs. Slidell, Bright & Corcoran (the Banker) assume the right to dispose of all the patronage. If this purpose is carried out & I am the object of attack I shall fight all my enemies and neither ask nor give quarter. I do not decline to urge friends, provided the opportunity is presented, to do so under any prospect of success. My advice is not invited nor will my wishes probably be regarded.

Douglas proved correct. Buchanan gave control of the patronage to Slidell and Bright, the latter distributing the federal jobs throughout the Northwest, bailiwick of Douglas. The Kansas question added fuel to the Democratic dissension.

In Kansas Territory a constitutional convention was chosen by a minority of those having the right to vote; many "free state" elements refused to participate in the gathering. Meeting at Lecompton, the convention adopted a "pro-slavery" constitution. The people were permitted only to vote for the "constitution with slavery," or for the "constitution with no slavery." If they should decide on the latter course, slavery was not to exist any longer in Kansas, except that the right of property in slaves then in the Territory was not to be abridged. All this indicated that only the pro-slavery element had a ballot. The official vote taken in December, 1857, resulted in over 6,000 votes for the "constitution with slavery" and less than 600 for the constitution "with no slavery." Most "free state" men had declined to cast ballots.[5]

The Lecompton constitution created havoc among the Democrats and precipitated a permanent break between Buchanan and Douglas.[6] The President urged Congress to admit Kansas into the Union under the Lecompton constitution. Douglas, incensed, had a show-down with Buchanan; he informed the latter that he would oppose the administration's Lecompton policy. "Mr. Douglas," the adamant President warned, "I desire you to remember that no Democrat ever yet differed from an administration of his own choice without being crushed."[7] Douglas—moved by a sense of honor, outraged at Buchanan's failure to live up to the Democratic platform of 1856, and concerned with reëlection to the Senate—stood his ground.[8] One of Douglas's Senate colleagues declared: "I *know*, not only from conversations with Douglas himself—that he was opposed to Mr. Buchanan the moment he knew that Richardson was not made a member of the Cabinet."[9] On December 9, 1857 Douglas cast the die. For three hours on the Senate floor he denounced the Lecompton constitution.[10] The vehemence of his utterance carried Douglas farther than he had intended.[11]

Although the Senate finally approved the Lecompton constitution, the pro-Douglas Democrats and Republicans united to defeat it in the House. Congress then passed the measure of Representative William H. English, of Indiana, which provided for a referendum on the whole constitution and promised the future state of Kansas over 5,000,000 acres of land if the instrument were ratified. In August, 1858, the Kansas voters rejected the English proposition.

Henceforth the Democracy in nation and state was divided into two factions—Buchanan's "Lecomptonites" and Douglas's "Anti-Lecomptonites." [12]

Closely linked with the Buchanan-Douglas animosity and the Kansas issue in splitting the Democratic party was the federal patronage. Douglas became convinced that the President planned to discharge the pro-Douglas, anti-Lecompton federal officeholders. Douglas confided to a friend: [13]

I fear there is no hope of an amicable adjustment of the Kansas Question. . . . The administration is more anxious for my destruction than they are for the harmony & unity of the Democratic party. You have doubtless seen that they are removing all my friends from office. Of course my friends do not consider this course fair, honest, or Democratic, and will not be reconciled to the administration by this line of conduct. The administration is endeavoring to form an alliance with the Republicans of Ill. to beat me [for reelection to the Senate] with a Republican. . . . I am determined to stand firmly by my position and vindicate my principles and let the consequences take care of themselves. If the Party is divided by this course, it will not be my fault.

After repudiating Buchanan's leadership, Douglas returned to Illinois to stand for reëlection. He found the President's patronage axe had cut down many of his officeholding friends. The Little Giant carried thousands of Democrats with him. To stem the tide toward Douglas, Buchanan's Illinois supporters built up an administration Democratic press. Officeholders were recruited as publishers and editors. Despite the efforts of the "Buchaneers," the Democrats renominated the Little Giant on an "anti-Lecompton" platform. Douglas succeeded in besting Abraham Lincoln, his Republican opponent, in the senatorial campaign of 1858. Thus he would remain in the Senate to plague the Buchanan administration—and widen the breach within his party.[14]

The Democratic split was utilized by the Republicans in Illinois. Every time Buchanan's administration organ, the Washington *Union*, blasted away at Douglas, the Republican mouthpieces would reprint the fulmination, sometimes with crocodile tears that Douglas was assailed, but always predicting that the Illinois senator's days were done.[15]

As in Illinois, the Buchanan-Douglas controversy over Kansas and patronage disrupted the Democrats in Buchanan's own Pennsyl-

ania. Organized as the "People's party," the Republicans and
ther anti-Democratic elements in the populous Keystone State
ampaigned for a protective tariff, denounced the Lecompton
"frauds"—and captured the fall elections of 1858. Conspicuous in
"stabbing" the President in his home state was John W. Forney,
Philadelphia's leading Democratic editor, who broke with Buchanan
over federal patronage and public printing.[16] Republicans in Congress rewarded Forney. Horace Greeley advised a party associate in
Congress: "I consider Forney *entitled* to the Clerkship, no matter
how he may behave hereafter. I go for paying debts as we go
along."[17] In January, 1860, the Republicans in Congress joined with
the anti-Lecompton Democrats to elect Forney clerk of the House
of Representatives.[18]

The Buchanan-Douglas rift, the Lecompton struggle and rivalry
over distribution of patronage—kept alive partly by Republicans
working behind the scenes—were manifest not alone in Illinois and
Pennsylvania, but also in less populated states. California was a case
in point.

California had been traditionally Democratic. It wanted none of
Republican radicalism. The settlers were more concerned with ac-
quiring subsidies from the federal government for a Pacific railroad
than with the slavery controversy.[19] Besides, many Californians,
coming from southern states, constituted a militant pro-slavery
minority; the large lawless element attracted there by the gold rush
were generally not interested in anti-slavery crusades.[20] Except for
a brief dalliance with Know-Nothingism, California had always been
Democratic.[21] The state Republican party did not become organized until 1856, when it presented Frémont as the exponent of
the Pacific railroad and muffled anti-slavery utterances.[22] In the
following year the Republican gubernatorial candidate polled only
21,000 votes out of some 93,500 cast.[23]

Suddenly the dominant California Democracy was rent in twain
by a discordant medley of personalities, patronage and Lecompton
constitution. The fight centered about the rivalry of California's
two Democratic United States Senators, David C. Broderick and
William M. Gwin.

Early in 1857 both United States Senate seats were to be filled.
After fierce bargaining, Broderick, chieftain of the San Francisco
Democratic machine, having been elected for the six-year term,
supported his rival Gwin for the short-term Senate seat on con-

dition that the latter agree that he (Broderick) should handle Cali
fornia's share of federal patronage. The old Broderick-Gwin feud
was soon reopened wider than ever when Buchanan showered his
attention—and most of the jobs—on Gwin. An anti-Broderick hire
ling was given the coveted collectorship of the port of San Francisco. Broderick became a sworn opponent of the President, aligning
himself with Douglas and the Republicans in the Senate fight against
the Lecompton constitution. Broderick and Stuart, of Michigan,
were the only two Democratic senators who joined Douglas in
opposing Buchanan's Kansas policy.[24] The Republicans capitalized
on the situation and filled their press with flattering editorials concerning Broderick.[25] In the fall of 1858 the Broderick-Douglas
"anti-Lecompton" Democrats and the Gwin-Buchanan "Lecompton" Democrats nominated different candidates for state Supreme
Court justice—and the California Republicans (numbering only a
minority) endorsed the "anti-Lecompton" entry.[26] In 1859 the
Democratic break became wider when the Broderick wing fused
with the Republicans on a single candidate for Congress.[27] The
Republicans considered their *rapproachement* with Broderick wise
strategy, one of them declaring: [28]

Gwin . . . turned the tables on Broderick by wriggling into
Buchanan's favor and monopolizing the whole of the Executive
patronage. . . . From this act dates Broderick's hostility to the
Administration. We will not say how far his opposition to the
Lecompton swindle was predicated upon this prior enmity to Mr.
Buchanan.

Broderick aided the Republicans further by his tragic death in
a duel. David S. Terry of San Francisco, a native southerner, in-
sulted Broderick, who countered by making uncomplimentary statements about Terry, which resulted in a duel between them. Broderick fell, mortally wounded.[29]

In death Broderick's unsavory reputation was forgotten. He was
exalted by his friends, particularly the Republicans, as a victim of
the Slave Power; Buchanan's opponents alleged that the wounded
senator's last statement was that he had been wounded because of his
opposition to the "corrupt, southern-dominated" administration at
Washington. The Republicans' chief organizer in California, Colonel
Edward D. Baker—who was said to have "fairly rivaled Cicero
himself in persuasive eloquence" [30]—delivered the main funeral

oration.[31] Baker waxed morbidly loquacious over the senator's body and rang out the words: [32]

What was his [Broderick's] public crime? The answer is in his own words: *"I die because I was opposed to a corrupt administration, and the extension of slavery."* Fellow-citizens, they are remarkable words, uttered at a very remarkable moment; they involve the history of his senatorial career, and of its sad and bloody termination.

The Republican press throughout the nation, eager to accept Baker's interpretation, preached that Broderick had been hunted to his death because he dared resist the Slave Power.[33]

The Republicans, in anticipation of 1860, did not relax in their efforts to widen the Democratic rift, as evidenced in their inauguration of the "Covode Committee." In March, 1860, Representative John Covode sponsored in the House a resolution to inquire "whether the President of the United States, or any other officer of the Government, has, by money, patronage, or other improper means, sought to influence the action of Congress" for or against the passage of any law.[34] Covode's pretext was a charge by two members of Congress that the President had attempted to bribe them in the Lecompton affair.[35] Under Cavode's chairmanship, voluminous testimony was taken, but the House took no action on either majority or minority reports submitted by the Committee.[36] "In all probability," writes Professor Robert S. Cotterill, "the investigation was meant to produce nothing more serious than ammunition to be used by the Republicans in the presidential campaign of 1860; Covode was a member of the Republican Executive Congressional Committee for this campaign." [37]

At least two major witnesses before the Covode Committee, John W. Forney and Cornelius Wendell, bore grievances against Buchanan. Forney, having been elected clerk of the House by a Republican-anti-Lecompton coalition following his rift with Buchanan over the public printing, political patronage, and personal pique, testified that he was offered Post Office contracts on condition that he come out editorially in favor of the Chief Executive's Kansas policy. He also portrayed Buchanan as a man of rank ingratitude. Particularly damaging to the President was the testimony of Wendell, who declared that, with Buchanan's approval, he had expended "from $30,000 to $40,000" in an attempt to pass the Lecompton bill in Congress; that he (Wendell) had secured the money through government contracts and federal patronage.[38] The pro-Buchanan press charged that such accusations were not heard "while Mr. Wendell had the free run of the printing spoils and could squander large sums of public money." [39]

The split between the Buchanan-dominated "Lecomptonites" and the Douglas-led "anti-Lecomptonites" was fast disintegrating the national Democratic party. The bad blood existing between the two factions was graphically expressed in 1858 by Buchanan's chief northwestern patronage-dispenser, Senator Bright, of Indiana: [40]

I have not, nor shall I ever regard a set of men in this Country who call themselves "anti-Lecompton Democrats," in any other light than Abolitionists, and most of them, rotten in every sense of the term.

I court and defy the opposition of every one of them, from their lying hypocritical Demagogical master Douglas, down to the scurviest puppy in the kennel.

Not alone were the Democrats split on the personalities of Buchanan and Douglas, on the issue of Kansas, and rivalry over federal appointments. The party was also at odds over Constitutional interpretations regarding the measure of protection which the Constitution gave to Negro slavery. In particular the Dred Scott case, handed down by the Supreme Court in 1857, precipitated additional wrangling among the Democrats.

The Douglas Democrats could not accept the Dred Scott decision because it was incompatible with their doctrine of popular sovereignty. (Popular sovereignty decreed that the people of the territories had the right either to permit or reject slavery in their respective regions.) And popular sovereignty was the Douglasites' political capital. On the other hand, the "southern rights" Democrats would not surrender to Douglas, since popular sovereignty was viewed by them as quite as deadly to the institution of slavery as the Republican creed of Congressional prohibition of slavery in the territories. Douglas's lieutenants labored to restore party harmony, but without avail.[41] "Southern rights" had come to mean racial security and self-determination by the whites whether in or out of the Union. A program had been framed to make the most of state sovereignty, whether it was needed to safeguard the South as a minority within the Union or to legitimatize its exit into national independence. Legal sanction for the spread of slaveholding became the touchstone of "southern rights." The meteoric rise of the Republican party, which denied this sanction, gave a driving force to this intense pro-southern feeling. Militant southerners were primed for action in 1856 in case Frémont should be elected president. And although the Pathfinder was defeated by Buchanan, the strength shown by the Republicans increased the zeal of "south-savers." [42]

The "southern rights" movement attracted its strongest support in the lower South—particularly in South Carolina, Alabama, and Mississippi.

Militant states' rights sentiment in South Carolina dated from Andrew Jackson's day. During the late 1840's this states' rights viewpoint protested against the North's attempted prohibition of slavery in the territory acquired by the Mexican War. Under John C. Calhoun's leadership it became an effort to unite the South in a demand for equality of the slave interests with the "free" states; otherwise the southern states should seek protection outside the Union. The refusal of other southern states to follow her was the main reason why the Palmetto state did not secede in 1850–1852. When Calhoun died in 1850, leadership passed to the even more radical Robert Barnwell Rhett, editor of the Charleston *Mercury*, under whose direction the secession-minded faction of South Carolina Democrats went into the ascendancy.[43] John Brown's Harpers Ferry raid in 1859, moreover, had convinced even the anti-secession Democrats that there might be little safety in their state remaining in the Union.[44] Rhett found a staunch ally in William L. Yancey, of Alabama. By 1858 both Rhett and Yancey were determined that the issue must be faced in the presidential campaign of 1860, even if the national Democractic party must be destroyed. To this end Yancey worked in Alabama, as did Rhett in South Carolina.[45]

The southern-rights movement in Alabama, headed by Yancey, had dated from the days of the Wilmot Proviso, which in the 1840's had sought to commit Congress to the policy of excluding slavery from the territory acquired from Mexico.[46] Often Democratic and Whig leaders in Alabama compromised their pro-slavery principles for the sake of party orthodoxy. Not so Yancey, who had resigned his seat in Congress in 1846 because he believed that loyalty to the Democratic party and coöperation with the North were not protecting the South's vital slave interests. "If this foul spell of party which binds and divides and distracts the South can be broken," he concluded, "hail to him who shall break it." In 1848 he had presented for consideration the so-called "Alabama Platform," in answer to the Wilmot Proviso. The Alabama Platform was a statement of abstract principles presenting the southern demands for protection of slavery in the territories.[47] Yancey had carried it into the Democratic National Convention of 1848, which rejected it. But he was not discouraged. During the next dozen years he agitated for the radical pro-southern cause in the deep South: the union of all southern men in a sectional party could come only with the national Democratic party's disintegration.[48]

When Douglas set forth his "Freeport doctrine" of unfriendly legislation, the Buchanan faction of Democrats, led by Jefferson Davis and Slidell, seized the opportunity of crushing the Illinois senator by destroying his southern support. The "Buchaneers" below the Potomac demanded that the Democratic party formally repudiate the Douglas doctrine of "squatter sovereignty" and that Congress accept responsibility for the protection of slavery in the territories. Born more of the Buchanan-Douglas factional conflict than of any strong southern demand, the territorial issue was seized on by Yancey and Rhett in order to unite the South and split the Democratic party. They took counsel together. Yancey journeyed to South Carolina to lend support to Rhett, who was preaching the radical southern gospel in his Charleston *Mercury*. At Columbia in July, 1859, the fiery Alabamin presented a definite program: states' rights men should go to the Democratic National Convention at Charleston in April, 1860; but if the convention failed to uphold the South's rights in the territories, they should leave and organize a new convention. If the Republicans won the Presidency, the southern states should secede from the Union before the inauguration.[49]

Yancey largely dominated the Democratic party in Alabama. His was the viewpoint of most influential Alabamans, who desired to free themselves from economic dependence on the North.[50] Non-slaveholders, who constituted the bulk of Alabama's white population, feared the social consequences of abolition.[51] The latest historian of the Alabama secession movement concluded: [52]

The Southern Rights Party, headed by W. L. Yancey in Alabama, and having its counterpart in every Southern state, demanded equal rights for the slavery interests in the territories. The Kansas-Nebraska Act, the organization of the Republican Party as a sectional and anti-Southern body, and the heightened violence of the abolition agitation which seemed to take root in the Northern mind during this time rapidly drove all Alabamians, as well as the citizens of other Southern states, into the Southern Rights Party.

When the time arrived for Alabama to select delegates to the Democratic National Convention at Charleston in 1860, the state was largely dominated by Yancey's radical pro-southern faction. The Whig party, usually a conservative and nationalizing influence, was almost completely destroyed.[53] Yancey, the guiding force at the Democratic convention at Montgomery in January, resurrected his "Alabama Platform" of 1848. Resolutions were adopted which declared that the United States Constitution was a compact between sovereign and co-equal states; that citizens of every state were entitled to entry into the territory with their property of every description (i.e., slaves included), and to protection by the federal government; that neither Congress nor its creature, a territorial legislature, could abolish slavery in a territory; that the people of a territory held no constitutional power to do so until they framed a state constitution preparatory to entry into the Union. The tenth resolution directed the Alabama delegates to secede from the national convention if these resolutions were not substantially accepted.[54]

In Alabama's neighboring state, Mississippi, the "southern rights" faction were also in control by 1860. John C. Frémont's huge northern vote in 1856 persuaded Mississippians that the Constitution was not an adequate safeguard for the protection of slavery and other southern institutions; that the North, through the Republican party, would even carry into practice the dreaded equality of the white and black races. By 1858 Democrats were shrieking for disunion and serving notice that the election of a "Black" Republican to the presidency two years hence would be the "overt act" for secession.[55]

In addition to the radical pro-southern feeling, another factor in brewing secessionism and splitting the Democratic party in Mississippi was Douglas himself, who had alienated much of his support by his warfare against the Buchanan administration over the Lecompton constitution.[56] By 1858 the Mississippi Democracy was as determined to destroy the Little Giant's candidacy as it was insistent upon a "southern rights" plank in the national platform.[57]

Douglas agreed to accept the presidential nomination if the plat-

form adopted embodied the principles of the Compromise of 1850;
but if the party adopted "such new issues as the revival of the
African slave trade, or a Congressional slave code for the territories
—it is due to candor to say, that, in such an event, I cannot accept
the nomination if tendered to me." [58] Mississippi turned unalterably
against the Little Giant. The Democratic machinery was now in
the hands of those who would disrupt the national party rather than
have Douglas nominated.[59] One Mississippi historian concludes:
"There was, therefore, no chance to prevent the selection of delegates to Charleston who would be pledged to withdraw from the
convention rather than accept an 'unsound' platform or an 'unsound' candidate." [60]

Although the "southern rights" movement was strongest in South
Carolina, Alabama and Mississippi, it became powerful in other
lower slave states which proceeded to send strongly pro-southern
(and, incidentally, anti-Douglas) delegations to Charleston.[61] Professor Dwight L. Dumond concludes: "South Carolina, Florida,
Mississippi, Louisiana, Texas, and Arkansas endorsed the Alabama
platform and, rallying behind Yancey, went into the Charleston
convention determined to force the issue to a conclusion." [62]

In addition to the "constitutional" opposition of Yancey and his
"southern rights" doctrinaires towards the Douglasites' popular-
sovereignty doctrine, a striking feature of the Democratic schism
was the personal element: the Buchanan faction's hatred of Douglas.
This was apparent from the delegation sent to Charleston by
Buchanan's own Pennsylvania, among whom were such Buchanan-
appointed officeholders as the collector and the naval office of the
Port of Philadelphia; the postmaster of Philadelphia; the postmaster
of Lancaster, and the collector and postmaster of Pittsburgh.[63]

The selection of a "packed" anti-Douglas delegation and the personal factor were also obvious in Louisiana, home state of Buchanan's ally Senator Slidell. A Louisiana scholar observes: "The
faction of the Democrats in Louisiana which . . . was allied with
the Buchanan or radical element in the national party was the conservative wing headed by Slidell; while the group which followed
Stephen A. Douglas and other northern conservatives was in Louisiana the ultra-southern faction of Pierre Soulé. This indicates,
perhaps, that the personal element counted for quite as much if not
more than fundamental principles." [64] Slidell's anti-Douglas faction,
controlling the federal patronage, prevailed over Soulé's pro-

Douglas group in the state Democratic convention. Delegates loyal to the Buchanan administration were chosen to go to Charleston. Sildell was endorsed for President.[65] Slidell himself went to Charleston to work for Douglas's defeat.[66]

As the crowds descended on the South Carolina city in April, 1860, it was recognized that Douglas "was the pivot individual of the Charleston convention. Every delegate was for or against him." [67] The anti-Douglasites' chief task was to concentrate on a single candidate. Hosts of "favorite sons" appeared, making united action against the Little Giant difficult. Douglas's opponents had sought to convert certain candidacies into efforts of more than home-state importance.[68]

The personal bitterness between the Douglas and Buchanan partisans—added to the conflict of constitutional opinions between the popular-sovereignty men and the "southern rights" champions—was intense as the Charleston convention assembled. Word came from Washington: "The city is full of Federal officeholders whom Mr. Buchanan is rallying around him to defeat Douglas. He has brought them here from every part of the country, and insists that they shall all go to Charleston, whether they are delegates or not." [69] Now, at Charleston, the Douglasites found, "by actual count," 507 United States government job-holders on the scene.[70] Slidell arrived early to direct the Buchanan forces. "His appearance here means war to the knife," it was observed. "It means also, that the Administration is uneasy on the Douglas question—and feels constrained to exert every influence against the Squatty Giant of Illinois, whose nomination would be perdition to Buchanan, Slidell & Co." [71] Yancey was there, "the prince of fire-eaters . . . who proposes according to common report to precipitate the cotton States into a revolution, dissolve the Union and build up a Southern empire." [72] The anti-Douglas delegates constituted a formidable bloc: the Buchanan administration leaders who opposed the Little Giant, both because of personal hatred and because they knew too well that, once he succeeded, their sun had set; the southern political oligarchy, which similarly realized that Douglas in the White House would bring into power in the South a new group which would take over the federal patronage there; and the "southern rights" doctrinaires, sincere if shortsighted men of the lower South who convinced themselves that their section's interests required the full protection for slavery.[73]

The Douglasites were equally primed for battle, controlling many northern delegations and having minority support in the South. Douglas had denounced seemingly all who differed with him as traitors to the party principles.[74] His followers had journeyed to Charleston determined to support no man except him.[75]

The selection of Charleston as the national convention site was not a judicious one [76] but the anti-Douglas Democratic National Committee had chosen that secession-minded city because it would be less propitious for the Douglasites to accomplish his nomination.[77] One effect was to draw northern and southern delegates farther apart.[78]

New York proved to be the first disrupting force of the Charleston convention. The New York Democrats were divided. Tammany Hall, controlling the party machinery in the metropolis, had elected Fernando Wood as mayor. In dispensing the municipal patronage Mayor Wood neglected the Wigwam leaders, for which the latter ousted him from Tammany and defeated him for reëlection. Thereupon Wood organized his personal following as "Mozart Hall," which secured Wood's third election as mayor in 1859.

Now, in April, 1860, the ambitious Wood, on friendly terms with President Buchanan and certain southern leaders, turned up at Charleston with a delegation of his own. He demanded admission to the convention for his group, which, he claimed, represented his state's "true" Democracy. Contesting Wood's claims at Charleston was the regular or "Albany Regency" faction, which comprised Tammany Hall and most of the upstate groups. The Regency chieftain, Dean Richmond, demanded that Wood's delegation be refused recognition.[79] News came from Charleston: "The Southern delegations are standing together for the Wood delegation." [80] The matter was referred to the Committeee on Credentials.[81] It was reported from Charleston that "unless the Wood delegates are admitted, and the whole of the Richmond delegates rejected, the delegations of several Southern States will take this opportunity of seceding and forming a separate Convention with the Wood delegates and those of some other Southern States." [82]

The third day of the convention produced no harmony, for the Committee on Credentials brought in a majority report recommending that Dean Richmond's delegation be recognized in the casting of New York's huge bloc of thirty-five votes. A minority report was submitted—signed by the committeemen from the South—which recommended that the two contesting delegations (Richmond's and Wood's) each select thirty-five delegates to cast seventeen votes, the odd vote to be cast alternately. The sitting (Richmond's) delegates, comprising a majority of Douglas men, were to cast their vote first, which under the unit rule would mean the casting of New York's entire thirty-five votes for the Illinois senator. Wood's rival delegation was almost solidly against Douglas. Although the Wood-ites were staunchly defended by the "southern rights" men, the convention voted to reject the minority report. Richmond was in, and Wood was out. The "southern rights" men became more furious than ever.[83]

The importance of the Wood-Richmond contest subsequently became apparent in the vote on the platform. And it was controversy over the platform that wrecked the convention.

Yancey and his "southern rights" ultras demanded that the platform be adopted before the balloting for president and vice-president. "The platform issue was the Ultras' last chance to blow up the convention," [84] concludes one historian. What harassed Yancey most was the possibility of a southerner being nominated, which would make the platform seem less vital and prevent any "bolt" in Yancey's wake. But Douglas's supporters played into Yancey's hands when they, too, for their own reasons, voted, contrary to the usual procedure, to adopt the platform before making the nominations. Having a majority but not the two-thirds necessary for a nomination, the Little Giant's followers welcomed the platform struggle in order to bring about the withdrawal of a few "ultras." [85] Senator Robert Toombs, of Georgia, maintained: "Douglas's men made a great mistake in voting to go to the platform before nominating a Prest. A rupture then became inevitable; but he and his friends expected to profit by the secession of two or three states and therefore urged it in common with the various elements of combustion in the So. West." [86] One who attended the Charleston convention recorded: [87]

The determination of the New York contest, and the adoption of a rule allowing individual delegates from uninstructed States to vote as they pleased, gave the friends of Mr. Douglas a majority in the Convention. They proceeded to use that majority, for the purpose of making sure of their game. They joined the ultra-Southern States in demanding the test fight upon the platform. . . .

The Douglas men had discovered, that whereas they had just

about a majority, it would be impossible for them to obtain a two-thirds vote in a full Convention. They were willing, therefore, that a few ultra-Southern States might go out, and allow them to nominate their man. All at once they became very cheerful on the subject of a disruption of the Convention. They could go North and get two votes (electoral) for their nominee, for every Southern vote that would leave the Convention. Their game then was, to have three or four States, at most, go out. They wanted a little eruption, but not a great one.

Thus, by agreement of both the Douglasites and the "southern rights" men, the platform was to be adopted before the balloting for candidates. The lines upon which the Charleston convention was at bitter odds were sharply drawn by a series of resolutions presented to the Senate by Jefferson Davis back in February: the right of either Congress or a territorial legislature to impair the constitutional right of property in slaves was denied. In case of unfriendly legislation it was declared to be the duty of Congress to provide adequate protection to slave property. Douglas's doctrine of popular sovereignty was completely discarded by the assertion that the people of a territory might pass upon the question only when they formed a state constitution. What the southerners demanded above all else was Congressional protection of slavery in the territories—and they insisted that this principle be written into the platform.[88] Some believed that Davis introduced his resolutions "merely to have the political effect of killing off the great non-interventionist, Douglas, before the Charleston Convention." [89]

The Democratic factions at Charleston fought fiercely over the platform. Two platforms were submitted to the convention by the Platform Committee: a "majority" one, which called for the protection of slavery in the territories; and a "minority" one, which maintained that the party must abide by the decisions of the Supreme Court. When the convention adopted the minority platform, Yancey led the Alabama and other lower southern delegations out of the convention hall. The Charleston conclave was disrupted. Unable to choose a presidential candidate—the Douglasites would accept none other than their idol—the remaining delegates adjourned and made arrangements to reassemble at Baltimore. In the Maryland metropolis in June they named Douglas for President. Subsequent conventions of southern "bolters" were held at Baltimore and Richmond at which a "southern" Democratic ticket was nominated: Vice-President John C. Breckinridge, a Kentuckian, for President, and Senator Joseph Lane, of Oregon, for Vice-President.[90]

Meanwhile, in the interval between the Democratic conventions at Charleston and Baltimore, the Republicans in high glee assembled in their national gathering at Chicago to select candidates for president and vice-president.

CHAPTER NINE

The Triumph of Availability

IN MID-MAY 1860 four hundred and sixty-six Republican delegates and thousands of party leaders, newspaper correspondents and observers convened in Chicago.

The Republican National Convention met in a building specially built for its use—the co-called "Wigwam," a two-story wooden structure erected at Lake and Market Streets by enthusiastic Chicago Republicans. Construction of the Wigwam was barely finished when the convention assembled on May 16. The city's forty-two hotels were taxed to the limit.[1]

Some of the delegates and spectators were in a festive mood. Drinking and "singing songs not found in hymn books" had started on the trains, and in Chicago it was observed that "the Republicans are imbibing the spirit as well as the substance of the old Democratic party."[2] One delegate was awakened by his noisy roommates in an overcrowded hotel: "I was aroused by a vehement debate among them, and rubbing my eyes, discovered that they were sitting up in bed playing cards to see who should pay for gin cock-tails all around, the cock-tails being an indispensable preliminary to breakfast."[3] When Mayor "Long John" Wentworth made his weekly police raid on resorts of ill repute he discovered several delegates.[4] Most of the delegates, however, were absorbed in more serious business.

The complexion of the convention was most heterogeneous—an indication that the Republican party of 1860 comprised diverse groups brought together by common hostility to the Democrats. There were former Whigs such as Caleb B. Smith of Indiana and Judge David Davis of Illinois, erstwhile Free Soil Democrats such as Preston King of New York and David Wilmot of Pennsylvania, German leaders such as Carl Schurz of Wisconsin and Gustave Koerner of Illinois, abolitionists such as Joshua R. Giddings of Ohio, conservative Union-lovers such as the Blairs, former political re-

formers like Horace Greeley of New York, protective-tariff devotees such as Thomas H. Dudley of New Jersey, and anti-slavery
men from border-slave states such as George D. Blakey of Kentucky.[5] Then there was a bogus "Texas" delegation, recruited from
Seward enthusiasts in a Michigan town, pretending to represent the
Lone Star State! [6]

A unique delegation was that from far-off Oregon, at least three
of whose five delegates—Horace Greeley, Eli Thayer, and Franklin
Johnson—were not residents of that state. The time required to
travel from Oregon in 1860 had necessitated enlisting the services of
eastern Republicans as "proxies." Greeley declared later: "I intended to stay away from Chicago, till I received my most unexpected appointment from Oregon, then it seemed that I could not
without absolute cowardice." [7] Eli Thayer was a member of Congress from Massachusetts.[8] Franklin Johnson, although having once
lived in Oregon, was then a student at Colgate Theological Seminary
in up-state New York.[9] "My older brother was a member of the
[Oregon] executive committee," Johnson explained, "and I discovered later that he was responsible for my receiving a commission
as a delegate." [10]

Indeed, a very diverse group comprised the Chicago convention.
One Democrat caustically described the gathering: [11]

Probably no deliberative body ever came together, even in
France, during the old revolutionary period, composed of such
miscellaneous elements. There were Free Soil Whigs in the largest
proportion, and with them Free Soil Democrats, Native Americans,
and foreign adventurers; abolitionists, and their lifelong opponents;
those for saving the Union, and those for dividing it; professed
conservatives and the most thoroughgoing radicals; sentimentalists;
ideologists; "economists and calculators"; a sprinkling of delegates
pretending to represent some sort of constituency, in two or three
of the border slave States; and, to crown all, Mr. Horace Greeley,
of the New York *Tribune*, as an accredited deputy from the somewhat distant regions of Oregon.

The amount of talking, loud and low, was amazing. Men gathered
in small groups, often with arms about each other, chatting and
whispering "as if the fate of the country depended upon their
immediate delivery of the mighty political secrets with which their
imaginations are big." [12] Rumor ran riot, and "things of incalculable
moment are communicated to you confidentially, at intervals of

five minutes." [13] Behind the scenes was the maneuvering of managers for their respective candidates.

Most conspicuous of the aspiring King-makers was Thurlow Weed, exerting every nerve to capture the nomination for Seward. Weed established headquarters at the Richmond House and started operations immediately. He won Mayor Wentworth's favor, and the latter's newspaper declared for Seward.[14] Carl Schurz, chairman of the pro-Seward Wisconsin delegation, found Weed surrounded by hirelings whom the Albany politician had brought from New York: [15]

They were New York politicians, apparently of the lower sort, whom Thurlow Weed had brought with him to aid him in doing his work. . . . They had marched in street parades with brass bands and Seward banners to produce the impression that the whole country was ablaze with enthusiasm for Seward. They had treated members of the other delegations with no end of champagne and cigars, to win them for Seward, if not as their first, then at least as their second choice, to be voted for on the second or third ballot. . . . They had spent money freely and let everybody understand that there was a great deal more to spend. Among these men moved Thurlow Weed as the great captain, with ceaseless activity and noiseless step, receiving their reports and giving new instructions in his peculiar whisper, now and then taking one into a corner of the room for a secret talk, or disappearing with another through a side door for transactions still more secret.

The entire Michigan delegation, led by Austin Blair, assisted Weed and set up headquarters at the Adams House. Chicago was "alive with Michigan men. . . . One meets them everywhere. They have contributed not a little to keep up the courage of the Seward ranks." [16]

Bates men were also active. The Blairs, Greeley "of Oregon," and others argued that the Missourian's nomination would refute charges of sectionalism and would dissolve the Constitutional Union party which had just nominated John Bell.[17] Blair, with his Missouri delegation, rented rooms in the Tremont House.[18]

Simon Cameron's strategists were operating among the arriving delegates as early as May 10.[19] They preached: "Cameron is the *only* man that can carry Pennsylvania." [20]

Chase men were also active, but all too few. A handful of the Ohio governor's admirers—among them the anti-Seward New

Yorkers, Hiram Barney, David Dudley Field, James A. Briggs, and George Opdyke—urged Chase's name upon all who would listen. But it was soon evident that Chase would not bulk large as a contender. Not all Ohioans presumably pledged to him were active in his behalf.[21] One ardent Chase worker reported to the Ohio governor: "There is lots of *good feeling*, afloat for you. The lukewarmness of those who should not be lukewarm is your misfortune. . . . The hardest kind of death to die is that occasioned by indecisive lukewarm friends."[22] But Chase's "corporal's guard" did not lose hope.

Other candidates of lesser prestige had their agents too. Chief among these candidacies were those of Governor Banks, Justice McLean—and Abraham Lincoln. Anson Burlingame arrived in Chicago on May 14 to work for his friend Banks.[23] Congressman Thaddeus Stevens, of Pennsylvania, taking charge of McLean's interests, argued with Indiana delegates that the Supreme Court jurist could carry conservative Pennsylvania.[24] Most energetic of all the floor managers were those working for Lincoln. Their problem was to unite the anti-Seward forces on Lincoln and to accomplish as much as possible before the convention formally assembled.

Judge David Davis, Lincoln's loyal friend, had established headquarters at his own expense in the Tremont House, five blocks from the Wigwam.[25] Working in close coöperation with Davis for Lincoln were Norman B. Judd; Leonard Swett, a friend and fellow-townsman of Judge Davis; Joseph Medill and Charles H. Ray, both of the Chicago *Press & Tribune;* Richard Yates, Republican candidate for governor of Illinois; Lincoln's one-time law partner, Stephen T. Logan; State Auditor Jesse K. Dubois; Illinois' Secretary of State Ozias M. Hatch; Orville H. Browning, of Quincy; State Senator John M. Palmer; State Treasurer William Butler; Jackson Grimshaw; Burton C. Cook; and the German leader, former Lieutenant-Governor Gustave Koerner.[26] They made little noise, but operated effectively.[27]

Upon arriving at Chicago on May 13 an Illinois leader reported: "Our delegation will stick to Lincoln as long as there is a chance to prevent Seward getting any votes from us at all."[28] This "stop-Seward" technique was the negative approach. On the positive side the Lincoln strategy was to prove that Lincoln alone could carry Illinois, Indiana, New Jersey and Pennsylvania. These four states held a most strategic position. And for good reason.

If an imaginary line were drawn from the Atlantic coast to the Mississippi at the forty-first degree of north latitude the portions of the free states of New Jersey, Pennsylvania, Ohio, Indiana, and Illinois lying below that line would be found to have differed in their politics from the portions above the line. The southern halves of these states sympathized with their neighbors in slave-holding Delaware, Maryland, Virginia and Kentucky more than with the northern regions of their own states. This fact arose from the influences of proximity and also from the fact that the southern regions of those free states were settled largely by emigrants from slave states. The southern portion of the free states mentioned and the northern portion of the border slave states, neighboring on each other, may arbitrarily but correctly be termed the "conservative zone"—a great mid-segment of the nation which, while it might have had some anti-slavery feeling, nevertheless had no tolerance for the extreme Republican point of view. Such sentiment had been apparent in the election of 1856: Frémont had carried the northern parts of Pennsylvania, Ohio, Indiana and Illinois, but had lost the southern portions to Buchanan, and in these states (Ohio excepted) the moderate, nationally-minded Fillmore had polled a huge vote.[29]

The states south of this line of 41° cast 111 electoral votes; the true northern states, 98; the central states, New Jersey, Ohio, Indiana, Illinois, Missouri, and California, 94. Oregon was believed sure to vote Democratic, so the Republicans would require all the rest of the North, plus Ohio of which they were certain. In addition, they would need 34 electoral votes from that conservative zone, which Pennsylvania and New Jersey could give them. If they lost Pennsylvania, they would have to carry New Jersey, Indiana, Illinois, and Missouri. But Missouri could not be had, despite the Blairs' protests that Bates could carry it. The decision of November 1860 rested with four states—Pennsylvania, New Jersey, Illinois, and Indiana—all of which the Democrats had carried for Buchanan in 1856. Republican leaders throughout the North realized this.[30]

Lincoln's managers concentrated upon the doubtful states. "State pride," plus the maneuvering of Judd, had made Lincoln first choice in Illinois. With Lincoln's home state secure, his managers approached the delegates from Indiana.

There was considerable Bates sentiment among the Indiana delegates but other Hoosiers had open minds.[31] One of the four Indiana delegates-at-large believed: "If we can ascertain who would be most likely to carry the four doubtful States of N. J., Penn., Ind. and Ill. we ought to act as a unit at Chicago. . . . Seward, Lincoln and Bates all have their friends." [32] But Seward had few friends in Indiana, because he symbolized anti-slavery radicalism.[33] Henry S. Lane, Republican nominee for governor of Indiana, determined that his chances should not be jeopardized by having a "radical" head the national ticket, went about among the delegates insisting that Seward could not carry Indiana.[34] Mrs. Lane wrote in 1891: [35]

I was with my husband in Chicago. . . . Thurlow Weed, in his anxiety for the success of Seward, took Mr. Lane out one evening and pleaded with him to lead the Indiana delegation over to Seward, saying they would send enough money from New York to ensure his election for Governor, and carry the State later for the New York candidate.

His proposal was indignantly rejected, as there was neither money nor influence enough in their State to change my husband's opinion in regard to the fitness and availability of Mr. Lincoln for the nomination.

Indiana's choice narrowed down to Bates or Lincoln. And the final decision rested primarily with Caleb B. Smith.

Caleb B. Smith had served in Congress with Lincoln during 1847–1849. Like Lincoln, he had been a Whig. As one of Indiana's four delegates-at-large and chairman of the delegation, Smith threw his influence behind Lincoln, stifling the pro-Bates element at the Hoosier caucus on May 15. He was able to do this despite the efforts of Colfax and Frank Blair to swing the delegation to Bates.[36] Gleefully Medill reported to the Tremont House that "half" of the Hoosier delegation had been won over even before the convention met.[37] He might have added that the entire delegation was already in the Lincoln column.

Strong evidence appears that Judge David Davis and other Lincoln managers, anxious for Indiana support, promised Smith a Cabinet position in the event of Lincoln's election. The secretary of the Republican State Central Committee of Illinois, Jesse W. Fell, in recommending later that Cabinet positions be given to Indiana and Pennsylvania, wrote Lincoln: "Such a disposition of favors was a good deal spoken of at Chicago, in a quiet way, though of course no improper pledges—so far as I know or believe—were asked—as I am very sure they were not, and could not be given." [38] Lincoln's law partner, William H. Herndon, maintained that Judge Davis promised Smith a Cabinet position in return for Indiana's support.[39] A manager for Edward Bates at Chicago, Charles Gibson, made the same assertion.[40] Moreover, Davis's biographer has located among Davis's private papers two letters written by Smith which convince him that such a "bargain" was made.[41] In addition, an Indiana delegate-at-large, Judge William T. Otto, informed Mrs. Matilda Gresham (wife of the later Secretary of State of the United States) that Smith was offered a Cabinet post: [42]

I have frequently heard Judge Otto tell how Caleb B. Smith imposed on Judge David Davis and Joseph Medill when the latter during the convention was pledging everything in sight to insure Mr. Lincoln's nomination. "Mr. Smith," Judge Otto said, "made Judge Davis believe that the Indiana delegation would go to Seward unless Smith was promised a place in the Cabinet; when the truth was that none of us cared for Smith and after we got to Chicago and looked over the ground all were for Lincoln."

Moreover, William P. Fishback (friend and law partner of the Republican state chairman of Indiana) later wrote confidentially: "There was a determination and promise on the part of Mr. Lincoln to give Mr. C. B. Smith a place in his *Cabinet*." [43] Lincoln himself was grateful for Smith's services; after receiving the presidential nomination, he wrote Smith a note of special thanks.[44]

The day before the convention assembled, the Lincolnites had won over almost the entire Hoosier delegation. Under that date an Indianapolis correspondent reported from Chicago: "Illinois is for Lincoln always, and all the time. Indiana leans in the same direction. At a caucus of the delegation held this morning, the expression was in the main for Lincoln." [45] Another correspondent reported: "Illinois and Indiana are for Abe Lincoln." [46]

With Indiana almost certain, the Lincolnites approached another doubtful and conservative state, New Jersey. The opposition to the Democrats in New Jersey had been the Know-Nothings, who were moderate on the sectional issue. Not until 1858 did the New Jersey Know-Nothings and Republicans unite with the "Opposition" party, judiciously avoiding the label "Republican." [47] Seward sentiment in the New Jersey delegation was only lukewarm. Besides,

Judge William L. Dayton was a favorite son. This did not discourage Judge Davis, however. He visited the New Jersey delegates and was told that they were for Seward! Davis thereupon dispatched Illinois State Senator John M. Palmer to see the New Jersey delegates who now suggested Seward for President and Lincoln for Vice-President. Whereupon, Palmer relates, "I told them that there were forty thousand Democrats who would vote the Republican ticket, but who would not consent to do so if two old Whigs were placed upon the ticket." [48]

Actually, the nativistic Jerseymen were not strong for Seward: his anti-slavery record was too advanced and he had been too friendly with the New York Catholics. Furthermore, there was Dayton to be considered. Lincoln's supporters finally discerned that, although the New Jersey delegation was not ready to forsake Dayton and go for Lincoln, it at least was opposed to Seward.

With Lincoln certain of Illinois, reasonably assured of Indiana and confident of New Jersey's opposition to Seward, he was in a strong position. For Illinois, Indiana and New Jersey were three of the four "doubtful" states required for Republican success—states which Frémont had lost to Buchanan in 1856 and had decided the presidential contest in the latter's favor. Moreover, the action of Illinois and Indiana now impressed the New England delegates. [49]

Massachusetts was mostly for Seward. The boom for Governor Banks had collapsed, primarily because his close connections with the Know-Nothings made him unacceptable to the Germans. [50] Furthermore, many Bay State leaders did not wish to press their personal preference for Seward to the point of jeopardizing success in November. That the New York senator would alienate conservative votes in the four "doubtful" states was feared by such Banks supporters as Samuel Bowles, editor of the Springfield (Massachusettes) *Republican*. [51] This same fear was shared by John A. Andrew, chairman of the Massachusetts delegation. Accordingly, on the eve of the convention, a committee from Massachusetts visited the delegates of the four "doubtful" states. Andrew pointed out that all desired victory in November, that he and other New Englanders were for Seward but that, in the words of a New Jersey delegate, "they preferred the success of the party rather than the election of any particular individual." [52] Andrew, therefore, admitting that Seward could not carry Pennsylvania, New Jersey, Illinois and Indiana, suggested that delegates from those states concentrate upon a single candidate. Andrew is quoted as having made the following declaration: [53]

> You delegates all say that William H. Seward cannot carry the doubtful States. When we ask you who can, you from New Jersey give us the name of William L. Dayton, a most excellent and worthy man in every way, and entirely satisfactory to us; but when we go to Pennsylvania they name Simon Cameron; and Indiana and Illinois, Abraham Lincoln. Now it is impossible to have all these three candidates, and unless you delegates from the four doubtful states can agree upon some one candidate, who you think can carry these States, we from New England will vote for our choice, William H. Seward of New York; but if you will unite upon some one candidate and present his name, we will give him enough votes to place him in nomination.

These words undoubtedly reflected Massachusetts opinion at Chicago. The Bay State leaders did indeed request the four "doubtful" delegations to designate three men who, in their opinion, could carry their respective states.[54]

Meanwhile, the lesser New England states were in caucus. Vermont was tied to its "favorite son," Senator Jacob Collamer; but Maine, New Hampshire, Connecticut and Rhode Island were uninstructed. Judge Davis and Orville H. Browning visited the Maine and New Hampshire delegations.[55]

Although majority opinion in Maine was for Seward, two shrewd Down East strategists, Senator Hannibal Hamlin and James G. Blaine, were opposed to Seward because of his "unavailability." They believed that Seward could not be elected. Hamlin did not attend the Chicago convention, but he had cautioned Maine delegates to canvass opinion among the Pennsylvania, Indiana, and Illinois delegations and be guided by their decision.[56] Blaine, although not a delegate, went to Chicago to work against Seward.[57] Blaine wrote later: "Governor [Lot] Morrill and myself worked hard for Lincoln from the time we reached Chicago. . . . All the way out in the cars I tried to persuade Lot that Lincoln was the man, but he would not believe it until after he reached Chicago." [58] It was apparent that a militant anti-Seward minority was cutting down Seward's support in the Pine Tree State.

The New Hampshire delegates were cautious. The Republican candidate for governor of that state had recently defeated his Democratic opponent by less than 5,000 out of a total of over

71,600 votes cast.[59] When the Granite state Republicans had held their state convention, they prudently refrained from expressing a preference for any particular candidate.[60] "They are all expediency men," declared a Democratic editor of New Hampshire, "holding that 'success is a duty,' no matter by what means it is secured."[61] Moreover, Lincoln had become somewhat known in New Hampshire since his visit there following his Cooper Institute address.[62]

In Connecticut, anti-slavery feeling was not ardent. The conservative Know-Nothings had been the chief opposition to the Democrats since 1855, and they continued to be a major factor until early in 1860.[63] The Republicans had been unable to organize as a state party before 1856.[64] In 1858 and 1859 Governor William A. Buckingham had been elected easily by a Republican-Know-Nothing coalition; but in the Spring elections of 1860 he had been returned to office by less than 600 votes out of almost 90,000.[65] His narrow margin of victory was disappointing to Republicans everywhere,[66] and made them think that Connecticut wanted no part of advanced Republicanism.[67]

The same indifference to crusading anti-slavery doctrines and consequent Republican weakness prevailed in Rhode Island, where Know-Nothingism and temperance had for long overshadowed the slavery issue.[68] Although Frémont had carried Rhode Island in 1856 by virtue of a Republican-Know-Nothing endorsement,[69] the state election held in April, 1860, resulted in the defeat of the Republican gubernatorial candidate.[70]

Immediately after the Connecticut and Rhode Island verdicts, Lincoln remarked that "the close votes in Conn. and the quasi defeat in R. I. are a drawback upon the prospects of Gov. Seward."[71] And this was the view of even more neutral observers.[72] More significant, the result convinced Connecticut and Rhode Island delegates to Chicago that Seward, with his long anti-slavery record, would be a poor candidate. United States Senator James Dixon, Republican of Connecticut, corresponded with Gideon Welles, the leader of the state's delegation to Chicago, advising him that Seward, if nominated, could not win: "He cannot be elected";[73] "Do not give us Seward";[74] "Seward's nomination would at once destroy our present bright prospect for success";[75] "I am more & more convinced that to nominate Seward will be a fatal policy."[76] Before Welles left for Chicago, Dixon introduced him by letter to United States Senator James F. Simmons, a Rhode Island delegate to Chicago. "I trust you will hold free conferences [with Simmons]," [77] Dixon requested. The chief Republican organ of Connecticut, the Hartford *Courant*, was likewise opposed to the nomination of a radical.[78]

On Tuesday evening, May 15, the delegations of Rhode Island, Connecticut, and New Hampshire met separately in caucus and all three came to the same decision: "Rhode Island, Connecticut and New Hampshire decided not to support Seward." [79]

Ohio, third largest state in convention votes, was divided on the candidacies of Justice McLean, Governor Chase, and Senator Wade—none of whom was friendly to Seward. The three Ohio candidates canceled each other's prospects and the large Buckeye delegation would probably settle upon another choice.

McLean was too old and colorless to satisfy the party's younger element.[80] A Minnesota delegate, arriving in Chicago, observed for the upper Northwest: "The putting up of an old 'granny' like McLean . . . will be a perfect wet blanket to all our zealous, working reliable Republicans." [81]

Chase also was handicapped by numerous weaknesses. He had little support in Indiana, New Jersey, or Pennsylvania, since he was even more radically anti-slavery than Seward.[82] He was distrusted in the East because of his erstwhile low-tariff views.[83] Chase had furthermore cultivated the German-American vote, which made him unpalatable to Know-Nothing elements in the Republican ranks.[84] Moreover, Chase was viewed with suspicion by old Whigs, who never forgave his "irregular" deal of 1849 which had resulted in the defeat of an orthodox Whig as Federal Senator.[85] Chase also lacked both skilled lieutenants and a political machine. Nor could Chase expect support from McLean. Although Chase and McLean were bound by family ties, McLean observed that Chase "is the most unprincipled man politically that I have ever known. He is selfish, beyond any other man. And I know from the bargain he has made in being elected to the Senate, he is ready to make any bargain to promote his interest." [86] The Chase men had endeavored to persuade Wade to withdraw in favor of the Ohio governor. But "Honest Ben" replied that, although he was a Chase man, he could not withdraw until there was something to withdraw from.[87]

Wade's refusal to withdraw was based on his hope that the Ohio delegation, after dropping Chase and McLean, would line up solidly for him.[88] "The reason that Chase was so soon dropped," wrote Joshua R. Giddings, who was an Ohio delegate, "was that his leading friends appointed by his request wanted to substitute Wade for him, and gave out notice as soon as we reached Chicago that we were to give Chase only a complimentary vote and then go for Wade." [89] Prior to this, Chase had requested the Ohio delegation to vote as a unit, in the belief that he had a majority of the delegation and might thus gain the state's unanimous vote. Many delegates who were only tepid toward Chase and wished to vote for Wade were willing to adopt the unit rule, seeing in it a chance to strengthen Wade. But the loyal Chase men at Chicago realized that following Chase's unwise instructions would defeat their favorite, and so they proceeded to defeat the unit system. To forestall further activity in behalf of Wade, Chase's managers threatened to vote for Seward if Wade's name were introduced in the convention.[90] Chase and Wade succeeded admirably in knifing each other. This rivalry within the Ohio delegation produced jubilation in the Lincoln camp, for Lincoln appeared to be Ohio's second choice.[91]

As the convention assembled on May 16 the paramount issue was Seward; all else sank into insignificance. The states in which the Republican party commanded large majorities and which it felt confident of carrying in November, regardless of the candidate, were strongly for Seward—New York, Michigan, Wisconsin, Minnesota, and most of Massachusetts and Maine. But the argument was advanced that only a conservative candidate could carry the "doubtful" states—Illinois, Indiana, Pennsylvania, and New Jersey—where anti-slavery sentiment was weak. Lincoln already had the first two of these and was regarded favorably in the latter two. Chase's boom had sagged beyond repair. Bates was growing weaker largely because the Germans were alienated by his Know-Nothing and conservative record. The race was narrowing down to Seward and Lincoln. An Illinois leader now reported: [92]

The nomination at present lies between Seward and Lincoln. . . . Indiana will go for Lincoln. New Hampshire & Connecticut are the same way. Ohio after getting through with Chase is for Lincoln, Chase's friends not desiring to nominate Wade so as not to hurt Chase for the succession. Pennsylvania also has many who are for Lincoln as their second choice. The Lincoln movement has become a serious thing and our state [Illinois] will stick to him to the last. Greeley is working hard against Seward. He is for Bates but if he can't get him will take Lincoln.

As the crowd drifted into the Wigwam this observer wrote: "The Convention is about to meet. The great struggle will be to beat Seward. Now it looks as if it cannot be done." [93] But some of the Sewardites were pessimistic. "The Seward men," a reporter noted "are as blue as Lake Michigan. He may yet succeed, but how, with Pennsylvania, New Jersey, Indiana, Illinois and Ohio against him, it is difficult to see." [94]

On Wednesday, May 16, the convention met in the Wigwam called to order by Governor Edwin D. Morgan of New York Chairman of the Republican National Committee. Morgan appointed David Wilmot, of Pennsylvania, temporary chairman. A Committee on Permanent Organization was appointed. The name of each state in the Union was called. Laughter and hisses greeted mention of the unrepresented slave states of Tennessee, Arkansas, Mississippi, Louisiana, Alabama, Georgia, North Carolina, and South Carolina. After the selection of a "Committee on Business," the convention adjourned until five P.M. Upon reassembling, the report of the Committee on Permanent Organization was received. The tactful George Ashmun, of Massachusetts, was chosen as permanent chairman—a "cool clearheaded" executive whose "emotions did not get the better of him." In his address to the convention Ashmun praised the "brotherly kindness" he had seen displayed everywhere.[95] Then a Committee on Resolutions was appointed and the convention adjourned until the following day.[96] The King-makers retired to organize their forces and the Committee on Resolutions went into closed session to draw up the platform.

The Committee on Resolutions, which met in the parlor of the Tremont House, was too large and unwieldy to function harmoniously. A sub-committee of seven members was directed to draw up the platform and report at nine o'clock the next morning. The members of the sub-committee were Horace Greeley "of Oregon," John A. Kasson of Iowa, Carl Schurz of Wisconsin, Gustave Koerner of Illinois, William T. Otto of Indiana, George S. Boutwell of Massachusetts, and William Jessup of Pennsylvania as chairman.[97]

The sub-committee's planks on the slavery issue were conservative At the party's first national gathering four years earlier the prohibition of slavery in the territories by Congressional action was strongly demanded. The campaign of 1856 had been waged largely on this territorial issue. Now, with anti-slavery Republicans in control of most northern states, the revolutionary work was over; the time no longer demanded sectional denunciation of slaveholders. Less than a third of the platform drawn up at the Tremont House concerned slavery, whereas five-sixths of the document of 1856 touched upon the subject. The right of Congress to prohibit slavery in the territories was not asserted, although it was not denied. Instead, the committee used the colorless statement: "We deny the authority of Congress, of a Territorial legislature, or of any individuals, to give legal existence to slavery in any Territory of the United States." The intention of this clause was not defined except by inference and understatement. The whole issue was evaded in an effort to attract conservative support and at the same time not alienate the radicals. As a sop to the latter, the platform indirectly favored the admission of Kansas as a free state. This appeasement of conservative sentiment dismayed the abolition-minded minority, who searched the platform in vain for denunciations of the fugitive-slave law and of slavery in the District of Columbia.[98]

The politicians who comprised the Resolutions sub-committee likewise avoided alienating those who sympathized with the Democratic doctrine of "states' rights." Even Wisconsin, a cradle of the Republican party, had become excited over the interference of the federal authorities—particularly when the Supreme Court rendered an unpopular decision in the famous Booth case involving the fugitive-slave law. In March, 1859, the Wisconsin legislature denounced the nation's highest tribunal, and Carl Schurz had delivered a state's rights speech in Milwaukee only the year previous with the late John C. Calhoun as the principal authority quoted![99] Accordingly, the platform makers at the Tremont House inserted as the fourth plank: [100]

Resolved . . . That the maintenance inviolate of the rights of the States, and especially the right of each State to order and control its own domestic institutions according to its own judgment exclusively, is essential to that balance of powers on which the perfection and endurance of our political fabric depends; and we denounce the lawless invasion by armed force of the soil of any State or Territory, no matter under what pretext, as among the gravest of crimes.

The last part of this plank was a condemnation of John Brown's raid. The plank as a whole was a concession to states'-rights sentiment. Wilmot admitted it.[101]

It was recognized at Chicago that slavery as an exclusive issue could not hold up the party, let alone assure victory in November. In 1854–1856 Negro slavery had been practically the only solid timber out of which the opponents of the Democracy could build a platform, but the defeat of Frémont in 1856 had proved that hostility to slavery extension by itself was insufficient. Greeley, now one of the two most active platform builders at Chicago, had written the year before: "I don't believe the time ever has been, or soon will be, when on a square slavery issue the Republicans could or can poll one hundred electoral votes." [102] To another he had recently confided: "An Anti-slavery man *per se* cannot be elected; but a tariff, River and Harbor, Pacific Railroad, Free Homestead man may succeed. . . . I wish the country were more anti-slavery than it is." [103] Thus the sub-committee turned to material problems after disposing of slavery in the territories.

The tariff was a live issue. Pennsylvania's convention vote was coveted by all presidential contenders. A Harrisburg observer had written: "The opposition [anti-Democratic] politicians here say you may cry nigger, nigger, as much as you please, only give us a chance to carry Pennsylvania by crying tariff. Without this state you cannot elect your President." [104] Philadelphia's leading Republican daily had declared: "We tell the convention, so soon to meet at Chicago, squarely, roundly, and in every other shape that means earnestness, that their candidates cannot carry the States of Pennsylvania and New Jersey unless they stand publicly on protective ground. . . . This State [Pennsylvania] cannot be carried on an anti-slavery issue only. Frémont proved that." [105] One delegate now wrote home from Chicago: "Penn. demands a tariff plank in the platform. Her delegation is active and urgent." [106] Delaware, with growing industrial interests, gave support to a protective tariff.[107] Western Virginia, with vast mineral deposits, also clamored for protection. [108] Western regions like Illinois and Oregon, eager to conciliate Pennsylvania, agreed to accept higher rates as the price of Republican success.[109]

The platform makers, however, had to recognize free-trade sentiment among the former Democratic members of the Republican party, one leader warning: "Our brethren of democratic antecedents were tender footed on this [tariff] subject & had to be handled very carefully. Their faith is too new to bear the imposition of new articles of the old Whig creed directly tendered at our hands." [110] Thus the out-and-out protectionists found it impossible to obtain a frank endorsement of high-tariff principles. Thomas Dudley, New Jersey member of the Platform Committee, who lived in the industrial region of Camden, "was determined that the question of protection should be squarely met, and he therefore notified his fellow-members that if they did not then and there adopt a resolution to that effect, they should be compelled to fight it upon the following day on the floor of the convention. In that he, representing New Jersey, was sustained by the member from Delaware." [111] But the former Democrats had to be considered, and the tariff declaration ultimately adopted was very mild. Gustave Koerner, the Illinois member of the Platform sub-committee, explained: [112]

The only trouble was given us by Greeley, who insisted upon a strong protective plank. We did not consider the tariff question at this particular time as one of primary importance, and we humored him by declaring that "while providing revenue for the support of the general government by duties upon imports, sound policy requires such an adjustment as to encourage the development of the industrial interests of the whole country." This amounted to no more than the establishment of a revenue tariff bill with incidental protection, and did not differ essentially from former Democratic declarations on the same subject.

The tariff resolution constituted the twelfth plank of the platform. Political expediency prevented an unequivocal protectionist declaration since the Democratic element of the Republican party leaned toward free trade or "tariff-for-revenue-only." But the wording, calling for an "adjustment" to "encourage the development of the industrial interests" was accepted by the Pennsylvanians and other protectionists as the best obtainable under the circumstances." [113]

What the tariff was to Pennsylvania, homestead was to the Northwest. After the homestead bill had been reintroduced in the lame-duck Congress of 1859 the issue had become a major one.[114] According to Delegate Stephen Miller, of Minnesota: "This Homestead measure overshadows everything with us, and throughout the West." [115] The German-Americans were particularly aggressive in agitating for free land, and southerners condemned homestead as the "most conspicuous part of German philosophy transplanted to the shores of America." [116] Nevertheless, the German vote was recognized as vital.[117] An Ohio chieftain observed: "In Ohio & Illinois we cannot afford to lose the German vote." [118] A party editor emphasized: "[In] Wisconsin, Iowa, Minnesota, and Michigan . . . the Germans hold the balance of power." [119] Such sentiment was prevalent among the Northwestern leaders.[120] The Platform sub-committee had on it two German-born leaders, Carl Schurz and Gustave Koerner, who demanded both a homestead declaration and a resolution against legislation prejudicial to the foreign-born. The Germans, obviously, were still suspicious of the large number of Know-Nothings in the Republican party. Their demands were met in the so-called "Dutch planks." [121] The thirteenth plank read in part: "We demand the passage by Congress of the complete and satisfactory Homestead measure which has already passed the House." [122] The fourteenth plank declared: "That the Republican party is opposed to any change in our Naturalization Laws or any State legislation by which the rights of citizenship hitherto accorded to immigrants from foreign lands shall be abridged or impaired." [123]

The West also demanded internal improvements, the Pacific railroad and a daily overland mail.

Chicago and Detroit ardently favored the improvement of rivers and harbors.[124] They received satisfaction in the fifteenth plank: "That the appropriation by Congress for River and Harbor improvements of a National character, required for the accommodation and security of an existing commerce, are authorized by the Constitution, and justified by the obligation of Government to protect the lives and property of its citizens." [125] The Pacific railroad and a daily overland mail were demanded especially by residents of the proposed termini of those projects, in Missouri, Iowa, California and Oregon.[126] Their demands were gratified by the sixteenth plank of the Chicago platform: "That a Railroad to the Pacific Ocean is imperatively demanded by the interests of the whole country; that the Federal Government ought to render immediate and efficient aid in its construction; and that as a preliminary thereto, a daily Overland Mail should be promptly established." [127]

Horace Greeley, "of Oregon," was one of the most energetic members of the sub-committee.[128] He took for himself entire credit for framing the homestead plank which, he claimed, "I fixed exactly to my own liking." [129] He was ably assisted by the Iowa member, John A. Kasson.[130]

The platform reported to the convention May 17 began with a preamble of the Declaration of Independence. On the slavery issue it was moderate compared with the platform of 1856.[131] The "Naturalization" plank condemned by implication the Massachusetts "Two Year" Amendment so as to please the Germans, yet nothing was mentioned by name lest the Know-Nothings be offended. Appeal was made to advocates of states' rights. Homestead, rivers and harbors, the Pacific railroad, and a daily overland mail were dealt with to satisfy the West. A mild tariff declaration won the approbation of doubtful eastern states. "The Pennsylvania and New Jersey delegations," one observer reported, "were terrific in their applause over the tariff resolution, and their hilarity was contagious, finally pervading the whole vast audience."[132] The platform concluded by inviting all groups to support the Republican ticket: "Finally, having thus set forth our distinctive principles and views, we invite the coöperation of all citizens, however differing on other questions, who substantially agree with us in their affirmance and support."[133] The platform was indeed a rare piece of mosaic, designed to appeal to numerous groups. Republicanism became a latitudinarian creed, broad enough to suit anyone but a southern slaveholder. If there yet remained in the North a disposition not to coöperate with the Republicans, it was no fault of the Chicago platform makers.

After the platform was adopted with almost hysterical enthusiasm, the convention adjourned without taking a ballot for president.[134]

At this stage in the proceedings, Seward appeared certain of the party's nomination: "So confident were the Seward men, when the platform was adopted, of their ability to nominate their great leader, that they urged an immediate ballot, and would have had it if the clerks had not reported that they were unprovided with tally-sheets."[135] Even Greeley, although bitterly opposed to the New York senator, telegraphed on May 17: "My conclusion, from all that I can gather tonight, is, that the opposition to Gov. Seward cannot concentrate on any candidate, and that he will be nominated."[136]

The question before the delegates the night of May 17 was not that of choosing between Seward and Lincoln, or between Seward and Bates, but it was the question of Seward himself. The New Yorker's opponents, although preferring different men and disagreeing on specific grounds, were united in their opposition to him. They utilized Seward's connection with Weed's unsavory New York organization to block his nomination. Although Weed, anticipating this maneuver, had brought along the respectable William M. Evarts to place Seward in nomination, the New York senator's opponents, led by William Cullen Bryant, scattered among the delegates, spreading charges of Weed's "corruptions" in Albany.[187]

Lincoln's supporters, led by Davis, Judd and Medill, now worked furiously. With Illinois pledged to their man, with Indiana almost certain and the smaller New England states at least anti-Seward, the key to the situation was Pennsylvania, second only to New York in convention votes. The Lincolnites concentrated their attention on the Keystone delegation.

Pennsylvania's "favorite son" was Simon Cameron, but he had no strength outside his own state. Considerations of expediency, or "availability," were not sufficient to give his candidacy strength. He did not represent dominant opinion on the major issue, extension of slavery, and his stock-in-trade, the tariff, was important only in Pennsylvania and New Jersey. In addition, Cameron had a reputation for corruption and sharp practices that made party leaders fear to nominate him. However satisfactory he might be to spoilsmen and protective-tariff devotees, his nomination could not arouse the enthusiasm of Republicans throughout the nation, let alone win new adherents to the party's standard. Moreover, he did not command united support even from Pennsylvania: Andrew C. Curtin and Curtin's chief aide, Alexander K. McClure, actively fought the Cameron movement at Chicago. By the second day of the convention Cameron's managers had all but given up.[188]

When Cameron's weakness became apparent, the managers of the other contenders engaged in intense rivalry to attract the huge Pennsylvania delegation. Weed approached them, fortified with immense amounts of cash.[189] Word came from Chicago: "The flood of Seward money promised for Pennsylvania was not without efficacy. The phrase used was, that Seward's friend 'would spend oceans of money.'"[140] But Seward was unacceptable. Cameron's followers, despite their chief's pretension of favoring Seward previously, would not support him.[141] Curtin's adherents were even more hostile to the New Yorker. Curtin felt that he could not be elected governor in Pennsylvania if the radical Seward were placed at the head of the national ticket.[142]

Prior to the convention Curtin had been in touch with Henry S.

Lane, candidate for governor of Indiana. Both men were determined that Seward should not be nominated, since he would weaken
the party in their respective states. At Chicago Curtin and Lane
were in constant communication with each other. Through their
efforts the Pennsylvania and Indiana delegations met for consultation on Thursday evening—May 17.[143]

With Seward and Cameron ruled out by the Pennsylvanians, the
contest for their votes narrowed down to Bates and Lincoln. Thaddeus Stevens was still stubbornly backing the colorless McLean.[144]
But Bates had great strength among the Pennsylvanians because of
his conservatism and high-tariff views.[145] The Lincoln men became
alarmed at the Bates activity among the Indiana and Pennsylvania
delegations then meeting together at the Court House. Gustave
Koerner relates his own work at this juncture: [146]

The Bates men, having learned of this meeting, appeared there
in force, and [Frank] Blair had already commenced making a speech
for Bates when word was sent to our [Lincoln] headquarters of
what was going on. Browning and myself were immediately dispatched to counteract the movement. I heard the last part of
Blair's speech. He was followed by Fred Muench, who promised
the vote of Missouri for Bates, and Judge Krekel closed in a rather
able speech for Bates.

I now asked leave to speak for Lincoln. The court house was
crowded with many other delegates and with citizens of Chicago.
The moment I named Lincoln the cheers almost shook the court
house. I controverted the idea that Bates could carry Missouri, said
that outside of St. Louis and a few German settlements represented
by Krekel and Muench no Republican could get a vote; that the
State was for Douglas . . . that I was astonished that my German
friends from Missouri talked of supporting Bates, who in 1856
had presided over a Whig National Convention at Baltimore, which
had nominated Fillmore and Donelson, after they had been nominated by the Know Nothings; that Bates in the municipal elections
of St. Louis had several times supported the Know Nothing ticket;
that I would tell this meeting in all candor that if Bates was nominated, the German Republicans in the other States would never vote
for him; I for one would not, and I would advise my countrymen
to the same effect.

Koerner was shrewd in emphasizing the German hostility to
Bates. German leaders had begun agitating against Bates as early
as March. They had even called a "Conference of the German

Republican Clubs" at the Deutsches Haus, Chicago, May 14–15, the eve of the National Convention.[147] Seward, Lincoln, Chase, and Wade were the candidates favored by the German leaders.[148] One resolution adopted declared: "We pledge ourselves to support any aspirant for the presidency and vice-presidency who . . . has never opposed the republican platform of 1856, nor has ever been identified with the spirit of the Massachusetts Amendment."[149] This resolution was aimed not only at Governor Banks of Massachusetts (who had deliberately done nothing to prevent passage of the "Two Year" Amendment in 1859) but also at Bates. The latter, besides having coöperated with Know-Nothing groups in St. Louis, had supported Fillmore in 1856.[150]

The Germans' hostility to Bates had been manifest at the state Republican convention in St. Louis on March 10.[151] This had made a deep impression even in the East. "You have doubtless seen that at the Missouri Convention there was a German demonstration against Bates," a New York Republican leader had written. "It is indicative of German feeling everywhere, and inasmuch as we depend upon them to carry the western states if we are to carry them at all, it seems to me that it ought to be conclusive in respect to his nomination."[152] Also in March an Indiana leader reported: "Germany is with us for any Republican outside of Massachusetts, except Bates."[153] And Koerner wrote in April: "Bates . . . would drive off . . . the radical or I should rather say the German element."[154] Medill also emphasized the anti-Bates sentiment among the Germans.[155] During the two days preceding the National Convention even the Indiana Republicans, among whom Bates was popular, admitted that the Germans would not support the Missourian.[156]

The question now was: If the Germans would not accept Bates, and the conservative Republicans would not take the Germans' first choice, Seward, who would be the Germans' second choice? For several years Lincoln had been a favorite of the Illinois Germans and had cultivated their support, even to the point of owning part interest in a German-language newspaper. He had not joined the Illinois "American" party following the crack-up of the Whigs, but had made a slow metamorphosis directly into the Republican fold in 1856. In that year he had helped George Schneider, editor of the Chicago *Staats-Zeitung*, frame an anti-Know-Nothing plank, which was incorporated in the Illinois Republican platform.[157] In

April (1860) the widely circulated Baltimore *Turn-Zeitung* opposed Bates and declared for Seward, but added: "If on the score of expediency we pass Mr. Seward by, then will Mr. Lincoln be *the* man, as a matter of course."[158] Medill reprinted this editorial May 2, and other pro-Lincoln newspapers followed his example.[159]

On other counts, besides German hostility, Bates was not "available." His conservatism was frowned upon by the more radical Republicans; moreover, he could not carry his own state, which was considered certain to go Democratic.[160] An Iowa leader flippantly declared: "I am for the man who can carry Pennsylvania, New Jersey, and Indiana, with this reservation, that I will not go into the cemetery or catacomb";[161] and "I don't know why we should go into the state of Missouri for a President. As to carrying that, or any other slave state, it is folly to think of it."[162] Still another handicap to Bates's cause was the nomination of John Bell by the "Constitutional Unionists" at Baltimore the week previous. Bell's candidacy meant that most Whigs, "Americans," and other anti-Democratic conservatives would vote for Bell rather than for Bates.[163]

Bates was dropped from consideration.[164] "There were hundreds of Pennsylvanians, Indianians and Illinoisans, who never closed their eyes that night," wrote one correspondent on the scene. "I saw Henry S. Lane at one o'clock, pale and haggard, with cane under his arm, walking as if for a wager, from one caucus-room to another, at the Tremont House."[165] Curtin did the same. After hours of wrangling, the Pennsylvania delegation reached an agreement early in the morning of the 18th day of the balloting for president. The final vote in caucus gave Lincoln a majority of six votes over Bates.[166] Thurlow Weed continued to dangle bait before certain Pennsylvanians, and Horace Greeley wrote a few days later: "If you had seen the Pennsylvania delegation and known how much money Weed had in hand, you would not have believed we could do so well. Give Curtin thanks for that."[167] Probably David Wilmot helped Curtin. Wilmot had written: "Seward seems to be gaining ground. . . . I cannot feel that he is an available candidate. I believe Lincoln of Ill. a much stronger man."[168] At the caucus it was agreed that, as a courtesy gesture, Pennsylvania would cast its vote for Cameron on the first ballot and for Judge McLean on the second before swinging to Lincoln on the third. Since neither Cameron nor McLean now stood any chance, the third ballot was really the only one that mattered.[169]

In all probability Judge Davis and other Lincoln managers did not secure the support of Cameron's followers without promising Cameron a Cabinet position in event of Lincoln's election.[170] Davis's biographer concludes: "The support of Pennsylvania was assured to Lincoln by a promise to place Simon Cameron at the President's council table." [171] Joseph Medill's biographer writes: [172]

In Medill's account, he stated that after the Illinois delegates had gone to sound out the Pennsylvania group, he waited in the Tremont House for the final word. About midnight, Judge Davis came down the stairs and told Medill, "Damned if we haven't got them." To the query "how" was returned the answer, "By paying their price." Ray [Charles H. Ray, Medill's associate editor], who had been in attendance at the conference, told Medill that Cameron had been promised a cabinet position, remarking that such was a small price when playing for the presidency.

Curtin's lieutenant, Alexander K. McClure, a participant in the midnight caucus that swung Pennsylvania to Lincoln, insisted that the shift to Lincoln was made before the promise of a Cabinet post to Cameron. Later McClure declared that as soon as the Pennsylvania delegation had decided to support Lincoln, one of Cameron's confidential advisers, John P. Sanderson, of the Philadelphia *Daily News*, obtained a conference with Judge Davis and Leonard Swett, and secured this promise in behalf of his chief from them.[173]

At the midnight caucus the Lincolnites also won over most of the New Jersey delegates, largely through the efforts of Thomas H. Dudley, delegate-at-large. An associate of Dudley related: [174]

The committee met at six o'clock in Mr. Wilmot's room, and were in session until nearly ten P.M., before anything was accomplished. . . . Mr. Dudley took the floor, and proposed that it should be ascertained which one of the three candidates [Lincoln, Cameron and Dayton] had the greatest actual strength before the convention, and could carry the largest number of delegates from the four States in the event of dropping the other two. Judge Davis stated as to Mr. Lincoln's vote on the first ballot, and the probable vote of the Illinois delegates, in the event of Mr. Lincoln being dropped—that is, how they would break. The committee from Indiana and Pennsylvania also reported how the votes of their States would be cast if Lincoln and Cameron were both dropped. The New Jersey committee made a similar statement as to the strength of Judge Dayton. It was understood that a portion of the New Jersey delegates would drop Mr. Dayton after giving him a complimentary vote, and go for Mr. Seward. This examination revealed the fact, that of the three candidates, Mr. Lincoln was the strongest. Mr. Dudley then proposed to the Pennsylvania committee, that for the general good and success of the party, they should give up their candidates, and unite upon Mr. Lincoln. After some discussion, Mr. Dudley's proposition was agreed to, and a programme arranged to carry it into execution. A meeting of the Dayton delegates, from New Jersey, was immediately called, at James T. Sherman's room, at one o'clock that night. . . . Mr. Dudley . . . explained what had been accomplished, and after talking the matter over, they approved his action. It was understood that Judge Dayton was to receive one or more complimentary votes, and then the strength of the delegation to be thrown for Mr. Lincoln, and then they were to follow. The Pennsylvania delegation likewise adopted the plan, first giving Mr. Cameron a complimentary vote. The agreement of the committee was not generally known the next morning when the convention assembled.

With Illinois and Indiana lined up, and with the other two "doubtfuls," Pennsylvania and New Jersey, agreeing to vote for Lincoln after casting complimentary ballots for the respective favorite sons, Cameron and Dayton, the Lincoln managers were in a formidable position. They went to work among the smaller state delegations immediately. An Ohio delegate reported: "Ind. Illinois & Pa have been here in force determined to accomplish the defeat of Seward." [175] He might have added that there was now the positive purpose of nominating Lincoln.

Even while the midnight caucuses were in progress, Halstead observed: [176]

Henry S. Lane . . . in connection with others . . . had been operating to bring the Vermonters and Virginians to the point of deserting Seward. Vermont would certainly cast her electoral vote for any candidate who could be nominated, and Virginia as certainly against any [such] candidate. The object was to bring the delegates of those States to consider success rather than Seward, and join with the battleground States—as Pennsylvania, New Jersey, Indiana and Illinois insisted upon calling themselves. This was finally done, the fatal break in Seward's strength having been made in Vermont and Virginia, destroying at once, when it appeared, his power in the New England and slave State delegations. . . .

The cry of a want of availability which was from the start raised against Seward, now took a more definite form than heretofore.

. . . Henry S. Lane . . . asserted hundreds of times that the nomination of Seward would be death to him, and that he might in that
case just as well give up the canvass.

The Lincolnites' efforts to enlist Virginia had the support of Alfred Caldwell, of Wheeling, chairman of the Old Dominion delegation, who supported the Springfield man because "Mr. Lincoln
was not a sectional man . . . and would make a better run than
the courtly and distinguished William H. Seward." [177] Horace
Greeley, coöperating with the anti-Seward forces, declared: "Virginia had been regularly sold out; but the seller could not deliver.
We had to rain red-hot bolts on them, however, to keep the majority from going to Seward." [178] Although Seward had some support among the Virginians, Lincoln had most of the delegation.

On Friday morning Medill's Chicago Press & Tribune contained
a last appeal to discard Seward and nominate Lincoln. One enthusiastic Lincolnite now exulted: "Lincoln will be nominated. I
think he is the second choice of everybody." [179]

The Sewardites, however, abounded in confidence. They believed
firmly that the opposition of the doubtful states to their candidate
was an old story; it was hardly possible that their protests would
suddenly become effective. The Seward men marched as usual behind their brilliantly uniformed band. "They were about a thousand
strong, and protracting their march a little too far, were not all able
to get into the wigwam," one correspondent observed. "This was
their first misfortune. They were not where they could scream with
the best effect in responding to the mention of the name of William
H. Seward." [180]

There was good reason why the Sewardites could not crowd into
the convention hall. "While the friends of the other candidates held
processions and marched around with bands of music," declared
Gustave Koerner, "we had made arrangements that the Wigwam
should at the earliest opening every morning be filled with Illinoisans. We had them provided with tickets before tickets were
distributed to others." [181] Medill related that it was the Lincolnites' plan to pack the convention hall with Lincoln "shouters" and to
exclude as many Seward followers as possible. To this end Judd, a
railroad attorney as well as Illinois state chairman, had arranged with
his clients to carry Lincoln men to Chicago free of charge. On the
night preceding the balloting men sat far into the small hours

printing hundreds of duplicate tickets of admission to the Wigwam, to be distributed to Lincoln's followers with instructions to report early at the doors. "As a result of the activity of these men," Medill admitted, "the Seward 'Irrepressibles' found many of their number excluded from the hall on the morning of the third day." [182] In later years older residents of Illinois reminisced that tickets to the Wigwam had been monopolized by the Sewardites and that Lincoln's friend, Jesse W. Fell, provided for the printing of duplicate tickets to be distributed to the Lincolnites; that when the Seward contingent returned from their parade they found the Wigwam filled with westerners "ready to shout for Lincoln." [183] On this point Fell's son wrote: [184]

Father as Secretary of the Republican State Central Committee of the campaign of 1860 had the printing of *all* of the tickets of admission on account of the convention being held in Chicago and this State, and they [were] apportioned to the several delegations by the National Committee, and were delivered by father to them. They were easily duplicated. . . .

The New York delegation came by train loads, with bands and banners—filled the streets with their marching crowds, and the air with cries of Seward. Father and the rest of the Committee had a rush meeting, at which it developed that through some underhand work that all the Seward adherents had been furnished tickets of admission and that if they all got in there would be no room for the Lincoln "rooters." So father suggested that he would have plenty more tickets printed, and that they would be put in the hands of their friends, at the same time cautioning their friends to be on hand early—which was done. Amongst some of the first New York tickets presented at the door were some that were not regular, and as a consequence, the door-keepers held them back until father could be seen, and meanwhile the Lincoln friends were getting the seats, and had done it so well that they concluded to let technicalities go and admit all those holding tickets.

When Chairman Ashmun called the convention to order on Friday morning, May 18, 1860, the Wigwam was packed full; thousands outside clamored to gain entrance. The Seward men won the first test of strength. A rule had been adopted that no delegation should cast more votes than there were duly accredited delegates. The Maryland delegation had not been full, and Montgomery Blair, still fighting for Bates, wanted to fill it up with three Bates

men. The Seward forces checked this. But the convention was impatient to get to the nominations.[185]

The eminent New York lawyer William M. Evarts, who lent
respectability to the Seward-Weed organization, nominated Seward.
The applause was enthusiastic. Judd placed Lincoln in nomination.
The response was deafening. Dudley named Dayton. Andrew H.
Reeder, of Pennsylvania, presented Cameron. David K. Cartter, of
Ohio, did the same for Chase. Caleb B. Smith, of Indiana, seconded
the nomination of Lincoln. The Lincolnites shook the rafters. Frank
Blair, of Missouri, "gave" Edward Bates to the convention. Austin
Blair, of Michigan (no relation to the other Blairs), seconded
Seward's nomination. The Sewardites yelled themselves hoarse.
Tom Corwin, erstwhile Whig, nominated McLean. Carl Schurz
followed Michigan's example and seconded Seward's nomination.
New York, Wisconsin, Michigan and Minnesota shrieked their delight. Columbus Delano, of Ohio, countered by seconding the name
of Lincoln. Pandemonium broke loose. It was observed that "the
only names that produced 'tremendous applause' were those of
Seward and Lincoln. Everybody felt that the fight was between
them, and yelled accordingly." [186] When Delano spoke and it was
realized that the Lincolnites had even made inroads into the Ohio
delegation, "the uproar was beyond description. Imagine all the hogs
ever slaughtered in Cincinnati giving their death squeals together,
a score of big steam whistles going." [187] The Sewardites became
glum: "The New York, Michigan and Wisconsin delegations sat
together, and were in this tempest very quiet. Many of their faces
whitened as the Lincoln *yawp* swelled into a wild hozanna of
victory." [188]

The convention proceeded to ballot.

The New England states were called first. Seward had not his
expected strength there. Maine gave him ten votes and Lincoln
six. New Hampshire presented him with only one, John C. Frémont
one, and Lincoln nine. Vermont gave her ten to her Senator Jacob
Collamer, which was understood to be merely complimentary. Massachusetts, expected to go solidly for Seward, gave him twenty-
one and Lincoln four. The other two New England states did not
deliver Seward a single vote: Rhode Island gave five of her eight
votes to McLean. Connecticut cast seven of her twelve for Bates,
and two each for Lincoln and Chase, and one for Wade. Then came
the Empire State. Evarts, with pride in his voice, announced: "The

State of *New York* casts her seventy votes for *William H. Seward!*"
Applause. Next came New Jersey—fourteen votes for Dayton, as
planned. The huge Pennsylvania vote was then cast: 47½ votes for
Cameron, four for Lincoln, 1½ for Seward, and one for McLean.
The Blair-controlled Maryland delegation presented eight to Bates
and three to Seward. Delaware, also conservative and under Blair
influence, went solidly for Bates. The Sewardites were then ad-
ministered a blow by Virginia, which they had considered unanimous for the New Yorker. The Old Dominion announced eight
for Seward, one for Cameron—and 14 for Lincoln! The New
Yorkers looked nervously at each other. Kentucky divided its
twenty-three votes among Seward, Lincoln, Chase, McLean, and
Senator Charles Sumner. Ohio gave Chase thirty-four of its forty-
six, with four for McLean—and eight for Lincoln. The Lincolnites
went wild when Indiana gave her twenty-six to their man. "This
solid vote was a startler," one observer reported, "and the keen little
eyes of Henry S. Lane glittered as it was given. He was responsible
for it." [189] That is—he and Caleb B. Smith.

After the pivotal Hoosier vote, Missouri was called. Eighteen
for its son, Bates. Pro-Seward Michigan announced twelve for her
favorite. Illinois came next. Twenty-two for Lincoln. The bogus
Texas delegation gave four for Seward and two for Bates. Wisconsin, a Seward bailiwick, presented ten to the New Yorker. Iowa
had only eight votes but distributed them among Seward, Lincoln,
Cameron, Bates, McLean, and Chase. California, loyal to Seward,
cast her eight for him, as did Minnesota, the next state called.
Oregon, the last state, went all-out for Bates with her five. Then
came the territories—Kansas, Nebraska, and the District of Columbia
—with a total of fourteen votes. Of these Seward received ten, and
Lincoln, Cameron, and Chase divided the rest. The secretary announced the result of the first ballot: Seward 173½; Lincoln, 102;
Cameron 50½; Chase, 49; Bates, 48; Dayton, 14; McLean, 12; Collamer, 10; Wade, 3; Judge Read, 1; Sumner, 1; John C. Frémont,
1. The total number of votes cast was 465, of which 233 (a majority)
were necessary to nominate. [190] The result of the ballot "caused a
fall in Seward stock. It was seen that Lincoln, Cameron and Bates
had the strength to defeat Seward, and it was known that the
greater part of the Chase vote would go for Lincoln." [191] Few
knew what the Pennsylvanians were planning to do on the next
ballot.

Every man was fiercely enlisted in the struggle, the partisans of the respective candidates keyed to such a pitch of excitement as to cast all patience to the winds. "Call the roll!" they shrieked. The convention proceeded to a second ballot. The first gain for Lincoln was in New Hampshire, the scattered Chase and Frémont votes giving him nine out of the Granite State's ten votes. Vermont was then called. Collamer was dropped and Vermont's ten given to Lincoln. This was a terrible blow to Seward. Lincoln gained one in Massachusetts. Moreover, he had a gain of five from Rhode Island and Connecticut. New York, called next, maintained its unbroken line for Seward. Seward picked up in New Jersey: Seward, 4; Dayton, 10. But even this was indirectly helpful to Lincoln, since Dayton was being torn down as a favorite son—and his votes would apparently swing to Lincoln on the next ballot.[192] The decisive break came when Pennsylvania was called. In tomb-like silence all awaited the decision of the Keystone state. Then: Cameron was dropped. The Sewardites' spirits sagged hopelessly as the Pennsylvania vote was announced: Cameron, 1; Seward, 2½; McLean, 2½—and Lincoln, 48! Weed sickened as he perceived "the change in the vote of Pennsylvania startling the vast auditorium like a clap of thunder." [193]

Pennsylvania's decision tipped the scales in favor of Lincoln. The bandwagon was about to be wheeled out. Although Maryland continued to give most of its votes to Bates, Delaware transferred its six votes from the Missouri jurist to Lincoln. Most of Virginia remained loyal to Lincoln. Although Seward gained two votes from Kentucky, Lincoln gained three. Following Kentucky came Ohio; Chase lost five votes, McLean dropped one, and Lincoln gained six as the Buckeye State answered: Chase, 29; McLean, 3; and Lincoln, 14. The following remained behind their respective favorites: Indiana, twenty-six for Lincoln; Missouri, eighteen for Bates; Michigan, twelve for Seward; and Illinois, twenty-two for Lincoln. Seward gained the two Bates votes from "Texas." Wisconsin again gave its ten votes to Seward. But Lincoln picked up three votes in Iowa, while Seward had two, the same as on the first ballot. Seward held his own in California and Minnesota. Oregon stayed with Bates. The three territories gave Seward a gain of one, but it was at the expense of Cameron, not Lincoln. Great confusion reigned as the vote was being counted. The secretary announced the official count: Seward, 184½, and Lincoln, 181. Seward had gained only eleven votes by the desertion from favorite sons—but Lincoln had increased his vote by seventy-nine! The other votes were: Chase, 42½; Bates, 35; Dayton, 10; McLean, 8; Cameron, 2; Cassius M. Clay, of Kentucky, 2.[194]

Two hundred and thirty-three votes were necessary to nominate a candidate. Everyone realized that, while Seward's and Lincoln's strength was almost equal at this stage, the reserved votes by which the contest must be decided were more inclined to Lincoln. Bates's thirty-five, McLean's eight and Dayton's ten largely represented votes cast by bona-fide conservatives or by those practical Republicans who believed that Seward was too radical and controversial a personality. Chase's forty-two and one-half votes, while coming from advanced anti-slavery men, could not all be cast for Seward, principally because of Chase's personal dislike of the New York senator. Later Joseph Medill declared that Lincoln's managers feared such a defection of Chase support to Seward and had sent him (Medill, who formerly lived in Ohio) to prevent it. Medill seated himself among his friends in the Ohio delegation as the second ballot was taken, only to be unceremoniously ordered out by Giddings, but the Wade men, seeing in Medill anti-Chase strength, allowed him to stay.[195]

The third ballot began amid an atmosphere that strained the nerves of all. The first three New England states voted as on the preceding ballot: Maine, ten for Seward, six for Lincoln; New Hampshire, one for Seward, nine for Lincoln; Vermont, ten for Lincoln. Massachusetts, eighteen for Seward, eight for Lincoln—four votes going over from Seward to Lincoln.[196] The Sewardites were gloomier than ever—and Weed was long in forgiving certain men on the Massachusetts delegation.[197] Seward and Lincoln each gained one in Rhode Island. Seward gained one in Connecticut, but Lincoln held his four here. New York remained solidly for Seward. Then came New Jersey. Dayton was dropped, Seward gained one, but eight of the votes went to Lincoln, whereas he had had none on the preceding ballot. Pennsylvania, polled next, announced fifty-two for Lincoln and two for McLean—a net gain of four for Lincoln. Then Maryland. The Blairs saw the direction of the current. Bates was discarded. And Maryland cast nine of its eleven for Lincoln; only two for Seward. Delaware again declared its six for Lincoln. Seward, Lincoln and Bates held their respective second-ballot strength in the Virginia delegation and substantially in the states following: Kentucky, Ohio, Indiana, Missouri, Michigan, Illinois, "Texas," and Wisconsin. Iowa announced two for Seward and five for Lincoln—a gain of three for the Rail Splitter. California, Minnesota, Oregon, Kansas Territory, Nebraska Territory, and the District of Columbia—all these distributed their votes as on the second ballot.[198] Even while the roll was being called the delegates kept tally, and before the secretary announced the result they knew it: Lincoln had 231½ votes—only one and a half short of the necessary 233 to nominate. Seward had 180, Chase 24½, Bates 22, McLean 5, and Dayton and Cassius M. Clay one each. Hundreds of pencils had told the same story—and the news spread. The bandwagon was rolling around the Wigwam.[199] "I looked up to see who would be the man to give the decisive vote," Murat Halstead, reporting for the Cincinnati *Commercial*, relates. "In about ten ticks of a watch, Cartter of Ohio was up. . . . Every eye was on Cartter. . . . He said, 'I rise (eh), Mr. Chairman (eh), to announce the change of four votes of Ohio from Mr. Chase to Mr. Lincoln.' The deed was done."[200] Abraham Lincoln of Illinois was Republican candidate for President of the United States.

Later Medill claimed that he whispered to David K. Cartter to swing the Wade votes to Lincoln and Ohio would be well cared for.[201] Cartter later maintained that the governorship of Nebraska Territory had been promised him. Lincoln subsequently found a way out by tendering Cartter the post of minister to Bolivia.[202]

Following Lincoln's nomination, managers of the other contenders did the graceful thing and requested that the nomination be made unanimous.[203] The Sewardites were "so overcome by their favorite's defeat that they cried like heart broken children."[204] A Wisconsin leader wrote: "Tears flowed like water among the vast throng. I never saw a scene so truly affecting, & which showed a greater depth of feeling."[205]

The nomination of a vice-presidential candidate was not particularly exciting. Kentucky's Cassius M. Clay was Senator Hannibal Hamlin's only formidable rival. Since Hamlin was an ex-Democrat and Clay a former Whig, the former better balanced the national ticket, inasmuch as Lincoln had been a Whig. It was deemed judicious to patronize the Democratic element and combat charges that the Republican party was an "old Whig concern."[206] Hamlin, too, was from Maine, which would balance Lincoln's Illinois geographically. Moreover, the Democratic element of the

New York delegation, led by Senator Preston King, was partial to Hamlin.[207] On the second ballot the Maine senator was chosen Lincoln's running-mate. The convention had blended almost all elements opposed to the Democrats, and a Minnesota delegate rejoiced that "the ticket is such a one as promises to command the main body of all shades of the opposition." [208]

The story of Lincoln's nomination was essentially the familiar one unfolded in several previous (and later) American national party conventions. The most prominent candidate had strong and concentrated support, sufficient to enable him to give some direction to the affairs of the convention, in the absence of any union among his opponents. Beyond this strength, already secured, he had nothing to gain, and the leading position was his only so long as his opponents, divided in their loyalties, failed to unite. When they did unite, the leading candidate was dropped and a lesser known but less controversial figure was chosen. Considerations of expediency, grouped together under the familiar term "availability," had triumphed at Chicago.

CHAPTER TEN

Organizing for Victory

W HEN LINCOLN WAS NOMINATED for president he was largely unknown outside Illinois. "Who is Abraham Lincoln?" [1] many demanded. Newspapers called him "Abram" Lincoln[2] and his first campaign biography was entitled *The Life, Speeches and Public Services of Abram Lincoln.*[3] Lincoln corrected the error: [4]

Springfield, Ill., June 4, 1860.

Hon. George Ashmun—

My Dear Sir:

It seems as if the question whether my first name is "Abraham" or "Abram," will never be settled. It is "Abraham," and if the letter of acceptance is not yet in print, you may, if you see fit, have my signature thereto printed "Abraham Lincoln." Exercise your own judgment about this.

Yours as ever

A. LINCOLN

Republican leaders advised: "There should be at least one million copies of some cheap Life of Lincoln. . . . There are thousands . . . who do not yet know Abraham Lincoln." [5]

The Republicans went into the campaign united. Lincoln's chief rivals at Chicago did not long fret. Seward publicly announced himself for Lincoln's and Hamlin's election.[6] Edward Bates wrote a public letter to Old Line Whigs and "Americans," lauding Lincoln as a "sound and safe man. He could not be sectional if he tried." [7] It was recognized that the Republicans needed the votes of these conservatives.[8] Salmon P. Chase, a power among the former Free Soil Democratic element, held Senator Wade primarily responsible for his defeat and pledged his support to Lincoln.[9] And Simon Cameron also went down the line for Lincoln, informing his constituents: "The high office, which you, together with the people of this great State, would have conferred upon me, has for me no charms." [10] He forwarded $800 to Lincoln's state—"to assist in getting out votes," [11] he explained.

Despite Lincoln's obscurity, he proved a strong candidate. Around him clustered the pioneer and democratic tradition.

The Jacksonian era of the 1830's had been one of ardent belief in the democratic ideal and of distrust of aristocrats. In 1840 the log cabin had emerged as a symbol of the American spirit when the Whigs successfully transformed William Henry Harrison into a plain, simple inhabitant of a log cabin.[12] Henceforth the log cabin became a semi-sacred place from whence Providence might call a beloved President.[13] Lincoln had actually been born in a log cabin. One Republican worker exulted: "It has also afforded me sincere pleasure to think of Mr. Lincoln taking possession of the White House; he, who was once the inmate of the log cabin— were he the pampered, effeminated child of fortune, no such pleasing emotions would be inspired." [14]

Another feature of Lincoln's popular appeal was his "rail-splitter" background. This idea had originated at the State Republican convention in Decatur on May 9-10, when a Lincoln admirer produced two old fence rails, labeled with the inscription that they had been cut by Lincoln some thirty years before, with the words: "Abraham Lincoln, the Rail Candidate for President in 1860." The effect on the audience was "electrical." [15] During the National Convention two rails had been exhibited in the office of Medill's Chicago *Press & Tribune*.[16] In a newspaper interview during the campaign Lincoln replied: "Yes, sir, here is a stick I received a day or two since from Josiah Crawford, of Gentryville, Indiana. He writes me that it is one of the rails that I cut for him in 1825." [17] A campaign newspaper, *The Rail Splitter*, was established at Chicago and became the Northwest's outstanding campaign sheet.[18]

The Republicans went heartily into the campaign. The plain, rather bare-looking parlor in the modest Springfield home, the customary little table in the center of the room, and on it the silver plated water pitcher, the Bible, and photographs—all these were noted and publicized.[19]

On May 26, Lincoln wrote his letter formally accepting the Republican presidential nomination: "The declaration of principles and sentiments which accompanies your letter meets my approval; and it shall be my care not to violate or disregard it in any part."

Beyond this Lincoln refused to make political statements for publication, although the subsequent pressure upon him to say or
write something was heavy. During the entire campaign he remained in Springfield, and established an office in the State House,
where he remained for several hours each day seeing callers.[20] On
one occasion he supposedly declared to a Democratic reporter that
he would like to go into Kentucky to discuss issues but was afraid
of being lynched—a statement which, magnified by his opponents,
brought him much embarrassment and convinced him that he should
be more discreet. He requested one Republican manager to publish
an anonymous correction of the "lynching" story which he himself
drafted.[21] Lincoln held no illusions about carrying any border slave
state. To one Missouri relative he wrote: "There is now a Republican electoral ticket in Missouri, so that you can vote for me if
your neighbors will let you. I would advise you not to get into
any trouble about it." [22]

Lincoln agreed with his managers that he should not commit
himself publicly. In June he disclaimed authorization of a certain
campaign biography, explaining: "But in my present position, when
by the lessons of the past, and the united voice of all discreet
friends, I am neither [to] write or speak a word for the public,
how dare I to send forth, by my authority, a volume of hundreds
of pages, for adversaries to make points upon without end—Were
I to do so, the Convention would have a right to re-assemble, and
substitute another name for mine." [23] Lincoln's letter of October 27,
1860, to one correspondent is significant: [24]

Mr. Dubois has shown me your letter of the 20th, and I promised
him to write you—What is it I could say which would quiet alarm?
Is it that no interference by the government, with the slaves and
slavery within the states, is intended? I have said this so often already, that a repetition of it is but mockery, bearing an appearance
of weakness, and cowardice, which perhaps should be avoided—
Why do not uneasy men *read* what I have already said and what
our *platform* says? If they will not read, or heed these, would they
read or heed, a repetition of them? Of course the declaration that
there is no intention to interfere with slaves or slavery, in the states,
with all that is implied in such declaration, is true; and I should
have no objection to make, and repeat the declaration a thousand
times, if there were no danger of encouraging bold bad men to
believe they are dealing with one who can be scared into anything.

I have some reason to believe the Sub-National Committee, at the Astor House, may be considering this question; and if their judgment should be different from mine, mine might be modified by theirs–

The "Sub-National Committee" mentioned by Lincoln, recruited from the regular Republican National Committee, had been chosen at the Chicago Convention to conduct the campaign. It included seven members with Governor Edwin D. Morgan, of New York, as chairman and George G. Fogg, of New Hampshire, as secretary. The committee opened headquarters at the Astor House, New York City. Upon Fogg, an able strategist, fell the bulk of the committee's work, which consisted of "providing, arranging with and meeting the expenses of speakers" in coöperation with the various state committees.[24]

The state committees, eager for victory, generally worked harmoniously with the "Sub-National Committee." Fogg kept in close touch with the strategy pursued in each state, occasionally leaving his work at the Astor House to visit distant regions where blunders were being made.[25] Appropriate speakers and literature were sent to the various localities. Seward was dispatched to New England and the Northwest to appeal to his thousands of radical followers.[26] Massachusetts' United States Senator Henry Wilson, the "Natick Cobbler," a former shoemaker's apprentice, was ordered on the stump to enlighten the working classes.[27] Wilson's colleague, Senator Charles Sumner, was brought to the metropolis to speak to the "Young Men's Republican Club."[28] Salmon P. Chase went into Michigan to persuade the erstwhile Free Soil Democrats that their hope lay in Lincoln.[29] Carl Schurz was engaged to tour the German-American communities.[30] William L. Dayton, conservative Republican of New Jersey, preached to the Whig-minded moderates of the East.[31] And Edward Bates, although declining to go on the hustings, continued to write letters for circulation in the Whig and "American" regions.[32]

Monster Republican rallies were sponsored throughout the North, although some leaders cautioned: "The farmer or mechanic who gives a day and spends a dollar attending a mass meeting might better save the day and spend the dollar in the best documents, to be quietly circulated among his neighbors."[33]

Opposing Lincoln in the contest for the White House was his old Illinois rival, Senator Stephen A. Douglas. From everywhere the

Little Giant had received appeals to run for president as a "national" Democrat to combat the Buchanan officeholders and save the Union alike from dissolution by southern Democratic hot-spurs and northern "Black" Republicans. For vice-presidential candidate, the Douglas Democrats had named Herschel V. Johnson, Union-minded former governor of Georgia.[34]

Following the Democratic split into Douglas and Buchanan factions, Douglas's supporters were faced with countless problems. The major task was to erect the machinery for effective organization. For National Chairman the Douglasites chose the New York financier August Belmont, who, it was hoped, could make funds flow. Since the Democratic party committees in the southern states were under the Buchanan men's control, the Illinois senator's supporters had to build up organizations in every cotton and border state. For weeks their energies were absorbed in overcoming legal obstacles, calling new conventions, organizing state committees and launching electoral tickets. The Buchanan administration, by virture of the federal patronage, controlled the Democratic machinery in a few northeastern states and in California and Oregon. Elsewhere in the North it was the Buchanan forces who had to build the new local organizations. Belmont began a drive for funds, personally contributing one thousand dollars; but he found the merchants and business men apathetic. In July, Douglas, persuaded that he had a chance to win, broke precedent and visited various localities.[35]

The Buchanan men had decided on Vice-President John C. Breckinridge as their presidential candidate. Breckinridge had been nominated by the majority faction of southern Democrats and a minority bloc of anti-Douglas northern Democrats. He had agreed to step aside if harmony were restored in the party, but when that proved fruitless he remained in the field, insisting that he, not Douglas, was the true "national" Democratic standard-bearer.[36] He declared that he "never did an act nor cherished a thought that was not full of devotion to the Constitution and the Union." [37] As Breckinridge's running-mate his supporters named the ubiquitous Joseph Lane, native North Carolinian, former Indiana politician, and then United States senator from Oregon.[38]

In late June the Breckinridge-Lane supporters met in Washington and formed a "National Democratic Committee," including such pro-southern leaders as Senator Jefferson Davis of Mississippi, such bitter personal enemies of Douglas as Senator Jesse D. Bright of Indiana, such intimate friends of Buchanan as the Washington banker, George W. Riggs, and such federal officeholders as Augustus Schell, collector of customs of the port of New York.[39] On the 28th the committee called at the White House, where they were received by Buchanan.[40] In early July Breckinridge's letter of acceptance was released to the press—a message in which he insisted that "the citizens of all the States may enter the Territories of the Union with their property of whatever kind." [41] The Breckinridge adherents opened their campaign with a monster demonstration in Washington on July 9th. They called on Buchanan, who declared himself in favor of the Breckinridge-Lane ticket.[42] This announcement was the signal for federal office-holders to work for Breckinridge. The President was urged to remove those employees favorable to Douglas, and this was done to some extent.[43] In August, Buchanan wrote: "I do not indulge a proscriptive spirit, and have not removed one in twenty of the Douglas office-holders. His father-in-law [Cutts] and his brother-in-law [Granger] are still in lucrative offices in this city, and I have no present intention of removing either. There are peculiar cases, however, which I cannot overlook." [44]

In addition to Lincoln, Breckinridge and Douglas, a fourth entry in the presidential race was sixty-three year old Whig-minded Senator John Bell, of Tennessee, who frowned upon all sectionalism. In May, Bell had been nominated as standard-bearer of the "Constitutional Union" Party, a body of elderly conservative Old Line Whigs and "Americans" who still hoped to strike a middle course and avert disunion. Edward Everett, of Massachusetts, was nominated as Bell's running mate. Throughout the campaign the Constitutional Unionists became known as "Bell Men" or "Bell Everetters." [45] Republicans accused them of being the Know-Nothing party transformed into the "do nothing party." [46]

Two other presidential candidates appeared in the field—the New York abolitionist Gerrit Smith on a strong anti-slavery and temperance platform; and Texas's famed Sam Houston, who agreed to run on a personal "Texas" Unionist ticket. Neither cut any figure nor took his candidacy seriously.[47]

As the campaign progressed seemingly every conceivable vote-getting technique was resorted to. The Republican "Wide-Awakes" were a spectacular feature. This semi-military organization had originated accidentally in Hartford, Connecticut, during the Spring gubernatorial campaign, when ardent young Republicans formed a group to escort the visiting Cassius M. Clay, of Kentucky, to the lecture hall. To protect their garments from the dripping oil of lamps which they carried, they wore caps and capes of glazed cloth. On the way home one was attacked by a sturdy Democrat, but a blow from a Republican torch stretched him on the ground and stopped further disturbance. Resolved to combat Democratic interference with their rallies, this Hartford group organized the original Wide-Awake club and settled on a standard uniform. Other such clubs sprang up. The idea "took." From all over the North came requests for information. Soon notices were inserted in Republican journals that all inquiries should be addressed to the Hartford Wide-Awakes.

The torch used by the estimated several hundred thousand Wide-Awakes comprised a rail surmounted with a tin swinging lamp; fastened on the rail was a small American flag, on which were the names of Lincoln and Hamlin. "Privates" carried the torches while officers had colored lanterns.[48] Merchants did a thriving business in paraphernalia, and advertised: *"Wide Awake Uniforms: Prices Reduced:* Cap, Cape and torch with flags will be furnished at the cost price of $1.15." [49] In Western regions the "Rail Splitters" appeared as auxiliaries. In some localities "Rail Maulers" was the name applied.[50]

Lincoln's rivals in the election also had squads. The "Bell Ringers," supporters of Bell and Everett, imitated the Wide Awake's style of organization; they wore a different colored uniform than their Republican rivals and carried torches and large varieties of bells. The "Bell-Everetters" were another branch of the Constitutional Union organization. Other Bell supporters were the "Union Sentinels" and the "Minute Men." The most numerous group among Douglas's supporters were the "Little Giants," also drilled by their captains and lieutenants; in some localities they became known as the "Little Dougs." In Brooklyn a Douglas group started called "the Chloroformers"—their sworn object being to "put the Wide Awakes to sleep." [51] Those fighting for Breckinridge and Lane worked under the banner of "National Democratic Volunteers"—a name consistent with their claim as the true "National" Democrats who would save the Union from the sectionalism of Douglas Democrats and Lincoln Republicans.[52]

Another colorful aspect of the contest were the various campaign sheets—pages of spicy reading portraying the party enemy as drunkards and blackguards. Cartoons, jokes, quips, puns, and ballads were utilized.[53]

Songs were especially used in the Northwest, one Michigan leader cautioning: "Let no one underestimate the value of good songs in a political campaign." [54] Poets and lyricists began writing madly. *Hutchinson's Republican Songster for 1860* made its appearance. Some songs were humorous as the "New Nursery Ballads" inscribed to the hated Douglas: [55]

> There was a little Senator
>   Who wasn't very wise,
> He jumped into conventi-on
>   And scratched out both his eyes:
> And when he found his eyes were out,
>   With all his might and main,
> He bolted off to Baltimore
>   To scratch them in again.

In other election songs patriotism and Lincoln were made synonymous, as in "Lincoln, the Pride of the Nation," sung to the tune of "The Red, White and Blue," [56] and "Honest Abe of the West" to the air of "The Star Spangled Banner." [57]

Even while Lincoln, Douglas, Breckinridge and Bell were being nominated, public sentiment was dividing sharply on issues and the candidates' personalities. There were radical sectionalists in North and South; Republicans of various degrees throughout the North enthusiastically for Lincoln; Breckinridge men in control of the South but having minority strength in the North; Douglasites holding the affections of most northern Democrats but having minority support below Mason and Dixon's Line; and Bell-Everett adherents in all sections with the border regions as their main bailiwick. Each was bitterly arrayed against the others.[58]

In Congress the Republicans became particularly busy in assailing their opponents. As Breckinridge's lieutenant, Jefferson Davis, made warfare upon Douglas in the Senate,[59] the Republicans opened fire on the Buchanan administration. Much of their ammunition was supplied by testimony given to the Covode Committee which investigated the administration's use of money and patronage in influencing the vote on the Lecompton constitution. The sweeping powers, granted the committee by a House of Representatives controlled by an anti-Buchanan fusion of Republicans and Douglas Democrats, included in their scope almost every branch of the federal government. Chairman Covode and his Republican colleagues unearthed much damaging testimony.[60]

The old Whig elements were particularly attracted by the Republicans' emphasis on the administration's "extravagance" and "corruption." For at least two years Republican platforms had denounced the Democrats on these points. In 1859 an Ohio leader had even urged his Republican associates in Congress to appropriate money freely, letting Buchanan bankrupt the Treasury: "Nothing will open the people's eyes wider in 1860 than the proclamation from the stump and the press that the old scamp has involved them in a debt of $200,000,000." [61] The Covode Committee's weighty report, exhibiting alleged corruption in several government departments and made available by the summer of 1860, was too bulky for campaign use; but an abridgment was distributed throughout the North. In August Senator Preston King of New York, chairman of the Republican Congressional Campaign Committee, reported that one printer was supplying them with 40,000 copies of the Covode Committee tract every day.[62]

Particularly vigilant in keeping the Covode testimony before the public was Horace Greeley's New York *Tribune*, the nation's most widely-circulated Republican newspaper.[63] In conformity with the national platform Greeley also agitated for the admission of Kansas as a free state, for a homestead bill, for a Pacific railroad appropriation, for a river-and-harbor bill and for a protective tariff—all in the face of Democratic opposition.[64] Other Republican organs followed suit. Declared one Northwestern party organ: [65]

Congress has adjourned. The following popular measures were defeated by the action of the Democratic party:
1. The bill for the admission of Kansas.
2. The Free Homestead Bill.
3. The Pacific Railroad Bill.
4. The River and Harbor Improvement Bill.
5. The Tariff Bill.
The Senate is now in executive session.

Before adjournment of Congress in June, of all these measures only one—a homestead bill in emasculated form—was approved by a Democratic-dominated Senate and acquiesced in by a Republican-anti-administration-controlled House of Representatives. This bill did not give free land but set the cost at the nominal price of twenty-five cents per acre with the preëmptor having two years to pay.[66] Buchanan played directly into the Republicans' hands by vetoing the bill.[67] All this gave Greeley, a pioneer "free land" agitator, much ammunition against the administration and the Democratic party. In the *Tribune* he charged: [68]

Veto of the Homestead Bill

The bill which he [President Buchanan] vetoed on Saturday was not the Republican or House Free Homestead bill, but that of the Senate, which nearly every Republican voted against on its first passage and only acquiesced in at the last moment, in deference to the tens of thousands in Iowa, Minnesota, Kansas etc., who are liable to be ejected from their rude homes at any moment, because, in the pecuniary condition of the Northwest, it is morally impossible that they should pay $1¼ per acre for the quarter-section each [the prevailing price of land] which is or contains their all. . . . Does anybody suppose that Abraham Lincoln would ever veto such a bill?

Greeley was indeed touching the popular heart in the Northwest, which had not yet fully recovered from the baneful effects of the panic of 1857. Thousands of pioneers had no money with which to pay for the land which they had bought under the then existing Preëmption Law; some blamed the "preëmption" land system for "hard times." [69] As if to make matters worse, Buchanan, by proclamation, had opened the lands to public sale. Immediately the cry was set up that the administration was deliberately trying to injure the Northwest.[70] Greeley was influential in the region; in Minnesota his weekly edition had a larger circulation than any local sheet. He continued to emphasize that persistent opposition by the Democratic President and a majority of the Democrats to a free homestead law and the erratic policy pursued by the administration relative to land sales proved that their salvation lay in the Republican party, which "saves them from the spoliation of their homes." [71]

Homestead was, indeed, a vote-luring issue for Lincoln and the Republicans.

CHAPTER ELEVEN
The Safe States

THE LAND QUESTION completely overshadowed the slavery question in Minnesota. "People had gone there to make homes, not to fight the Southern tiger," [1] commented a St. Cloud abolitionist. In 1859 Republicans and Democrats had adopted homestead planks, but the administration's attitude placed the Democrats at distinct disadvantage. [2] The Minnesota Republicans had wanted Seward for President, but they accepted Lincoln. [3] The St. Paul Republican organ exhorted: "Let us marshal our forces and when we strike, let it be for a gallant champion of Freedom, for Free Land, Free Men, and a Glorious Cause." [4] The path was made easier for the Republicans because the Buchanan forces were using the federal patronage to combat Douglas. The Republicans, controlling the state government, had Governor Alexander Ramsey's officeholders working for Lincoln. [5] The Republicans also brought Seward into the state to make a speech from the State Capitol in St. Paul. [6] By election day the campaigns for Douglas and for Breckinridge had bogged down. John Bell was nowhere. Governor Ramsey, jubilant, declared that it was unnecessary for Republicans to make more speeches. [7] The Democratic split, plus Buchanan's policy of ordering public-land sales during a period of depression, assured the Gopher State for the Republicans. A student of ante-bellum Minnesota politics has concluded: "Whatever the causes elsewhere in the United States for the great political upheaval of 1860 and the election of Abraham Lincoln, the first Republican president, the decision in Minnesota turned upon distinctly local and western issues relating directly to the federal land policy, rather than upon such matters as Negro slavery." [8]

Minnesota's neighbor, Iowa, was another state where homestead was a live issue and where the New York *Tribune* wielded tremendous influence. [9] Although Iowa contained many ex-southerners,[10] James W. Grimes had been elected the state's first Republican governor in 1854 by fusing Native American groups, who were anti-slavery and wanted prohibition, with the German elements, who were free-land advocates.[11] The Iowa Republicans continued to strengthen their organization, largely by virtue of the Democratic split. In 1859 the Republicans elected Samuel J. Kirkwood governor on an anti-slavery and homestead platform.[12] Kirkwood summed up the vital issues:[13]

The passage by Congress of the measure commonly known as Homestead Bill, would, in my opinion, be productive of much good. . . . The building of a Railroad to the Pacific Ocean is a measure which, in my opinion, is demanded by the best interests in our whole country.

Following Lincoln's nomination, the homestead issue continued to occupy public attention, one Iowan even charging that the administration's land policy was "the primary cause of the great commercial depression that now sits like a nightmare on the pulseless cities and idle fields of the Northwest." [14] The Democratic rupture widened, the Douglasites attacking Buchanan for his veto of the homestead bill. Commented the vitriolic pro-Douglas Dubuque *Herald:* "The Slave Propagandists demanded that the Bill should be vetoed, and the pliant tool was swift to obey them. Let the pimps and hirelings of the old sinner defend this last act of his, if they dare." [15]

Although the Republicans were certain of carrying Iowa for Lincoln, they sent a galaxy of oratorical stars on the stump. Editors left their desks for the platform and scores of minor speakers were enlisted. In September Seward visited Dubuque and pleaded earnestly for Republican victory. Douglas came into the state and found all hope lost.[16]

Adjoining Iowa was the pioneer Republican citadel of Wisconsin. Here, too, the homestead issue was of primary interest. For several years the German population in Wisconsin had been agitating for free land.[17] The state Republican platform called for a homestead law,[18] and Carl Schurz, upon returning home from the Chicago convention, emphasized to his fellow Teutons that they had secured their demands—free land and protection of the rights of naturalized citizens.[19]

Lincoln's nomination was quite acceptable to Wisconsin, al-

though the state was grieved at Seward's defeat.[20] Lincoln sent
soothing words to Schurz: [21]

> I beg you to be assured that your having supported Governor
> Seward, in preference to myself, in the Convention, is not even
> remembered by me for any practical purpose, or the slightest un-
> pleasant feeling. I go not back of the Convention to make distinc-
> tions among its members; and, to the extent of our limited ac-
> quaintance, no man stands nearer my heart than yourself.

Other ardent Wisconsin Sewardites besides Schurz quickly came
out for Lincoln, including Seward's close friend Rufus King, who
placed his Milwaukee *Sentinel* behind the Republican national
ticket.[22] By 1860 the Badger State was well supplied with Republican
newspapers.[23] Often two Republican orators spoke simultaneously
from a huge platform, one in English, the other in German.[24]

Bordering on Wisconsin was another pioneer Republican strong-
hold—Michigan. As elsewhere in the Northwest, the Republicans
there strained every nerve to prove that they were the "free land"
party.[25]

The Democratic party in Michigan had been badly torn by the
Buchanan-Douglas feud. By 1860 the Democratic division became
so wide that the Republicans went into the campaign with little
over which to worry.[26] In Detroit one Douglas leader had already
reported to his chief: "You cannot carry Michigan, but you are
the only man that can make any show." [27] Michigan Republicans
had been for Seward but, when Lincoln emerged the victor, they
quickly supported him. Lincoln, after all, spoke the language of
the frontier. "Lincoln and Hamlin" became the war-cry of the
widely read Detroit *Tribune*, which exhorted the party faithful:
"Republicans of Michigan! Do your duty!" [28] At Ann Arbor early
student demonstrations for Lincoln disturbed slumbering profes-
sors.[29] On June 7 the Republicans nominated the popular Austin
Blair for governor. Seward's friend, Christopher Morgan, traveled
from Auburn, New York, to Detroit to bestow the Sewardites'
benediction on "Old Abe." [30] The state platform condemned the
Buchanan administration for not favoring appropriations for rivers
and harbors, and called for a Pacific railroad.[31]

Austin Blair proved to be a tireless campaigner, stressing state
economy. Senator Zachariah Chandler, who accompanied him, fired
away at Douglas.[32] The Democrats were handicapped because they

had no one to frank documents, since Michigan's delegation in Congress consisted entirely of Republicans.[33] The Democrats attempted to label Lincoln as an abolitionist—all of which did not take so well in radical Michigan.[34] Then they attacked the Republicans for having recruited a bogus "Texas" delegation to the Chicago convention.[35] The Republicans protested that they did not know at the time that the "Texans" came from Michigan.[36] The Republicans used the Covode Committee disclosures to substantiate their charge that no Democrat could be trusted to head the federal government.[37] Salmon P. Chase went into Michigan to speak for Lincoln. The greatest Republican meeting, however, was held by the "Wide-Awakes" in September, when Seward spoke at Detroit. The New York senator was given a similar reception at Lansing and Kalamazoo. In October Douglas followed Seward into Michigan, but his was a lost cause. Lincoln was carrying all before him in Michigan.[38]

The selection of Chase, McLean or Wade might well have left party wounds unhealed in Ohio. Lincoln, a former Whig and not an ultra, satisfied McLean's conservative followers, while at the same time Chase's radical supporters preferred him to Chase's traditional rival, Seward. Chase had campaigned for Lincoln in the Illinois senatorial contest against Douglas in 1858. Lincoln, following his nomination, made sure, through mutual friends, to inform the Ohio governor of his high regard for him. On May 26 he wrote Chase: "Holding myself the humblest of all whose names were before the convention, I feel in especial need of the assistance of all; and I am glad—very glad—of the indication that you stand ready." [39] Chase blamed Wade, rather than Lincoln, for his defeat at Chicago. Ohio rank-and-file Republicans, with frontier love of rustic simplicity, were satisfied with Lincoln. His speeches in Ohio during the campaign of 1859 had gained admirers. The Republican state convention heartily endorsed the national nominees and platforms while nominating Jacob Brinkerhoff for State Supreme Court Justice. With a united state party behind him, Lincoln enjoyed the support of 126 Ohio newspapers, whereas Douglas had the backing of 80.[40]

The campaign in Ohio resolved itself into a struggle between the Douglas Democrats and the Republicans. The Douglasites upheld the principle of non-intervention in the territories and attacked the Republicans and Breckinridge groups as interventionists. The Republicans favored confining slavery to the states where it existed.[41] The Republican *State Journal* of Columbus insisted that Lincoln's election "will effectually and forever silence this nauseating disunion twaddle." [42] The Ohio Republicans presented their candidates as moderates. The veteran Thomas Ewing, "the Last of the Whigs," was persuaded to make a speech for Lincoln at Chillicothe; his address made an effective appeal to elect Lincoln "the Whig." Ewing emphasized that time-honored Whig doctrine, the tariff.[43a] The tariff played a part in the iron and coal regions in the southern counties that bordered on the slaveholding region.[43b]

The October election was proof that Republicanism was supreme in Ohio. Brinkerhoff was elected supreme court justice over an opponent supported by both the Douglas and Breckinridge wings of the Democracy. Thirteen Republicans and eight Democrats were elected to Congress.[44] Attempts by the Douglas men to form a conservative Unionist alliance with the Bell men were to prove abortive, primarily because in an era of strong past party loyalties Democrats and Whigs could not agree.[45] However, even if the Douglas and Bell factions had been able to effect a basis of union, the popular vote polled indicates that Lincoln would still have carried the rock-ribbed Republican Buckeye State.[46]

Of only less importance than Ohio was Lincoln's own Illinois. Here also the homestead issue was of vital concern. The Republicans charged that Douglas and all Democrats were holding up passage of homestead in the Senate.[47] Owen Lovejoy, Illinois Republican congressman, had been the most militant of agitators for free land. Illinois had been incensed when Buchanan vetoed the emasculated homestead bill in June. The Republicans made the most of it; of ten Republican county conventions in 1860 whose records have been preserved, seven demanded free land.[48] The personality of Lincoln, however, seemed to overshadow all.[49]

The night of Lincoln's nomination was one the like of which had never been seen in Illinois. Cannon boomed, tar barrels were set afire and semi-hysterical men marched along carrying rails. "The cry is already 'Rails, Rails, Rails,'" wrote one observer. And Lincoln's son Robert was dubbed the "Prince of Rails." [50] Springfield did a brisk trade in wooden souvenirs made from the "identical Rails" split by the Republican standard-bearer; the city's streets "resemble a Hindoo Bazaar." [51] For years the Northwest had been demanding the presidency. The Northwest had not been represented in the White House since William Henry Harrison's brief tenure of one month in 1841. Lewis Cass of Michigan and Douglas had seemed within sight of it, but had failed. Now Lincoln was nominated, with an excellent chance of election. Republicans vied with each other in praise of their candidate's homely virtues.[52]

There were delicate situations to be faced. The Illinois of 1860 was composed of at least two distinct political communities—the upper part settled largely by people from other northern states and by immigrants, chiefly Germans and Irish; the lower counties were inhabited primarily by people originally from the slave states.[53] Lincoln's state was thus a smaller prototype of the nation as a whole. The Republican strategists conducted their campaign accordingly, one of them advising: "I believe the most effective Document for all the region North of Rock River will be Lovejoy's last speech—then for the whole state prepare a Document composed of choice selections from Lincoln's. . . . I think Jeff Davis' last speeches would be good to distribute down in Egypt—vs Douglas Democracy."[54]

The Republicans made determined efforts to win back the conservative anti-Democratic vote which had turned from them in 1858. Their national platform of 1860 could be used to attract this element more satisfactorily than that of 1858. Several new planks had been inserted in the 1860 document. Consequently, it was not surprising that the Republicans stressed economic issues to win the votes of those Illinoisans who were not rabidly anti-slavery.[55] At one grand rally in Springfield, twenty-seven inscribed banners were carried in the procession, only two of which referred to slavery. Among the inscriptions were: "River and Harbor Improvements," "A Pacific Railroad," "Liberty of Speech and Press," "Protection to American Labor," "Protection to Home Industry," "Free Homes for the Homeless" and "Abraham Lincoln, the Friend of Henry Clay."[56]

In efforts to attract the conservative vote, especially the Old Line Whigs, both Republicans and Douglas Democrats conjured much with Henry Clay's name. Douglas deplored the fact that the compromising Whig party of Harry of the West had been succeeded by a purely sectional party of bitter hatreds; naturally Douglas did not allude to his own action of 1854 in repealing Clay's Missouri Compromise which had brought forth the issue on which the Republicans originated. In reply, the Republican *Illinois State Journal* of Springfield published Lincoln's memorial oration on Clay and an alleged statement by Douglas that Clay was "an old black hearted traitor." But the old-line Whigs wanted no part of Douglas or any other Democrat, and those who did not go for Bell were soon flocking to their old partner Lincoln. After all, Lincoln was a former Whig.[57]

The Democrats continued to emphasize to Union-loving Whig bitter-enders that the Republicans were a sectional party who would cause disunion; but their arguments lost their force when the Charleston and Baltimore conventions indicated that Douglas would be as unpalatable to the South as Lincoln. And Lincoln continued his silence during the campaign.[58] Soon Lincoln's law-partner Herndon commented: "We are fast gaining ground out West: the 'old line Whigs' are fast coming out for us—are going almost unanimously and wildly for Lincoln." [59]

Still keeping an office in the State House, Lincoln received callers there, told stories to people, talked over the conduct of the campaign with the party leaders, and kept up his correspondence. But nothing escaped him on the issues of the day. On August 8 he attended a Republican rally at the State Fair. The crowd spied him immediately. He was hauled from his carriage, raised upon the shoulders of the people, and landed safely upon a speaker's stand. Cheers continued and a demand was made that he speak. Addressing the audience, Lincoln declared his intentions of making no speech; he had appeared only to see his fellow-citizens and allow them to see him. He had not anticipated such an enthusiastic reception. He begged to be allowed to remain silent and requested the audience to listen to other speakers. Descending from the platform, he was surrounded by a dense mass who hailed him with "Give us your hand, Old Abe!" [60] He escaped on horseback from the pressing crowd.[61]

Lincoln took occasion to deny in writing to his Jewish friend of Quincy, Abraham Jonas, that he had ever been in a Know-Nothing lodge, as charged by Democrats.[62] He also denied authorship of a letter, which, the Democrats charged, spoke of Thomas Jefferson in derogatory terms. It was "a base forgery," he declared, adding: "I never said anything like it, at any time or place. . . . I wish my name not to be used; but my friends will be entirely safe in denouncing the thing as a forgery, so far as it is ascribed to me." [63] In October Lincoln assured Secretary Fogg of the Republican National Sub-Committee: "Allow me to beg you will not live in much apprehension of my precipitating a letter upon the public." [64]

All the while Lincoln helped to map strategy. On one occasion he wrote: "What you say about the Northern 30 counties of Illinois pleases me—Keep good your promise that they will give as much majority as they did for Fremont, and we will let you off." [65] To an old Whig friend he directed: "The *time* we must fix according to your own suggestion; and the *places*, I wish to have a hand in fixing myself—My judgment is to have you in the old Whig region—I shall consult with Judd, have the appointments made, and you duly notified. *We really want you.*" [66]

On July 25, the Democrats of Springfield staged a parade. They claimed that Lincoln watched the procession from the State House dome. The Republicans denied this and for weeks a meaningless press controversy ensued between the Lincolnites and Douglasites as to the exact "spot" from which he viewed the Democratic procession. [67]

In October Seward, on his northwestern tour, stopped at Springfield. Lincoln met him at the station—and crowds cheered both. [68] That Seward was unreservedly supporting Lincoln was shown when the New York senator's friend, the banker-lawyer Richard M. Blatchford, sent $3,000 to Illinois. [69]

Republicans and Democrats contended for the huge foreign-born vote of Illinois. The Democrats had some claim to the German vote, since so many Know-Nothings had gone into the Republican ranks; moreover, Douglas had bitterly assailed the nativists and stood as the champion of the naturalized citizens. [70] But the Germans had won their fight in the Chicago convention for homestead and anti-alien planks. George Schneider's Chicago *Staats-Zeitung* and the *Belleviller Zeitung* were powerful influences. German campaigners were kept in the field; among the most effective were former Lieutenant-Governor Gustave Koerner, Frederick Hassaurek of Ohio, the ubiquitous Carl Schurz of Wisconsin, and Theodore Hielscher of Indiana. [71] In July Schurz arrived in Springfield to be Lincoln's guest. Both were escorted by American and German Wide-Awakes to the State House, where Schurz spoke. [72] A study of the election returns in Illinois and the federal census indicates that Lincoln received the bulk of the German vote in his own state. [73]

The Republicans soon despaired of attracting the Irish. The religious issue was injected into the campaign when the Chicago *Press & Tribune* asserted that Douglas's chief strength lay in his Roman

Catholic support. Douglas had married a Catholic, Adele Cutts, and his children were brought up in that faith; the Republicans alleged that the Little Giant had become converted to Catholicism.[74] The Irish stood loyally by Douglas.[75]

Throughout the Illinois canvass huge carnival-like meetings and barbecues were held. One account reads: [76]

> The [Republican] procession was formed . . . The Springfield Turner band led off, followed by some three hundred ladies and gentlemen on horseback; then came seventy-five or eighty wagons loaded with old and young of both sexes, each carrying some banner or flag on which "Old Abe" could be seen; again came some fifty or sixty horsemen, followed in turn by a decorated wagon in which were thirty-three young girls, all dressed in white, with pink and blue sashes, bearing flags on which were inscribed the names of each separate State of the Union, and they were followed in turn by thirty-three small boys on horses, bearing like flags; then came a section of "Old Abe's" fence with the stakes set . . . The Bloomington Republican Club, carrying a banner on which "Old Abe" is represented as making rails some thirty years ago.

In Illinois the Republicans had the advantage. Their campaign was well under way before Douglas's nomination was accomplished. The Douglas leaders waged a spiritless campaign while their candidate bounded about the country. The personality of Lincoln was enough to tip the scales in his favor over the old hero Douglas.[77]

In capturing the Northwest homestead proved to be an indispensable issue for the Republicans. Owen Lovejoy maintained that if free land had not been pledged, "the Republicans never could have elected their President." [78] "Free land" was of distinct advantage in attracting the German vote to Lincoln.

In the Northwest, aptly described as "not a melting pot . . . but rather a mixing bowl," [79] the foreign-born constituted about one-fifth of the population of 1860.[80] Since the Irish were perennially Democratic and the Scandinavians numbered but less than two per cent of the nation's foreign-born,[81] it was on the Germans that the Republicans concentrated their efforts. Koerner had assumed charge of compiling lists of German voters,[82] for, as one leader declared: "Without the German vote we lose the North West." [83] At the Chicago convention the Republicans had made a bid to the Germans by declaring for homestead and against any change in the existing naturalization laws. The Republicans made extensive use of

German translations of the proposed homestead bill. Speeches of Republican Congressmen were circulated in pamphlet form, among them "Frei Heimath für Frei Männer" and "Land für Landlose." [84] Soon sixty-nine of eighty-one German-language newspapers were supporting Lincoln; only nine of these had been behind Frémont in 1856.[85]

Probably Lincoln received the votes of most naturalized Germans and because of this was victorious in the Northwest and consequently in the nation—such, at least, is the finding of Professor Arthur C. Cole,[86] Professor Donnal V. Smith,[87] the late Professor William E. Dodd,[88] and Dr. Ernest Bruncken.[89] The late Dr. Joseph Schafer questioned these conclusions, contending that most Germans in Wisconsin, particularly among the Roman Catholics, voted for Douglas.[90] Later the New York *Herald* stated: "In Ohio, Illinois, Indiana, Iowa and Wisconsin, native Republicans now openly acknowledge that their victory was, if not wholly, at least to a great extent, due to the large accessions they received in the most hotly contested sections from the German ranks." [91] The Germans always contended that Lincoln received most of their votes. The Cincinnati leader, F. Oberkline, greeted Lincoln as President-elect: "You earned our votes as the champion of free labor and homesteads," and Lincoln replied: "In regard to the Homestead Law, I have to say that in so far as the Government lands can be disposed of, I am in favor of cutting up the wild lands into parcels, so that every poor man may have a home." [92]

Besides homestead and the slavery question, other issues aided in turning the Northwest to Lincoln.

In the depression-born resentment against wealth and the wealthy stemming from the panic of 1857, the slaveholder became a symbol of the overbearing aristocrat. The money shortage further tended to make men critical of government expenditures, the national deficits being viewed as the result of executive extravagance and debauchery. Economic collapse gave new significance to old issues and sharpened western resentment against southern and Democratic policies.

In the Buchanan administration's policy on slavery extension— implying augmented slaveholder power and competition in Kansas —there was ample evidence with which Republicans could demonstrate the South's intent to dominate free men. One scholar has well concluded: "The Northwesterner fought for freedom in Kansas for the simple reason that if he did not the hated power of slavery would gain ascendancy in the Federal Government and thus control the legislation and policy of the West." [93] Senator Trumbull of Illinois viewed the contest as one "between the contending principles of Democracy and Aristocracy." [94] And at Dubuque, Seward also emphasized this eternal conflict between the southern aristocrat and the northwestern democrat: [95]

The controversy is not with the negro at all, but with two classes of white men, one who have a monopoly of negroes, and the other who have no negroes. One is an aristocratic class, that wants to extend itself over the new territories and so retain the power it already exercises; and the other is yourselves, my good friends, men who have no negroes and won't have any, and who mean that the aristocratic system shall not be extended. There is no negro question about it at all. It is an eternal question between classes—between the few privileged and the many unprivileged—the eternal question between aristocracy and democracy.

Insistence upon the Republicans as the "White Man's Party" appears repeatedly in the northwestern press. [96]

The Northwest was also attracted to Republicanism by the Pacific railroad issue. Many looked to the day when the Democratic party would be ousted from national power and be replaced by a group who could command a majority in Congress favorable to a transcontinental railroad along the northern route.[97]

Internal improvements, although a lesser factor than in earlier Whig days, were still somewhat important in the Northwest in 1860. The railroads were carrying more and more of the freight— but the bulk of grain continued to be exported by water through at least a part of the transfer. To requests for federal appropriations to improve river and Great Lakes transportation the national Democratic party continued to turn a deaf ear. Thousands of northwesterners believed that only through a change at Washington could assistance be secured. When early in 1860 Buchanan pocket-vetoed an appropriation for improving navigation on the St. Clair River, the Republican journals insisted that this was "but one of a series of acts of injustice" which necessitated a change in the White House.[98]

The overland-mail issue also figured in the campaign to some extent. The main Republican contention was that Buchanan's "pro-slavery" administration, in linking the Mississippi River with the

Pacific by mail, was discriminating against northern and central routes in favor of southern ones.[99]

The tariff figured as an issue in northwestern regions. Greeley strove valiantly to show how the Northwest's interests were tied to the industrial East, even circulating a *Tribune* tract entitled *American Agriculture and Its Interest in the Protective Policy*.[100]

Western Republicans' acceptance of the tariff plank in the Chicago platform was based partly on staunch old Whiggery. Moreover, there were interests which had suffered under the tariff of 1857, such as the iron groups in Ohio and those in the lead districts of Wisconsin. There were regions in the upper Mississippi Valley where, in a period of depression, the tariff was looked to for the stimulus of manufactures. In addition, there was a widespread disposition to accept the tariff as a dose which must be swallowed to obtain the reward of homestead legislation. There was also the protectionists' allegation that the federal treasury, following the panic of 1857, was in need. Most of all, there was the belief, steadily urged upon all loyal Republicans everywhere, that Pennsylvania could be won, and with it the presidency, by a gesture toward upward tariff revision.[101]

Some eastern Republicans, like those in the Northwest, acquiesced in the tariff plank of the Chicago convention primarily because Pennsylvania demanded it. New England woolen manufacturers were quite satisfied with existing tariff rates since it provided them with low duties on incoming raw wool from abroad.[102] A New England delegate to the Chicago convention even spoke of the Pennsylvanians: "Dam[n] their iron and coal." [103]

With Massachusetts woolen-manufacturing interests apathetic toward a higher tariff, the party strategists sought to persuade them that the Morrill bill, passed by a Republican-controlled House of Representatives and awaiting action by the Senate, was beneficial to Bay State interests.[104] Action on the Morrill measure having meanwhile been blocked by a Democratic-dominated Senate, the Republicans maintained that this was a blow at the interests of the New England laboring man.[105]

Regardless of the popularity or unpopularity of the Morrill tariff bill, the result in Massachusetts was never in doubt.

The Bay State Republican organization—a fusion of erstwhile "Conscience" Whigs, radical Jeffersonian Democrats, anti-liquor reformers, anti-Irish Know-Nothings and assorted anti-slavery groups

—was full of the vitality that came with lusty growth. By 1860 no opposition party was formidable enough to challenge its supremacy. For years the Democratic party had been sterile, comprising only a small minority; as one critic observed: "Their leaders have always acted on the principle of keeping the party in Massachusetts 'conveniently small' . . . in order to have fewer competitors for the federal offices." [106] The old-line Whig element was likewise negligible in numbers. Their chief organ, the Boston *Courier*, was in financial difficulties.[107] The remnants of Whigs had persuaded Edward Everett to accept the vice-presidential nomination on the Constitutional Union ticket, and he had done so reluctantly; James Russell Lowell commented: "Mr. Everett in his letter accepting the nomination gave only a string of reasons why he should not have accepted it at all." [108] The Bell-Everett ticket was "universally respectable," the Republicans conceded, but it is "worthy to be printed on gilt-edged satin paper, laid away in a box of musk, and kept there. . . . It is the party of no idea and no purpose." [109] One Boston observer related the Constitutional Unionists' feeble electioneering efforts: [110]

I heard a great ding-donging. . . . A vehicle drawn by several horses and containing an immense *bell*, the rope of which a stout man was vigorously pulling and from which the clapper-trap was proceeding. "Oh, Bell and Everett!" said I; "meeting at Roxbury tonight." People . . . wagged their heads, rolled their eyes, shifted their quids from one side to the other, chuckled or sneered, and passed on. It was too bad to laugh at it. A more orderly and respectful funeral procession I have never seen, though the mourners were few.

Since Lincoln was conceded by all to carry Massachusetts, major interest centered in the candidacy of John A. Andrew for Governor. Neither Lincoln nor Andrew had anything to worry about in Massachusetts.[111]

The situation in Connecticut was similar to that in Massachusetts insofar as the Republicans had a comfortable majority. The weakness of the two Democratic groups and of the Constitutional Unionists was such that by late July the Republican United States Senator, James Dixon, declared at a Wide Awake rally in Hartford: "The success of the Republican cause seems now so certain that we may almost consider the election of Lincoln and Hamlin decided and begin to prepare for their inauguration." [112] Lincoln was destined to receive from Connecticut a most impressive majority. [113]

Adjacent to Connecticut was Rhode Island, where the Republicans opened their campaign on June 19 with a giant ratification meeting. A delegate to the Chicago convention, Benjamin T. Eames, eulogized Lincoln and Hamlin for their "sterling integrity, distinguished ability and lofty patriotism." [114] The Democrats never imperiled Lincoln's chances in Rhode Island. [115]

Lincoln proved a popular candidate in the other New England states.

Directing the Republican campaign in Maine, Hamlin's home, was James G. Blaine in his capacity of chairman of the Republican State Committee. Blaine had gone to the Chicago convention, had added his voice to Lincoln's supporters and had visited the standard-bearer in Springfield following his selection. "I think the nomination the very best that could have been made in every way," Blaine wrote from Springfield, "and I have no more doubt of the election of the ticket than I have Maine will be carried by the Republicans." [116] Blaine proved a good prophet. [117]

The Republicans encountered even less trouble in Vermont than in Maine. The abolitionist Gerrit Smith said: "Vermont is acknowledged to be the most anti-slavery of all the states." [118] In the 1840's the Liberty party had carried on a vigorous campaign and found a ready response because, writes one New England scholar: [119]

Vermont had practically no commercial dealings with the South. There were no shipping interests involved in the slave trade. Vermont had almost no social intercourse with Southern people. . . .
Vermont . . . was probably somewhat more individualistic than the older New England states. . . .
The Liberty Party planted the seed in fertile soil, and cultivated it with painstaking care; then the Republican Party stepped in to harvest the record-breaking crop.

Another reason why the Green Mountain State was so strongly Republican was the fact that Jacksonian Democracy had never secured a foothold there. She had been ardently Whig, devoted to Clay's American System; especially the protective tariff which would protect her wool-growing industry. [120] Vermont's own Representative Justin S. Morrill, who introduced the high tariff in

1860, declared: "My constituents . . . are more largely engaged in the wool-growing business than in any other one pursuit which can be affected by the tariff." [121]

Lincoln's nomination was acceptable to Vermont Republicans who preferred him since he was a former Whig. As if to make the state more top-heavily Republican, the Democratic minority was split between Douglasites and Breckinridgers. The Vermont result proved to be even more impressively Republican than anticipated. Lincoln carried every county by huge majorities. He polled almost 34,000 votes to Douglas's 8,649. Breckinridge received only 1,866 and Bell trailed with a mere 217.[122]

It was much the same story in Vermont's neighbor, New Hampshire. The Republicans had nothing to fear. As early as 1856 the Granite State had wiped out most of the Democratic strength.[123]

By the end of July, Horace Greeley analyzed the political scene. In Vermont and Massachusetts "all the factions opposed to the Republican party cannot, whether separately or combined, pull forty per cent of the whole vote." Maine, New Hampshire, Rhode Island, Connecticut, Ohio, Michigan, Wisconsin, Minnesota, and Iowa were each "sure for Lincoln by a larger majority than it has ever yet given." Illinois, while close, "will give Lincoln from Five to Ten Thousand majority, in spite of the most desperate exertions of the Douglas men." But—Greeley warned the party faithful —"Indiana is the most evenly contested of any of the Free States." He despaired of California; [124] indeed, the Breckinridgers were claiming both California and Oregon.[125] He was more hopeful of New Jersey and Pennsylvania. And then there was New York, with thirty-five electoral votes. The *Tribune* editor thought the Empire State would roll up a Lincoln majority but cautioned Republicans to be alert to any upsurge of Democratic strength there.[126]

So far the progress of the campaign had justified Greeley's observation following Lincoln's nomination: "New England stands like a rock, and the Northwest is all ablaze." [127] But there loomed uncertainties in California, Oregon, New Jersey and in the pivotal states of Indiana, Pennsylvania, and New York.

CHAPTER TWELVE

The Doubtful States

GREELEY HAD LISTED California as one of the "most doubtful" states.[1] Few Californians were indeed interested in anti-slavery. Republicans were enabled to grow only because the Democrats had been torn asunder by Senator Broderick's feud with his colleague, Senator Gwin, over federal patronage and the Lecompton constitution. When Broderick had fallen in a duel with a native Southerner, Lincoln's old Illinois friend, Edwin D. Baker, had seized on the tragic occasion to bolster the Republicans' claim that the Buchanan administration, which Broderick had opposed, was controlled by blood-thirsty slaveocrats. Broderick's death, added to agitation for a Pacific railroad, strengthened California Republicanism.[2] In their state platform California Republicans acclaimed "Abraham Lincoln of the great West."[3] They did not even mention slavery but merely invited "all the opponents of the present corrupt administration to join with us in hurling it from power."[4]

Although the California Republicans had lost their most effective orator when Baker had been enticed away to Oregon, they were aided by the circumstance that the Buchanan administration, as elsewhere, was working quite as hard against Douglas as against Lincoln.[5] The pro-Douglas Governor John G. Downey complained: "We have all the federal patronage working against us."[6] The Bell-Everett forces were only a negligible factor.[7]

The Democratic split and the Pacific railroad and daily overland mail issues convinced the Republicans that they had a chance to carry California. Baker was invited down from Oregon to take the stump, and on October 26 he spoke at San Francisco. Thousands poured into the city to hear the silver-tongued spell-binder appeal for Lincoln's election, and his speech was acclaimed as "the most eloquent that had ever been heard in California."[8] Baker emphasized that the Democrats had retarded construction of the Pacific railroad; that the Republican national platform pledged government funds to build a transcontinental "iron horse." [9] Then Baker again invoked the memory of the lamented Broderick.[10]

When the votes were counted in November, it was found that Lincoln had carried California by a mere plurality of 657 votes over Douglas. Breckinridge polled almost as many popular votes as Douglas. Bell's showing was slight.[11] "The Electoral vote of California is secured for *Lincoln and Hamlin*," a Republican county chairman reported gleefully. "Many of our own Friends in our confidential conferences were positive it could not be accomplished." [12] A pioneer California historian explained Lincoln's triumph: [13]

It was the result, so far as Breckinridge was concerned, of the killing of Broderick by Terry. It was the consequence, so far as Douglas was concerned, of the impression upon the anti-Lecompton mind in California that Douglas had been untrue to Broderick. It was the use made by the Republicans of the action of the California [Democratic] senators in dragging the state into the quarrel between the North and South, against which the whole population, except the Lecomptonites, had always protested, and of the fact of their having grossly neglected the welfare of their state.

The situation in Oregon was similar to that in California—a divided Democratic party, a state-conscious population not too concerned with the anti-slavery movement, and the personality of Edward D. Baker.

Oregon Republicans had pleaded with Baker to locate in their state, and he had done so. Baker arrived in Salem in January, 1860, and mapped Republican strategy. He was aided by the fact that Republicans held the balance of power between Douglas and Buchanan Democrats. In the state assembly were 19 "Buchaneers," 18 Douglasites—and 13 Republicans. Baker maneuvered his party into coöperation with the Douglasites.[14]

By summer of 1860 the Douglas faction was in the ascendancy, though Breckinridge's running-mate was Oregon's own Senator Joseph Lane. The Breckinridge men waged a vigorous campaign, one Douglas leader reporting to the Little Giant: [15]

In Oregon an active effort is already inaugurated by the Breckinridge-Lane office holders and lackeys to carry the State for Breckinridge and Lane. The whole patronage of the federal government distributed here will be prostituted to that end. For the past year the State has been flooded with Documents by Lane and Stout [Congressman Lansing Stout] assailing you.

With the Douglasites showing unexpected strength, the Republican strategy now was to join the Breckinridge-Lane forces in the fight against Douglas. The Portland *Advertiser* observed that Republicans were shouting "Hurrah for Joe Lane"; and Douglas's state manager, Asahel Bush, remarked: "We have noticed this somewhat remarkable sympathy for the Yancey bolters on the part of the Republicans." [16]

Primarily because the two Democratic factions were fairly evenly matched, Lincoln carried Oregon. The November talley revealed: Lincoln, 5,270; Breckinridge, 5,006; Douglas, 3,951; Bell, 183.[17] Baker's biographer gives him credit for tipping the scale in favor of Lincoln.[18]

In addition to California and Oregon, another of the smaller doubtful states was New Jersey.

New Jersey was necessary to the Republicans should either New York or Pennsylvania go Democratic. The situation in New Jersey, however, was full of uncertainty. In 1859 the "Opposition" party— the label "Republican" was carefully avoided—had elected its candidate for governor, Charles S. Olden, by a small majority; but both houses of the legislature were Democratic. The Republicans at the Chicago Convention had revealed that they considered New Jersey, as well as Pennsylvania, doubtful ground by adopting a tariff plank essentially protective and by discarding Seward in favor of the more moderate Lincoln.

Both Douglas and Breckinridge had strong support and John Bell's strength was unknown. In late October an anti-Republican "fusion" meeting was held in New York City, attended by the chairmen of the New Jersey Douglas, Breckinridge, and Bell state committees, the result of which was a coalition against the Lincoln-Hamlin ticket. A "Fusion" electorate ticket was entered in the field. The anti-Lincolnites predicted a withdrawal of southern trade from the North and possible secession of the southern states if Lincoln were successful. The Republicans, not "abolitionist" enough to suit their more extreme adherents and too "abolitionist" to attract the conservative groups, stressed the tariff and the dangers involved in the extension of slavery to the Territories. The usual procession of uniformed Wide-Awakes marched and policed Republican meetings. The Republicans were indeed fortunate that their opponents were late in "fusing." When the votes were counted, so close was New Jersey that for several days thereafter neither Republican nor Democratic papers ventured to declare the result: Lincoln and Douglas shared the state's vote, Lincoln receiving four electoral votes and Douglas three. The Republican Newark *Mercury* explained its party's semi-defeat: The result was due to the proximity of New York and Philadelphia, the great centers of southern trade, whose money had affected New Jersey politics; and to the lack of an efficient straight-out organization; also, the Republicans placed too much reliance on the Democratic division, and the Fusion ticket had been presented so late that there had been no time to organize effectively against it.[19]

More vital to Lincoln's success than New Jersey were Pennsylvania and Indiana. In electoral votes Pennsylvania held second place in the Union and Indiana fifth. Each was considered "doubtful"; each was an "October" state, holding its gubernatorial contest one month before the presidential election. Both states had been carried by Buchanan in 1856 and had thus decided the presidency against Frémont. The wishes of the Pennsylvania and Indiana delegates at Chicago had been a mighty factor in defeating Seward and nominating the more available Lincoln. Republican strategists were quite alive to the situation. "Should Indiana and Pennsylvania go right in October," wrote one shrewd Republican leader, "the Presidential election in November will go by default." [20] Thus all groups exerted titanic efforts in the Hoosier and Keystone states.[21]

Indiana was conservative on the slavery question. The Republicans had named for governor the moderate Henry S. Lane. The Democrats chose the equally moderate Thomas A. Hendricks to oppose him.[22] Not until all parties had nominated Presidential candidates did the campaign get into full swing.

The Republicans contended that they were fighting for free land for the landless; for laborer against the aristocrat; for a Pacific railroad; to rescue the government from the corrupt Democrats; for the extension of freedom; for the preservation of the Union; to put "Old Abe" in the chair; against a slave code; against Douglasian squatter sovereignty; against polygamy (a thrust at the Mormons). Lincoln was presented as a moderate, whereupon the Democrats stigmatized all Republicans as abolitionists. The Democratic Indianapolis *State Sentinel* set the pace in the onslaught on Lincoln.[23]

Lincoln, watching developments from Springfield, became concerned. To Caleb B. Smith he wrote: "From present appearances we might succeed in the general result, without Indiana; but *with* it, failure is scarcely possible. Therefore put in your best efforts. I see by the despatches that Mr. Clay had a rousing meeting at Vincennes." [24] To Cassius M. Clay Lincoln sent word in July: [25]

I see by the papers, and also learned from Mr. Nicolay, who saw you at Terre-Haute, that you are filling a list of speaking appointments in Indiana. I sincerely thank you for this; and I shall be still further obliged if you will at the close of the tour, drop me a line, giving your impression of our prospects in that State.

In a great Republican rally at Indianapolis on August 29, fifty thousand crowded into the city to watch the antics of Wide-Awakes, "Rail Maulers," and "Abe's Boys." Crowds listened to Thomas Corwin of Ohio, Frank Blair of Missouri, Caleb B. Smith, Lane, and other Republican conservatives hail the virtues of Lincoln.[26]

Lincoln's friend, Judge David Davis, after a visit to Indiana in early August, returned home alarmed. To Lincoln he wrote: "I got home yesterday having gone through Indiana at the request of the National Committee—Will be down Monday and report—I should like two or three hours conversation." [27] Following the Judge's visit to Lincoln we find him (Davis) writing Thurlow Weed: [28]

Am in receipt of a letter from Caleb B. Smith of Indiana. He says "that the greatest fears I have in reference to our state election arise from the efforts now making to induce the Bell men to vote for the Dem. State ticket. The Louisville Journal is appealing to the Bell men in this state to defeat the Republican State ticket, as the prestige of the success will give the state to Lincoln in November. This paper circulates extensively in Southern Indiana, where the Bell men mostly live. I fear that many of them will follow its advice. I have very strong faith that we shall carry the State in Oct. I do not think it possible to give half the Bell men to the Democratic ticket. I *think* we can stand this."—Still, Indiana is in great danger.

I hope the National Committee will do all they can for the State. The whole money they asked (and more if it can be raised) should be sent at once. *Men work better with money in hand.*

The first order of German speakers are needed in Indiana. . . .
I believe in God's Providence in this Election, but at the same
time we should keep our powder dry.

The veteran Republican leader of Indiana, John D. Defrees, had
previously appealed to Weed: "To injure our prospects in November, I am afraid a majority of Bell men will vote against us in our
State in October. . . . We need money very much." [29]

In emphasizing the necessity for competent German campaigners
Davis was cognizant of a delicate situation in Indiana—the Know-
Nothing tradition. Indiana still contained nativistic influences. The
Hoosier Republican party had recruited much of its membership
from former "Americans" and "anti-foreign" conservative Whigs.[30]
To alienate the Teutonic element from the Republican standard,
the Democrats resurrected the Massachusetts "Two Year" Amendment so obnoxious to all naturalized groups [31] and charged the
Republican gubernatorial candidate, Henry S. Lane, with having
supported the anti-liquor law passed by the Indiana legislature of
1855.[32] A Democratic appeal was directed at the Germans.[33]

The Republicans, to hold the Indiana Germans, pointed to Buchanan's veto of the twenty-five cents an acre bill as proof that
the Democrats were hostile to free land.[34] Finally, Republican State
Chairman Alexander H. Conner called upon Carl Schurz to stump
Indiana.[35] The Wisconsin German leader made an extensive tour,
extolling the virtues of Lincoln, Hamlin and Lane.[36] In late August,
Defrees requested Weed: [37]

The amount sent by the National Committee ($2,000) has been
exhausted in the payment of Carl Schurz and other speakers and on
a few German Republican papers. Could you not influence the
Committee to send a few thousand more? It ought to be sent immediately to A. H. Conner, the Chairman of our Committee, who
will use it faithfully and efficiently.

Late, Schurz asserted that for his services he received "$500 from
Indiana." [38]

With the German element fairly certain to go for Lane in the
October election, another worry loomed for the Republicans: the
abolitionist label that the Democrats had pinned on them. Throughout September the Indianapolis *State Sentinel* continued its assault
on Lincoln,[39] and other Democratic organs persistently appealed

to "conservative, Union-loving citizens of Indiana" to defeat Lane and elect Hendricks governor.[40] But suddenly a ray of hope appeared in the split within the Democratic ranks.

The personal and political enmity between Douglas and Senator Jesse D. Bright, of Indiana, had started when President Buchanan made the Indiana senator chief patronage-dispenser for the Northwest. Bright remained doggedly loyal to the President throughout the Lecompton controversy and denounced Douglas at every turn. When Douglas voted against the seating in the Senate of Bright and Graham N. Fitch, both of whose elections were being contested by the Republicans, the breach became wider. The pro-Douglas, anti-Lecompton forces captured control of the state Democratic convention at Indianapolis in January. When the Baltimore convention named Douglas for President, unrestricted warfare was on between the two Democratic factions.[41] The Republicans were in high glee, one leader reporting: "Senator Bright said last week that if Douglas was nominated he would take the stump against him in Indiana . . . [and] that if the contest was to be between Douglas and Lincoln he would vote for the latter." [42] For long the autocrat of the Hoosier Democracy and Buchanan's Northwestern swordsman, Bright now threw his organization behind the Breckinridge-Lane ticket. Bright's biographer declares: "Bright was too shrewd a politician to believe that Breckinridge would carry the state; his paramount object was to impair Douglas' chance to the full extent of his ability." [43]

At the Breckinridge-Lane convention in late July, Bright sounded the keynote: "I go into this fight now under the banner of those heroes and statesmen—Breckinridge and Lane. . . . The names of Douglas and Johnson were forced upon the party by a fragment of a packed National Convention. . . . Douglas! The President knows him too well to reward his treason by giving him aid and comfort." [44] The Bright forces started a tri-weekly campaign sheet, the *Old Line Guard*, whose editorial policy was more strongly anti-Douglas than anti-Lincoln.[45] The *Old Line Guard's* arguments portrayed the Republican standard-bearer not as a "mauler of rails" but as a "grog-shop keeper" who "sold red-eye at a picayune a nip" [46]—an inference to Lincoln's youthful years as a general store-keeper in New Salem, Illinois, when he sold liquor with other merchandise. In early September, Bright, with Senator Fitch and others, stumped the state for Breckinridge and Joe Lane.[47] It was soon recognized that Indiana would be carried by Lincoln or Douglas. To vote the Breckinridge ticket was viewed as strengthening Lincoln's chance of success.[48] Yet the embittered Bright said frankly: "If I were to tell you that I believe that we are going to carry the State, I should tell you that which I don't believe. . . . Let the breach be as wide as possible between us; and let the sound and rotten men of the Democratic party be separated." [49] To make matters gloomier for the Douglasites, the Breckinridge State Central Committee decided that it would be inexpedient to place a state ticket in the field. This left the Breckinridge men free to support whomever they pleased at the Lane-Hendricks gubernatorial election in October.[50]

With Indiana conceded to go for either Lincoln or Douglas in November and with Bright's pro-Buchanan Lecomptonites knifing the Little Giant, the Douglasites became alarmed. They had appealed to Douglas: "Important that you visit Indianapolis about the Middle of September." [51] Other such urgent requests continued to pour in on Douglas.[52] On September 28, Douglas and his running-mate, Herschel V. Johnson, spoke at a monster rally in Indianapolis. The Illinois senator blasted the Buchanan administration for deserting the Cincinnati (1856) platform and pleaded with his audience to resist both northern and southern sectionalism.[53] Then Douglas went to other parts of the state.[54] But he was being blocked by Bright's organization, which would even prefer the election of Lincoln to his own.

Destiny was smiling on Lincoln in the circumstance that the Whig-minded Constitutional Union men wanted no part of the Democratic party.

The Constitutional Union state convention had been held in Indianapolis on August 15 and endorsed the Bell-Everett ticket. The attendance was disappointingly small and it was evident that Bell could not carry Indiana. Soon Richard W. Thompson, heading the Hoosier Constitutional Unionists, denounced all Democrats as the authors of all the mischief that had been done. Thompson stated that none could be elected except Lincoln! He feared that if none of the candidates—Lincoln, Douglas, Breckinridge or Bell—received a majority of the electoral college and the election should be decided by Congress, the House of Representatives would be unable to elect. In such an eventuality the presidential office would fall on Breckinridge's running-mate, Joseph Lane, in his capacity as President *pro tempore* of the Senate. To the Union-minded Old-Line Whig Thompson, the "disunionist" Democratic Joe Lane was to be avoided at all costs—even if Lincoln should be the next President.[55] Rather than run the risk of Joe Lane's selection, Thompson declared, "I tell you frankly, I would prefer the election of Lincoln." [56] Thompson added further: "I would greatly prefer seeing Mr. Bell elected, but he shall never be elected, with my consent, nor shall any man, by a bargain with Mr. Douglas or his friends, or Mr. Breckinridge or his friends." [57] Thereupon Thompson issued a circular addressed to the "Conservative Men of Indiana," contending that the selection of Joe Lane as President would be a triumph for disunion. Thompson was for the Republican Henry S. Lane for governor, since his election would revive the spirit of Whiggery, for which Thompson had long been laboring. Other Constitutional Unionists shared Thompson's views and drifted toward the Republican state ticket "not because they believed in its principles but because of the desire to defeat the Democrats." By early October most Bell men were in Henry S. Lane's camp.[58] Too, Lincoln's freedom from anti-slavery radicalism and the comparative conservatism of the Republican national platform had induced hosts of Bell men to go over to Lincoln. Surveying the situation, one Constitutional Unionist leader confided: [59]

The result of the Chicago Convention in their candidate and platform was more moderate than was apprehended or anticipated. It is quite a comedown from 1856. . . . Many of our men here have given in. . . . Lincoln however to my mind is so much better than Seward and Co., that I have no opposition to him.

The state election was held October 9. With the Bell men supporting Lane and with the Bright Democrats doing likewise rather than go for the pro-Douglas Hendricks, Henry S. Lane was elected Governor by almost 10,000 votes in over 260,000 cast. The enraged Douglasites correctly blamed Bright's organization.[60]

An even more important "October" state than Indiana was Pennsylvania, largest of the "doubtful" states with twenty-seven electoral votes—second only to New York.

Lincoln, although little known, proved acceptable to the conservative nativistic groups of the anti-Democratic coalition in Pennsylvania, since he proved a welcome contrast to Seward. One Keystone Republican chieftain observed: "The Americans appear

well satisfied and the Bell movement is backward. . . . Our people are happy to have escaped the infliction of Seward." [61] The
Constitutional Unionists were indeed nowhere. The Philadelphia
Evening Bulletin began the campaign as a Bell organ but finally
went into the Lincoln camp.[62] The Republican presidential candidate, as a former Henry Clay Whig, was also acceptable to the
powerful high-tariff interests.[63]

Despite Lincoln's general popularity in Pennsylvania, the diverse
anti-Democratic elements in the "People's Party" were not mar-
shalled under the Republican banner without serious threats of
revolt. The feud between Senator Cameron and Andrew G. Curtin,
the gubernatorial candidate, was not buried even during the
campaign. Cameron endeavored to secure control of the state organization. The chairman of the People's Party State Committee,
Alexander K. McClure, was a Curtin follower but a majority of its
members were Cameron men. A plan was devised whereby control
of the campaign would be placed in the hands of an executive
committee and a treasurer, and the position of chairman rendered
ornamental. When the state committee held its first meeting, every
friend of Curtin and Cameron was on hand the evening before, and
a roistering frolic held. Wine flowed freely. The Curtinites controlled the meeting. McClure never felt that another meeting was
necessary, although Cameron's faction demanded one.[64] McClure's
action in raising funds aroused the Cameronians' ire, one com-
plaining: "McClure is at New York, and has been since Friday,
begging for money. I fear the whole crew are more active in getting money for themselves, than they are in securing success at the
election." [65]

Two Cameron leaders, James Casey and one Putnam, now consulted with Lincoln's friend Leonard Swett, of Bloomington, Illinois,
and suggested that Swett and Judge David Davis visit Pennsylvania, in order to tame the Curtinites. Swett communicated with
Lincoln, who had been closely watching Pennsylvania.[66] In mid-
July Lincoln instructed Swett: [67]

Herewith I return the letters of Messrs. Putnam and Casey. I
thank you for sending them—in the main, they bring good news.
And yet that matter mentioned by Mr. Casey about want of confidence in their Central committee pains me. I am afraid there is
a germ of difficulty in it. Will not the men thus suspected, and
treated as proposed, rebel, and make a dangerous explosion? When

you write Mr. Casey, suggest to him that great caution and delicacy of action is necessary in that matter.

I would like to see you and the Judge [Davis], one or both, about that matter of your going to Pennsylvania.

Lincoln consented that Davis and Swett visit Pennsylvania. The two Illinois emissaries, after ascertaining that the Pennsylvania campaign was well organized,[68] met Cameron and Thurlow Weed —presumably in Saratoga Springs, New York. Unknown to Lincoln, an agreement was supposedly reached that they should be the controlling element in the new administration if Lincoln should be victorious. Davis's offer of a Cabinet post to Cameron, made at the Chicago convention, was probably discussed.[69] Davis, Swett, and Cameron found a willing ally in Weed: Cameron had convinced Weed that Curtin, and not he, was responsible for Seward's defeat at Chicago,[70] and the Sewardites heartily detested Curtin.[71] McClure later complained that Weed would not provide him with funds for Curtin's campaign.[72]

Curtin's followers feared that Davis and Swett would persuade Lincoln to recognize only the Cameron faction.[73] The Curtinites' anxiety was relieved only when Lincoln reassured a friend of McClure: [74]

Yours of the 27th is duly received. It consists almost exclusively of a historical detail of some local troubles, among some of our friends in Pennsylvania; and I suppose its object is to guard me against forming a prejudice against Mr. McC–. I have not heard near so much upon that subject as you probably suppose; and I am slow to listen to criminations among friends, and never expose their quarrels on either side. My sincere wish is that both sides will allow by-gones to be by-gones, and look to the present and future only.

The Republican feud, however, was indeed mild when compared with the Democrats' family quarrels. The Republican troubles were grounded in the rivalry of two state leaders, Cameron and Curtin. The Democratic rupture was based on the friction between two national chieftains, Buchanan and Douglas.

Buchanan had already thrown his administration's influence behind Breckinridge, but most Democrats in western Pennsylvania supported Douglas. On July 2 the Democratic State Central Committee met in Philadelphia and recommended that Henry D. Foster should be supported for governor. The committee also proposed that all Democrats unite upon the electoral ticket formed at Reading in March, with the understanding that if the ticket should be elected and if, in view of the results in other states, it was found that Douglas's election could be effected by having the electors cast Pennsylvania's entire vote for him, this should be done; if, on the other hand, the state's vote would not elect Douglas but would win for Breckinridge, the electors were to vote for the latter. But if Pennsylvania's united vote could determine the success of neither, then the electors were to be permitted to divide their votes. Buchanan endorsed this arrangement.[75]

But the Douglas faction, led by John W. Forney (who had broken with Buchanan), would have none of such compromise with the Breckinridgers. Forney declared in his Philadelphia *Press:* [76]

No true friend of Douglas, in Pennsylvania or elsewhere, can touch an electoral ticket which contains upon it the single name of a Breckinridge Disunionist . . . precisely as a single drop of subtle poison thrown into a goblet of pure and crystal water might render the whole a deadly potion.

Some anti-Buchanan Democrats, fearful of certain defeat if harmony were not restored, tried to place fusion electoral tickets in the field supported by both the Douglasites and Breckinridgers. Not so Forney, who owed his election as clerk of the House of Representatives to a coalition of Douglas Democrats and Republicans. Throughout the campaign he continued his vindictive campaign against "fusion," charging the Breckinridge party with "disunionism." [77] The Breckinridge men were furious, and charged Forney with supporting Douglas only to aid Lincoln; [78] their editorials were often entitled, "Forney Paying Off His Debts to the Republican Party," [79] and "Bought and Paid For By the Republicans." [80] Forney admitted later: "I had done my utmost to elect him [Lincoln] President by the only way in my power, and that was by supporting the straight Douglas electoral ticket in Pennsylvania." [81] And so the campaign proceeded—the Breckinridge men assailing Douglas and his "chief imp, Forney" as the destroyers of the party; and the Douglasites accusing their opponents of being "seceders" who had blasted Democratic unity.[82] Commented one Republican leader gleefully: "The Douglas and Breckinridge men would give it [Pennsylvania] to us to spite each other." [83]

All groups in the national contest centered their heaviest artillery in the fight for governor of Pennsylvania. The Republican National Committee sent its best oratorical talent into the state. Congressmen Morrill of Vermont and John Sherman of Ohio, because of their association with the Republicans' protectionist stand, were especially welcome.[84] Carl Schurz came from Wisconsin to speak to the men of his blood and speech and then boasted that the "old Pennsylvania Dutch" followed him like children.[85] Schurz's Pennsylvania fee was $600.[86]

While providing forensic talent, the Republican high command did not neglect the sinews of war. Republican National Committeeman John Z. Goodrich of Massachusetts instructed a co-worker: [87]

After all Pennsylvania is the Sebastopol we must take. Every needed help—so far as the help can be used legitimately and properly—should be furnished. A great deal of work must be done in that State, and it should be shared in by other strong Republican states.

The legitimate and proper expenses of an election so sharply contested as it will be in that State, are heavy. Toward them New York and Massachusetts ought to contribute. . . . I would be glad to possess myself of the fullest information from Pa. So that when I ask A. B. and C. in Mass. to contribute toward discharging such expenses as must necessarily be incurred, I may be able as far as possible to explain the actual state of things.

In October the Democratic press charged: "The Republican financial clubs of Boston, Providence and other New England cities, warned of the necessity, have been sending on their remittances to Philadelphia, by hundreds and thousands of dollars." [88] One Republican journal admitted that $5,000 was donated to Curtin's campaign, besides payment for 200,000 documents; that $100,000 more was sent into the Keystone State by the New York Republican Committee.[89] There is little foundation for McClure's claim that he received no aid from the National Committee.[90] The Breckinridge forces had financial support from the federal office-holders.[91] The Republican Pittsburgh *Gazette* even charged that the pro-Buchanan Senator William Bigler had arrived in Philadelphia armed with $100,000 to elect Foster governor.[92] The Douglasites found it almost impossible to raise funds, since many of the New York merchants who usually opened their purses became convinced that Douglas stood no chance of election.[93]

McClure found it difficult to raise funds in Philadelphia. For business men believed that if Lincoln and Curtin should triumph, that city would lose its profitable southern trade; moreover, merchants were disgusted with politics and politicians. At this time many below the Potomac were closing their northern accounts and cancelling orders, and discriminations were made against commercial houses of Republican leanings. A Georgia journal published a list of northern firms under two headings: a black list of "Abolition Houses" and a white list of "Constitutional Houses." Only two leading Philadelphia business organizations are said to have contributed to the Republican chest in 1860.[94]

This conservatism in Philadelphia and elsewhere throughout the state furnished the Democrats with what they hoped would be their most effective campaign argument. They charged the Republicans with abolitionism. Most Republican journals seemed reluctant to discuss the slavery question *per se*. Between September 1 and November 6 the Philadelphia *North American* printed only six editorials relating to slavery; between September 3 and October 11, this sheet contained sixteen lengthy editorials advocating a higher tariff.[95]

Immediately following Lincoln's nomination, the *North American* proceeded to make protectionism the paramount issue in Pennsylvania, lauding Lincoln as an old Henry Clay Tariff Whig and praising the Chicago tariff resolution. Buchanan's Philadelphia organ, the *Pennsylvanian*, denounced the "ambiguous" language of the Republican tariff plank. And so began the fierce editorial controversy between the *North American* and the *Pennsylvanian*.[96] Other important journals opposed to the Democrats followed the *North American*.[97] Lincoln, pressed by Pennsylvanians for his views, referred his correspondents to the national platform and pointed to the Whig papers of 1844 to prove his adherence to Clay's protective policy.[98]

In preaching upward revision of the tariff of 1857, the Republicans were following a popular line. For in 1860, Pennsylvania produced one-half of the nation's iron.[99] Even the Democrats inserted in their state platform a plank in favor of "adequate" protection.[100]

Suddenly Keystone State Republicans were given a magnificent opportunity by the fate of their Morrill tariff bill in Congress.

Shortly before Lincoln's nomination, the House of Representatives passed the Morrill bill raising the rates in the existing Tariff of 1857: of the 113 Republican members, 89 voted for the bill, 8 announced themselves as paired with opponents of it, and only 4 voted against it. Of the 93 administration Democrats, only 60 voted on the measure—57 against and 3 for the bill.[101] The Pennsylvania Douglas leaders begged the Little Giant to support the Morrill legislation.[102] Foster left the stump long enough to journey to Washington in efforts to persuade Democratic senators to vote for it.[103] The Pennsylvania Breckinridge leaders appealed to their national leaders not to embarrass them by voting against upward revision. On June 8 (1860) the Democratic postmaster of Pottsville implored Senator Robert M. T. Hunter, Democrat of Virginia: [104]

> I refer to the Tariff bill now under consideration in Committee of which you are chairman. With its solution depends the success or defeat of the Democratic party. . . . If a proper Tariff bill passes the United States Senate it will make a difference of 20,000 votes in Pennsylvania, to the Democratic Party. If it is defeated we cannot hope to succeed. This is conceded by all who know the feelings of the people. . . .
> You sir, have the key to the solution. Can you fail to be impressed of the necessity of saving our party from annihilation and defeat? The masses of this state think and speak of nothing else but the Tariff. . . . *All* are looking with anxious eyes to the democratic Senate for its solution.

On the same day Curtin turned up in Washington to agitate the question. He gave out the statement that he found the Republicans fighting for the Morrill bill and the Democrats resisting it.[105]

Five days later, on June 13, Hunter, as chairman of the Senate Committee on Finance, reporting out the Morrill bill, moved that its consideration be postponed until the next session—after the election! Two days later the Senate, by a strict party vote, passed Hunter's resolution. William Bigler of Pennsylvania, alone among the Democrats, opposed postponement. A bill for increased tariff rates had passed the House under Republican leadership only to be blocked in the Senate by Democrats.[106]

The Republicans now denounced Breckinridge as the "exponent of the anti-tariff party and the candidate of the radical free-traders." They treated Bell, a recognized old Whig protectionist, less harshly but emphasized that "as he relies chiefly on Southern States for support, he will have to conform to a considerable extent to Southern policy, which favors free trade." [107] They turned their heaviest fire on Douglas. They combed the Illinois senator's record in the Senate and distributed a pamphlet that portrayed Douglas as a rank free-trader. [108]

The Republican campaign diet was most unpalatable to the Douglasites. "The Republicans, in their speeches, say nothing of the nigger question," one complained to Douglas, "but all is made to turn on the Tariff." [109] Douglas was advised to favor higher import duties when he visited Pennsylvania. [110] One appealed to the Little Giant: "If you could advert to that subject in your speech at Harrisburg or Reading it would do immense good." [111] On September 7 at Harrisburg Douglas came out publicly for protection. [112] The next day at Reading he did the same. [113] But Douglas's solicitude for Pennsylvania's industry was denounced alike by Lincoln and Breckinridge men as "the most unblushing effrontery" and as "a signal instance of political trickery" that deceived no one. [114]

Protectionism and the split in the Democratic party proved to be the deciding factors in the gubernatorial contest in October. Curtin defeated Foster—262,396 to 230,312. [115] Cameron reported happily: "Our people here are tired of 'bad times' and are becoming disgusted with the miserable conduct of Mr. Buchanan; they could no longer be held by the leaders of the Democratic party, who had so often deluded them with the promises of a tariff." [116]

Lincoln could now send the glad tidings to his law-partner, Herndon: "I cannot give you details, but it is entirely certain that Pennsylvania and Indiana have gone Republican very largely. Pennsylvania 25,000, and Indiana 5,000 to 10,000. Ohio of course is safe." [117] Douglas was crestfallen. "Mr. Lincoln is the next President," he remarked dejectedly. "We must try to save the Union. I will go South." [118] The Little Giant headed southward. "Hot-spur" papers resented his presence. [119] Breckinridge was sweeping the lower slave regions. [120] Bell would attract the border states. New England and the Northwest were certain for Lincoln. The Republicans now emphasized to wavering conservatives that their state victories in Indiana and Pennsylvania had resulted in no outbreaks below the Potomac. [121]

Only one obstacle would now seem to block Lincoln's path to the White House—New York. [122] One Republican observed anxiously: [123]

But while doubtful States are rendered sure, it may be asked are there none of the heretofore sure Republican States rendered doubtful. I can fix my eye on but one State where a shadow or cloud is likely to appear. The battle ground, instead of being the Keystone State, *may be* the Empire State.

With the Pennsylvania, Indiana and Ohio victories behind them, the Lincolnites concentrated on New York.

CHAPTER THIRTEEN

New York – and the Decision

T O LINCOLN'S OPPONENTS New York presented the only chance to defeat him. If the Empire State's thirty-five electoral votes could be kept from the Republican standard-bearer he would be deprived of a majority in the electoral college even if he carried every other Northern state; in such an eventuality the presidential contest would be thrown into Congress, where the Democrats believed they had a chance. This could be said of no other state.[1] Lincoln realized this and wrote Thurlow Weed: [2]

I think there will be the most extraordinary effort ever made to carry New York for Douglas. You and all others who write me from your State think the effort cannot succeed, and I hope you are right. Still it will require close watching and great efforts on the other side.

For a period following the Chicago convention the New York Republicans were sharply divided into the Seward-Weed faction and the anti-Weed or former Free Soil Democratic faction led by William Cullen Bryant. Horace Greeley coöperated with the latter wing. The pro-Seward Henry J. Raymond, editor of the New York *Times*, charged that Greeley was largely responsible for blocking Seward's nomination; he declared that some six years previous the *Tribune* editor had written a letter to Seward dissolving the political firm of "Seward, Weed and Greeley" because he had not been offered public office by his two partners. Greeley angrily demanded that Raymond produce the letter—and Raymond printed it in the *Times*. A bitter controversy ensued.[3] Thus passed into history the interpretation that Greeley was instrumental in stopping Seward at Chicago.[4]

The wrangling was interrupted to hold a monster Lincoln-Hamlin ratification meeting in Cooper Institute on June 7. The "angel" of the Weed organization, Richard M. Blatchford, presided—and cheers were given in turn for Seward and Greeley.[5] In late August the Republicans met in convention at Syracuse and reiterated that the hatchet had been buried for the duration. The pro-Weed Governor Edwin D. Morgan and the anti-Weed Lieutenant Governor Robert D. Campbell were renominated. Presidential electors were chosen representing the different groups.[6] A week later a new Republican State Central Committee was organized at Albany—with the pro-Weed Simeon Draper as chairman and the anti-Weed leader, George Opdyke, as a member. A vigorous campaign was mapped.[7] The Republicans were out for victory.[8]

A major Republican objective was to attract the large "American" element. Millard Fillmore as the latter group's presidential candidate in 1856 had polled 124,000 votes in New York, or 21 per cent of the whole. The 1859 election had indicated that the "Americans" held the balance of power between Republicans and Democrats; if enough of the nativists voted for Bell, Douglas would carry New York. Thus the Republicans worked feverishly to attract the "Americans" to Lincoln.[9]

There were thousands of "Americans," most of them former Whigs, who recognized that Bell could not possibly be elected and that even Lincoln would be preferable to any of the hated Democrats. Although Fillmore himself would have none of Lincoln,[10] many of his supporters took a more practical view. The ex-President's organ, the Albany *Statesman*, even defended the plank in the Chicago platform that declared against changes in the naturalization laws.[11] The erstwhile pro-Fillmore Buffalo *Commercial Advertiser* declared: [12]

With the knowledge of the little strength belonging to John Bell in this State . . . and with the Old Whig hatred of Democracy, nursed in with our mother's milk, and strong today as in 1844, in our hearts, we conceive it to be our duty to place the names of Lincoln and Hamlin at the head of our columns.

Most influential of all pro-Lincoln "Americans" was the Buffalo leader James O. Putnam, who feared that Old Line Whigs and "Americans" might give New York to Douglas by voting for Bell. Invoking the memory of Harry of the West, Putnam emphasized: "Mr. Clay . . . was ever the target for all their [the Democrats'] hunters, and he went into his grave covered with their poisoned arrows. He was hardly at rest in his tomb before it undid the most glorious act of his life [the Missouri Compromise]." [13] Lincoln, grateful for Putnam's services, wrote the Buffalo man: "I have just read the speech you sent me with your note of the 23rd attached. I do not mean to flatter you when I say it is, indeed, a very excellent one." [14]

The Republican strength, as demonstrated by the truce between Weed and anti-Weed factions and by the defection of some "Americans" from Bell to Lincoln, alarmed the Democrats, one of whom warned: "New York is the key to the White House, and if not seized to shut out Lincoln, it will be used to let him in." [15]

Mayor Fernando Wood of New York City, fearful of Republican success if a coalition of all anti-Lincoln factions were not effected, tendered the olive branch to his arch-foes, Dean Richmond and the Tammany leaders. His overtures were graciously received, and Wood's Mozart Hall, Richmond's Albany Regency, and Tammany agreed to support Douglas.[16] Wood endeavored to bring in the Breckinridge element, led by Daniel S. Dickinson of Binghamton, on this basis: since Douglas was strong in the North and Breckinridge was powerful in the South, only the Douglas electoral ticket should be run in the North and only the Breckinridge slate in the South. Between them they could obtain a majority of the electoral college and thus defeat Lincoln, which was the Democracy's first duty. How the votes should be apportioned among Douglas, Breckinridge or some other candidate, could be arranged later. Wood's plan was coldly received—primarily because of the feud between Richmond and Dickinson.[17]

Richmond's "soft" faction and Dickinson's "hard" faction were at bitter odds. The "softs" had trapped the "hards" into allegiance with a promise of solid support for Dickinson for President—and then gagged them by a rigid unit rule at the Charleston convention in April. Dickinson was enraged at Richmond, who professed devotion to Douglas although waiting for a chance to put across Horatio Seymour as Democratic standard-bearer.[18] On returning home following Douglas's nomination at Baltimore in June, the embittered "hards" held a monster mass-meeting at Cooper Institute, at which Dickinson denounced Richmond: "There is no fox so crafty but his hide finally goes to the hatter." [19]

The "hards," in open rebellion, met in convention at Syracuse on August 8, appointed a state committee, denounced Richmond's leadership at Charleston and Baltimore, nominated James T. Brady for governor—and selected a Breckinridge-Lane electoral ticket and adopted a pro-southern platform. Since Breckinridge would secure one hundred and twenty-seven electoral votes in the South and on the Pacific coast, according to Dickinson, this made the election depend on New York. Dickinson called upon the "national" Democrats to force Douglas out of the race.[20]

In hoisting the pro-southern standard in the Empire State, the "hards" recognized that New York City had social and commercial relations with the South.[21] Merchants, wanting peace between the sections, were by 1860 viewing Republicanism with alarm.[22] Moreover, there were numerous Irish groups, traditionally loyal to the Democratic party, whose religion frowned upon anti-slavery agitation; moreover, sons of Erin hated the former Know-Nothing element within the Republican party.[23] Brady's nomination was expected to attract the Celtic vote.[24] The federal patronage was utilized for the Breckinridge ticket: Collector Schell and Surveyor Hart, of the port of New York, and Sub-Treasurer Cisco attended Breckinridge meetings.[25]

Conservative New Yorkers, such as James Gordon Bennett, editor of the *Herald*, backed Breckinridge against the "abolitionist" Lincoln.[26] Bennett waged a bitter campaign against union with the Douglasites: "The Albany Regency want to get Breckinridge into their clutches, that they may cheat him as they . . . cheated Dickinson." [27] This did not discourage Mayor Wood, who redoubled his efforts to fuse all anti-Lincoln forces into a Douglas organization.[28]

The Douglasites' appeals now struck a sympathetic note among the Bell leaders. Ex-Governor Washington Hunt and other Constitutional Unionists, recognizing that they could not make a respectable showing for Bell, prepared to unite with the Douglas groups.[29] The defection of the Buffalo *Commercial Advertiser* to Lincoln had been a severe blow and Hunt wrote Bell dejectedly: "We have but one or two remaining (and those obscure weeklies) west of the Hudson River. We had an organ at Albany but it has been bought by the Republicans. In New York City we have nothing but the Express . . . We have realities to deal with and must look them in the face, as they are." [30] Later Hunt informed Bell: "My instincts are rather in favor of doing whatever is fair and honorable to carry the election to the House of Representatives." [31]

In still another letter to Bell, Hunt indicated that he nurtured ambitious hopes: [32]

> Some of the leading Douglas men have said to me in confidence that if we succeed, and it shall appear that the whole College of New York is necessary and sufficient to elect you their men will vote for you rather than send the election to the House of Reps. In reply, I have said to them in confidence that they ought to do it, and in that event that you will not fail to appreciate their patriotism and to exhibit your proverbial sense of justice. I deem it my duty to inform you of these things at this early stage. You need make no answer to the suggestion, but in the course of human events I may have to ask you to remember it.

The Douglas leaders were quite willing to accept the aid of the Bell-Everett men. This they did at the "soft" Democratic convention held at Syracuse on August 15. The customary contest between Tammany Hall and Wood's Mozart Hall was compromised by admitting both delegations upon an equality, much to Tammany's indignation. When the report recommending this settlement was adopted, Tammany withdrew for consultation. Later the braves returned; but presented a protest setting forth Tammany's exclusive claims to regularity and stating that in view of the crisis threatening the party and nation, they would retain their seats in convention and support its nominees, but would cast no vote therein. William Kelley, of Dutchess county, was nominated for governor. The Douglas Democrats and Constitutional Unionists agreed on a joint electoral ticket, whereby the Bell men were given ten electors. The resolutions adopted condemned northern Republican and southern Democratic extremism.[33]

Three candidates for governor were now in the field—Morgan, Republican; Brady, Breckinridge Democrat; and Kelley, Douglas Democrat. The campaign went into full swing. But overshadowing all was the presidential contest.

Following the Syracuse convention a controversy arose within the anti-Lincoln coalition. Hunt now declared that the ten Constitutional Union electors, if chosen in the election, would be free to vote for Bell for President. On the other hand, a Douglas chieftain, the German Oswald Ottendorfer, asserted that the distinct understanding was that all on the electoral ticket, if elected, should vote for Douglas. Irish papers claimed the same. Underneath was the German and Irish distrust of the Know-Nothing–tainted Constitutional Unionists. Greeley's New York *Tribune* aptly labelled the arrangement the "confusion ticket." Meanwhile, the ten Constitutional Union candidates for elector remained silent.[34]

As if to add to the Douglasites' troubles, the old feud between Tammany and Mozart halls flared up again. August Belmont, a Tammanyite and chairman of the Douglas Democratic National Committee, had been opposed to admitting Wood and his group to the Syracuse convention, but Richmond had his way and the Mozart delegation had been recognized on an equal footing with Tammany. Belmont called Richmond's action a *"fatal* mistake" and a "gross injustice to Tammany" which would lose Douglas "many thousands" of votes in New York City.[35] Wrote Belmont: "You know the feeling against Wood amongst our respectable and monied men. It is this aid and countenance which we want now at all hazards." [36] Belmont was indeed having his troubles in raising funds. He confided to Douglas discouragingly: [37]

My efforts to collect money in the City have met with but little success, and unless we can give to our merchants and politicians some *assurance of success* I fear that it will be impossible to raise the necessary funds for our campaign. There is at present an apathy and indifference, of which it is difficult to form an idea—the opinion has gained ground, that nothing can prevent the election of Lincoln and that it is consequently useless to spend any money in a hopeless cause—others, who usually contribute freely to our funds, are afraid to lose their southern customers by siding with us. I have made a most *urgent personal appeal* to G. Low, but he positively declines: the fact is he wants another Republican Legislature in Albany, which will help him in his schemes to plunder the public. Aspinwall and others, upon whom I calculated, keep also aloof. . . .

My opinion is that if we could only demonstrate to all those lukewarm and selfish money-bags, that we have a strong probability to carry the State of New York, we might get from them the necessary sinews of war. This, I think, can be done and no time ought to be lost in going to work to bring it about.

Belmont ended his letter by requesting Douglas to speak in New York.[38]

There were those who did not lose hope of forming an effective anti-Lincoln coalition in early September. Representatives of Douglas, Bell and Breckinridge factions met in conference but their efforts were in vain because, it was said, "the real difficulty in the way of the Breckinridge men coöperating on the fusion ticket in New York springs from the absolute disgust and distrust felt towards the Albany [Regency] clique." [39] But the Breckinridgers alone were not responsible for failure to achieve fusion. Douglas himself put a damper on such an anti-Republican union when, at Belmont's solicitation, he spoke at a Democratic barbecue in New York City. "I do not charge all the Breckinridge men in the United States with being disunionist," the Illinois senator declared heatedly, "but I do express my firm conviction that there is not a disunionist in America who is not a Breckinridge man." A heckler demanded, "Is the honorable Senator in favor of fusion?" Douglas shouted back: [40]

If Major Breckinridge is in favor of enforcing the laws against disunionists, seceders, abolitionists and all other [such] classes of men, in the event the election does not result to suit him, then I am willing—but I tell you that I am utterly opposed to any union or any fusion with any man or any party who will not enforce the laws, maintain the constitution, and preserve the Union in all contingencies. . . .
Make no bargain, no combination, no fusion, no compromise with the friends of any candidate who will not first publicly pledge himself to the maintenance of the Union, the inviolability of the constitution and the enforcement of the laws in all cases and under all circumstances.

Some Douglas and Breckinridge leaders realized that they could ill afford the odium of throwing New York's vote to Lincoln. Accordingly on September 17 they held a meeting, presided over by one Joshua J. Henry, a merchant in the southern dry-goods trade. A resolution was adopted for appointment of a committee of fifteen which would form a fusion electoral ticket. Ultimately this resulted in an electoral ticket comprising eighteen Douglas, ten Bell and seven Breckinridge adherents. But it was mid-October before this partial union was effected. The Republican victory in Pennsylvania spurred the anti-Lincoln forces into agreement. [41] "As things now appear in Pennsylvania," a Douglas leader bemoaned on October 10, "we will have to save the Union and keep the rail splitter out of the White House." [42] Yet the Breckinridge committee acceded to the coalition with recriminations and reproaches. Since

Douglas had no chance of election in Congress a union on the state ticket was the kind of fusion which alone would have been of value to the Albany Regency; but the Breckinridge men refused to withdraw Brady from the governorship race. The prolonged mutual bickerings could not but weaken Democratic prospects even more.[43]

The Republicans, compared with their opponents, were harmonious. On the stump they argued that the Democrats and the Bell-Everett men had no possible chance of electing their candidates but were, on the contrary, engaging in obstructionist work of preventing an election by popular vote. Thurlow Weed, directing strategy from his Albany headquarters, formulated the party line: [44]

The Republicans are the only party this year who advocate the election of a President by the People, or offer a feasible means of doing it. All the other parties are seeking not to *effect*, but to *prevent* such an election! By their own confession, this is all that any one of them is capable of doing.

The Republicans continued to assail and ridicule their opponents' incongruous coalition. They reminded naturalized Irish and German citizens of the former Know-Nothing records of the Constitutional Unionists. The Republicans were inspired with new vigor by the anti-Lincoln union. From upstate came reports of hostility and disgust on the part of both wings of the Democracy toward the ticket. Many Democratic votes were destined to be cast for Lincoln, some preferring Republicans to the opposing faction within their own party. The New York *Herald*, now an ardent advocate of anti-Lincoln fusion, asserted that there was no genuine union between the two Democratic wings and that the breach had widened since the October elections in Pennsylvania, Indiana, and Ohio. On October 16 Dickinson, having reluctantly come to favor the fusion ticket, declared that he did so because it might make possible the choice of Breckinridge. Brady expressed the same sentiments.[45]

Although the great New York City mercantile interests supported the anti-Lincoln ticket, the Republicans had the advantage of better organization. Weed in his day had few if any equals in the election craft. The Lincolnites also had better forensic talent. For many months they had been conducting a campaign of education at Cooper Institute, where meetings had been addressed by Lincoln himself, Frank Blair, Cassius M. Clay, and John Sherman. After the battle proper was joined other talented spell-binders were imported, among them Salmon P. Chase, Senator Doolittle, and Senator Henry Wilson. The popular Seward also took the stump in New York City and upstate.[46]

Weed's confidence remained undimmed when he received reports from the various precincts. "The fusion leaders have largely increased their fund," he wrote Lincoln as the fateful November day neared, "and they are now using money lavishly. This stimulates and to some extent inspires confidence, and all the confederates are at work. Some of our friends are nervous. But I have no fear of the result in this state." [47] On November 5—night before the Election— Weed gave instructions to his well-drilled organization: [48]

Close Up The Work Of Preparation To-Night: Leave nothing for tomorrow but direct work. Pick out and station your men. . . . Let there be an assigned place for every man, and, at sunrise, let every man be in his assigned place. Don't wait until the last hour, to bring up delinquents. Consider every man a "delinquent" who doesn't vote before 10 o'clock. *At That Hour Begin To Hunt Up Voters!*

November 6, 1860—a momentous day in the nation's destiny— came. Weed's men worked frantically from dawn to late evening. Returns came in rapidly. Before midnight a Lincoln victory in New York was forecast. The next morning's *Tribune* gave the news of the Republican triumph. Official figures fixed Lincoln's majority in New York state at over 50,000.[49] The astute Democrat, Samuel J. Tilden, analyzed Lincoln's victory: [50]

Masses went for Lincoln, from habit and association,—as a lineal succession from Whiggism. Masses from mere opposition to the Democratic party—and from all the causes which gradually operate to make a revolution between the ins and the outs. The drift created by the disorganization of the Democratic party—and our inability to present any single candidate as a point of union to the conservative sentiment—and the concession from April till October that we must inevitably be beaten; I say this drift alone might fail by 24,000 out of 675,000 voters or 3½ per cent, which would have changed the result in New York and in the Union.

In Springfield, Illinois, crowds mobbed the telegraph offices on Election night. Republicans crowded into the state House of Representatives to hear the returns. As the different dispatches came over the wires, yells of victory went up. The hours passed. Reports came in, showing that Lincoln had carried the West. "News from New York was anxiously awaited." [51]

Late in the night Senator Trumbull and his friend, Henry McPike, proceeded to the Hall of Representatives, where Lincoln and his close associates, including State Treasurer Jesse K. Dubois and Edward L. Baker, Springfield editor, eagerly awaited the all-important returns from the Empire State. Finally a dispatch came. Lincoln had carried New York! McPike describes the scene: [52]

Dubois jumped to his feet. "Hey," he shouted, and they began singing as loud as he could (sic) a campaign song, "Ain't You Glad You Jined the Republicans?"

Lincoln got up and Trumbull and the rest of us. We were all excited. There were hurried congratulations. Suddenly old Jesse grabbed the dispatch . . . out of Ed. Baker's hands and started for the door. We followed, . . . Lincoln last. The staircase was narrow and steep. We went down it still on the run. Dubois rushed across the street toward the meeting, so out of breath he couldn't speak plain. All he could say was "Spetch. Spetch.". . . Lincoln, coolest of the lot, went home to tell his wife the news.

Springfield's popular citizen and lawyer was President-elect of the United States. A Chief Executive had been elected by the Republican party.

CHAPTER FOURTEEN

Summing Up

EARLY REPUBLICANISM WAS A SECTIONAL, almost purely northern, movement. The cohesive force within the new political party, however, was not anti-southern sentiment, but opposition to the Democrats. It was this common antagonism to the dominant political organization, the eagerness of the "outs" to get "in," that made possible coöperation between the diverse elements who joined forces under the Republican standard.

The formal organization of the new party was preceded by a short period involving dissolution of previous political loyalties and the crystallization of new issues. This was a period during which the national Whig organization disintegrated consequent upon declining interest in traditional Whig doctrines and upon the Seward-Fillmore feud, followed by the disastrous defeat of General Scott in 1852. It was a period when thousands of northern Democrats became disgruntled over their exclusion from patronage rewards, and became disappointed over the pro-southern bias of their national leadership. Moreover, it was a period during which the demand for internal improvements was revived as a sectional issue in the Northwest and during which a moral issue was injected into the anti-Democratic movement by the repeal of the Missouri Compromise in the Kansas-Nebraska Act.

Any study of Republican organization in these formative years will reveal the wide variety of issues involved and the divergent emphases placed upon them in different localities. In New York and New England, the major issues were Americanism, temperance and opposition to slavery extension; the Pope, John Barleycorn, and Stephen A. Douglas were the targets of the anti-Democratic attack. In lower Illinois and Indiana "Unionism" was an issue; and the Democrats were "disunionist." In California, the Pacific railway, the overland mail and the personal feud between Senators Gwin and Broderick over patronage were the issues. In Pennsylvania and New Jersey the issue was the tariff. In the Northwest, it was the twin issues of homestead and opposition to the spread of slavery to the Territories.

In spite of this diversity of aim among Republicans, it cannot be denied that the major issue, when the party was considered as a whole, was that of slavery extension. This does not mean any overwhelming ethical condemnation of slavery as an institution. This is not to say that abolitionist sentiment was universal within the Republican ranks. It was not. Vast numbers among Republican leaders were amazingly indifferent toward the problem of slavery. Nevertheless, they were aware of the psychological or emotional factors surrounding slavery as a vote-getting issue. They exploited these possibilities to the full, and without them they could hardly have built a party or won a national election.

Republican anti-slavery agitation aroused the jealous defenders of the declining slave economy and excited fierce partisanship on both sides of Mason and Dixon's Line. The resulting agitation was remarkable first because the natural limits of slavery expansion had probably already been reached,[1] and second because the fierceness of the struggle compelled even the indifferent to take sides and become emotionally aroused. Nearly every political issue of national importance during the 1850's was affected by the bias of the opposing interests regarding slavery. Kansas "bled" all over the floors of Congress and over the pages of the country's press; the Republicans blamed the Democrats for it. Cuba, in the propaganda of the Republicans, became no mere object of simple imperialistic expansion; but the tool of sinister Democratic politicians eager for the expansion of the evil institution of slavery. The Dred Scott decision, according to Republicans, was not the honest opinion of an impartial tribunal, but one further example of the machinations of the Democratic administration to extend the Slave Power. Senator Sumner was attacked in the Senate not by a young hot-blood with a warped sense of honor, but by a champion of slavocracy.

This Republican campaign was aided and abetted by disagreement among the Democrats themselves, which frequently arose over personal and patronage differences. These disagreements did not remain unaffected by genuine differences over slavery which were exacerbated by the intensity of Republican party propaganda. Furthermore, the Democratic party itself, with curious short-sightedness, advanced the Republican cause by its continued opposition to homestead, tariff protection and internal improvements and thus antagonized elements without whose support the Republican cause was hopeless.

Any evaluation of the causes of Republican strength by 1860 cannot disregard the economic, physiographical, cultural and temperamental reasons for northern sectionalism, upon which Republicanism rested. Yet all of this could have availed little without the driving energy of politicians anxious for power and without the spellbinding oratory, inflammatory press and word-of-mouth campaign of propaganda which the Republicans astutely waged against Democratic leaders and policies especially as the protectors of slavocracy.

This whole Republican strategy was accurately analyzed on the eve of the 1860 elections by James Gordon Bennett: [2]

The work was fairly commenced with the Democratic repeal of the Missouri compromise in 1854, from which we date the commencement of the practical disintegration of the Democratic party. Hence, but for the distracting element of Know-Nothingism in 1856, the opposition would have buried the Democracy in that campaign. . . . But the knowledge acquired in that campaign by the Republicans of the secret of their strength was not thrown away. On the contrary, they have employed it with unflagging industry ever since. This secret of their power is the slavery agitation.

A powerful auxiliary in 1856 to "bleeding Kansas" had been furnished in the exciting anti-slavery romance of "Uncle Tom's Cabin," and these things, with the deplorable outrage upon Senator Sumner in the Senate Chamber, and the political consequences thereof, suggested to the Republicans their future programme of operations, to wit: a moral, religious and political crusade against the slave system of the South as a diseased excrescence upon the body politic which must be taken out by the roots. And so, in resuming their work for 1860, after having fed the anti-slavery prejudices of the North for several years with the sufferings of "Uncle Tom," the border ruffianism of Kansas, the assault upon Sumner, "the Lecompton infamy," and what not, a more enlarged and systematic distribution of political anti-slavery documents was commenced. . . . Altogether, we dare say that a million of dollars would not cover the Republican contributions expended in the distribution of their anti-slavery documents, agents, and orators in Pennsylvania and the Western States during the last three years.

It is questionable, of course, whether all the Republican agitation and organization could have prevailed against a united Democratic party. The belligerent attitude of southern extremists, however, made unity impossible. Slavery advocates in the South for a decade had been possessed by one exclusive idea—federal protection of slavery in the territories. When in 1860 Yancey and other "southern rights" doctrinaires determined to force the issue, the party became divided. Their demand for protection of slavery in the territories sabotaged the Charleston convention, and they coöperated with Buchanan in opposing Douglas. On the other hand, Douglas's supporters were equally inept in refusing to withdraw the Little Giant's candidacy, although it was obvious that his nomination would lead to division within the party, and a probable Republican victory. In this respect, extremists in the Democratic ranks were less far-sighted than the Republicans who cast aside controversial personalities to unite behind a more moderate, and therefore "available," candidate.

The action of the Republican convention in rejecting the radical candidacy of Seward, and the eagerness for victory which kept party lines tight in spite of major disappointments, provide the key to the Republican victory. The Democrats were not capable of similar action; they had tasted too long of success to appreciate the value of compromise and sacrifice.

The story of the remarkable Republican success is contained in the story of the Chicago convention. Here many of the presidential aspirants were discarded quickly because, for one reason or another, each was too radical, too doctrinaire, too conservative, or too much the representative of special interests to serve the party as a whole. Seward was too radical on the slavery question to suit conservatives; too partial to immigrants to satisfy "Americans"; too tainted with Weed's alleged corruption to please reformers; too long in politics to have made few enemies. Bates was too "American" to suit the Germans; too old to appeal to the younger bloods, and too conservative to satisfy the radicals. Chase was too radical to suit conservatives; too partial to the Germans to please the "Americans"; too much a Democrat to please the former Whigs; too much associated with free trade to suit protectionists. Cameron was too much the politician and spoilsman and too much the candidate of a single state. Banks was too much like Bates and was no competition for Seward. McLean was too aged and colorless. Collamer and Dayton came from states too small to affect the election. Wade was too much disliked by Chase. There remained Abraham Lincoln.

Lincoln was hardly known in the East at all, except for his debates with Douglas, his Cooper Institute address and his New England tour. He had been endorsed as the favorite son of Illinois scarcely a week before the national convention met. He was the first choice of very few outside his own state, but he was disliked by none. Therefore he was the second choice of many, and herein lay his strength. As he himself wrote to an Ohio supporter: "My name is new in the field, and I suppose I am not the first choice of a very great many. . . . Our policy, then, is to give no offense to others—leave them in a mood to come to us if they shall be compelled to give up their first love." [3]

This was the strategy of "availability."

Furthermore, Lincoln owed much of his success at Chicago to the work of his managers, who were ever active in capitalizing on the other candidates' "stop-Seward" maneuvers. They were not averse to making promises in return for support from hesitant delegations. Judge David Davis's promises of Cabinet positions to Caleb B. Smith and Simon Cameron are illustrative. Two days following the nomination, William Jayne—Lincoln's Springfield friend, brother-in-law of Senator Trumbull, and governor of Dakota Territory during Lincoln's administration—could well comment: "Logan & Davis, Butler & Dubois, Judd, Cook & Palmer, & Jack Grimshaw worked like Turks for Lincoln's nomination." [4]

The stature which Lincoln later demonstrated in the White House was not obvious at the time of the Chicago convention. Indeed, it was his relative obscurity compared with his rivals that contributed so heavily to his success. Lincoln's nomination was procured through the familiar channels of applied politics.

The sagacity of those in control at the Chicago convention was indicated not only in Lincoln's selection but also in the platform adopted. Realizing that anti-slavery radicalism could not carry the entire North, they limited themselves to a comparatively conservative stand, only declaring the undesirability of the extension of slavery into the territories. Non-extension was only one of the planks approved. Tariff revision was called for—in words strong enough to satisfy Pennsylvania and New Jersey but weak enough so as not to offend the erstwhile Free Soil Democratic low-tariff elements within the Republican party. A demand for river-and-harbor improvements was adopted—to satisfy the old Whig elements and to attract the Great Lakes regions. A homestead act was championed—to appeal to Northwestern farmers, both American and German-born. Pacific-railroad and daily-overland-mail planks were included—to court particularly the California and Oregon vote. Proscription against the foreign-born was disapproved—to satisfy the Germans, but in language that would not alienate the Know-Nothings.

As Lincoln's campaign opened it became apparent that he was a strong candidate. About him clustered the tradition of the pioneer and the log cabin. He was radical enough to appease the advanced anti-slavery Republicans, yet conservative enough to be satisfactory to the more moderate Republicans. The former Whigs accepted him because he had been one of them; so did even many of the more conservative Old Line Whigs for the same reason. He was thus able to make inroads into Bell's strength. The former Free Soil Democratic element acquiesced in his nomination, partly because he was by far more anti-slavery than Douglas, Bell, or Breckinridge, partly because Chase supported him; and partly because Hamlin had been given a place on the national ticket. In a word, Lincoln could unite the diverse anti-Democratic elements behind him. And he judiciously refrained from quoting his opinions for the public during the campaign.

By August it was generally agreed that Lincoln would be the next president. The Republicans were united for the duration of the campaign while the superior numbers of the opposition were divided into three hostile camps, apparently more intent upon destroying each other than upon defeat of the Republicans, who they all agreed might split the Union if successful. The Douglas orators denounced Breckinridge as a secessionist and charged him and Buchanan with being under the influence of southern fire-eaters. The Breckinridge forces, on the other hand, repudiated Douglas as the destroyer of Democratic unity, a traitor and semi-abolitionist who played away his own hopes and followers into the Republican receiving basket. Meanwhile Douglas broke tradition and entered the hustings in person. He was soon engulfed in a most extraordinary canvass throughout the country, attempting to stem the northern tide toward Lincoln and the southern current toward Breckinridge—advocating his sure-cure medicine of popular sovereignty. Often the issue between the Democrats was merely one of personality—an embittered exchange of charges, denials and countercharges about the claims to party "regularity" and support of the rival Democratic "National" conventions which nominated Douglas and Breckinridge, respectively. Breckinridge wandered into questions touching himself. Douglas did the same. By their criminations and recriminations they were, as one Democrat complained, "doing more to elect Lincoln than all the republican presses and republican orators in the land." [5] As for the Bell-Everetters, they cut in and out, combining with or opposing Douglas, or Breckinridge, or both as the occasion seemed to demand; in New York they combined with the Douglasites, in Indiana with the Republicans.

The Republican state victories in pivotal Pennsylvania and indispensable Indiana in October—made possible by the split in the Democratic party and, in Pennsylvania, by the tariff issue—all but marked the inevitability of Lincoln's victory. To the anti-Lincoln forces there remained only one hope of stopping Lincoln—New York. If the Empire State could be kept out of the Lincoln column, the presidential contest would be decided by Congress. The Douglas and Bell men succeeded in "fusing." Efforts were now made to bring the Breckinridge men, led by Daniel S. Dickinson, into the anti-Republican front. But each wing of the Democracy detested the other. It was estimated that a popular anti-Republican majority of 50,000 existed in New York. But, as in other states, the materials which made up this hypothetical majority comprised diverse factions, each hating the other. Moreover, Lincoln was Whig enough to draw some of the Fillmore "American" strength that would have gone to Bell. With the largest of all states, and Pennsylvania, Indiana, New England and the Northwest in the Republican column, there could be only one result—Lincoln's election.

The campaign of 1860, besides being one of the most momentous in American history, was one of the most remarkable insofar as the winning candidate, Abraham Lincoln, did not represent a majority of the voters—his popular vote reveals that. Moreover, it is doubtful if the party which he headed represented what was in the minds of the American people. The conservative sense of the country stood arrayed against a northern and sectional minority—but the Republicans were united for the duration of the contest, while their opponents were divided. Yet through the jealousy and personal enmity of political leaders, through quarrels over constitutional doctrines and distrust of the past party antecedents of each other following the break-up of the Whig party in the mid-fifties and the division in the Democracy, the opposition to the Republicans was divided three ways—two separate and distinct factions of the Democracy combatting each other, running their separate candidates, Douglas and Breckinridge, respectfully; and the remnants of the old Whigs and "Americans," most of whom hated all Democrats and shunned sectional Republicans, placing Bell in the field. The majority of the northern Democracy would not drop Douglas, the Constitutional Unionists would not withdraw Bell—neither of whom could possibly be elected, since most of the northern states were conceded to Lincoln and most of the southern states were conceded to Breckinridge. The Republicans would not forsake Lincoln and the southern Democrats would not abandon Breckinridge. In the process Lincoln became President of the United States.

Notes

1. Andrew W. Crandall, *The Early History of the Republican Party, 1854–1856*, pp. 18–19, 35–37, 43, 47–61, 138–141; James L. Sellers, "The Make-up of the Early Republican Party," *Transactions of the Illinois State Historical Society*, 1930, pp. 41–42.

2. George W. Julian, "The First Republican National Convention," *American Historical Review*, IV, 313–322.

3. H. Waldron to May, *Private*, April 26, 1856, Charles S. May Papers; Fred Wadsworth to Wade, February 25, 1856, Benjamin F. Wade Papers.

4. Albany *Atlas & Argus*, December 3, 1856.

5. B. F. Williams to Chase, February 7, 1856, Salmon P. Chase Papers, Library of Congress.

6. Allison to McLean, June 2, 1856, John McLean Papers.

7. Alexander Harris, *A Review of the Political Conflict in America*, pp. 171–172; William E. Smith, *The Francis Preston Blair Family in Politics*, I, 345–350.

8. Harry J. Carman and Reinhard H. Luthin, "The Seward-Fillmore Feud and the Disruption of the Whig Party," *New York History* (July, 1943), XXIV, 353–354; *Tribune Almanac*, 1857, p. 46.

9. W. H. Furness to Sumner, November 9, 1856, Charles Sumner Papers.

10. Speech after the Election of Buchanan, November, 1856, MS., Richard Yates Papers.

11. George T. Curtis, *Life of James Buchanan*, II, 185.

12. Philip G. Auchampaugh, *James Buchanan and His Cabinet on the Eve of Secession*, pp. 29–30.

13. F. H. Hodder, "Some Phases of the Dred Scott Case," *Mississippi Valley Historical Review* (June, 1929), XVI, 3–19; Philip G. Auchampaugh, "James Buchanan, the Court and the Dred Scott Case," *Tennessee Historical Magazine* (January, 1926), IX, 232–239; Francis P. Weisenburger, *The Life of John McLean*, pp. 195–210.

14. J. G. Randall, *The Civil War and Reconstruction*, p. 155.

15. *Congressional Globe*, 35th Cong., 1st sess., p. 941. Seward did not substantiate his charge of a pro-slavery conspiracy between Buchanan and the Supreme Court justices.

16. Auchampaugh, "James Buchanan, the Court and the Dred Scott Case," *loc. cit.*, p. 239; Randall, *The Civil War and Reconstruction*, p. 156.

17. Chase to Sumner, May 1, 1857, Sumner Papers.

18. Henry M. Field, *The Story of the Atlantic Telegraph*, pp. 23–31, 34–37, 43, 44, 50–58, 69–72, 80–95; Charles F. Briggs and Augustus Maverick, *The Story of the Telegraph and a History of the Great Atlantic Cable*, pp. 46–47, 49–52.

19. Joseph B. Bishop, *A Chronicle of One Hundred & Fifty Years: The Chamber of Commerce of the State of New York, 1768–1918*, pp. 128–129.

20. Allan Nevins, *Abram S. Hewitt, With Some Account of Peter Cooper*, p. 166.

21. *Congressional Globe*, 34th Cong., 3rd sess., p. 397.

22. *Ibid.*, p. 425.

23. *Ibid.*, p. 754.

24. *Ibid.*, p. 1086; 11 *U. S. Statutes at Large*, 187.

25. John G. Van Deusen, *Economic Bases of Disunion in South Carolina*, pp. 67–74, 84–94; Jesse T. Carpenter, *The South as a Conscious Minority, 1789–1861*, pp. 19, 29–30, 56; Ulrich B. Phillips, *The Life of Robert Toombs*, p. 148.

26. Robert R. Russel, *Economic Aspects of Southern Sectionalism, 1840–1861*, pp. 151–156, 178.

27. Frank W. Taussig, *The Tariff History of the United States*, 6th edition, pp. 112–114.

28. Edward Stanwood, *American Tariff Controversies in the Nineteenth Century*, II, pp. 99, 101–104.

29. *Congressional Globe*, 34th Cong., 3rd sess., Appendix, p. 345.

30. Stanwood, *American Tariff Controversies*, II, 106–108. The vote is in *Congressional Globe*, 34 Cong., 3rd sess., Appendix, p. 358.

31. See George W. Van Vleck, *The Panic of 1857*.

32. Malcolm R. Eiselen, *The Rise of Pennsylvania Protectionism*, pp. 246 ff.

33. H. Winter Davis to Morrill, August 20, 1859, Justin S. Morrill Papers.

34. Thomas M. Pitkin, "Western Republicans and the Tariff in 1860," *Mississippi Valley Historical Review* (December, 1940), XXVII, 402–404; Reinhard H. Luthin, "Pennsylvania and Lincoln's Rise to the Presidency," *Pennsylvania Magazine of History and Biography* (January, 1943), LVII, 62–65, 78–81.

35. Indianapolis *Daily Journal*, March 16, 1860.

36. Chicago *Press & Tribune*, March 30, April 3, 1860.

37. *Ibid.*, April 4, 1860.

38. Thomas M. Pitkin, "The Tariff and the Early Republican Party," MS., p. 185; Reinhard H. Luthin, "Abraham Lincoln and the Tariff," *American Historical Review* (July, 1944), XLIX, 615 ff.

39. Samuel B. Ruggles to Seward, October 20, 1852, William H. Seward Papers.

40. E. C. Nelson, "Presidential Influence on the Policy of Internal Improvements," *Iowa Journal of History and Politics* (January, 1906), IV, 47–50, 67–68.

41. Kirk H. Porter, *National Party Platforms*, p. 49.

42. Mildred C. Stoler, "Influence of the Democratic Element in the Republican Party of Illinois and Indiana, 1854–1860," MS., p. 137.

43. Henry G. Wheeler, *History of Congress . . . Comprising a History of Internal Improvements*, II, 533–563; O. J. Hollister, *Life of Schuyler Colfax*, p. 111; Wilmer C. Harris, *Public Life of Zachariah Chandler*, pp. 17–18, 46.

44. Stoler, "Influence of the Democratic Element in the Republican Party of Illinois and Indiana, 1854–1860," MS., pp. 139, 179.

45. *Congressional Globe*, 34th Cong., 3rd sess., pp. 84, 635, 636, 638.

46. Harris, *Public Life of Zachariah Chandler*, p. 46.

47. *Congressional Globe*, 35th Cong., 1st sess., pp. 2159, 2348–2353, 2403.

48. Ulrich B. Phillips (ed.), *The Correspondence of Robert Toombs, Alexander H. Stephens, and Howell Cobb*, p. 278.

49. Chicago *Press & Tribune*, March 5, 1860.

50. *Ibid.*

51. *Ibid.*, April 16, May 16, 1860; *Congressional Globe*, 36th Cong., 1st sess., p. 850.

52. Paul W. Gates, *The Illinois Central Railroad and Its Colonization Work*, pp. 31–34; 39–41; Howard K. Brownson, *History of the Illinois Central Railroad to 1870*, chap. i.

53. Robert R. Russel, "The Pacific Railroad Issue in Politics Prior to the Civil War," *Mississippi Valley Historical Review* (September, 1925), XII, 189–194.

54. Wilford L. Wilson, "The Contest Between the North and South Over the Building of the Pacific Railway," MS.; *The Public and Diplomatic Correspondence of James M. Mason. . .*, p. 138; Crandall, *The Early History of the Republican Party, 1854–1856*, pp. 197, 260; George T. Clark, *Leland Stanford*, pp. 72–74.

55. Alvin F. Harlow, *Old Wires and New Waves*, pp. 306–317; James D. Reid, *The Telegraph in America*, pp. 488–497; *Congressional Globe*, 36th Cong., 1st sess., pp. 494, 1292, 1345, 2353, 2375, 2422, 3032, 3063, 3113; 12 *U. S. Statutes at Large*, 41.

56. *Congressional Globe*, 36th Cong., 1st sess., p. 1345.

57. Curtis Nettels, "The Overland Mail Issue During the Fifties," *Missouri Historical Review* (July, 1924), XVIII, 521–532; Joseph Ellison, *California and the Nation, 1850–1869*, pp. 136–141, 156–163.

58. Nettels, *loc. cit.*, p. 524; Le Roy R. Hafen, *The Overland Mail, 1849–1869*, pp. 81–88.

59. *Congressional Globe*, 34th Cong., 3rd sess., Appendix, p. 321.

60. Le Roy R. Hafen, "Butterfield's Overland Mail," *California Historical Society Quarterly* (1923), II, 211–222; Hafen, *The Overland Mail*, pp. 88–94; Nettels, *loc. cit.*, pp. 524–529.

61. *Congressional Globe*, 35th Cong., 1st sess., pp. 3002–3003.

62. *Ibid.*, p. 3003.

63. *Ibid.*, p. 3004.

64. *Ibid.*, p. 3005.

65. San Francisco *Daily Evening Bulletin*, July 14, 1858.

66. Winfield J. Davis, *History of Political Conventions in California, 1849–1892*, p. 98.

67. Hafen, *The Overland Mail*, pp. 165–170.

68. *Congressional Globe*, 35th Cong., 2nd sess., Appendix, p. 1500.

69. St. Louis *Daily Missouri Democrat*, August 16, 1859.

70. Nettels, *loc. cit.*, p. 534.

71. Joseph G. Rayback, "Land for the Landless: The Contemporary View," MS.

72. George M. Stephenson, *The Political History of the Public Lands from 1840 to 1862*, pp. 19–20, 97–114, 149–156, 161–162; John B. Sanborn, "Some Political Aspects of Homestead Legislation," *American Historical Review* (October, 1900), VI, 19, 31–33; James C. Ballagh, "Southern Economic History: Tariff and Public Lands," *Annual Report, American Historical Association, 1898*, pp. 241–242.

73. Rayback, "Land for the Landless," MS., pp. 31–32.

74. *Ibid.*, pp. 53, 58–59, 59 n., 97.

75. John G. Stephenson to Trumbull, March 25, 1860, Lyman Trumbull Papers.

76. Stephenson, *The Political History of the Public Lands from 1840 to 1862*, p. 193.

77. *Congressional Globe*, 35th Cong., 2nd sess., p. 1076.

78. *Ibid.*

79. Rayback, "Land for the Landless," MS., p. 81.

80. St. Louis *Daily Missouri Democrat*, July 2, 1859, pp. 1, 2.

81. *Ibid.*

82. Johnson Brigham, *James Harlan*, p. 136.

83. *Ibid.*, pp. 137–138.

84. Stephenson, *The Political History of the Public Lands from 1840 to 1862*, pp. 214–219, 227–228; Sister Evangeline Thomas, *Nativism in the Old Northwest, 1850–1860*, pp. 81–82, 241; Indianapolis *Daily Journal*, March 14, 1860; Chicago *Press & Tribune*, March 13, 14, 27, April 23, 1860.

85. *Congressional Globe*, 35th Cong., 2nd sess., p. 852.

86. Alfred C. True, *A History of Agricultural Education in the United States, 1785–1925*, pp. 99–102; George W. Knight, "History and Management of the Land Grants for Education in the Northwest Territory," *Papers of the American Historical Association* (1885), I, 22–24.

87. *Congressional Globe*, 35th Cong., 2nd sess. p. 718.

88. *Ibid.*, pp. 94–95.

89. *Ibid.*, pp. 186–187.

90. *Ibid.*, p. 857.

91. Greeley to Schuyler Colfax, February 18, 1859, Greeley-Colfax Papers.

92. William B. Parker, *The Life and Public Services of Justin Smith Morrill*, pp. 267–268.

93. Charles H. Ambler (ed.), *Correspondence of Robert M. T. Hunter, 1826–1876*, p. 265.

94. Amos A. Ettinger, *The Mission to Spain of Pierre Soulé, 1853–1855*, chaps. i–x.

95. New York *Daily Times*, March 6, 19, April 9, 1855.

96. Kirk H. Porter, *National Party Platforms*, p. 49.

97. George E. Baker (ed.), *Works of William H. Seward*, IV, 270.

98. Ambler (ed.), *Correspondence of Robert M. T. Hunter, 1826–1876*, p. 201.

99. John Bassett Moore (ed.), *The Works of James Buchanan*, X, 252.

100. Louis M. Sears, *John Slidell*, pp. 152–153; John H. Latané, "The Diplomacy of the United States in Regard to Cuba," *Annual Report, American Historical Association, 1897*, pp. 250–251; Ballagh, "Southern Economic History: Tariff and Public Lands," *loc. cit.*, pp. 244–245.

101. Frederic Bancroft, *The Life of William H. Seward*, I, 478.

102. J. Fred Rippy, *The United States and Mexico*, 1926 edition, pp. 149 ff.; Paul N. Garber, *The Gadsden Treaty*, pp. 118, 133–134.

103. Ulrich B. Phillips (ed.), *The Correspondence of Robert Toombs, Alexander H. Stephens, and Howell Cobb*, p. 399.

104. Rippy, *The United States and Mexico*, pp. 212–221, 223–226; James M. Callahan, "The Mexican Policy of Southern Leaders Under Buchanan's Administration," *Annual Report, American Historical Association*, 1910, pp. 135–151; Howard L. Wilson, "President Buchanan's Proposed Intervention in Mexico," *The American Historical Review* (July, 1900), V, 687–701.

105. New York *Daily Tribune*, January 26, 1860.

106. See Chapter VIII of the present volume.

107. James L. Sellers, "The Make-up of the Early Republican Party," *Transactions of the Illinois State Historical Society, 1930*, p. 45.

108. Rayback, "Land for the Landless," MS., p. 79 n.

109. Harrisburg (Pa.) *Daily Telegraph*, August 13, 1859.

110. Copies in New York Public Library.

111. Henry B. Stanton, *Random Recollections*, 2nd edition, p. 97.

112. David R. Barbee, "Hinton Rowan Helper," *Tyler's Quarterly Historical and Genealogical Magazine* (January, 1934), XV, 135–172; Hugh H. Lefler, "Hinton Rowan Helper: Advocate of a 'White America,'" *Southern Sketches*, No. 1, pp. 5–25. See also: John Spencer Bassett, *Anti-Slavery Leaders of North Carolina*, pp. 11–29. For a scholarly account of the speakership fight, see Ollinger Crenshaw, "The Speakership Contest of 1859–1860," *Mississippi Valley Historical Review* (December, 1942), XXIX, 323–328.

113. Oswald Garrison Villard, *John Brown, 1800–1859*; Allen Johnson (ed.), *Dictionary of American Biography*, III, 131–134.

114. Villard, *John Brown*, pp. 471–472, 474; James Ford Rhodes, *History of the United States from the Compromise of 1850*, II, 402; New York *Herald*, October 19, 1859.

115. *House Report* No. 278, 36th Cong., 1st sess., Vol. II, serial no. 1040, p. 254.

116. Villard, *John Brown*, p. 502.

117. Ambler (ed.), *Correspondence of Robert M. T. Hunter, 1826–1876*, pp. 278–286.

118. *Indiana Magazine of History* (September, 1928), XXIV, 206–207.

119. John G. Nicolay and John Hay (eds.), *Complete Works of Abraham Lincoln*, Gettysburg Edition, V, 314.

120. *Congressional Globe*, 36th Cong., 1st sess., pp. 552–554.

121. Arthur C. Cole, *The Whig Party in the South*, pp. 328, 331–336; Henry T. Shanks, *The Secession Movement in Virginia, 1847–1861*, pp. 46, 58–65; Marguerite B. Hamer, "The Presidential Campaign of 1860 in Tennessee," *The East Tennessee Historical Society Publications* (January, 1931), III, 3–5; Clement Eaton, "The Resistance of the South to Northern Radicalism," *New England Quarterly* (June, 1935), VIII, 215; Washington Hunt to Winthrop, February 8, 1860, Robert C. Winthrop Papers.

122. Dunbar Rowland (ed.), *Jefferson Davis, Constitutionalist: His Letters, Papers, and Speeches*, IV, 87.

123. New York *Herald*, December 22, 1859.

124. *Memoirs of Gustave Koerner*, II, 80; Charles Gibson, "Edward Bates," *Collections, Missouri Historical Society* (January, 1900), II, 55; Chicago *Press & Tribune*, December 27, 1859.

125. Malcolm R. Eiselen, *The Rise of Pennsylvania Protectionism*, pp. 247 ff.; Charles M. Knapp, *New Jersey Politics During the Period of the Civil War and Reconstruction*, pp. 17, 24 n., 35 n.

126. James L. Sellers, "James R. Doolittle," *Wisconsin Magazine of History* (March, 1934), XVII, 288–290.

127. *Ibid.*, p. 289; Burton A. Konkle, *The Life and Speeches of Thomas Williams*, I, 391–392, 392 n.

128. Konkle, *Thomas Williams*, I, 292–293; New York *Herald*, December 23, 1859, p. 1.

129. See Chapter VIII.

130. A. H. Bullock to Samuel Bowles, October 6, 1859, in Harry J. Carman and Reinhard H. Luthin, *Lincoln and the Patronage*, p. 6.

CHAPTER II

1. James S. Pike, *First Blows of the Civil War*, p. 483; Henry G. Pearson, *The Life of John A. Andrew*, I, 112.

2. *Reminiscences of Carl Schurz*, II, 34; Lewis D. Campbell to Schouler, February 15, 1855. William Schouler Papers.

3. The best biography of Seward is Frederic Bancroft, *The Life of William H. Seward*, 2 vols. Dean Harry J. Carman and Dr. Reinhard H. Luthin, of Columbia University, are now preparing a new life of Seward.

4. Harry J. Carman and Reinhard H. Luthin, "The Seward-Fillmore Feud and the Crisis of 1850," *New York History* (April, 1943), XXIV, 163–184; Harry J. Carman and Reinhard H. Luthin, "The Seward-

Fillmore Feud and the Disruption of the Whig Party," *New York History* (July, 1943), XXIV, 335–357.

5. New York *Daily Tribune*, July 2, 18, 26, August 11, 15, 1853.

6. Albany *Evening Journal*, May 20, 1853.

7. Seward to Weed, January 8, 1854. Thurlow Weed Papers, University of Rochester Library.

8. *New York State Senate Journal* (1854), 77th sess., pp. 123, 159–160, 179, 205–208.

9. New York *Daily Tribune*, February 18, May 13, 1854; New York *Herald*, January 30, February 1, 1854.

10. New York *Herald*, January 31, 1854.

11. *Congressional Globe*, 33rd Cong., 1st sess., Appendix, p. 151.

12. James Ford Rhodes, *History of the United States from the Compromise of 1850*, I, 453.

13. De Alva S. Alexander, *A Political History of the State of New York*, II, 193; *Congressional Globe*, 33rd Cong., 1st sess., p. 442.

14. *Congressional Globe*, 33rd Cong., 1st sess., pp. 1708–1709.

15. Seward to Weed, May 29, 1854, Weed Papers.

16. Bancroft, *Seward*, I, 366 n.

17. Frederick W. Seward, *Seward at Washington*, II, 232. For a brilliant biography of Parker, see Henry Steele Commager, *Theodore Parker*.

18. Horace Greeley, *Recollections of a Busy Life*, p. 315. Greeley erroneously gives the date of the Saratoga Anti-Nebraska Convention as September instead of August.

19. A. Hunt to Weed, August 16, 1854. Weed Papers.

20. New York *Daily Tribune*, September 21, 1854; John A. Krout, "The Maine Law in New York Politics," *New York History* (July, 1936), XVII, 262 ff.; Louis D. Scisco, *Political Nativism in New York State*, pp. 113 ff.

21. Scisco, *Political Nativism in New York State*, pp. 130–132; New York *Herald*, January 10, 11, February 2, 3, 7, 8, 1855; New York *Evening Post*, January 4, 9, 1855.

22. Seward, *Seward at Washington*, II, 245.

23. Alexander, *A Political History of the State of New York*, II, 217–218.

24. Gideon Welles, *Lincoln and Seward*, p. 11; Carman and Luthin, "The Seward-Fillmore Feud and the Disruption of the Whig Party," *op. cit.*, p. 353.

25. William E. Smith, *The Francis Preston Blair Family in Politics*, I, 323, 324.

26. Seward to Weed, December 31, 1855, Weed Papers.

27. Seward, *Seward at Washington*, II, 259.

28. Crandall, *The Early History of the Republican Party*, pp. 47–61.

29. Ralph V. Harlow, "The Rise and Fall of the Kansas Aid Movement," *American Historical Review* (1935), XLI, 1 ff.; James C. Malin, "The Proslavery Background of the Kansas Struggle," *Mississippi Valley Historical Review* (1923), X, 288 ff.

30. *Congressional Globe*, 34th Cong., 1st sess., p. 693.

31. Seward to Weed, April 4, 1856, Weed Papers.

32. *Congressional Globe*, 34th Cong., 1st sess., Appendix, p. 403.

33. Seward, *Seward at Washington*, II, 270.

34. Allan Nevins, *Frémont: The West's Greatest Adventurer*, II, 478 ff.; Ruhl J. Bartlett, *John C. Frémont and the Republican Party*, pp. 16 ff.

35. Seward to Weed, May 4, 1856, March 13, 18, 24, 1858, Weed Papers.

36. New York *Daily Tribune*, October 24, 1856; Seward, *Seward at Washington*, II, 291 ff.

37. *Morning Courier and New York Enquirer*, November 13, 1856; Alexander, *A Political History of the State of New York*, II, 240.

38. *Morning Courier and New York Enquirer*, September 25, 1856.

39. Albany *Atlas and Argus*, December 3, 1856; New York *Herald*, November 10, 1856; January 27, 1857.

40. Weed to Cameron, November 12, 1856, Simon Cameron Papers.

41. Preston King to Weed, January 29, 1857, Weed Papers.

42. Fish to William Kent, December 11, Letter Book P, pp. 98–101. Hamilton Fish Papers; Allan Nevins, *Hamilton Fish*, p. 78.

43. *Congressional Globe*, 35th Cong., 1st sess., p. 941.

44. George E. Baker (ed.), *The Works of William H. Seward*, IV, 292.

45. *The American Whig Review*, XI, 637; Smith to Carey, November 4, 1858, Henry C. Carey Papers.

46. Alexander, *A Political History of the State of New York*, II, 255, 255 n.

47. Malcolm R. Eiselen, *The Rise of Pennsylvania Protectionism*, pp. 244 ff.; Reinhard H. Luthin, "The Democratic Split during Buchanan's Administration," *Pennsylvania History* (January, 1944), XI, 17.

48. John Allison to McLean, December 7, 1858, John McLean Papers.

49. Thomas M. Pitkin, "The Tariff and the Early Republican Party," MS., pp. 151–153, 244–245.

50. *Congressional Globe*, 35th Cong., 2nd sess., pp. 277, 1351–1354.

51. *Dictionary of American Biography*, III, 487–489.

52. Smith to Carey, July 25, 1858, Carey Papers.

53. Same to same, September 12, 1858, *ibid.*

54. Same to same, September 18, 1858, *ibid.*

55. Same to same, November 4, 1858, *ibid.*

56. Philadelphia *Public Ledger*, April 2, 1859.

57. Seward to Weed, April 11, 1859, Weed Papers.

58. New York *Herald*, April 17, May 3, 1859.

59. New York *Daily Tribune*, May 9, 1859.

60. Seward, *Seward at Washington*, II, 360.

61. New York *Daily Tribune*, May 7, 9, 1859.

62. New York *Herald*, December 30, 1859.

63. E. Peshine Smith to Carey, January 25, 1860, Carey Papers.

64. J. Dixon to Welles, January 31, 1860, Gideon Welles Papers.

65. Villard, *John Brown, 1800–1859*, pp. 471–472, 474; James Ford Rhodes, *History of the United States from the Compromise of 1850*, II, 402.

66. *House Report No. 278*, 36th Cong., 1st sess., Vol. II, serial no. 1040, p. 254.

67. Portland (Maine) *Daily Eastern Argus*, January 24, 1860.

68. Howard K. Beale (ed.), *The Diary of Edward Bates (Annual Report, American Historical Association*, 1930, Vol. IV), pp. 93–94.

69. Sumner to Chase, February 7, 1860, Salmon P. Chase Papers.

70. *Congressional Globe*, 36th Cong., sess., p. 913.

71. Providence *Daily Post*, March 2, 1860.

72. Alexander, *A Political History of the State of New York*, II, 268.

73. Thurlow Weed Barnes, *Memoir of Thurlow Weed*, p. 260.

74. Rochester *Union and Advertiser*, April 19, 1860.

75. James E. Harvey to McLean, September 5, 1859, John McLean Papers.

76. E. G. Spaulding to Weed, January 24, 25, 1860, Weed Papers.

77. F. H. Herriott, "Republican Presidential Preliminaries in Iowa—1859–1860," *Annals of Iowa* (January, 1910), Series III, Vol. 9, pp. 267–268.

78. Allan A. Craig to Weed, "Confidential," November 19, 1859; Frank M. Cooley to Weed, January 2, 1860; Read to Weed, January 30, 1860; Bradford to Weed, January 30, 1860, Weed Papers.

79. Thomas Webster, Jr., to Weed, March 28, April 11, 1860, Weed Papers, Library of Congress.

80. G. Milton Allen to Weed, January 7, 1860, Weed Papers.

81. E. G. Spaulding to Weed, March 13, 1860, Weed Papers.

82. J. Dixon to Welles, February 17, 1860, Welles Papers: Dan R. Tilden to Wade, March 27, 1860, Benjamin F. Wade Papers; E. Peshine Smith to Carey, April 15, 1860, Carey Papers.

83. Seward to Weed, April 5, 1860, Weed Papers.

84. Weed to Cameron, April 8, 1860, Cameron Papers.

85. A. K. McClure to Cameron, April 24, 1860, *ibid.*

86. Weed to Cameron, April 27, 1860, *ibid.*

87. Weed to Cameron, May 7, 1860, *ibid.*

88. Later Cameron said: "The nomination of Seward for the presidency . . . would have happened if Thurlow Weed had been at pains to travel to Chicago by way of Harrisburg." See Albany *Evening Journal*, May 19, 1890.

89. J. Dixon to Welles, February 27, May 8, 1860, Welles Papers; Preston King to Fish, March 26, 1860, Hamilton Fish Papers.

90. Donnal V. Smith, "Salmon P. Chase and the Election of 1860," *Ohio Archaeological and Historical Quarterly* (1930), XXXIX, 516, 521.

91. Bangor *Daily Whig and Courier*, March 2, 1860; Louis C. Hatch (ed.), *Maine: A History*, II, 420.

92. Worcester *Daily Spy*, March 8, 1860, p. 2; Henry G. Pearson, *The Life of John A. Andrew*, I, 111-112.

93. Robert H. Morris to Fish, February 11, 1860, Fish Papers; James S. Pike, *First Blows of the Civil War*, p. 443.

94. Winona (Minn.) *Democrat*, February 27, 1860; Eugene V. Smalley, *A History of the Republican Party . . . To Which Is Added a Political History of Minnesota from a Republican Point of View*, p. 166.

95. Appleton (Wis.) *Crescent*, March 10, 1860; Alexander Graham to Weed, November 26, 1859, Weed Papers.

96. Detroit *Free Press*, May 4, 1860.

97. F. I. Herriott, "Iowa and the First Nomination of Abraham Lincoln," *Annals of Iowa* (July, 1907), Series III, Vol. 8, pp. 94-95.

98. H. Kreismann to Washburne, May 7, 1860, Elihu B. Washburne Papers.

99. Topeka *Kansas State Record*, April 14, 1860; D. W. Wilder, *The Annals of Kansas*, pp. 243-244.

100. Hubert H. Bancroft, *History of California*, VII, 257.

101. *Collections, Cayuga County Historical Society* (1893), X, 51-54; William E. Barton, *President Lincoln*, I, 96.

CHAPTER III

1. The best biography of Chase is still Albert Bushnell Hart, *Salmon Portland Chase*. See also Reinhard H. Luthin, "Salmon P. Chase's Political Career Before the Civil War," *Mississippi Valley Historical Review* (March, 1943), XXIX, 517-540.

2. Theodore Clarke Smith, *The Liberty and Free Soil Parties in the Northwest*, pp. 138-142; Chase to John Van Buren, July 19, 1848, Samuel J. Tilden Papers, Box No. 18.

3. Margaret L. Plunkett, "A History of the Liberty Party with Emphasis upon Its Activities in the Northeastern States," MS., pp. 171-172.

4. Erwin H. Price, "The Election of 1848 in Ohio," *Ohio Archaeological and Historical Quarterly* (1927), XXXVI, 300.

5. Annie A. Nunns (ed.), "Some Letters of Salmon P. Chase, 1848-1865," *American Historical Review* (April, 1929), XXXIV, 536 ff.; Albert G. Riddle, "The Election of Salmon P. Chase to the Senate," *The Republic* (Washington, D. C.), IV, 179-183 (March, 1875).

6. *Diary and Correspondence of Salmon P. Chase*, 1902, Vol. II, p. 135; Floyd P. Gates, "Salmon P. Chase and the Independent Democrats," MS., pp. 22-23.

7. Ben Perley Poore, *Reminiscences*, I, 307; *Diary and Correspondence of Salmon P. Chase*, p. 189.

8. *Congressional Globe*, 32nd Cong., 1st sess., Appendix, p. 1125.

9. Smith, *The Liberty and Free Soil Parties in the Northwest*, pp. 239-241.

10. Eugene H. Roseboom, "Ohio in the 1850's," MS., p. 252.

11. Smith, *The Liberty and Free Soil Parties in the Northwest*, pp. 261–276, 286.

12. *Ibid.*, p. 287.

13. *Congressional Globe*, 33rd Cong., 1st sess., pp. 221–222.

14. *Ibid.*, pp. 239–240.

15. Allen Johnson, *Stephen A. Douglas*, pp. 240–241; George Fort Milton, *The Eve of Conflict*, pp. 117–122.

16. Milton, *The Eve of Conflict*, p. 117.

17. Joshua R. Giddings, *History of the Rebellion: Its Authors and Causes*, p. 366 n.

18. *Diary and Correspondence of Salmon P. Chase*, p. 263.

19. *Congressional Globe*, 33rd Cong., 1st sess., p. 275.

20. *Ibid.*, p. 276.

21. For Douglas's maneuvers in enacting his Kansas-Nebraska Act, see Roy F. Nichols, *Franklin Pierce*, pp. 322–323; Mrs. Archibald Dixon, *The True History of the Missouri Compromise and Its Repeal*.

22. Cincinnati *Daily Gazette*, February 25, 1854.

23. *Quarterly Publication of the Historical and Philosophical Society of Ohio*, XIII, 53.

24. *Ibid.*, pp. 555–56.

25. Roseboom, "Ohio in the 1850's," MS., p. 286.

26. Chase to Schouler, May 28, 1854, William Schouler Papers.

27. Roseboom, "Ohio in the 1850's," MS., pp. 286–290.

28. *Ibid.*, pp. 292–321.

29. *Ibid.*, pp. 313–317.

30. Edgar Holt, "Party Politics in Ohio, 1840–1850," *Ohio Archaeological and Historical Quarterly* (1929), XXXVIII, 312–313.

31. Annie A. Nunns (ed.), "Some Letters of Salmon P. Chase, 1848–1865," *The American Historical Review* (April, 1929), XXXIV, 561.

32. Chase to James W. Grimes (copy), April 29, 1854, Chase Papers, Historical Society of Pennsylvania.

33. James S. Pike, *First Blows of the Civil War*, p. 296.

34. Joseph P. Smith, *History of the Republican Party in Ohio*, I, 15.

35. Harry J. Carman and Reinhard H. Luthin, "Some Aspects of the Know-Nothing Movement Reconsidered," *The South Atlantic Quarterly* (April, 1940), XXIX, 225–226.

36. Chase to ———— (copy), October 31, 1854, Chase Papers, Historical Society of Pennsylvania.

37. Eugene H. Roseboom, "Salmon P. Chase and the Know-Nothings," *Mississippi Valley Historical Review* (December, 1938), XXV, 340–341.

38. L. B. Hamlin (ed.), "Selections from the Follett Papers," *loc. cit.*, XIII, 75.

39. Chase to Giddings, *Private*, May 5, 1858, Joshua R. Giddings Papers.

40. Roseboom, "Salmon P. Chase and the Know-Nothings," *loc. cit.*, pp. 341–345.

41. Chase to Sumner, October 15, 1855, Charles Sumner Papers.

42. Roseboom, "Salmon P. Chase and the Know-Nothings," *loc. cit.*, pp. 347–349; Ernst Bruncken, "German Political Refugees in the United States During the Period from 1815 to 1860," *Deutsch-Amerikanische Geschichtsblätter* (1904), IV, 52.

43. L. B. Hamlin (ed.), "Selections from the Follett Papers," *loc. cit.*, XIII, 75.

44. Chase to Kingsley S. Bingham (copy), October 19, 1855, Chase Papers, Library of Congress.

45. G. Bailey to Chase, February 21, 1856, in *ibid.*

46. Andrew W. Crandall, *The Early History of the Republican Party, 1854–1856*, pp. 18–19, 35–37, 47–52; William E. Smith, *The Francis Preston Blair Family in Politics*, I, 323–324.

47. Chase to Sumner, May 3, 1856, Sumner Papers.

48. Allan Nevins, *Frémont: Pathmarker of the West*, p. 427; Smith, *The Francis Preston Blair Family in Politics*, I, 353–355.

49. Roseboom, "Salmon P. Chase and the Know-Nothings," *loc. cit.*, pp. 340, 346–348.

50. Hart, *Chase*, pp. 158–161.

51. Chase to Sumner, May 1, 1857, Sumner Papers.

52. Roseboom, "Ohio in the 1850's," MS., pp. 368–374, 374 n.

53. William Slade to Banks, May 8, 1859, Nathaniel P. Banks Papers, Illinois State Historical Library, Springfield.

54. Chase to Henry Wilson, November 9, 1857, Nathaniel P. Banks Papers, Essex Institute, Salem, Mass.

55. Chase to Giddings, May 5, 1858, Joshua R. Giddings Papers, Ohio Archaeological and Historical Society, Columbus.

56. Chase to Sumner, January 18, 1858, Sumner Papers.

57. James Birney to Chase, January 23, 1860, Chase Papers, Library of Congress.

58. Smith, *The Liberty and Free Soil Parties in the Northwest*, pp. 291–294; Floyd B. Streeter, *Political Parties in Michigan, 1837–1860*, pp. 200–201, 230–255, 267, 280–282.

59. Michigan's population in 1860 was 749,113. Of these, 191,128 were born in New York and 34,235 in Ohio. See *Eighth Census of the United States, 1860: Population*, p. 248.

60. Earl O. Smith, "The Public Life of Austin Blair, War Governor of Michigan, 1845–1863," MS., pp. 1–37; Detroit *Free Press*, May 4, 1860.

61. Theodore Clarke Smith, "The Free Soil Party in Wisconsin," *Proceedings, State Historical Society of Wisconsin* (1894), Vol. 42.

62. William F. Rainey, *Wisconsin: A Study of Progress*, p. 147.

63. Joseph C. Cover, "Memoirs of a Pioneer County Editor," *The Wisconsin Magazine of History* (March, 1928), XI, 250–251.

64. Joseph Schafer, "Prohibition in Early Wisconsin," in *ibid.* (1924–1925), VIII, 298–299.

65. The population of Wisconsin in 1860 was 775,881. Of these, 123,879 were born in the German states. See *Eighth Census of the United States, 1860: Population*, p. 544. The late Joseph Schafer concluded, however, that most German voters in Wisconsin voted for Douglas in 1860.

See Joseph Schafer, "Who Elected Lincoln?" *American Historical Review* (October, 1941), XLVII, 51–63.

66. Joseph Schafer, "Carl Schurz, Immigrant Statesman," *Wisconsin Magazine of History* (June, 1928), XI, 380.

67. Chase to Robert Hosea, *Private and Confidential*, January 14, 1860, Chase-Hosea Papers.

68. *Ohio State Journal* (Columbus), March 19, 1860.

69. *Reminiscences of Carl Schurz*, II, 169, 171–172.

70. Chase to Robert Hosea, March 18, 1860, "Private and Confidential," Chase-Hosea Papers.

71. *Ibid.*

72. Charles King, "Rufus King," *Wisconsin Magazine of History*, IV.

73. *Eighth Census of the United States, 1860: Population*, p. 554.

74. Appleton (Wis.) *Crescent*, March 10, 1860.

75. John A. Bingham to Chase, January 14, 1860, Chase Papers, Library of Congress.

76. Pike, *First Blows of the Civil War*, p. 443.

77. Schuckers, *Chase*, p. 99.

78. Smith, "Salmon P. Chase and the Election of 1860," Ohio *Archaeological and Historical Quarterly* (1930), XXXIX, 518.

79. Charles M. Knapp, *New Jersey Politics*, pp. 17, 24, 24 n, 54 n, 185.

80. James A. Briggs to Chase, October 19, 1859, Chase Papers, Library of Congress.

81. *Ibid.*

82. R. P. Lowe to Chase, December 12, 1859; J. W. Ashley to Chase, December 19, 1859, Chase Papers, Library of Congress.

83. In Chicago *Press & Tribune*, January 25, 1860.

84. Dawson's Fort Wayne *Daily Times*, February 28, 1860.

85. John A. Gurley to Chase (Private), April 13, 1860, Chase Papers, Library of Congress.

86. See Chapter VI.

87. James A. Briggs to Chase, April 13, 1860, Chase Papers, Library of Congress.

88. William H. Bissell to Chase, February 14, 1860, Chase Papers, Library of Congress.

89. Roseboom, "Ohio in the 1850's," MS., pp. 399–400; Chase to Sumner, June 20, 1859, Sumner Papers.

90. J. M. Ashley to Chase, January 14, 1860, Chase Papers, Library of Congress.

91. See Chapter IV.

92. *Ohio State Journal* (Columbus), February 28, 1860.

93. *Ibid.*, March 2, 1860, p. 2.

94. *Ibid.*, Joseph P. Smith, *History of the Republican Party in Ohio*, I, 101–102.

95. James Elliott to Chase, February 23, 1860, Chase Papers, Library of Congress; Caleb B. Smith to Cassius M. Clay, April 22, 1860, in R. Gerald McMurtry, "Disappointed Presidential Hopefuls in 1860," *Lincoln Herald*, October, 1943, pp. 35–36.

96. George H. Porter, *Ohio Politics During the Civil War Period*, pp. 43–44.

97. Francis Weisenburger, *The Life of John McLean*, pp. 212–214.

98. Chase to R. C. Parsons (copies), April 5, 10, 17, 25, 1860, Chase Papers, Historical Society of Pennsylvania.

99. Chase to James A. Briggs (copy), April 27, 1860, *ibid*.

100. *Ibid*.

101. James Walker to Chase, October 3, 1859; George Hoadley to Chase, February 6, 1860; George R. Morton to Chase, April 19, 1860, Chase Papers, Library of Congress.

102. Smith, *The Liberty and Free Soil Parties in the Northwest*, pp. 240–241.

103. Gamaliel Bailey to Chase, January 16, 1859, Chase Papers, Historical Society of Pennsylvania.

104. Chase to Bailey (copy), January 24, 1859, *ibid*.

105. Galloway to John Covode, March 19, 1860, John Covode Papers.

106. Pike, *First Blows of the Civil War*, p. 503.

CHAPTER IV

1. There is no published biography of Bates. See, however, Floyd A. McNeil, "Lincoln's Attorney General: Edward Bates," MS. See also Reinhard H. Luthin, "Organizing the Republican Party in the 'Border-Slave' Regions: Edward Bates's Presidential Candidacy in 1860," *Missouri Historical Review* (January, 1944), XXXVIII, 138–161.

2. Bates to Fillmore, August 1, 1850, Millard Fillmore Papers.

3. Edward Bates Diary, MS., March 6, 1850, July 4, 1851.

4. *Ibid*., May 31, 1851.

5. *Ibid*., November 27, 1850.

6. McNeil, "Edward Bates," MS., pp. 173–174.

7. George J. McHugh, "Political Nativism in St. Louis, 1840–1857," MS., pp. 51–53, 95–124.

8. New York *Herald*, September 18, 1856.

9. For the warfare between Bentonites and anti-Bentonites see Clarence H. McClure, *Opposition in Missouri to Thomas Hart Benton*; P. Orman Ray, *The Repeal of the Missouri Compromise*, Chapters I–IV.

10. Allan Nevins, *Frémont: The West's Greatest Adventurer*, II, 504–505; Theodore Roosevelt, *Thomas Hart Benton*, p. 354.

11. McClure, *Opposition in Missouri to Thomas Hart Benton*, p. 219.

12. Sceva B. Laughlin, "Missouri Politics During the Civil War," *Missouri Historical Review* (April, 1929), XXIII, 414–416.

13. Walter H. Ryle, *Missouri: Union or Secession*, pp. 75–76, 75 n.

14. F. P. Blair, Jr., to F. P. Blair, Sr., December 23, 1860, Blair Papers.

15. See William E. Smith, *The Francis Preston Blair Family in Politics* (2 vols.).

16. Lucy L. Tasher, "The *Missouri Democrat* and the Civil War,"

MS., pp. 1–19; Lucy L. Tasher, "The *Missouri Democrat* and the Civil War," *Missouri Historical Review* (July, 1927), XXXI, 402–403; Gertrude O'Connell, "St. Louis in the 'Thirties and 'Forties," MS., pp. 147–149.

17. Tasher, "The *Missouri Democrat* and the Civil War," MS., p. 23.

18. Blair to Stone, "1855," John H. Gundlach Collection.

19. *Congressional Globe*, 35th Cong., 1st sess., pp. 293–298.

20. R. J. Robertson to Snyder, March 4, 1860, John F. Snyder Papers; Sceva B. Loughlin, "Missouri Politics During the Civil War," *Missouri Historical Review* (April, 1929), XXIII, 414, 419–422; Harrison A. Trexler, *Slavery in Missouri, 1804–1865*, p. 165. Benton had endeared himself to the Germans. See McHugh, "Political Nativism in St. Louis, 1840–1857," MS., p. 145.

21. St. Louis *Daily Missouri Democrat*, December 13, 1859.

22. Edward L. Pierce to Sumner, April 18, 1859, Sumner Papers.

23. Howard K. Beale (ed.), *The Diary of Edward Bates, 1859–1866*, p. 11.

24. St. Louis *Daily Missouri Democrat*, December 2, 1859.

25. *Ibid.*, December 20, 1859.

26. Boston *Daily Advertiser*, April 18, 1859.

27. *Ibid.*

28. Chauncey S. Boucher, "*In Re* That Aggressive Slavocracy," *Mississippi Valley Historical Review* (June–September, 1921), VIII, 69; Arthur C. Cole, *The Whig Party in the South*, pp. 327–336; Henry T. Shanks, *The Secession Movement in Virginia, 1847–1861*, pp. 64–65, 101.

29. Beale, *Bates Diary*, pp. 29–30.

30. St. Louis *Daily Missouri Democrat*, August 30, 1859.

31. *Ibid.*

32. *Ibid.*, July 12, 1859.

33. *Ibid.*, October 20, 1859.

34. *Ibid.*, July 18, 1859.

35. *Ibid.*, July 22, 1859.

36. *Ibid.*, July 26, 1859.

37. *Ibid.*, August 15, 1859.

38. *Ibid.*, July 29, 1859.

39. *Ibid.*, October 21, 1859.

40. *Loc. cit.*

41. St. Louis *Daily Missouri Democrat*, November 28, 29, 1859.

42. *Ibid.*, December 22, 1859.

43. *Ibid.*, December 24, 1859.

44. Broadhead to Newland, December 6, 1859, James O. Broadhead Papers.

45. St. Louis *Daily Missouri Democrat*, December 13, 1859.

46. Beale, *Bates Diary*, p. 89.

47. St. Louis *Daily Missouri Republican*, March 1, 11, 1860.

48. *Ibid.*

49. W. F. Switzler to Smith, March 5, 1860, Sol Smith Papers; St. Louis *Daily Missouri Republican*, March 9, 11, 1860; Sceva B. Laugh-

lin, "Missouri Politics During the Civil War," *Missouri Historical Review* (April, 1929), XXIII, 417–418.

50. Bates's letter in St. Louis *Daily Missouri Republican,* January 20, 1860.

51. St. Louis *Daily Missouri Republican,* March 11, 1860.

52. F. I. Herriott, "Senator Stephen A. Douglas and the Germans in 1854," *Transactions, Illinois State Historical Society* (1912), No. 17, pp. 144–156; George M. Stephenson, *The Political History of the Public Lands from 1840 to 1862,* pp. 113, 175–177, 221, 225; Harrison A. Trexler, *Slavery in Missouri, 1804–1865,* p. 165; H. Von Holst, *The Constitutional and Political History of the United States,* IV, 429 n.; Ernst Bruncken, "German Political Refugees in the United States During the Period from 1850 to 1860," *Deutsch-Amerikanische Geschichtsblätter* (January, 1904), IV, 57.

53. *Eighth Census of the United States: Population,* 1860, pp. 300, 301.

54. Sceva B. Laughlin, "Missouri Politics During the Civil War," *Missouri Historical Review* (April, 1929), XXIII, 411, 420–422.

55. Walter H. Ryle, *Missouri: Union or Secession,* p. 111.

56. *Ibid.,* p. 166.

57. H. Kreismann to Banks, April 2, 1859; C. H. Ray to Banks, April 2, 1859, *Private,* Nathaniel P. Banks Papers, Essex Institute, Salem, Mass. (in volume marked "II, 1858"); Edward L. Pierce to Sumner, April 18, 1859, Sumner Papers; Boston *Daily Advertiser,* May 10, 11, 1859; *The Reminiscences of Carl Schurz,* II, 116, 117.

58. E. R. Harlan to Missouri Historical Society, February 7, 1908, Bates Papers; F. I. Herriott, "The Germans of Davenport and the Chicago Convention of 1860," in Harry E. Downer, *History of Davenport and Scott County, Iowa,* I, 839, 846.

59. F. I. Herriott, "The Conference in the Deutsches Hause, Chicago, May 14–15, 1860," *Transactions, Illinois State Historical Society* (1928), No. 35, p. 135.

60. St. Louis *Daily Missouri Republican,* March 11, 1860.

61. Detroit *Free Press,* March 13, 1860.

62. St. Louis *Daily Evening News,* March 21, 1860.

63. Beale, *Bates Diary,* pp. 111–114; Ryle, *Missouri: Union or Secession,* pp. 133–134.

64. Laughlin, "Missouri Politics During the Civil War," *loc. cit.,* p. 419.

65. Louisville *Journal* clipper in Indianapolis *Daily Journal,* March 24, 1860.

66. Mary Scrugham, *The Peaceable Americans of 1860–1861,* pp. 14–15; James L. Sellers, "The Make-Up of the Early Republican Party," *Transactions of the Illinois State Historical Society, 1930,* pp. 50–51.

67. Greeley to Colfax, February 18, 24, 1859, February 3, 1860, Greeley-Colfax Papers.

68. Greeley to Seward, November 11, 1854 (copy), Seward Papers; Ralph R. Fahrney, *Horace Greeley and the Tribune in the Civil War,* pp. 32–33.

69. New York *Daily Tribune*, February 20, 1860.

70. Greeley to Chase, September 29, 1863, Chase Papers, Historical Society of Pennsylvania, Philadelphia.

71. Greeley to Colfax, February 28, 1860, Greeley-Colfax Papers.

72. Willard H. Smith, "Schuyler Colfax: Whig Editor, 1845–1855," *Indiana Magazine of History* (September, 1938), XXXIV, 262–282.

73. O. J. Hollister, *Life of Schuyler Colfax*, pp. 142–143.

74. Theodore C. Smith, *The Liberty and Free Soil Parties in the Northwest*, p. 303; James R. Robertson, "Kentucky's Contribution to Indiana," *Publications, Indiana Historical Society* (1919), VI, 82–97; Dale Beeler, "The Election of 1852," *Indiana Magazine of History* (1915–1916), XI, 314–315; XX, 39.

75. Orth to Colfax, September 25, 1854, Colfax-Orth Papers.

76. Hollister, *Colfax*, p. 74.

77. Greeley to Colfax, May 4, 1857, Greeley-Colfax Papers.

78. Charles Kettleborough, "Indiana on the Eve of the Civil War," *Publications, Indiana Historical Society* (1919), VI, 137–138.

79. Donohue to Pratt, March 31, 1860, Daniel D. Pratt Papers; Indianapolis *Daily Journal*, April 12, 1860; Reinhard H. Luthin, "Indiana and Lincoln's Rise to the Presidency," *Indiana Magazine of History* (December, 1942), XXXVIII, 385–387.

80. Mildred C. Stoler, "Influence of the Democratic Element in the Republican Party of Illinois and Indiana, 1854–1860," MS., pp. 26–31.

81. Carl F. Brand, "The History of the Know Nothing Party in Indiana," Indiana Magazine of History (1922), XVIII, 300–301; W. H. Gregory to Thompson, January 17, 1860, Richard W. Thompson Papers.

82. Rollins to Broadhead, February 17, 1860, James O. Broadhead Papers.

83. Indianapolis *Daily State Sentinel*, February 23, 24, 1860.

84. Indianapolis *Daily Journal*, February 21, 1860.

85. Hielscher to Julian, November 20, 1860, George W. Julian Papers.

86. Indianapolis *Daily Journal*, February 23, 1860.

87. *Ibid.*

88. Fort Wayne *Sentinel*, February 25, 1860; A. H. Davidson to Thompson, February 24, 1860, Thompson Papers.

89. Beale, *Bates Diary*, p. 102.

90. Theodore C. Pease and James G. Randall (eds.), *The Diary of Orville Hickman Browning, 1850–1864*, I, 380.

91. *Ibid.*, p. 381.

92. *Ibid.*, p. 407.

93. *Ibid.*, p. 382.

94. *Ibid.*, p. 395.

95. *Ibid.*, p. 396.

96. Arthur C. Cole, *The Whig Party in the South*, pp. 2–4, 44, 62, 133; Frank R. Rutter, *South American Trade of Baltimore*, p. 7.

97. Laurence F. Schmeckebier, *History of the Know Nothing Party in Maryland*, pp. 37, 69; Sister Mary St. Patrick McConville, *Political*

Nativism in the State of Maryland, 1830–1860, pp. 116, 121–122, 124; Benjamin Tuska, "Know-Nothingism in Baltimore, 1854–1860," *Catholic Historical Review* (July, 1925), New Series, V, 217–251; Reinhard H. Luthin, "A Discordant Chapter in Lincoln's Administration: The Davis-Blair Controversy," *The Maryland Historical Magazine* (March, 1944), XXXIX, 25 ff.

98. Davis to Morrill, August 20, 1859, Justin S. Morrill Papers.

99. J. Thomas Scharf, *History of Maryland,* III, 346.

100. *Congressional Globe,* 36th Cong., 1st sess., pp. 641, 650.

101. *Ibid.,* p. 663; Indianapolis *Daily State Sentinel,* February 7, 1860, p. 2.

102. Steiner, *Davis,* p. 145; Schmeckebier, *op. cit.,* pp. 107, 107 n.

103. Steiner, *Davis,* pp. 150–151.

104. Notice the hostile criticism leveled at the pro-Republican policy of the Baltimore *Patriot* in Baltimore *Daily Clipper,* February 25, 27, March 13, April 5, 1860. Also Springfield (Mass.) *Republican,* February 22, 1860.

105. Baltimore *Patriot,* cited in Springfield (Mass.) *Republican,* January 9, 1860.

106. George S. York to Douglas, Private, June 30, 1860, Stephen A. Douglas Papers; L. P. Henninghausen, "Reminiscences of the Political Life of the German-Americans in Baltimore During 1850–1860," *Seventh Annual Report of the Society for the History of the Germans in Maryland* (1892–1893), pp. 55–59.

107. *Studies in Southern History and Politics Inscribed to William Archibald Dunning,* p. 10.

108. Matthew P. Andrews, *History of Maryland: Province and State,* p. 505.

109. Marshall to Blair, May 30, 1860, Blair Papers.

110. Andrews, *op. cit.,* p. 505; Baltimore *Sun,* April 27, 1860.

111. The campaign of 1860 was waged by the Republicans in Delaware under the banner of the "People's Party." See Henry C. Conrad, *History of the State of Delaware,* I, 194–195.

112. Wilmington *Delaware Republican,* February–May, 1860.

113. Milford (Del.) *News and Advertiser,* clipped in Chicago *Press & Tribune,* February 3, 1860; *Peninsula News,* clipped in Harrisburg (Pa.) *Daily Telegraph,* August 8, 1859; Philadelphia *North American and United States Gazette,* July 1, 1858; Walter A. Powell, *A History of Delaware,* p. 238.

114. Wilmington *Delaware Republican,* January 30, 1860.

115. *Ibid.,* February 27, 1860.

116. *Ibid.,* February 6, 1860.

117. *Ibid.,* April 26, 30, 1860.

118. *Ibid.,* April 19, 1860.

119. *Loc. cit.*

120. Corwin to Schouler, April 28, 1860, William Schouler Papers; Eugene H. Roseboom, "Ohio in the 1850's," MS., pp. 387–388, 387 n., 407 n.

121. Wilmington *Delaware Republican*, May 3, 1860.
122. William T. Smithers, "Nathaniel B. Smithers," *Papers, Historical Society of Delaware* (1899), XXIII, 24–25.
123. *Life of Cassius Marcellus Clay: Memoirs, Writings, and Speeches*, I, 244–246.
124. *The Moorsfield Antiquarian* (August, 1937), I, 105–106.
125. Beale, *Bates Diary*, pp. 105–106.

CHAPTER V

1. The best of the modern Lincoln biographies are those by Albert J. Beveridge, Carl Sandburg, Ida M. Tarbell, and William E. Barton. The most worthwhile of the very early lives of Lincoln are those by William H. Herndon, Isaac N. Arnold, Ward H. Lamon, and Josiah G. Holland. Outstanding special studies are William Baringer, *Lincoln's Rise to Power*, and T. Harry Williams, *Lincoln and the Radicals*. For an intelligent guide to Lincoln material, see Paul M. Angle, "Basic Lincolniana," *Bulletin of the Abraham Lincoln Association*, June, 1936, and September, 1936.
2. See Professor James G. Randall's brilliant sketch of Lincoln in *Dictionary of American Biography*, XI, 242–259; R. Gerald McMurtry, "The Lincoln Migration from Kentucky to Indiana," *Indiana Magazine of History* (December, 1937), XXIII, 385–421; Benjamin P. Thomas, *Lincoln's New Salem*, pp. 41–90.
3. Albert J. Beveridge, *Abraham Lincoln, 1809–1858*, I, 96–99, 115; Louis A. Warren (ed.), "The Lone Whig from Illinois," *Lincoln Lore* (May 20, 1940), No. 580; Reinhard H. Luthin, "Abraham Lincoln and the Massachusetts Whigs in 1848," *New England Quarterly* (December, 1941), XIV, 619–632.
4. John G. Nicolay and John Hay (eds.), *Complete Works of Abraham Lincoln*, Gettysburg Edition, II, 105–106. (Hereafter cited as *Complete Works of Abraham Lincoln*.)
5. Thomas Ewing, "Lincoln and the General Land Office, 1849," *Journal of the Illinois State Historical Society* (October, 1932), XXV.
6. Paul I. Miller, "Lincoln and the Governorship of Oregon," *Mississippi Valley Historical Review* (December, 1936), XXIII, 391–394.
7. Emanuel Hertz, *Abraham Lincoln: A New Portrait*, II, 604.
8. Earl W. Wiley (ed.), *Four Speeches by Abraham Lincoln Hitherto Unpublished or Unknown*, pp. 35–83.
9. Arthur C. Cole, *The Era of the Civil War, 1848–1870*, p. 101; Hubbart, H. C., *The Older Middle West, 1840–1880*.
10. Mildred C. Stoler, "Influence of the Democratic Element in the Republican Party of Illinois and Indiana, 1854–1860," MS., pp. 26–31.
11. *Ibid.*, pp. 32, 44–47; Arthur C. Cole, *The Era of the Civil War*, pp. 119–120, 125–126; *Journal of the Illinois State Historical Society* (1923–1924), XVI, 20–22; "Address of Gen. John M. Palmer," *Trans-*

actions of the McLean County Historical Society (1900), III, 120–122;
F. I. Herriott, "The Germans of Chicago and Stephen A. Douglas in
1854," *Deutsch-Amerikanische Geschichtsblätter* (1912), XII, 388 ff.;
Dugger to Yates, January 22, 1854, Selby to Yates, April 8, 1854, Richard
Yates Papers.

12. H. L. Breese to Sidney Breese, September 26, 1854, Sidney Breese
Papers.

13. Ward H. Lamon, *The Life of Abraham Lincoln*, p. 348.

14. Paul M. Angle (ed.), *Herndon's Life of Lincoln*, pp. 298–299,
299 n.; *Complete Works of Abraham Lincoln*, II, 264; Horace White,
"Abraham Lincoln in 1854," *Transactions of the Illinois State Historical
Society*, 1908, pp. 35–38; Harry J. Carman and Reinhard H. Luthin,
"Some Aspects of the Know-Nothing Movement Reconsidered," *The
South Atlantic Quarterly* (April, 1940), XXXIX, 222–223.

15. Herndon to ———, January 15, 1874, in Emanuel Hertz, *The
Hidden Lincoln*, pp. 82–83.

16. Paul M. Angle (ed.), *New Letters and Papers of Lincoln*, p. 166;
John D. Barnhart, "The Southern Influence in the Formation of Illinois,"
Journal of the Illinois State Historical Society (September, 1939),
XXXII, 358–378; Solon J. Buck, *Illinois in 1818*, pp. 93–95.

17. William H. Lambert, "A Lincoln Correspondence," *The Century Magazine*, February 1909, p. 619.

18. John G. Nicolay, "Abraham Lincoln," *Transactions of the
McLean County Historical Society* (1900), III, 98.

19. Paul M. Angle (ed.), *Herndon's Life of Lincoln*, p. 318; Rankin to Yates, August 23, 1856, Yates Papers.

20. Henry B. Rankin, *Personal Recollections of Abraham Lincoln*,
p. 196.

21. *Complete Works of Abraham Lincoln*, II, 315–316; Angle (ed.),
Herndon's Life of Lincoln, p. 319; Gilbert A. Tracy, *Uncollected Letters of Abraham Lincoln*, p. 78.

22. William H. Lambert, "A Lincoln Correspondence," *op. cit.*,
p. 620; *Journal of the Illinois State Historical Society* (1923–1924), XVI,
40, 40 n.; Angle (ed.), *Herndon's Life of Lincoln*, p. 322; Hertz, *The
Hidden Lincoln*, pp. 113–114.

23. Edwin E. Sparks (ed.), *The Lincoln–Douglas Debates of 1858*.

24. Cole, *The Era of the Civil War*, p. 179. Lincoln's opponents
asserted that the apportionment law in effect when the Illinois legislature
elected Douglas over Lincoln was the same under which a legislature
had been elected which chose Lyman Trumbull, a party associate of
Lincoln, for the U. S. Senate; and that Governor Bissell, a Republican,
had vetoed a new apportionment bill in the session of 1856–1857. See
Sparks (ed.), *The Lincoln–Douglas Debates of 1858*, p. 535.

25. Lincoln to Dr. B. C. Lundy (Facsimile), November 26, 1858,
Chicago Historical Society, Chicago.

26. Jesse W. Weik, *The Real Lincoln*, pp. 2–3.

27. Gilbert A. Tracy (ed.), *Uncollected Letters of Abraham Lincoln*, p. 99.

28. *Ibid.*, pp. 100–101.

29. *Complete Works of Abraham Lincoln*, V, 114–124.

30. *Daily Illinois State Journal*, March 14, 1859.

31. Sandusky (Ohio) *Register*, November 6 (or 9), 1858, in Daniel J. Ryan, "Lincoln and Ohio," *Ohio Archaeological and Historical Publications* (1923), XXXII, 104; Charles H. Workman, "Tablet to Abraham Lincoln at Mansfield," *Ohio Archaeological and Historical Publications* (1925), XXXIV, 510.

32. D. W. Wilder, *The Annals of Kansas*, p. 204.

33. Some Lincoln students are of opinion that Lincoln's goal in 1859 was to succeed Douglas in 1864.

34. *Complete Works of Abraham Lincoln*, V, 127–128.

35. *Ibid.*, p. 138.

36. Arthur C. Cole, "Abraham Lincoln and the South," *Lincoln Centennial Association Papers*, 1928, pp. 49–51.

37. Lincoln to Dummer, August 5, 1858, Henry E. Dummer Papers.

38. Daniel J. Ryan, "Lincoln and Ohio," *Ohio Archaeological and Historical Quarterly.*

39. Tracy, *Uncollected Letters of Abraham Lincoln*, p. 113.

40. *Complete Works of Abraham Lincoln*, V, 132.

41. Arthur C. Cole, "President Lincoln and the Illinois Radical Republicans," *Mississippi Valley Historical Review* (March, 1918), IV, 419.

42. Charles Roll, "Indiana's Part in the Nomination of Abraham Lincoln for President in 1860," *Indiana Magazine of History* (March, 1929), XXV, 2.

43. Tracy E. Strevey, "Joseph Medill and the *Chicago Tribune* in the Nomination and Election of Lincoln," in Paul M. Angle (ed.), *Papers in Illinois History*, 1938, pp. 45–47; Chicago *Press & Tribune*, October 7, November 16, 1859.

44. Medill to Archibald W. Campbell, October 30, 1859, in Reinhard H. Luthin, "Pennsylvania and Lincoln's Rise to the Presidency," *Pennsylvania Magazine of History and Biography* (January, 1943), LXVII, 63. For Campbell, see Charles H. Ambler, *West Virginia; Stories and Biographies*, pp. 237–238. See also Philip Kinsley, *The Chicago Tribune: Its First Hundred Years*, I, 90 ff.

45. Stanton L. Davis, *Pennsylvania Politics, 1860–1863*, pp. 47–48, 106–107; Malcolm R. Eiselen, *The Rise of Pennsylvania Protectionism*, chap. xii; Charles M. Knapp, *New Jersey Politics During the Period of the Civil War and Reconstruction*, pp. 17, 24, 24 n.; Newark *Daily Advertiser*, January 4, 29, February 2, 1859; Trenton *State Gazette*, September 10, October 15, 22, 1859.

46. William E. Dodd, "The Fight for the Northwest, 1860," *American Historical Review* (July, 1911), XVI, 775, 781–785.

47. Strevey, "Joseph Medill and the *Chicago Tribune* in the Nomination and Election of Lincoln," *loc. cit.*, p. 42.

48. Angle (ed.), *New Letters and Papers of Lincoln*, p. 206.

49. Ward H. Lamon, *The Life of Abraham Lincoln*, p. 423. See also

Reinhard H. Luthin, "Abraham Lincoln and the Tariff," *American Historical Review* (July, 1944), XLIX, 613–614.

50. Springfield *Daily Illinois State Journal,* November 7, 1859.

51. *Kansas Historical Collections* (1901–1902), VII, 536–538.

52. *Complete Works of Abraham Lincoln,* V, 257–258.

53. Frances M. I. Morehouse, *The Life of Jesse W. Fell,* pp. 9–59; Harry E. Pratt, "Abraham Lincoln in Bloomington, Illinois," *Journal of the Illinois State Historical Society* (April, 1936), XXIX, 64–65; *Complete Works of Abraham Lincoln,* V, 286. For the rôles of Fell and other residents of Bloomington, Illinois, in sponsoring Lincoln for the presidency, see Sherman D. Wakefield, *How Lincoln Became President.*

54. Morehouse, *The Life of Jesse W. Fell,* p. 60.

55. Lewis to Fell, January 30, 1860, Transcript, Jesse W. Fell Transcripts.

56. Morehouse, *The Life of Jesse W. Fell,* p. 60; *Complete Works of Abraham Lincoln,* V, 286–289.

57. Tracy (ed.), *Uncollected Letters of Abraham Lincoln,* p. 123.

58. Chicago *Press & Tribune,* October 4, 1859.

59. *Ibid.,* October 14, 1859.

60. *Ibid.,* October 20, 1859.

61. *Ibid.,* November 21, 1859.

62. *Ibid.,* December 9, 1859.

63. *Ibid.,* January 21, 26, 1860.

64. *Ibid.,* January 9, 1860.

65. Strevey, "Joseph Medill and the *Chicago Tribune* in the Nomination and Election of Lincoln," *loc. cit.,* p. 45.

66. Chicago *Press & Tribune,* February 16, 1860, in *Ibid.,* p. 48.

67. For Judd, see *Dictionary of American Biography,* X, 230–231; Arthur Edwards, *Sketch of the Life of Norman B. Judd.*

68. *Diary of Orville Hickman Browning, 1850–1864,* I, 382; Hertz, *The Hidden Lincoln,* p. 338.

69. *Complete Works of Abraham Lincoln,* V, 281–282.

70. Lincoln to Messrs. Dole, Hubbard & Brown (Photostat), December 14, 1859, Lincoln Collection, Chicago Historical Society.

71. *Ibid.*

72. Lincoln to Grimshaw, December 15, 1859, Lincoln Collection, Illinois State Historical Library, Springfield.

73. Chicago *Press & Tribune,* December 27, 1859; Koerner to Trumbull, December 23, 1859, Trumbull Papers; Rufus Rockwell Wilson, "Learning About Lincoln," *Lincoln Herald,* October, 1943, p. 29.

74. Ward H. Lamon, *The Life of Abraham Lincoln,* p. 424.

75. Chicago *Press & Tribune,* January 30, 1860.

76. Isaac N. Arnold, *The Life of Abraham Lincoln,* p. 162 n.

77. *Journal of the Illinois State Historical Society* (June, 1939), XXXII, 231–232.

78. Chicago *Press & Tribune,* February 10, 1860.

79. Judd to Trumbull, April 2, 1860, Trumbull Papers.

80. Donald V. Smith, "Salmon P. Chase and the Election of 1860," *Ohio Archaeological and Historical Quarterly* (July, 1930), XXXIX, 516, 521.

81. Hertz, *The Hidden Lincoln*, pp. 75–76.

82. *Ibid.*, p. 76.

83. Emanuel Hertz, *Abraham Lincoln: A New Portrait*, II, 759.

84. James A. Briggs to the Editor of the *Evening Post*, undated, in pamphlet catalogued under title "James A. Briggs, *An Authentic Account of Hon. Abraham Lincoln Being Invited To Give An Address . . . February 27, 1860*" (reprinted from New York *Evening Post*, August 16, 1867).

85. New York *Evening Post*, January 24, 1860; Cephas Brainerd Broadsides, Lincoln National Life Foundation.

86. Cephas Brainerd Broadsides; George H. Putnam, *Abraham Lincoln: The People's Leader in the Struggle for National Existence*, p. 232.

87. Smith, "Salmon P. Chase and the Election of 1860," *loc. cit.*, p. 521.

88. Putnam, *Abraham Lincoln*, pp. 223–224.

89. Jesse W. Weik, *The Real Lincoln*, p. 258.

90. Lincoln to Cameron, February 26, 1860, Cameron Papers.

91. Printed in *Complete Works of Abraham Lincoln*.

92. Louis A. Warren, "Printing the Cooper Institute Address," *Lincoln Lore*, July 22, 1940.

93. *Ibid.*

94. "The Time Lincoln Needed Cheering Up," by E. J. Edwards, in St. Louis *Globe Democrat*, October 20, 1909.

95. *Proceedings, Massachusetts Historical Society* (1909), Vol. 42, p. 81; New York *Herald-Tribune*, July 27, 1926. Lincoln's tour through New England is treated in Percy C. Eggleston, *Lincoln in New England*.

96. Providence *Journal*, cited in Paul M. Angle, *Lincoln, 1854–1861*, p. 322.

97. Angle, *Lincoln, 1854–1861*, pp. 322–324.

98. *Ibid.*, p. 324.

99. Warren, "Printing the Cooper Institute Address," *loc. cit.*

100. Lincoln to John Pickering, April 6, 1860, in *Week By Week*, August 27, 1932, p. 8. (Clipping in "Unpublished Lincoln Letters," Lincoln National Life Foundation, Fort Wayne, Ind.)

101. Lincoln to A. Chester, March 14, 1860, Lincoln Collection, Chicago Historical Society.

102. Lambert, "A Lincoln Correspondence," *op. cit.*, p. 622.

103. Carroll J. Noonan, *Nativism in Connecticut, 1829–1860*, pp. 324–329; New Haven *Columbian Weekly Register*, April 28, 1860; Bridgeport *Republican Farmer*, April 27, 1860.

104. Providence *Daily Post*, January 5, April 2, 5, 1860; Newport *Advertiser*, January 11, 18, April 11, 1860.

105. Tracy (ed.), *Uncollected Letters of Abraham Lincoln*, pp. 141–142.

106. Weik, *The Real Lincoln*, p. 260.

107. Chicago *Press & Tribune*, March 2, 1860.
108. *Ibid.*, March 5, 8, 17, 1860.
109. *Ibid.*, March 6, 1860.
110. *Ibid.*, March 15, 1860.
111. *Ibid.*, March 6, 1860.
112. Chicago *Press & Tribune*, clipped in Boston *Daily Advertiser*, May 19, 1860.
113. Allmond to Douglas, March 29, 1860, Stephen A. Douglas Papers.
114. Chicago *Press & Tribune*, March 5, April 16, 1860.
115. *Ibid.*, March 10, 13, 14, 27, April 7, 23, 1860.
116. *Ibid.*, February 29, 1860.
117. *Ibid.*, March 5, 1860.
118. Koerner to Trumbull, March 15, 1860, Lyman Trumbull Papers.
119. Koerner to Yates, October 25, 1856, Yates Papers; Hertz, *Abraham Lincoln: A New Portrait*, II, 712, 716–717; George Schneider, "Lincoln and the Anti-Know-Nothing Resolutions," *Transactions of the McLean County Historical Society* (1900), III, 88–90.
120. Ferry to Welles, March 1, 1860, Welles Papers; Slade to Banks, May 8, 1859, Nathaniel P. Banks Papers, Illinois State Historical Library; Donnal V. Smith, "The Influence of the Foreign-Born Vote of the Northwest in the Election of 1860," *Mississippi Valley Historical Review* (September, 1932), XIX, 192 ff.
121. *Complete Works of Abraham Lincoln*, V, 132.
122. *Ibid.*, pp. 129–130.
123. F. I. Herriott, "The Premises and Significances of Abraham Lincoln's Letter to Theodore Canisius," *Deutsch-Amerikanische Geschichtsblätter* (1915), XV, 184, 249–254; J. G. Holland, *The Life of Abraham Lincoln*, pp. 196–197.
124. Photostatic copy in the Massachusetts Historical Society.
125. Angle (ed.), *New Letters and Papers of Lincoln*, p. 207.
126. Cited in Chicago *Press & Tribune*, May 2, 1860.
127. Chicago *Press & Tribune*, May 2, 1860.
128. *Ibid.*, April 26, 1860.
129. Frederic Bancroft, *The Life of William H. Seward*, I, 530 n.–531 n.
130. Hay to Trumbull, "Private," April 20, 1860, Trumbull Papers.
131. Wing to Trumbull, May 4, 1860, *ibid.*
132. Parks to Trumbull, May 4, 1860, *ibid.*
133. Weik, *The Real Lincoln*, p. 260.
134. *Ibid.*, p. 261.
135. Chicago *Press & Tribune*, April 30, May 1, 2, 3, 8, 1860.
136. Harry E. Pratt, "David Davis, 1815–1886," *Transactions of the Illinois State Historical Society*, 1930, p. 166.
137. Tracy (ed.), *Uncollected Letters of Abraham Lincoln*, p. 141.
138. Lambert, "A Lincoln Correspondence," *op. cit.*, p. 264.
139. Tracy (ed.), *Uncollected Letters of Abraham Lincoln*, p. 135.
140. *Ibid.*
141. Lambert, "A Lincoln Correspondence," *op. cit.*, p. 622.

142. Tracy (ed.), *Uncollected Letters of Abraham Lincoln*, p. 142.
143. Angle (ed.), *New Letters and Papers of Lincoln*, pp. 242, 243.
144. Hertz, *Abraham Lincoln: A New Portrait*, II, 771, 772.
145. *Ibid.*
146. Judd to Welles, March 8, 1860, Welles Papers.
147. Harry E. Pratt, "David Davis, 1815–1886," *Transactions of the Illinois State Historical Society*, 1930, p. 166.
148. Ida M. Tarbell, *The Life of Abraham Lincoln*, II, 337. For Taylor, see *Annals of Iowa* (1893–1895), Series III, Vol. I, p. 343; Benjamin F. Gue, *History of Iowa*, IV, 259.
149. Galloway to Covode, March 10, 1860, John Covode Papers; Washington Gladden, "Samuel Galloway," *Ohio Archaeological and Historical Quarterly* (1895), IV, 263–278.
150. Ryan, "Lincoln and Ohio," *Publications, Ohio Archaeological and Historical Society* (January 1923), XXXII, 116.
151. *Ibid.*, p. 117.
152. *Ibid.*
153. *Ibid.*, pp. 117–118.
154. Tracy, *Uncollected Letters of Abraham Lincoln*, p. 145.
155. James Sutherland, *Biographical Sketches of the Members of the Forty-first General Assembly of the State of Indiana*, pp. 78–79.
156. Tarbell, *The Life of Abraham Lincoln*, 1917 Edition, II, 347.
157. Harry J. Carman and Reinhard H. Luthin, *Lincoln and the Patronage*, pp. 56, 138, 253, 311.
158. Roll, "Indiana's Part in the Nomination of Abraham Lincoln for President in 1860," *loc. cit.*, pp. 4–5.
159. Indianapolis *Daily Journal*, April 19, 1860, quoted in Reinhard H. Luthin, "Indiana and Lincoln's Rise to the Presidency," *Indiana Magazine of History* (December, 1942), XXXVIII, 389.
160. Indianapolis *Daily Journal*, May 11, 1860.
161. Lamon, *The Life of Abraham Lincoln*, p. 444.
162. *Ibid.*, pp. 444–445.
163. *Ibid.*, pp. 445–445; Angle (ed.), *New Letters and Papers of Lincoln*, p. 253; Holland, *The Life of Abraham Lincoln*, p. 198.
164. Whiteley to Cameron, May 10, 1860, Cameron Papers; *Personal Recollections of John M. Palmer*, pp. 80–81.
165. Isaac N. Arnold, *The Life of Abraham Lincoln*, p. 163.
166. Tracy (ed.), *Uncollected Letters of Abraham Lincoln*, p. 145.
167. Harry E. Pratt, "David Davis, 1815–1886," *Transactions of the Illinois State Historical Society*, 1930, p. 166.

CHAPTER VI

1. See Lee Crippin, *Simon Cameron: Antebellum Years*; A. Howard Meneely, *The War Department, 1861*, pp. 74–78; Alexander Harris, *A Biographical History of Lancaster, Pennsylvania*, pp. 125–129. There are numerous letters in the Simon Cameron Papers, in the Library of Congress, indicating Cameron's extensive economic interests.

2. Henry R. Mueller, *The Whig Party in Pennsylvania*, pp. 115–117; Cameron to the "Whig Members of the Pennsylvania Legislature," March 13, 1845, Cameron Papers.

3. Sister M. Theophane Geary, *A History of Third Parties in Pennsylvania*, p. 111; Cameron to "Native Americans," March 12, 1845, Cameron Papers.

4. Eugene C. Savidge, *Life of Benjamin Harris Brewster*, p. 71.

5. *Pennsylvania Magazine of History and Biography* (1927), Vol, 51, p. 127.

6. *Ibid.* (1915), Vol. 39, p. 495.

7. Roy F. Nichols, *The Democratic Machine, 1850–1854*, pp. 59–63; Mueller, *The Whig Party in Pennsylvania*, pp. 143–144, 144 n., 194; Cameron to Coryell, February 19, 1853, Lewis Coryell Papers, Vol. 5, p. 15.

8. Black to Cameron, February 20, 1854, Cameron Papers.

9. Garrison to Helen E. Garrison, October 13, 1858, William Lloyd Garrison Papers.

10. Warren F. Hewitt, "The Know Nothing Party in Pennsylvania," *Pennsylvania History* (April, 1935), II, 73–77; Asa E. Martin, "The Temperance Movement in Pennsylvania Prior to the Civil War," *Pennsylvania Magazine of History and Biography* (July, 1925), Vol. 49, pp. 222–226.

11. Coffey to Covode, August 23, 1854, John Covode Papers.

12. Alexander Harris, *A Review of the Political Conflict in America Comprising Also a Resume of the Career of Thaddeus Stevens*, p. 172.

13. H. Waldron to May, April 26, 1856, Charles S. May Papers.

14. Cameron to Howell Powell (Copy), February 20, 1855, Cameron Papers.

15. Alexander K. McClure, *Old Time Notes of Pennsylvania*, I, 198.

16. Mueller, *The Whig Party in Pennsylvania*, pp. 215–217; Hewitt, "The Know Nothing Party in Pennsylvania," *loc. cit.*, pp. 78–79.

17. Harrisburg *Pennsylvania Telegraph*, June 13, 1855.

18. *Ibid.*, August 1, 1844.

19. *Ibid.*, August 8, 1855.

20. *Ibid.*, August 15, 1855.

21. Daily *Pittsburgh Gazette*, September 6, 1855.

22. *Ibid.*

23. *Ibid.*; Henry Wilson, *History of the Rise and Fall of the Slave Power in America*, II, 415–416.

24. Richard Hildreth, *Atrocious Judges . . . with an Appendix Containing the Case of Passmore Williamson*, pp. 389–432.

25. *Daily Pittsburgh Gazette*, September 6, 1855.

26. *Pittsburgh Daily Commercial Journal*, September 7, 1855.

27. Harrisburg *Pennsylvania Telegraph*, September 12, 1855.

28. Mueller, *The Whig Party in Pennsylvania*, p. 222.

29. Harrisburg *Pennsylvania Telegraph*, September 26, 1855.

30. *Ibid.*

31. Mueller, *The Whig Party in Pennsylvania*, pp. 222–223.

32. *Ibid.*, p. 224; Harrisburg *Semi-Weekly Telegraph*, February 15, 1856.

33. Harrisburg *Semi-Weekly Telegraph*, March 21, 1856.

34. J. Thomas Scharf and Thompson Westcott, *History of Philadelphia, 1609–1884*, I, 722, 722 n.; Burton A. Konkle, *The Life and Speeches of Thomas Williams . . . a Founder of the Whig and Republican Parties*, I, 296.

35. Allan Nevins, *Frémont: Pathmarker of the West*, pp. 433–434.

36. Roy F. Nichols, "Some Problems of the First Republican Presidential Campaign," *American Historical Review* (April, 1923), XXVIII, 495, 496.

37. Harrisburg *Weekly Telegraph*, September 4, 1856.

38. Mueller, *The Whig Party in Pennsylvania*, p. 235.

39. McClure, *Old-Time Notes of Pennsylvania*, I, 266–273.

40. Kirkpatrick to Cameron, August 24, 1857, Cameron Papers.

41. Frank H. Taylor, *Philadelphia in the Civil War, 1861–1865*, pp. 9–11.

42. Andrews to Banks, July 17, 1856, Nathaniel P. Banks Papers, Essex Institute, Salem, Mass. (In volume marked "V, 1856.")

43. Garrison to Helen E. Garrison, October 13, 1858, Garrison Papers.

44. Malcolm R. Eiselen, *The Rise of Pennsylvania Protectionism*, pp. 244–249; Reinhard H. Luthin, "Abraham Lincoln and the Tariff," *American Historical Review* (July, 1944), XLIX, 612 ff.

45. Roy F. Nichols, *Franklin Pierce*, pp. 408 ff., 415 ff., 432, 451–452.

46. Albert J. Beveridge, *Abraham Lincoln, 1809–1858*, II, 367.

47. New York *Evening Post*, September 18, 1856.

48. Sister Frances Loretto Conlin, "The Democratic Party in Pennsylvania from 1856 to 1865, *Records of the American Catholic Historical Society* (June, 1936), Vol. 47, p. 138.

49. Philip G. Auchampaugh, *James Buchanan and His Cabinet on the Eve of Secession*, p. 9.

50. *Ibid.*, pp. 9 n., 10 n.

51. Philip G. Auchampaugh, "John W. Forney, Robert Tyler and James Buchanan," *Tyler's Quarterly Historical and Genealogical Magazine* (October, 1933), XV, 71–89.

52. Hewitt, "The Know Nothing Party in Pennsylvania," *loc. cit.*, p. 85.

53. Philadelphia *North American and United States Gazette*, October 7, 1858.

54. Cameron Quoted in I. F. Boughter, Western Pennsylvania and the Morrill Tariff," *Western Pennsylvania Historical Magazine* (January, 1923), VI, 118.

55. Supplement, bound with Philadelphia *North American and United States Gazette*, June 16, 1858.

56. Helfenstein to Douglas, *Private*, January 18, 1860, Douglas Papers.

57. *Congressional Globe*, 35th Cong., 1st sess., p. 1898; Philadelphia *Evening Bulletin*, April 1, 1858.

58. *Ibid*. Cameron was "paired" with Jefferson Davis against the Lecompton bill. Harrisburg *Semi-Weekly Telegraph*, April 3, 1858.

59. Philadelphia *Evening Bulletin*, April 1, 1858.

60. Philadelphia *North American and United States Gazette*, July 16, 1858.

61. McQuaide to Covode, August 11, 1858, Covode Papers.

62. New York *Herald*, June 8, 1858.

63. Harrisburg Daily *Telegraph*, June 11, 1858.

64. Philadelphia Evening *Bulletin*, June 9, 1858.

65. New York *Herald*, June 24, 1858.

66. *Ibid*., June 28, 1858.

67. *Ibid*., June 30, 1858.

68. *Ibid*., July 17, 1858.

69. Danville *Democrat*, clipped in Harrisburg *Daily Telegraph* June 29, 1858; Bedford *Enquirer*, clipped in *ibid*., July 10, 1858.

70. *Miltonian*, clipped in Philadelphia *Evening Bulletin*, June 26, 1858.

71. Philadelphia *Evening Bulletin*, July 29, 1858.

72. New York *Herald*, August 3, 1858.

73. Malcolm R. Eiselen, *The Rise of Pennsylvania Protectionism*, pp. 244 ff.

74. New York *Herald*, October 14, 1858.

75. Hay to Cameron, October 29, 1858, Cameron Papers.

76. New York *Herald*, January 21, 1859.

77. *Ibid*., February 3, 1859.

78. Henry B. Stanton, *Random Recollections*, pp. 194–195; Weed to Cameron, January 15, 1857, Cameron Papers.

79. Harrisburg *Daily Telegraph*, April 1, 1859; Philadelphia *Public Ledger*, April 2, 1859.

80. Seward to Weed, April 11, 1859, Weed Papers.

81. New York *Herald*, May 3, 1859.

82. Harrisburg *Daily Telegraph*, April 18, 1859.

83. *Ibid*., April 29, 1859.

84. *Ibid*.

85. *Ibid*.

86. *Ibid*., May 4, 1859.

87. Adams kept Cameron posted. See Adams to Cameron, May 22, 28, 1859, Cameron Papers.

88. Harrisburg Daily *Telegraph*, May 31, 1859.

89. *Ibid*., June 1, 1859.

90. *Ibid*., June 3, 6, 8, 15, 17, 23, 1859.

91. Howard O. Folker, *Sketches of the Forney Family*, p. 88.

92. New York *Herald*, June 12, 1859.

93. New York *Herald*, June 12, 1859.

94. Philadelphia *Evening Bulletin*, June 9, 1858.

95. *Ibid*., January 27, February 16, 1859.

96. *Ibid.*, June 2, 6, 22, 24, 1859.

97. New York *Herald*, July 18, 1859.

98. *Ibid.*

99. Cameron to Nesbit, September 5, 1859, Cameron Papers.

100. Joseph H. Barrett to Cameron, September 7, 1859, Cameron Papers.

101. Casey to Barrett (copy), September 19, 1859, Cameron Papers.

102. Andrews to Doolittle, October 11, 1859, James R. Doolittle Papers.

103. John G. Nicolay and John Hay (eds.), *Complete Works of Abraham Lincoln*, Gettysburg edition, V, 257–258.

104. Edward F. Dunne, *Illinois*, I, 468.

105. Chicago *Press & Tribune*, November 14, 1859.

106. Lancaster *Examiner*, cited in Harrisburg *Daily Telegraph*, October 13, 1859.

107. Chicago *Press & Tribune*, November 9, 1859.

108. *Ibid.*, December 26, 1859.

109. *Ibid.*, January 20, 24, 27, 1860.

110. *Ibid.*, November 19, 1859.

111. Simon Whitely to Cameron, May 10, 1860, Cameron Papers.

112. Fisher to Pratt, March 13, 1860, Daniel D. Pratt Papers.

113. Jeremiah Nichols to Pratt, March 8, 1860, *ibid.*

114. Indianapolis *Daily State Sentinel*, February 8, 1860.

115. Edward L. Pierce to Sumner, April 20, 1860, Charles Sumner Papers.

116. Levering to Calif, April 28, 1860, Arthur B. Calif Papers.

117. Eugene V. Smalley, *A History to the Republican Party . . . to Which Is Added a Political History of Minnesota from a Republican Point of View*, p. 166; Ramsey to Cameron, March 15, 1860; Miller to Cameron, April 2, 1860, Cameron Papers.

118. J. Cutler Andrews, *Pittsburgh's Post-Gazette*, p. 149; Pittsburgh *Gazette* clipped in Harrisburg *Daily Telegraph*, April 1, 1859; Errett to Cameron, January 8, 1860, Cameron Papers.

119. Errett to "Dear Sir," *Private* (copy), April 17, 1860; Marsh to Errett, April 28, 1860; Andrews to Errett, April 30, 1860; Smith to Errett, April 30, 1860; Pease to Errett, April 30, 1860; French to Errett, April 30, 1860; Scholte to Errett, May 2, 1860; Paine to Errett, undated, Cameron Papers.

120. Errett to Cameron, May 8, 1860, Cameron Papers.

121. Casey to Cameron, January 28, 1860, *ibid.*

122. Philadelphia *Sunday Dispatch*, February 5, 1860.

123. Ida M. Street, "The Simon Cameron Indian Commission of 1838," *Annals of Iowa* (July–October, 1905), VII, 115–139, 172–195; *Collections of the State Historical Society of Wisconsin* (1873–1876), VII, 394–396; "Execution of Treaty with the Winnebagoes," *Executive Document* No. 229, 25th Cong., 3rd sess., serial no. 345.

124. Henry R. Mueller, *The Whig Party in Pennsylvania*, p. 117.

125. Morton to Thompson, March 26, 1860, Thompson Papers.

126. Brisbin to Covode, November 28, 1859, Covode Papers.
127. Stanton L. Davis, *Pennsylvania Politics, 1860–1863*, pp. 53–63.
128. *Ibid.*, pp. 64–65.
129. Casey to Cameron, May 7, 1860, Cameron Papers.

CHAPTER VII

1. Reinhard H. Luthin, "Abraham Lincoln and the Massachusetts Whigs in 1848," *New England Quarterly* (December, 1941), XIV, 620–624.

2. Fred Harvey Harrington, "Nathaniel Prentiss Banks: A Study in Anti-Slavery Politics," *New England Quarterly* (December, 1936), IX, 635–636.

3. *Ibid.*, p. 638.

4. William G. Bean, Party Transformation in Massachusetts with Special Reference to the Antecedents of the Republican Party, 1848–1860, MS., Chapters VII–X; Everett to Mrs. Charles Eames (copies), September 30, October 9, 21, November 13, 1854, Edward Everett Diary, MS., Vol. 173, pp. 215, 216.

5. Harrington, "Nathaniel Prentiss Banks," *loc. cit.*, pp. 641–647, 647 n.; Edward L. Pierce to Sumner, September [no day listed], 1857, Charles Sumner Papers.

6. Springfield (Mass.) *Republican*, July 12, 1860.

7. Harrington, "Nathaniel Prentiss Banks," *loc. cit.*, pp. 647–649.

8. Bean, Party Transformation in Massachusetts . . ., 1848–1860, MS., pp. 377–380.

9. *Eighth Census of the United States: Population, 1860*, p. 227.

10. *Reminiscences of Carl Schurz*, II, 116–117; Edward L. Pierce to Sumner, April 18, 1859, Sumner Papers.

11. Goodrich to Banks, April 27, 1859, Nathaniel P. Banks Papers, Illinois State Historical Library, Springfield.

12. Slade to Banks, May 8, 1859, *ibid.*

13. Ray to Banks, April 2 [1859], Private, Nathaniel P. Banks Papers, Essex Institute, Salem, Mass. (in volume marked "II, 1858").

14. Kreismann to Banks, April 2, 1859, *ibid.*

15. *Ibid.*

16. Pierce to Sumner, May 31, 1859, Sumner Papers.

17. *Ibid.* For the organization of the "Silver Grey" (or anti-Seward, pro-Fillmore) movement, see Harry J. Carman and Reinhard H. Luthin, "The Seward-Fillmore Feud and the Disruption of the Whig Party," *New York History* (July, 1943), XXIV, 335–357.

18. Pierce to Sumner, July 21, 1859, Sumner Papers.

19. Andrews to Banks, July 16, 1859, Madeira to Banks, August 26, 1859, Porter to Banks, September 4, 1859, J. S. Richardson to Banks, September 4, 1859, J. S. Richardson to Banks, December 9, 1859, Nathaniel P. Banks Papers, Illinois State Historical Library, Springfield.

20. Springfield (Mass.) *Republican*, March 5, 12, 22, 1860.

21. A. Burlingame to Banks, March 4, 1860, Nathaniel P. Banks Papers, Essex Institute, Salem, Mass. (in volume marked "IV, 1856").

22. W. C. Bryant, David Dudley Field, William Emerson, S. Draper, George W. Blunt, L. B. Wayman et al. to Banks, April [no day listed], 1860, Nathaniel P. Banks Papers, Essex Institute, Salem, Mass. (in folio marked "1860").

23. Samuel Bowles to Banks, April\30, 1860, *ibid.*

24. Bartlett to Banks, April 19, 1860, *ibid.*

25. Same to same, April 27, 1860, *ibid.*

26. New York *Herald*, April 25, 1860.

27. New York *Daily Tribune*, May 9, 1860.

28. Springfield (Mass.) *Republican*, April 19, 1860.

29. *Ibid.*, May 1, 1860.

30. *Ibid.*, May 8, 1860.

31. *Ibid.*, May 9, 1860.

32. *Ibid.*, May 10, 1860.

33. *Ibid.*, May 11, 1860.

34. E. Malcolm Carroll, *Origins of the Whig Party*, pp. 40–44, 132–133.

35. *Memoirs of John Quincy Adams*, VIII, 537.

36. William Salter (ed.), "Letters of John McLean to John Teesdale," *The Bibliotheca Sacra* (October, 1899), Vol. 56, p. 740.

37. Francis P. Weisenburger, *The Life of John McLean*, pp. 211–213; Reinhard H. Luthin, "Salmon P. Chase's Political Career Before the Civil War," *Mississippi Valley Historical Review* (March, 1943), XXIX, 530.

38. Teesdale to McLean, August 3, 1859, John McLean Papers.

39. Trumbull to McLean, "Private," April 21, 1860, *ibid.*

40. Daniel J. Ryan "Lincoln and Ohio," *Publications, Ohio Archaeological and Historical Society* (January, 1933), XXXII, 116–117.

41. Weisenburger, *John McLean*, p. 213.

42. A. G. Riddle, "Rise of Anti-Slavery Sentiment on the Western Reserve," *Magazine of Western History* (June, 1887), VI, 145.

43. Briggs to Wade, February 22, 1860, Benjamin F. Wade Papers; Luthin, "Salmon P. Chase's Political Career Before the Civil War," *op. cit.*, p. 530.

44. Paine to Wade, February 24, March 22, 1860, Wade Papers.

45. Tilden to Wade, March 27, 1860, *ibid.*

46. Frederic Bancroft (ed.), *Speeches, Correspondence and Political Papers of Carl Schurz*, I, 113.

47. Wade to "Cal," April 1, 1860, Wade Papers.

48. S. P. Chase to Wade, March 4, 1860, *ibid.*

49. Smith, "Salmon P. Chase and the Election of 1860," *loc. cit.*, p. 523.

50. Bingham to Chase, May 10, 1860, Salmon P. Chase Papers, Library of Congress.

51. Joseph P. Bradley, "A Memorial of the Life and Character of

Hon. William L. Dayton," *Proceedings, New Jersey Historical Society,* Series II, Vol. 4, pp. 71–118.

52. Henry S. Cooley, *A Study of Slavery in New Jersey,* pp. 27–29, 54.

53. Frank H. Taylor, *Philadelphia in the Civil War, 1861–1865,* p. 10.

54. *Eighth Census of the United States: Population, 1860,* p. 313.

55. James L. Sellers, "The Make-Up of the Early Republican Party," *Transactions of the Illinois State Historical Society,* 1930, p. 44.

56. Briggs to Chase, April 13, 1860, Salmon P. Chase Papers, Library of Congress.

57. For protective-tariff sentiment in New Jersey see Trenton *Daily True American,* January 12, 1859; Trenton *State Gazette,* October 22, September 10, October 15, 1858; Newark *Daily Advertiser,* January 4, 29, February 2, April 26, 1859.

58. Personal Reminiscences of Charles Perrin Smith, MS., pp. 172–173.

59. Dudley to Carey, November 24, 1859, Henry C. Carey Papers.

60. Charles M. Knapp, *New Jersey Politics During the Period of the Civil War and Reconstruction,* pp. 17, 24 n., 26–27.

61. Sherman to Welles, March 23, 1860, Gideon Welles Papers.

62. Erik Eriksson, "William Penn Clarke," *Iowa Journal of History and Politics* (January, 1927), XXV, 50.

63. Stanton L. Davis, *Pennsylvania Politics, 1860–1863,* p. 57.

64. Charles A. Hamlin, *The Life and Times of Hannibal Hamlin,* p. 335.

65. E. Merton Coulter, "The Downfall of the Whig Party in Kentucky," *Register, Kentucky State Historical Society* (1925), XXIII, 162.

66. James R. Robertson, "Sectionalism in Kentucky from 1855 to 1865," *Mississippi Valley Historical Review* (June, 1917), IV, 55.

67. William Ritchie, "The Public Career of Cassius M. Clay," MS., p. 91.

68. Henry Wilson, *History of the Rise and Fall of the Slave Power in America,* II, 511.

69. Ritchie, "The Public Career of Cassius M. Clay," MS., pp. 135–136.

70. *Ibid.,* pp. 131–132.

71. Dawson's Fort Wayne (Ind.) *Daily Times,* February 29, 1860.

72. Indianapolis *Daily Journal,* February 21, 1860.

73. Hackleman to Pratt, March 23, 1860, Daniel D. Pratt Papers.

74. Clay to Sumner, March 3, 1860, Charles Sumner Papers.

75. Same to same, March 18, 1860, *ibid.*

76. Lexington (Kentucky) *Observer & Reporter,* May 5, 1860; Dawson's Fort Wayne (Ind.) *Daily Times,* May 4, 1860.

77. Clay to Brainerd, May 7, 1860, in "The 1860 Presidential Campaign: Letters of Cassius M. Clay to Cephas Brainerd," *The Moorsfield Antiquarian* (August, 1937), I, 105–106.

78. Jane Grey Swisshelm, *Half a Century,* pp. 172–173; Greeley to Colfax, April 3, 1859, Greeley-Colfax Papers.

79. Joseph G. Rayback, "Land for the Landless: The Contemporary View," MS., pp. 79–82.

80. Franklin F. Holbrook, "The Early Political Career of Ignatius Donnelly, 1857–1865," MS., pp. 25–42.

81. King to Dawson, "Private," June 2, 1859, Thurlow Weed Papers, University of Rochester Library.

82. Winona (Minnesota) *Democrat*, February 27, 1860.

83. Jones to Wade, February 25, 1860, Wade Papers.

84. Smalley, *A History of the Republican Party . . . To Which Is Added a Political History of Minnesota from a Republican Point of View.*

85. Miller to Cameron, April 25, 1860, Cameron Papers.

86. Richard Webb, "William Pitt Fessenden," *Collections, Maine Historical Society* (1899), Series II, Vol. 10, pp. 227–232; George F. Talbot, "Lot M. Morrill," *Collections, Maine Historical Society* (1894), Series II, Vol. 5, pp. 231–232.

87. Warren to Washburne, February 6, 1860, Elihu B. Washburne Papers; James S. Pike, *First Blows of the Civil War*, pp. 482–483; Harvey to McLean, September 5, 1859, John McLean Papers; Fessenden, *Life and Public Services of William Pitt Fessenden*, I, 109–111.

88. Pike, *First Blows of the Civil War.*

89. *Proceedings of the Vermont Historical Society,* 1919–1920, p. 94.

90. Davis to Morrill, August 20, 1859, Justin S. Morrill Papers.

91. Pike, *First Blows of the Civil War,* pp. 499–500.

92. Paul R. Frothingham, *Edward Everett: Orator and Statesman,* pp. 408–409; Kirk H. Porter, *National Party Platforms,* p. 52.

93. New York *Daily Tribune,* May 11, 1860.

CHAPTER VIII

1. Philip G. Auchampaugh, "The Buchanan-Douglas Feud," *Journal of the Illinois State Historical Society* (April, 1932), XXV, 5–48; Richard R. Stenberg, "An Unnoted Factor in the Buchanan-Douglas Feud," *Journal of the Illinois State Historical Society* (1932–1933), XXV, 271–284. For a summary of the Democratic split, see Reinhard H. Luthin, "The Democratic Split During Buchanan's Administration," *Pennsylvania History* (January, 1944), XI, 13–35.

2. George Fort Milton, *The Eve of Conflict: Stephen A. Douglas and the Needless War,* pp. 84, 90–92, 211–229, 239–243, 255, 259, Louis M. Sears, *John Slidell,* pp. 121–124, 131–140.

3. S. A. Douglas to Treat, February 5, 1857, Samuel Treat Papers.

4. Jesse D. Bright to English, April 16, 1857, William H. English Papers, William Henry Smith Memorial Library, Indianapolis; Murat Halstead, *Caucuses of 1860,* p. 13.

5. J. G. Randall, *The Civil War and Reconstruction,* p. 158.

6. John Bassett Moore (ed.), *The Works of James Buchanan,* X, 183, 190 ff.

7. Milton, *The Eve of Conflict*, pp. 272–273; Allen Johnson, *Stephen A. Douglas*, pp. 327–328.

8. Johnson, *Stephen A. Douglas*, p. 334; Everett to Mrs. Charles Eames (copy), December 27, 1857, Edward Everett Papers.

9. Jones to Breese, September 7, 1858, Sidney Breese Papers.

10. Johnson, *Stephen A. Douglas*, p. 331.

11. *Ibid.*, p. 332.

12. Milton, *The Eve of Conflict*, pp. 288–293.

13. Douglas to Treat, February 28, 1858, Treat Papers.

14. Arthur C. Cole, *The Era of the Civil War, 1848–1870*, pp. 157–180; Milton, *The Eve of Conflict*, pp. 270 ff.

15. Milton, *The Eve of Conflict*, p. 295.

·16. Philip G. Auchampaugh, "John W. Forney, Robert Tyler and James Buchanan," *Tyler's Quarterly Historical and Genealogical Magazine* (October, 1933), IV, 71–90; Reinhard H. Luthin, "Pennsylvania and Lincoln's Rise to the Presidency," *Pennsylvania Magazine of History and Biography* (January, 1943), LXVII, 62, 75.

17. Greeley to Colfax, November 2, 1859, Greeley-Colfax Papers.

18. *Congressional Globe*, 36th Cong., 1st sess., pp. 662–663.

19. Joseph Ellison, *California and the Union, 1850–1869*, pp. 151, 152, 171, 180; Purdy to Chase, November 5, 1856, Chase Papers, Library of Congress; New York *Herald*, September 9, 22, 1856.

20. Imogene Spaulding, "The Attitude of California to the Civil War," *Publications, Historical Society of Southern California* (1912–1913), II, 104–106.

21. Harris Newmark, *Sixty Years in California, 1853–1913*, p. 91.

22. *Memoirs of Cornelius Cole*, pp. 112–113, 118, 129, 133; George T. Clark, *Leland Stanford*, p. 72; Zoeth Skinner Eldredge, *History of California*, III, 495–496; New York *Herald*, September 22, 1856.

23. Walter R. Bacon, "Fifty Years of California Politics," *Publications, Historical Society of Southern California* (1900–1901), V, 38.

24. Jeremiah Lynch, *A Senator of the Fifties: David C. Broderick of California*, pp. 29–36, 144–196.

25. James S. Pike, *First Blows of the Civil War*, p. 417; New York *Daily Tribune*, April 20, 1858.

26. Bacon, "Fifty Years of California Politics," *loc. cit.*, pp. 38–39.

27. Hubert H. Bancroft, *History of California*, VI, 722–723.

28. Chicago *Press & Tribune*, October 11, 1859.

29. Lynch, *A Senator of the Fifties*, pp. 201–224.

30. *Memoirs of Cornelius Cole*, p. 112.

31. Howard K. Beale (ed.), *The Diary of Edward Bates, 1859–1866*, p. 49.

32. Oscar T. Chuck (ed.), *Masterpieces of E. D. Baker*, pp. 74–75.

33. Washington *Era*, October 29, 1859, in Pike, *First Blows of the Civil War*, p. 446; St. Louis *Daily Missouri Democrat*, October 10, 1859; Harrisburg (Pa.) *Daily Telegraph*, October 14, 1859.

34. *Congressional Globe*, 36th Cong., 1st sess., p. 997.

35. *Ibid.*, p. 1017.

NOTES TO CHAPTER VIII

36. *House Report No. 648*, 36th Cong., 1st sess., serial no. 1071.

37. Allen Johnson and Dumas Malone (ed.), *Dictionary of American Biography*, IV, 470.

38. "Covode Investigation," *House Report No. 648*, 36th Cong., 1st sess., serial no. 1071, pp. 138–148, 296–299.

39. New York *Herald*, April 18, 1860.

40. Jesse D. Bright to Hamilton, December [no day listed], 1858, Allen Hamilton Papers.

41. Dwight L. Dumond, *The Secession Movement, 1860–1861*, pp. 19–21.

42. Ulrich B. Phillips, "The Central Theme of Southern History," *American Historical Review* (October, 1928), XXXIV, 35.

43. Philip M. Hamer, *The Secession Movement in South Carolina, 1847–1852*, Chapters I–VII.

44. Laura A. White, "The National Democrats in South Carolina, 1852–1860," *South Atlantic Quarterly* (October, 1929), XXVIII, 382.

45. Laura A. White, *Robert Barnwell Rhett: Father of Secession*, pp. 96, 111, 111 n., 113, 144, 146–49.

46. Clarence P. Denman, *The Secession Movement in Alabama*, p. 1.

47. Denman, *The Secession Movement in Alabama*, pp. 159–160.

48. Professor Dwight L. Dumond's sketch of Yancey in Dumas Malone (ed.), *Dictionary of American Biography*, XX, 592–593. Also John W. Dubose, "Yancey: A Study," *Gulf States Historical Magazine* (January, 1903), I, 241–245. The only biography of Yancey is John W. Dubose, *The Life and Times of William Lowndes Yancey*.

49. White, *Robert Barnwell Rhett*, pp. 154–155.

50. Denman, *The Secession Movement in Alabama*, pp. 65–72.

51. *Ibid.*, p. vii.

52. Lewy Dorman, *Party Politics in Alabama From 1850 Through 1860*, Preface.

53. J. E. D. Yonge, "The Conservative Party in Alabama, 1848–1860," *Transactions of the Alabama Historical Society* (1902), IV, 509–515.

54. James L. Murphy, "Alabama and the Charleston Convention of 1860," *Transactions of the Alabama Historical Society* (1904), V, 244–245.

55. Perry Lee Rainwater, *Mississippi: Storm Center of Secession, 1856–1861*, pp. 22–30, 40–44, 59.

56. James B. Ranck, *Albert Gallatin Brown: Radical Southern Nationalist*, pp. 156–157, 166.

57. Rainwater, *Mississippi: Storm Center of Secession, 1856–1661*, pp. 65–66, 109.

58. Natchez *Free Trader*, June 29, 1859, in *ibid.*, p. 111 n.

59. Rainwater, *Mississippi: Storm Center of Secession, 1856–1861*, pp. 111–112.

60. *Ibid.*, p. 113.

61. Dorothy Dodd, "The Secession Movement in Florida, 1850–1861," *Florida Historical Society Quarterly* (1933), XII, 46–47; Willie

M. Caskey, *Secession and Restoration of Louisiana*, pp. 1–2; Anna I. Sandbo, "Beginnings of the Secession Movement in Texas," *The Southwestern Historical Quarterly* (July, 1914), XVIII, 65–73; Eugene C. Barker (ed.), *A History of Texas and Texans*, by Frank W. Johnson, I, 528; David Y. Thomas, *Arkansas in War and Reconstruction, 1861–1874*, p. 32.

62. Dumond, *The Secession Movement, 1860–1861*, pp. 35–36.

63. Philadelphia *Press*, March 5, 14, 1860.

64. James K. Greer, "Louisiana Politics, 1846–1861," *Louisiana Historical Quarterly* (July, 1929), XII, 381; Amos A. Ettinger, *The Mission to Spain of Pierre Soulé, 1853–1855*, pp. 112–113, 127–131, 472; Louis M. Sears, *John Slidell*, pp. 90, 99, 142, 155–158.

65. Mary L. McLure, "The Elections of 1860 in Louisiana," *Louisiana Historical Quarterly* (October, 1926), IX, 644–650.

66. Murat Halstead, *Caucuses of 1860*, pp. 7, 13.

67. *Ibid.*, p. 1.

68. Milton, *The Eve of Conflict*, pp. 373–374, 376, 403, 414.

69. Philadelphia *Press*, April 12, 1860.

70. Milton, *The Eve of Conflict*, p. 428.

71. Halstead, *Caucuses of 1860*, p. 7.

72. *Ibid.*, p. 5.

73. Milton, *The Eve of Conflict*, pp. 420–421.

74. Rainwater, *Mississippi: Storm Center of Secession, 1856–1861*, p. 111 n.

75. James Guthrie to ——, May 21, 1860, Samuel J. Tilden Papers, Box No. 20.

76. Philadelphia *Press*, January 10, 1860.

77. Philip G. Auchampaugh, "The Buchanan-Douglas Feud," *Journal of the Illinois State Historical Society* (April, 1932), XXV, 33.

78. Mrs. Roger B. Pryor, *Reminiscences of Peace and War*, pp. 95, 96.

79. Milledge L. Bonham, Jr., "New York and the Election of 1860," *New York History* (April, 1934), XV, 124–127.

80. New York *Herald*, April 24, 1860.

81. *Ibid.*

82. *Ibid.*, April 25, 1860.

83. Dumond, *The Secession Movement, 1860–1861*, pp. 41–43.

84. Milton, *The Eve of Conflict*, p. 433.

85. White, *Robert Barnwell Rhett*, p. 163.

86. Ulrich B. Phillips (ed.), *Correspondence of Robert Toombs, Alexander H. Stephens, and Howell Cobb*, p. 468.

87. Halstead, *Caucuses of 1860*, pp. 68–69.

88. Allen Johnson, *Stephen A. Douglas*, pp. 415–416; Rainwater, *Mississippi: Storm Center of Secession, 1856–1861*, p. 114.

89. Natchez *Free Trader*, June 15, 1860, in Rainwater, *op. cit.*, pp. 115–116.

90. Randall, *The Civil War and Reconstruction*, pp. 175–176.

CHAPTER IX

1. P. Orman Ray, *The Convention That Nominated Lincoln*, pp. 5, 11.

2. Murat Halstead, *Caucuses of 1860*, p. 121.

3. *Ibid.*, p. 122.

4. E. Hempstead to Washburne, May 14, 1860, Elihu B. Washburne Papers; Bangor (Maine) *Daily Whig and Courier*, May 21, 1860.

5. Harry J. Carman and Reinhard H. Luthin, *Lincoln and the Patronage*, p. 7.

6. Detroit *Free Press*, May 29, 30, 31, June 3, 1860; Detroit *Daily Tribune*, June 20, 1860; Springfield (Mass.) *Republican*, May 29, 1860.

7. Greeley to Chase, August 5, 1860, Salmon P. Chase Papers, Historical Society of Pennsylvania, Philadelphia.

8. Franklin P. Rice, "The Life of Eli Thayer," MS.

9. For material on Johnson, see Dumas Malone (ed.), *Dictionary of American Biography*, X, 99–100.

10. Franklin Johnson, "Nominating Lincoln," *The Companion*, February 8, 1917. (Clipping in files of Lincoln National Life Foundation, Fort Wayne, Ind.)

11. George Lunt, *The Origins of the Late War*, p. 353. See Lawrence S. Mayo's sketch of Lunt in Dumas Malone (ed.), *Dictionary of American Biography*, XI, 507–508.

12. Halstead, *Caucuses of 1860*, p. 122.

13. *Ibid.*

14. Kreismann to Washburne, May 15, 1860, Elihu B. Washburne Papers.

15. *Reminiscences of Carl Schurz*, II, 176–177.

16. Detroit *Daily Tribune*, May 17, 1860.

17. Boston *Daily Advertiser*, May 15, 1860.

18. Smith, *The Francis Preston Blair Family in Politics*, I, 475–476.

19. Joseph Casey to Cameron, May 10, 1860, Simon Cameron Papers.

20. H. Kreismann to Washburne, May 13, 1860, Elihu B. Washburne Papers.

21. Donnal V. Smith, "Salmon P. Chase and the Election of 1860," *Ohio Archaeological and Historical Quarterly* (1930), XXXIX, 526–527; Reinhard H. Luthin, "Salmon P. Chase's Political Career Before the Civil War," *Mississippi Valley Historical Review* (March, 1943), XXIX, 531–532.

22. Erastus Hopkins to Chase, May 17, 1860, in *ibid.*, p. 526.

23. Philadelphia *Press*, May 15, 1860.

24. Francis P. Weisenburger, *The Life of John McLean*, p. 213.

25. Statement of Dr. Harry E. Pratt, biographer of Davis, to the present author.

26. Jayne to Trumbull, May 20, 1860, Trumbull Papers; *Memoirs of Gustave Koerner*, II, 84–85; Joseph Fort Newton, *Lincoln and Herndon*, p. 272; Henry C. Whitney, *Lincoln the Citizen*, p. 286; *Personal Recollections of John M. Palmer*, p. 81.

27. *Memoirs of Gustave Koerner*, II, 85.

28. Kreismann to Washburne, May 13, 1860, Elihu B. Washburne Papers.

29. Springfield (Mass.) *Republican*, January 4, 1860.

30. *Ibid.;* Stoler, "Influence of the Democratic Element in the Republican Party of Illinois and Indiana, 1854–1860," MS., p. 188; Reinhard H. Luthin, "Indiana and Lincoln's Rise to the Presidency," *Indiana Magazine of History* (December, 1942), XXXVIII, 390.

31. O. J. Holister, *Life of Schuyler Colfax*, p. 148; Bobb to Cameron, May 19, 1860, Cameron Papers; Conner to Pratt, April 23, 1860, Daniel D. Pratt Papers.

32. Hackelman to Pratt, March 23, 1860, Pratt Papers.

33. Dawson's Fort Wayne *Daily Times*, April 12, 18, May 2, 1860.

34. *Ibid.*, May 16, 1860, p. 2; Alexander K. McClure, *Abraham Lincoln and Men of War-Times*, pp. 24–30.

35. McClure, *Abraham Lincoln and Men of War-Times*, Second Edition, p. 25 n.

36. Louis J. Bailey, "Caleb Blood Smith," *Indiana Magazine of History* (September, 1933), XXIX, 220, 225–227; Indianapolis *Daily Journal*, May 16, 17, 1860; St. Louis *Daily Missouri Republican*, May 16, 1860.

37. Tarbell, *The Life of Abraham Lincoln*, 1900 edition, I, 347 n.

38. Fell to Lincoln, January 2, 1860, Jesse W. Fell Papers. (Copy in possession of Dr. Harry E. Pratt, of Ball State Teachers College, Muncie, Indiana.)

39. Paul M. Angle (ed.), *Herndon's Life of Lincoln*, p. 381.

40. Charles Gibson, "Edward Bates," *Missouri Historical Society Collections* (1900), II, 55.

41. Caleb B. Smith to David Davis, January 31, February 5, 1861, in Pratt, "David Davis, 1815–1884," *loc. cit.*, p. 167. Also conversation of the present author with Dr. Pratt.

42. Matilda Gresham, *Life of Walter Q. Gresham*, I, 110–111.

43. William P. Fishback to his brother "Tip" (Photostat), January 19, 1861, Miscellaneous Papers, Indiana State Library, Indianapolis.

44. *Complete Works of Abraham Lincoln*, VI, 21.

45. Indianapolis *Daily Journal*, May 16, 1860.

46. St. Louis *Daily Missouri Republican*, May 16, 1860.

47. Charles M. Knapp, *New Jersey Politics During the Period of the Civil War and Reconstruction*, pp. 1–28; Thomas Frazer to Douglas, Stephen A. Douglas Papers.

48. "Reminiscences of Charles Perrin Smith," MS., pp. 172–175.

49. Jayne to Trumbull, May 20, 1860, Trumbull Papers.

50. Springfield (Mass.) *Republican*, May 16, 1860; Pierce to Schurz, May 18, 1859, Pierce to Charles Francis Adams (copy), December 1, 1859, Carl Schurz Papers.

51. Springfield (Mass.) *Republican*, May 16, 1860; Wilson to Carey, April 16, 1860, Henry C. Carey Papers; Pierce to Sumner, April 20, 1860, Sumner Papers.

52. Thomas H. Dudley, "The Inside Facts of Lincoln's Nomination," *Century Magazine* (1890), Vol. 40, p. 478.

53. *Ibid.*

54. Kreismann to Washburne, May 16, 1860, Elihu B. Washburne Papers; Boston *Daily Advertiser*, May 17, 1860; Springfield (Mass.) *Republican*, May 17, 1860.

55. Pease and Randall (ed.), *The Diary of Orville Hickman Browning, 1850–1864*, I, 406.

56. Charles Hamlin, *The Life and Times of Hannibal Hamlin*, pp. 335–344; Louis C. Hatch (ed.), *Maine: A History*, II, 420–422.

57. David S. Muzzey, *James G. Blaine: A Political Idol of Other Days*, p. 31.

58. Gail Hamilton (Mary Abigail Dodge), *Biography of James G. Blaine*, p. 129.

59. Concord *New Hampshire Patriot*, March 28, 1860.

60. *Ibid.*, May 2, 1860.

61. *Ibid.*

62. Charles R. Corning, *Amos Tuck*, pp. 83–84.

63. Carroll J. Noonan, *Nativism in Connecticut, 1829–1860*, Chapters X, XI, XII, XVI; Gladys Franklin, "The Know Nothing Party in Connecticut," MS., Chapters II–V.

64. J. Hammond Trumbull, *The Memorial History of Hartford County, Connecticut, 1633–1884*, I, 610.

65. Noonan, *op. cit.*, pp. 313, 321 n., 324–329; New Haven *Columbian Weekly Register*, April 28, 1860; Bridgeport *Republican Farmer*, April 27, 1860.

66. Starkweather to Hawley, February 8, 1860, Joseph R. Hawley Papers.

67. Boston *Daily Advertiser*, clipped in Concord *New Hampshire Patriot*, April 18, 1860.

68. Charles Stickney, "Know Nothingism in Rhode Island," *Publications of the Rhode Island Historical Society* (1892–1894), pp. 243–257.

69. Thomas W. Bicknell, *The History of the State of Rhode Island and Providence Plantations*, II, 809.

70. Providence *Daily Post*, January 5, April 2, 5, 1860; Newport *Advertiser*, January 11, 18, April 11, 1809.

71. Tracy (ed.), *Uncollected Letters of Abraham Lincoln*, pp. 141–142.

72. Kreismann to Washburne, April 4, 1860, Elihu B. Washburne Papers; James H. Barrett to Chase, April 9, 1860, Salmon P. Chase Papers, Library of Congress; Philadelphia *News*, clipped in Baltimore *Clipper*, April 9, 1860.

73. Dixon to Welles, April 26, 1860, Gideon Welles Papers.

74. Same to same, May 1, 1860, *ibid.*

75. Same to same, May 4, 1860, *ibid.*

76. Same to same to May 8, 1860, *ibid.*

77. Same to same, May 7, 1860, *ibid.*

78. Hartford *Daily Courant*, April 7, 1860.

79. Springfield (Mass.) *Republican*, May 17, 1860.

80. Francis P. Weisenburger, *The Life of John McLean: A Politician on the United States Supreme Court*, p. 214.

81. Nourse to Trumbull, May 13, 1860, Lyman Trumbull Papers.

82. Stephenson to Trumbull, March 25, 1860, Trumbull Papers; Briggs to Chase, April 13, 1860, Chase Papers.

83. Pitkin, "The Tariff and the Early Republican Party," MS., pp. 195–197; John A. Gurley to Chase (Private), April 13, 1860, Chase Papers; Robert F. Paine to Wade, March 1, 1860, B. F. Hoffman to Wade, April 1, 1860, Benjamin F. Wade Papers.

84. Morton to Chase, April 19, 1860, Chase Papers; Eugene H. Roseboom, "Salmon P. Chase and the Know Nothings," *Mississippi Valley Historical Review* (1938), XXV, 540–541.

85. Luthin, "Salmon P. Chase's Political Career Before the Civil War," *op. cit.*, p. 531.

86. William Salter (ed.), "Letters of John McLean to John Teesdale," *The Bibliotheca Sacra* (October, 1899), LVI, 740.

87. Donnal V. Smith, "Salmon P. Chase and the Election of 1860," *Ohio Archaeological and Historical Quarterly* (1930), XXXIX, 528–529.

88. Daniel J. Ryan, "Lincoln and Ohio," *Ohio Archaeological and Historical Quarterly* (1923), XXXII, 118–121.

89. James L. Sellers, "The Make-Up of the Early Republican Party," *Transactions of the Illinois State Historical Society*, 1930, p. 50.

90. Smith, "Salmon P. Chase and the Election of 1860," *loc. cit.*, pp. 527–529.

91. Kreismann to Washburne, May 15, 1860, Elihu B. Washburne Papers.

92. *Ibid.*

93. Same to same, May 16, 1860, *ibid.*

94. New York *Herald*, May 17, 1860.

95. Halstead, *Caucuses of 1860*, p. 129.

96. *Ibid.*, p. 130.

97. *Reminiscences of Carl Schurz*, II, 3; *Memoirs of Gustave Koerner, 1809–1896*, II, 86; "John A. Kasson: An Autobiography," *Annals of Iowa* (July, 1920), Series III, Vol. 12, p. 349.

98. Emerson D. Fite, *The Presidential Campaign of 1860*, pp. 124–25; Halstead, *Caucuses of 1860*, pp. 138–139.

99. Dumond, *The Secession Movement, 1860–1861*, p. 5, 5 n.; James L. Sellers, "Republicanism and State Rights in Wisconsin," *Mississippi Valley Historical Review* (September, 1930), XVII, 213–229; Ernest Bruncken, "German Political Refugees in the United States During the Period from 1815 to 1860," *Deutsch-Amerikanische Geschichtsblätter* (January, 1905), IV, 54–55.

100. Halstead, *Caucuses of 1860*, p. 138.

101. Dumond, *The Secession Movement, 1860–1861*, p. 5 n.; Charles W. Johnson, *The First Three Republican National Conventions . . . 1856, 1860 and 1864*, p. 138.

102. George E. Baker, "Seward, Weed, and Greeley," *The Republic* (Washington, D. C.), I, 200 (June, 1873).

103. Ralph R. Fahrney, *Horace Greeley and the Tribune in the Civil War*, p. 131.

104. New York *Herald*, September 13, 1859.

105. Eiselin, *The Rise of Pennsylvania Protectionism*, p. 257.

106. Pitkin, "The Tariff and the Early Republican Party," MS., p. 190; Philadelphia *Press*, May 15, 1860.

107. Wilmington *Delaware Republican*, March 15, May 3, 1860; Wilmington *Delaware Gazette*, February 3, March 20, 1860.

108. Margaret K. Monteiro, "The Presidential Election of 1860 in Virginia," *Richmond College Historical Papers* (June, 1916), I, 245.

109. Chicago *Press & Tribune*, March 30, April 3, 4, 1860; Portland *Oregon Weekly Times*, April 30, 1859.

110. Smith to Carey, February 6, 1859, Henry C. Carey Papers.

111. Pitkin, "The Tariff and the Early Republican Party," MS., pp. 191 n.–192 n.; Dudley to Carey, Carey Papers.

112. *Memoirs of Gustave Koerner*, II, 87.

113. Pitkin, "The Tariff and the Early Republican Party," MS., pp. 190 ff. See Reinhard H. Luthin, "Abraham Lincoln and the Tariff," *American Historical Review* (July, 1944), XLIX, 616–617.

114. Rayback, "Land for the Landless; The Contemporary View," MS., pp. 78–82; Portland *Oregon Weekly Times*, April 30, 1859; Detroit *Free Press*, May 4, 1860; Indianapolis *Daily State Sentinel*, January 13, 1860; Columbus *Daily Ohio State Journal*, March 14, 1860; Wilmington *Delaware Republican*, May 3, 1860; Louis C. Hatch (ed.), *Maine: A History*, II, 414.

115. Stephen Miller to Cameron, April 2, 1860, Simon Cameron Papers; P. N. Town to Washburne, March 26, 1860, Elihu B. Washburne Papers.

116. *De Bow's Review* (1860), XXXIX, 287.

117. E. Peshine Smith to Carey, March 14, 1860, Carey Papers.

118. William Slade to Banks, May 8, 1859, Nathaniel P. Banks Papers, Illinois State Historical Library, Springfield.

119. James S. Pike, *First Blows of the Civil War*, p. 443.

120. Ray to Banks, April 2, 1859, *Private*, Nathaniel P. Banks Papers, Essex Institute, Salem, Mass. (erroneously inserted in volume marked "II, 1856").

121. Dudley to Schurz, August 24, 1860, Carl Schurz Papers; Donnal V. Smith, "The Influence of the Foreign-Born Vote of the Northwest in the Election of 1860," *Mississippi Valley Historical Review* (September, 1932), XIX, 192, 198–199; *Memoirs of Gustave Koerner, 1809–1896*, II, 87.

122. Halstead, *Caucuses of 1860*, p. 139.

123. *Ibid.*

124. Chicago *Press & Tribune*, March 5, April 16, 1860; Detroit *Daily Tribune*, May 3, 1860; Wilmer C. Harris, *Public Life of Zachariah Chandler, 1851–1875*, pp. 17–18, 46.

125. Halstead, *Caucuses of 1860*, p. 139.

126. John S. Phelps to Snyder, October 30, 1858, John F. Snyder Papers; Shambaugh, *Messages and Proclamations of the Governors of Iowa*, II, 229–247; Curtis Nettels, "The Overland Mail Issue During the

Fifties," *Missouri Historical Review* (July, 1924), XVIII, 532; Le Roy Hafen, *The Overland Mail;* Portland *Oregon Weekly Times,* April 30, 1859.

127. Halstead, *Caucuses of 1860,* p. 139.

128. Franklin P. Rice, "The Life of Eli Thayer," MS.; *American Series of Popular Biographies: Maine Edition,* p. 180.

129. Greeley to Schuyler Colfax, June 20, 1860, Greeley-Colfax Papers.

130. Burk, *Golden Jubilee of the Republican Party* . . ., pp. 218–219. See also "John A. Kasson: An Autobiography," *Annals of Iowa* (July, 1920), Series III, Vol. 12, p. 349.

131. Shelby Cullom, *Fifty Years of Public Service,* p. 59.

132. Detroit *Daily Tribune,* May 18, 1860.

133. Halstead, *Caucuses of 1860,* p. 139.

134. *Ibid.,* p. 140.

135. *Ibid.*

136. *Ibid.,* p. 142.

137. Springfield (Mass.) *Republican,* June 5, 1860; *Annals of Iowa* (October, 1920), Series III, Vol. 12, p. 465; Bryant to Bigelow, February 20, 1860, in John Bigelow Diary, MS., New York Public Library.

138. Roland to Cameron, May 16, 1860, Errett to Cameron, May 29, 1860, Cameron Papers; Jasm G. McQuaide to Covode, March 1, 1860, John Covode Papers; Morton to Thompson, March 26, 1860, Richard W. Thompson Papers; Pierce to Sumner, April 20, 1860, Sumner Papers; Philadelphia *Sunday Dispatch,* June 12, November 27, 1859; February 26, March 4, 18, 25, 1860; Alexander K. McClure, *Abraham Lincoln and Men of War-Times,* pp. 24 ff.

139. James S. Pike, *First Blows of the Civil War,* p. 520.

140. Halstead, *Caucuses of 1860,* pp. 142–143.

141. Weed to Cameron, May 7, 1860, Cameron Papers; Springfield (Mass.) *Republican,* May 30, 1860; Albany *Evening Journal,* May 28, 1860, Halstead, *Caucuses of 1860,* p. 142 n.

142. McClure, *Abraham Lincoln and Men of War-Times,* pp. 24 ff.

143. John G. Nicolay, *Short Life of Abraham Lincoln,* p. 186; Alexander K. McClure, *Abraham Lincoln and Men of War-Times,* pp. 24 ff., 138–139.

144. Weisenburger, *John McLean,* p. 213.

145. Pitkin, "The Tariff and the Early Republican Party," MS., p. 199; Reinhard H. Luthin, "Organizing the Republican Party in the 'Border-Slave' Regions: Edward Bates's Presidential Candidacy in 1860," *Missouri Historical Review* (January, 1944), XXXVIII, 158.

146. *Memoirs of Gustave Koerner,* II, 88–89.

147. H. Kreismann to Banks, April 2, 1859; C. H. Ray to Banks, April 2, 1859, *Private,* Nathaniel P. Banks Papers, Essex Institute, Salem, Mass. (in column marked "II, 1858"); Pierce to Sumner, April 18, 1859, Sumner Papers; Chicago *Press & Tribune,* March 15, 1860; F. I. Herriott, "The Germans of Davenport and the Chicago Convention of 1860," in Harry E. Downer, *History of Davenport and Scott County, Iowa,* I, 839–846;

E. R. Harlan to the Missouri Historical Society, February 7, 1908, Edward Bates Papers.

148. F. I. Herriott, "The Conference in the Deutsches Haus, Chicago, May 14–15, 1860," *Transactions of the Illinois State Historical Society*, 1928, pp. 141–189; Philadelphia Press, May 15, 1860, p. 2.

149. Herriott, "The Conference in the Deutsches Haus, Chicago, May 14–15, 1860," *loc. cit.*, p. 189.

150. Harry J. Carman and Reinhard H. Luthin, "Some Aspects of the Know-Nothing Movement Reconsidered," *South Atlantic Quarterly* (April, 1940), XXXIX, 230–231.

151. St. Louis *Daily Missouri Republican*, March 11, 1860; Detroit *Free Press*, March 13, 1860.

152. E. Peshine Smith to Carey, March 14, 1860, Carey Papers.

153. Stephenson to Trumbull, March 23, 1860, Trumbull Papers.

154. G. Koerner to Trumbull, April 16, 1860, *ibid.*

155. Chicago *Press & Tribune*, March 15, 1860.

156. Indianapolis *Daily Journal*, May 16, 1860; Philadelphia *Press*, May 15, 1860.

157. Carman and Luthin, "Some Aspects of the Know-Nothing Movement Reconsidered," *loc. cit.*, pp. 222–223, 229–231; George Schneider, "Lincoln and the Anti-Know-Nothing Resolutions," *Transactions of the McLean County Historical Society* (1900), III, 87–91; Herriott, "The Conference in the Deutsches Haus, Chicago, May 14–15, 1860," *loc. cit.*, pp. 141–142.

158. Baltimore *Turn-Zeitung*, clipped in Chicago *Press & Tribune*, May 2, 1860.

159. *Ibid.*; Herriott, "The Conference in the Deutsches Haus, Chicago, May 14–15, 1860," *loc. cit.*, p. 155.

160. Nourse to Trumbull, May 13, 1860, Trumbull Papers; Edward L. Pierce to Sumner, April 20, 1860, Sumner Papers.

161. Pike, *First Blows of the Civil War*, p. 484.

162. Warren to Washburne, February 6, 1860, Papers.

163. Halstead, *Caucuses of 1860*, pp. 16 ff.

164. Springfield (Mass.) *Republican*, May 23, 1860.

165. Halstead, *Caucuses of 1860*, p. 142.

166. Stanton L. Davis, *Pennsylvania Politics, 1860–1863*, p. 105.

167. Pike, *First Blows of the Civil War*, p. 520.

168. Wilmot to Joseph Casey, March 10, 1860, Cameron Papers.

169. Davis, *Pennsylvania Politics, 1860–1863*, p. 105.

170. *Ibid.*, Otto Gresham, *The Greenbacks*, pp. 37–38; Matilda Gresham, *Life of Walter Quintin Gresham, 1832–1895*, pp. 565–566; Angle (ed.), *Herndon's Life of Lincoln*, p. 381; Charles Gibson, "Edward Bates," *Missouri Historical Society Collections* (January, 1900), II, 55.

171. Harry E. Pratt, "David Davis, 1815–1886," MS., p. 77.

172. Tracy E. Strevey, "Joseph Medill and the Chicago *Tribune* in the Nomination and Election of Lincoln," in Paul M. Angle (ed.), *Papers in Illinois History*, 1938, pp. 58–59.

173. Alexander K. McClure, *Old Time Notes of Pennsylvania*, I, 406–407.

174. "Reminiscences of Charles Perrin Smith," MS., pp. 174–175.

175. R. Hosea to Chase, May 18, 1860, Salmon P. Chase Papers, Library of Congress.

176. Halstead, *Caucuses of 1860*, pp. 142, 143.

177. Thomas C. Miller and H. Maxwell, *West Virginia and Its People*, II, 13.

178. Margaret K. Monteiro, "The Presidential Election of 1860 in Virginia," *Richmond College Historical Papers* (June, 1916), I, 245–246.

179. Farnsworth to Washburne, telegram, May 18, 1860, Washburne Papers.

180. Halstead, *Caucuses of 1860*, p. 144.

181. *Memoirs of Gustave Koerner*, II, 85.

182. Strevey, "Joseph Medill and the Chicago *Tribune* in the Nomination and Election of Lincoln," *loc. cit.*, p. 60.

183. Frances M. I. Morehouse, *The Life of Jesse W. Fell*, pp. 61 n.–62 n.

184. Henry C. Fell to the Misses Alice and Fanny Fell, February 10, 1909. A copy of this letter was furnished to the present author by Dr. Harry E. Pratt.

185. Halstead, *Caucuses of 1860*, p. 144.

186. *Ibid.*

187. *Ibid.*, p. 145.

188. *Ibid.*

189. *Ibid.*, p. 146. Cf. Charles W. Johnson (ed.), Official *Proceedings of the National Republican Conventions of 1856, 1860, and 1864*, p. 149.

190. Halstead, *Caucuses of 1860*, pp. 146–147.

191. *Ibid.*, p. 146.

192. *Ibid.*, p. 147.

193. Thurlow Weed Barnes, *Memoirs of Thurlow Weed*, p. 264.

194. Halstead, *Caucuses of 1860*, pp. 147–148.

195. Donnal V. Smith, "Salmon P. Chase and the Election of 1860," *Ohio Archaeological and Historical Quarterly* (1930), XXXIX, 530.

196. Halstead, *Caucuses of 1860*, pp. 148–149.

197. E. Lincoln to Weed, June 5, 1860, Weed Papers.

198. Halstead, *Caucuses of 1860*, p. 148.

199. *Ibid.*, p. 149.

200. *Ibid.*

201. H. I. Cleveland, "Booming the First Republican President: A Talk with Abraham Lincoln's Friend, the Late Joseph Medill," *Saturday Evening Post*, Vol. 172, pp. 84–85. Professor Roseboom doubts Medill's story. See Roseboom, "Ohio in the 1850's," MS., p. 419.

202. Harry J. Carman and Reinhard H. Luthin, *Lincoln and the Patronage*, pp. 92–93.

203. Halstead, *Caucuses of 1860*, pp. 150–151.

204. New York *Herald*, May 19, 1860, p. 3.

205. C. C. Washburn to Elihu B. Washburne, May 19, 1860, Washburne Papers.

206. Halstead, *Caucuses of 1860*, pp. 151–153.

207. Beale (ed.), *Bates Diary*, p. 130.

208. Miller to Cameron, May 27, 1860, Cameron Papers.

CHAPTER X

1. Emerson D. Fite, *The Presidential Campaign of 1860*, pp. 209–210.

2. Pontiac (Mich.) *Weekly Gazette*, May 25, June 1, 8, 15, 1860; Wilmington *Delaware Republican*, May 21, 1860.

3. Ernest J. Wessen, "Campaign Lives of Abraham Lincoln, 1860" in Paul M. Angle (ed.), *Papers in Illinois History*, 1937, p. 190.

4. Springfield (Mass.) *Republican*, June 12, 1860.

5. New York *Daily Tribune*, July 19, 1860.

6. Albany *Evening Journal*, May 25, 1860.

7. Floyd A. McNeil, "Lincoln's Attorney General: Edward Bates," MS., p. 213.

8. Kreismann to Banks, April 2, 1859, Nathaniel P. Banks Papers, Essex Institute, Salem, Mass.

9. Reinhard H. Luthin, "Salmon P. Chase's Political Career Before the Civil War," *Mississippi Valley Historical Review* (March, 1943), XXIX, 532.

10. Albany *Evening Journal*, May 28, 1860.

11. Cameron to Trumbull, October 25, 1860, Trumbull Papers.

12. Richard S. Elliott, *Notes Taken in Sixty Years*, p. 120.

13. Dixon Wecter, *The Saga of American Society*, p. 96.

14. Ryland Fletcher to Barrett, March 7, 1861, Lincoln Collection, John Hay Library.

15. J. M. Davis, "Origin of the Lincoln Rail," *The Century* (1900), Vol. 60, pp. 271–275; William E. Barton, *The Life of Abraham Lincoln*, 2 volume edition, I, pp. 413–415.

16. John Bach McMaster, *A History of the People of the United States*, VII, 456.

17. New York *Herald*, October 20, 1860.

18. William E. Baringer, "Campaign Technique in Illinois—1860," *Transactions of the Illinois State Historical Society*, 1932, p. 170.

19. Fite, *The Presidential Campaign of 1860*, pp. 211–212.

20. Paul M. Angle, "Lincoln's First Campaign for the Presidency," *Bulletin of the Abraham Lincoln Association* (September, 1932), No. 28, pp. 8–9.

21. Tracy, *Uncollected Letters of Abraham Lincoln*, pp. 157–159.

22. *Ibid.*, p. 163.

23. Lincoln to Samuel Galloway, June 19, 1860, Lincoln Collection, Illinois State Historical Library.

24. Lincoln to Davis, October 27, 1860, *ibid.*; Preston King to Washburne, August 3, 1860, Elihu B. Washburne Papers; Albany *Evening Journal*, May 30, 1860.

25. Lincoln to Medill, September 4, 1860, Newspaper clipping in Volume marked "1832–1860," unpublished Lincoln Letters, Lincoln National Life Foundation.

26. Theodore C. Blegen, "Campaigning with Seward in 1860," *Minnesota History* (June, 1927), VIII, pp. 150–171.

27. *How Ought Workingmen to Vote in the Coming Election: Speech of Hon. Henry Wilson, at East Boston, Oct. 15, 1860*, 2.

28. New York *Herald*, July 12, 1860.

29. Floyd B. Streeter, *Political Parties in Michigan, 1837–1860*, p. 289.

30. Joseph Schafer, *Carl Schurz, Militant Liberal*, pp. 135–146.

31. New York *Herald*, September 20, 1860.

32. McNeil, "Lincoln's Attorney General: Edward Bates," MS., p. 214.

33. New York *Daily Tribune*, July 27, 1860.

34. See especially the numerous letters from all sections of the country, May–June, 1860, in Stephen A. Douglas Papers. For Johnson, consult Percy Scott Flippin, *Herschel V. Johnson of Georgia, State Rights Unionist*.

35. Milton, *The Eve of Conflict*, pp. 481, 487 ff.

36. Professor E. Merton Coulter's sketch in Allen Johnson (ed.), *Dictionary of American Biography*, III, 7–10.

37. *Kentucky Statesman*, July 20, 1860, *ibid.*, p. 9.

38. Eldorah M. Raleigh, "General Joseph Lane," *Indiana History Bulletin* (December, 1926), IV, 71–82.

39. New York *Herald*, June 28, 1860.

40. *Ibid.*, June 30, 1860.

41. *Ibid.*, July 10, 1860.

42. George T. Curtis, *Life of James Buchanan*, II, 290–295.

43. New York *Daily Tribune*, July 16, 25, 30, 1860; New York *Herald*, June 29, 30, July 23, August 1, 16, 1860.

44. John Bassett Moore (ed.), *The Works of James Buchanan*, X, 466.

45. Allen Johnson (ed.), *Dictionary of American Biography*, II, 157–158. The only scholarly sketch of Bell is Joshua W. Caldwell, "John Bell," *American Historical Review*, IV, 652–664. For Everett see P. R. Frothingham, *Edward Everett*, Orator and Statesman.

46. Detroit *Daily Tribune*, June 6, 1860.

47. Ralph V. Harlow, *Gerrit Smith: Philanthropist and Reformer*, p. 427; New York *Daily Tribune*, May 31, July 17, 20, 1860.

48. Julius G. Rathbun, "The 'Wide Awakes': The Great Political Organization of 1860," *Connecticut Quarterly* (October, 1895), I, 327–335. Hartford *Daily Courant*, March 17, 1860; New York *Herald*, September 10, 19, 1860; Chicago *Press & Tribune*, May 7, 1860.

49. Fort Wayne *Daily Times*, September 21, 1860.

50. New York *Herald*, September 29, 1860.

51. See the article, "The Clubs of the Campaign," in New York *Herald*, September 29, 1860.

52. New York *Herald*, July 19, 1860.

53. Baringer, "Campaign Technique in Illinois—1860," *op. cit.*, p. 170.
54. Detroit *Daily Tribune*, June 5, 1860.
55. *Hutchinson's Republican Songster for 1860*, p. 72.
56. *Ibid.*, p. 46.
57. Osborn H. Oldroyd, *Lincoln's Campaign or the Political Revolution of 1860*, pp. 150–151.
58. Fite, *The Presidential Campaign of 1860*, p. 132.
59. Allen Johnson, *Stephen A. Douglas*, pp. 324–424.
60. The Covode Committee findings are printed in *House Report No. 648*, 36th Cong., 1st sess., serial #1071.
61. Madison Kuhn, "Economic Issues and the Rise of the Republican Party in the Northwest," MS., p. 153.
62. *Ibid.*, pp. 153–154, 154 n.
63. New York *Daily Tribune*, May 24, 26, 28, June 11, 1860.
64. *Ibid.*, May 25, June 4, 6, 9, 18, 1860.
65. Pontiac (Mich.) *Weekly Gazette*, July 6, 1860.
66. Helene S. Zahler, *Eastern Workingmen and National Land Policy, 1829–1862*, pp. 171–172, 171 n.
67. James D. Richardson (Comp.), *Messages and Papers of the Presidents, 1789–1897*, V, 607–614.
68. New York *Daily Tribune*, June 25, 1860.
69. Donnal V. Smith, "The Influence of the Foreign-Born Vote of the Northwest in the Election of 1860," *Mississippi Valley Historical Review* (September, 1932), XIX, 192; George M. Stephenson, *The Political History of the Public Lands From 1840 to 1862*, pp. 230–232.
70. *Ibid.*, pp. 231–232.
71. Ruby C. Karstad, "The 'New York Tribune' and the Minnesota Frontier," *Minnesota History* (December, 1936), XVII, 411, 416–417; Greeley to Colfax, April 3, 1859, Greeley-Colfax Papers.

CHAPTER XI

1. Jane Grey Swisshel, *Half a Century*, p. 172. See also Ben R. Brainerd, "Public Opinion on Federal Land Policies in Minnesota, 1837–1862," MS., M.A. thesis, University of Minnesota, 1935; Ruby G. Karstad, "Political Alignments in Minnesota, 1854–1860," MS., M.A. thesis, University of Minnesota, 1934, pp. 190 ff.
2. Stephenson, *The Political History of the Public Lands from 1840 to 1862*, p. 222.
3. Solon J. Buck, "Lincoln and Minnesota," *Minnesota History* (December, 1925), VI, 356.
4. St. Paul *Daily Minnesotian and Times*, May 22, 1860, in *ibid.*
5. Sibley to Douglas, *Private*, July 16, 1860, Stephen A. Douglas Papers.
6. Theodore C. Blegen, "Campaigning with Seward in 1860," *Minnesota History* (June, 1927), VIII, 150–171. See also William W. Folwell, *A History of Minnesota*, II, 66.

7. Ramsey to Donnelly, October 22, 1860, in Franklin F. Holbrook, "The Early Political Career of Ignatius Donnelly, 1857–1863," MS., p. 61 n.

8. Verne E. Chatelain, "The Federal Land Policy and Minnesota Politics, 1854–1860," *Minnesota History* (September, 1941), XXII, 227.

9. *Transactions of the Illinois State Historical Society*, 1928, pp. 113, 113 n.; *Iowa Historical Record* (July, 1895), XI, 296.

10. Theodore Clarke Smith, *The Liberty and Free Soil Parties in the Northwest*, pp. 75, 87, 96–97, 131, 219, 219 n., 297; William Salter, *The Life of James W. Grimes*, pp. 52, 54; *Annals of Iowa* (July, 1906), Series III, Vol. 7, pp. 446–465.

11. F. I. Herriott, "James W. Grimes Versus the Southrons," *Annals of Iowa* (October, 1926), Series III, Vol. 15, pp. 431–432; Salter, *James W. Grimes*, p. 39.

12. Louis Pelzer, "The History of Political Parties in Iowa from 1857 to 1860," *The Iowa Journal of History and Politics* (April, 1909), VII, 179–209.

13. Benjamin F. Shambaugh (comp.), *The Messages and Proclamations of the Governors of Iowa*, II, 242–244; Dan E. Clark, *Samuel Jordan Kirkwood*, p. 150.

14. Kuhn, "Economic Issues and the Rise of the Republican Party in the Northwest," MS., p. 136.

15. *Ibid.*, p. 143.

16. Pelzer, "The History of Political Parties in Iowa from 1857 to 1860," *loc. cit.*, pp. 219–229; Louis Pelzer, "The Disintegration and Organization of Political Parties in Iowa, 1852–1860," *Proceedings of the Mississippi Valley Historical Association* (1911–1912), V, 166.

17. *Collections of the State Historical Society of Wisconsin* (1898), XIV, 392–393.

18. Kuhn, "Economic Issues and the Rise of the Republican Party in the Northwest," MS., p. 161.

19. *Ibid.*, p. 160.

20. Schurz to Sumner, June 8, 1860, Sumner Papers.

21. Hertz, *Abraham Lincoln: A New Portrait*, II, 779.

22. Charles King, "Rufus King: Soldier, Editor, and Statesman," *Wisconsin Magazine of History* (1920–1921), IV, 375.

23. Kate Everest Levi, "The Wisconsin Press and Slavery," *ibid.* (1925–1926), IX, 433.

24. James L. Sellers, "James R. Doolittle," *ibid.* (March 1943), XVII, 293.

25. Detroit *Daily Tribune*, June 9, 18, 1860.

26. Floyd B. Streeter, *Political Parties in Michigan, 1837–1860*, pp. 270–282.

27. Bates to Douglas, February 23, 1860, Douglas Papers.

28. Detroit *Daily Tribune*, May 21, 1860.

29. *Ibid.*, May 22, 1860.

30. *Ibid.*, June 8, 1860; Earl O. Smith, "The Public Career of Austin Blair, War-Governor of Michigan," MS., p. 38.

31. Kuhn, "Economic Issues and the Rise of the Republican Party in the Northwest," MS., p. 161.

32. Smith, "The Public Career of Austin Blair, War-Governor of Michigan," MS., p. 40; Pontiac *Weekly Gazette*, October 5, 1860.

33. Sessions to Douglas, January 17, 1860, Stevens to Douglas, March 7, 1860, Douglas Papers; *Biographical Directory of the American Congress, 1774–1927*, p. 261.

34. Detroit *Free Press*, June 2, 1860.

35. *Ibid.*, June 6, 7, 19, 1860.

36. Detroit *Daily Tribune*, June 20, 1860.

37. *Ibid.*, June 2, 1860, p. 2.

38. Streeter, *Political Parties in Michigan, 1837–1860*, pp. 283–292; Henry M. Utley and Byron M. Cutcheon, *Michigan as a Province, Territory and State*, III, 427; T. Maxwell Collier, "William H. Seward in the Campaign of 1860," *Michigan History Magazine* (1935), XIX, 91–106.

39. *Complete Works of Abraham Lincoln*, VI, 20.

40. Eugene H. Roseboom, "Ohio in the 1850's," MS., pp. 419–420; George H. Porter, *Ohio Politics During the Civil War Period*, p. 48 n.

41. Roseboom, "Ohio in the 1850's," MS., pp. 427–428.

42. *Ibid.*, p. 428.

43. Paul I. Miller, "Thomas Eqing, Last of the Whigs," MS., pp. 259–261.

44. Roseboom, "Ohio in the 1850's," MS., pp. 430–433.

45. For the efforts to form a Douglas-Bell coalition, see Porter, *Ohio Politics During the Civil War Period*, p. 48.

46. *Ibid.*

47. Basting to Douglas, April 17, 1860, Douglas Papers. For an excellent account of the campaign of 1860 in Illinois, see H. Preston James, "Lincoln's Own State in the Election of 1860," MS.

48. Kuhn, "Economic Issues and the Rise of the Republican Party in the Northwest," MS., pp. 142, 143, 161; William E. Dodd, "The Fight for the Northwest, 1860," *American Historical Review* (July, 1911), XVI, 786.

49. *Bulletin of the Abraham Lincoln Association* (June 1, 1927), No. 7, p. 2.

50. J. H. Burnham to his father (photostat), May 19, 1860, Lincoln Collection, John Hay Library, Brown University.

51. Indianapolis *Daily State Sentinel*, June 16, 1860.

52. Walter E. Myer, "The Presidential Campaign of 1860 in Illinois," MS., pp. 44–45.

53. *Ibid.*, pp. 1–4.

54. Tomlin to Yates, May 23, 1860, Richard Yates Papers.

55. Myer, "The Presidential Campaign of 1860 in Illinois," MS., pp. 47–48.

56. *Ibid.*, p. 49.

57. Myer, "The Presidential Campaign of 1860 in Illinois," MS., pp. 49–50.

58. *Ibid.*, p. 51.

59. Herndon to Sumner, June 20, 1860, Sumner Papers.

60. New York *Herald*, August 14, 1860.

61. Paul M. Angle, *Lincoln, 1854–1861: Being the Day-by-Day Activities of Abraham Lincoln from January 1, 1854 to March 4, 1861*, p. 345.

62. *Complete Works of Abraham Lincoln*, VI, 45–47.

63. Tracy (ed.), *Uncollected Letters of Abraham Lincoln*, p. 161.

64. *Ibid.*, p. 167.

65. Lincoln to Medill, September 4, 1860, newspaper clipping in volume marked "1832–1860," Unpublished Lincoln Letters, Lincoln National Life Foundation.

66. Lincoln to Schenck, August 23, 1860, Lincoln Collection, Illinois State Historical Library, Springfield.

67. Angle, *Lincoln, 1854–1861*, p. 343.

68. *Ibid.*, p. 353.

69. Blatchford to Seward, August 8, 1861, William H. Seward Papers, in possession of Mr. W. H. Seward of Auburn, N. Y.

70. Johnson, *Stephen A. Douglas*, pp. 263, 318.

71. Theodore Hielscher to Julian, November 20, 1860, George W. Julian Papers; *Memoirs of Gustave Koerner, 1809–1896*, II, 97 ff.; New York *Daily Tribune*, July 24, 1860.

72. Angle, *Lincoln, 1854–1861*, p. 343.

73. Jay Monaghan, "Did Abraham Lincoln Receive the Illinois German Vote?" *Journal of the Illinois State Historical Society* (1942), XXXV, 133–139.

74. Myer, "The Presidential Campaign of 1860 in Illinois," MS., pp. 52–53.

75. Bessie Louise Pierce, *A History of Chicago*, II, 248.

76. Myer, "The Presidential Campaign of 1860 in Illinois," MS., pp. 56–57.

77. Arthur C. Cole, *The Era of the Civil War, 1848–1870* (Vol. III of *The Centennial History of Illinois*), pp. 199–200.

78. *Congressional Globe*, 37th Cong., 2nd sess., p. 39.

79. Frederick Jackson Turner, *The United States, 1830–1850*, p. 286.

80. *Census of the United States, 1860: Population*, pp. xxix, xxxi.

81. Madeleine H. Rice, *American Catholic Opinion in the Slavery Controversy*, pp. 84, 102, 114, 118, 154–155; George T. Flom, "The Scandinavian Factor in the American Population," *Iowa Journal of History and Politics* (January, 1905), III, 58.

82. Koerner to Trumbull, March 15, 1860, Trumbull Papers.

83. Ferry to Welles, March 1, 1860, Welles Papers.

84. Kuhn, "Economic Issues and the Rise of the Republican Party in the Northwest," MS., p. 160.

85. Rayback, "Land for the Landless," MS., p. 82 n.

86. Cole, *The Era of the Civil War, 1848–1870*, pp. 341–342.

87. Donnal V. Smith, "The Influence of the Foreign-Born of the

Northwest in the Election of 1860," *Mississippi Valley Historical Review* (September, 1932), XIX, 192–204.

88. William E. Dodd, "The Fight for the Northwest, 1860," *American Historical Review* (July, 1911), XVI, 785–788.

89. Ernest Bruncken, "German Political Refugees in the United States During the Period from 1815 to 1860," *Deutsch-Amerikanische Geschichtsblätter* (July, 1903), III, 36.

90. Joseph Schafer, "Who Elected Lincoln?" *American Historical Review* (October, 1941), Vol. 47, pp. 51–63.

91. New York *Herald*, December 9, 1860.

92. Kuhn, "Economic Issues and the Rise of the Republican Party," MS., p. 160 n.

93. Helen M. Cavanaugh," Antislavery Sentiment and Politics in the Northwest, 1844–1860," MS., p. 140.

94. Kuhn, "Economic Issues and the Rise of the Republican Party in the Northwest," MS., p. 137.

95. George E. Baker (ed.), *The Works of William H. Seward*, IV, 372.

96. Kuhn, "Economic Issues and the Rise of the Republican Party in the Northwest," MS., p. 163.

97. *Ibid.*, p. 144.

98. *Ibid.*, pp. 146–148.

99. Curtis Nettels, "The Overland Mail Issue During the Fifties," *Missouri Historical Review* (July, 1924), XVIII, 534.

100. New York *Daily Tribune*, July 19, 1860.

101. Thomas M. Pitkin, "Western Republicans and the Tariff in 1860," *Mississippi Valley Historical Review* (December, 1940), pp. 410–418.

102. Richard Hofstadter, "The Tariff Issue on the Eve of the Civil War," *American Historical Review* (October, 1938), XLIV, 50–55.

103. Gaillard Hunt, *Israel, Elihu and Cadwallader Washburn*, p. 72.

104. Boston *Daily Advertiser*, May 15, 1860.

105. *Ibid.*, October 29, 1860.

106. Everett to Mrs. Eames, September 30, 1854, Edward Everett Papers.

107. Lunt to Peabody, February 20, 1860, George Peabody Papers.

108. Paul R. Frothingham, *Edward Everett: Orator and Statesman*, pp. 410–412.

109. George S. Merriam, *The Life and Times of Samuel Bowles*, I, 264.

110. Mrs. W. S. Robinson (ed.), *"Warrington" Pen-Portraits . . . from the Writings of William S. Robinson*, pp. 243–244.

111. Springfield (Mass.) *Republican*, August 30, 31, 1860; Henry G. Pearson, "Massachusetts to the Front, 1860–1861," in Albert Bushnell Hart (ed.), *Commonwealth History of Massachusetts*, IV, 500–502.

112. Carroll J. Noonan, *Nativism in Connecticut, 1829–1860*, Chapters VIII–XVI; Gladys Franklin, "The Know Nothing Party in Connecticut," MS., Brother J. Robert Lane, *A Political History of Connecticut During the Civil War*, pp. 130–138.

113. Hartford *Daily Courant,* November 8, 1860.

114. Providence *Daily Journal,* June 20, 1860.

115. Edward Field, *State of Rhode Island and Providence Plantation* at the End of the Century, I, 372.

116. Gail Hamilton (Mary A. Dodge), *Biography of James C. Blaine* p. 129.

117. Portland (Maine) *Transcript,* August 18, September 8, 22, 1860.

118. New York *Herald,* July 23, 1860.

119. R. L. Morrow, "The Liberty Party in Vermont," *New England Quarterly* (April, 1929), II, 234–235.

120. Walter H. Crockett, *Vermont: The Green Mountain State,* III, 218–221, 234–236, 257, 277, 313, 342, 371, 401–402.

121. William B. Parker, *The Life of Justin Smith Morrill,* p. 86.

122. Crockett, *Vermont,* III, 486, 491.

123. Everett S. Stackpole, *History of New Hampshire,* III, 151–161; John N. McClintock, *History of New Hampshire,* p. 607.

124. New York *Daily Tribune,* July 27, 1860.

125. New York *Journal of Commerce,* clipped in Providence *Daily Journal,* July 21, 1860, p. 2.

126. New York *Daily Tribune,* July 27, 1860.

127. Pike, *First Blows of the Civil War,* p. 520.

CHAPTER XII

1. Greeley to Reavis, August 21, 1860, Logan U. Reavis Papers.

2. Milton H. Shutes, "Colonel E. D. Baker," *California Historical Society Quarterly* (September, 1938), XVII, 312–314; Jeremiah Lynch, *A Senator of the Fifties;* George T. Clark, *Leland Stanford,* pp. 165–166.

3. Winfield J. Davis, *History of Political Conventions in California, 1849–1892,* p. 117.

4. *Ibid.,* pp. 116–117.

5. Zoeth S. Eldredge, *History of California,* IV, 183.

6. Downey to Callan, August 3, 1860, Douglas Papers.

7. Walter R. Bacon, "Fifty Years of California Politics," *Publications, Historical Society of Southern California* (1900–1901), V, 40.

8. Eldredge, *History of California,* IV, 187; Hubert H. Bancroft, *History of California,* VII, 264 n.; Curtis Nettels, "The Overland Mail Issue During the Fifties," *Missouri Historical Review* (July, 1924), XVIII, 534.

9. Elijah R. Kennedy, *The Contest for California in 1861,* pp. 156–157.

10. *Ibid.,* p. 159.

11. *Tribune Almanac,* 1861, p. 64.

12. Houghton to Banks, November 10, 1860, Nathaniel P. Banks Papers, Essex Institute, Salem, Mass. (in Volume marked "II, 1860").

13. Bancroft, *History of California,* VII, 270.

14. Walter C. Woodward, *The Rise and Early History of Political Parties in Oregon,* 1843–1868, pp. 168–171.

15. Bush to Douglas, July 27, 1860, Douglas Papers.
16. Woodward, *op. cit.*, p. 179.
17. *Tribune Almanac*, 1861, p. 64.
18. Kennedy, *op. cit.*, p. 148.
19. Charles M. Knapp, *New Jersey Politics during the Period of the Civil War and Reconstruction*, pp. 24–37.
20. John D. Defrees to Weed, August 25, 1860, Weed Papers.
21. David Davis to Weed, September 11, 1860, *ibid.*, Joseph J. Lewis to Fell, September 25, 1860, Jesse W. Fell Papers (Transcripts), Illinois Historical Survey, University of Illinois, Urbana, Ill.
22. Indianapolis *Daily State Sentinel*, January 13, 1860; Indianapolis *Daily Journal*, February 24, 1860. For the conduct of the campaign in Indiana, see Reinhard H. Luthin, "Indiana and Lincoln's Rise to the Presidency," *Indiana Magazine of History* (December, 1942), XXXVIII, 396–405.
23. Charles Zimmerman, "The Rise of the Republican Party in Indiana from 1854 to 1860," *Indiana Magazine of History* (1917), XIII, 405–408; Indianapolis *State Sentinel*, May 25, 1860.
24. *Complete Works of Abraham Lincoln*, VI, 47.
25. Bess V. Ehrmann, *The Missing Chapter in the Life of Abraham Lincoln*, pp. 3–4.
26. Zimmerman, "The Origin and Rise of the Republican Party in Indiana from 1854 to 1860," *op. cit.*, p. 394.
27. David Davis to Lincoln, August 24, 1860. Copy in possession of Dr. Harry E. Pratt, of the Abraham Lincoln Association, Springfield, Ill. The original is supposed to be in possession of the Lincoln Tomb, Springfield.
28. David Davis to Weed, September 11, 1860, Thurlow Weed Papers.
29. John D. Defrees to Weed, August 25, 1860, *ibid.*
30. Harry J. Carman and Reinhard H. Luthin, "Some Aspects of the Know-Nothing Movement Reconsidered," *South Atlantic Quarterly* (April, 1940), XXXIX, 229; Luthin, "Indiana and Lincoln's Rise to the Presidency," *op. cit.*, p. 399.
31. Fort Wayne *Sentinel*, June 30, 1860.
32. *Ibid.*, September 8, 15, 22, 1860.
33. *Ibid.*, September 8, 1860.
34. Dawson's Fort Wayne *Daily Times*, June 28, 1860.
35. Conner to Pratt, July 26, 1860, Daniel Pratt Papers.
36. Dawson's Fort Wayne *Daily Times*, September 29, 1860.
37. John D. Defrees to Weed, August 25, 1860, Weed Papers.
38. Schurz to J. P. Sanderson, December 22, 1860, Carl Schurz Papers.
39. Indianapolis *Daily State Sentinel*, September 10, 1860.
40. Fort Wayne *Sentinel*, September 15, 1860.
41. Milton, *Eve of Conflict: Stephen A. Douglas and the Needless War*, pp. 259, 275, 278, 406, 420, 430, 469; Charles B. Murphy, "The Political Career of Jesse D. Bright," *Publications, Indiana Historical Society* (1931), Vol. X, no. 1, pp. 128–134.

42. John Woodruff to Calif, *Private*, June 18, 1860, Arthur B. Calif Papers.

43. Murphy, "The Political Career of Jesse D. Bright," *op. cit.*, p. 134.

44. Indianapolis *Old Line Guard*, August 9, 1860.

45. *Ibid.*, September 4, 1860.

46. *Ibid.*, July 24, 1860.

47. *Ibid.*, September 15, 1860.

48. Zimmerman, "The Origin and Rise of the Republican Party in Indiana from 1854 to 1860," *op. cit.*, p. 402.

49. *Ibid.*

50. *Ibid.*, p. 401.

51. Willard to Douglas, August 9, 1860, Douglas Papers.

52. Pierce to Douglas, August 10, 1860; J. J. Bingham to Douglas, August 12, 1860; Charles E. Sturgis to Douglas, September 1, 1860, Douglas Papers.

53. Indianapolis *Daily State Sentinel*, September 29, 1860.

54. Fort Wayne *Sentinel*, October 6, 13, 1860.

55. Zimmerman, "The Origin and Rise of the Republican Party in Indiana from 1854 to 1860," *op. cit.*, pp. 396–397.

56. *Ibid.*, p. 397.

57. *Ibid.*

58. *Ibid.*, pp. 297–298; Robert N. Lamb and F. J. Waldo to Thompson, August 11, 1860, Richard W. Thompson Papers.

59. W. K. Edwards to Thompson, June 4, 1860, Richard W. Thompson Papers.

60. Milton, *Eve of Conflict*, pp. 497, 497 n.; Murphy, "The Political Career of Jesse K. Bright," *op. cit.*, p. 134; Zimmerman, *op. cit.*, Indianapolis *Daily State Sentinel*, October 11, 1860; Indianapolis *Daily Journal*, December 4, 1860.

61. Lewis to Fell, May 28, 1860, Fell Papers (Transcripts). For the conduct of the campaign in Pennsylvania, see Reinhard H. Luthin, "Pennsylvania and Lincoln's Rise to the Presidency," *Pennsylvania Magazine of History and Biography* (January, 1943), LXVII, 71–82.

62. Edgar B. Cale, "Editorial Sentiment in Pennsylvania in the Campaign of 1860," *Pennsylvania History* (October, 1937), IV, 233.

63. Philadelphia *North American and United States Gazette*, May 19, 1860.

64. Stanton L. Davis, *Pennsylvania Politics, 1860–1863*, pp. 114–115.

65. J. P. Sanderson to Cameron, October 1, 1860, Simon Cameron Papers.

66. Gilbert A. Tracy, *Uncollected Papers of Abraham Lincoln*, pp. 152, 153, 156, 162.

67. Lincoln to Swett, July 16, 1860, in *ibid.*, p. 156.

68. Davis, *Pennsylvania Politics, 1860–1863*, p. 115.

69. Harry J. Carman and Reinhard H. Luthin, *Lincoln and the Patronage*, pp. 21, 22.

70. Allison to Trumbull, June 4, 1860, Trumbull Papers.

71. E. Peshine Smith to Carey, September 25, 1860, Henry C. Carey Papers.

72. McClure, *Old Time Notes of Pennsylvania*, I, 419 ff.

73. J. J. Lewis to Fell, September 25, 1860, Fell Papers.

74. Lincoln to John ———, August 31, 1860 in *Complete Works of Abraham Lincoln*, VI, 54.

75. Davis, *Pennsylvania Politics, 1860–1863*, pp. 107–108.

76. Philip G. Auchampaugh, "John W. Forney, Robert Tyler and James Buchanan," *Tyler's Quarterly Historical and Genealogical Magazine* (October, 1933), XV, 71–90; Philadelphia *Press*, February 8, 27, 29, March 6, 17, 31, April 3, 20, 26, 1860.

77. Davis, *Pennsylvania Politics, 1860–1863*, p. 50 ff.

78. Philadelphia *Press*, July 17, August 31, October 10, 1860.

79. Elwyn B. Robinson, The Public Press of Philadelphia during the Civil War, MS., p. 50.

80. New York *Herald*, August 16, 1850, p. 4.

81. Robinson, "The Public Press of Philadelphia during the Civil War," MS., p. 51.

82. Cale, "Editorial Sentiment in Pennsylvania in the Campaign of 1860," *op. cit.*, p. 232.

83. Greeley to Reavis, August 21, 1860, Logan U. Reavis Papers.

84. Pitkin, "The Tariff and the Early Republican Party," MS., pp. 210–211.

85. Frederic Bancroft (ed.), *Speeches, Correspondence and Political Papers of Carl Schurz*, I, 160–161.

86. *Ibid.*, p. 172.

87. J. Z. Goodrich to Dawes, June 8, 1860, Henry L. Dawes Papers.

88. New York *Herald*, October 2, 1860.

89. *Ibid.*, October 16, 1860, p. 6.

90. Alexander K. McClure, *Old-Time Notes of Pennsylvania*, I, 417 ff.

91. W. H. Egle, *Andrew Gregg Curtin*, p. 108.

92. Davis, *Pennsylvania Politics, 1860–1863*, p. 118.

93. Belmont to Douglas, July 28, 1860, Douglas Papers; Philip S. Foner, *Business and Slavery*, pp. 169–171; Henry R. Mueller, *The Whig Party in Pennsylvania*, pp. 230–231.

94. Davis, *Pennsylvania Politics, 1860–1863*, p. 116.

95. Cale, "Editorial Sentiment in Pennsylvania in the Campaign of 1860," *op. cit.*, pp. 221, 226–228.

96. Philadelphia *North American*, May 19, 21, 23, 1860.

97. Robinson, "The Public Press of Philadelphia during the Civil War," MS., pp. 127–128; Pitkin, The Tariff and the Early Republican Party, MS., pp. 212–213.

98. *Complete Works of Abraham Lincoln*, VI, 61–62.

99. James Ford Rhodes, *History of the United States from the Compromise of 1850*, II, 436.

100. Philadelphia *Press*, March 2, 1860.

101. Pitkin, "The Tariff and the Early Republican Party," MS., pp. 174–175.

102. Ellis to Douglas, May 22, 1860; Helfenstein to Douglas, June 1, 11, 1860, Douglas Papers.

103. New York *Daily Tribune*, June 4, 1860.

104. Charles H. Ambler (ed.), *Correspondence of Robert M. T. Hunter, 1826–1876*, pp. 333–334.

105. New York *Daily Tribune*, June 9, 1860.

106. Pitkin, "The Tariff and the Early Republican Party," MS., pp. 175–177, 208.

107. Malcolm R. Eiselen, *The Rise of Pennsylvania Protectionism*, p. 260.

108. *Record of Hon. Stephen A. Douglas on the Tariff*.

109. Helfenstein to Douglas, July 31, 1860, Douglas Papers.

110. *Ibid.*

111. Same to same, September 5, 1860, *ibid.*

112. New York *Herald*, September 8, 1860.

113. Eiselen, *The Rise of Pennsylvania Protectionism*, p. 263.

114. *Ibid.*

115. Pitkin, "The Tariff and the Early Republican Party," MS., pp. 187–246; Davis, *Pennsylvania Politics, 1860–1863*, pp. 128 ff.; James G. Blaine, *Twenty Years of Congress*, I, 206–207; C. Maxwell Myers, "The Influence of Western Pennsylvania in the Campaign of 1860," *Western Pennsylvania Historical Magazine* (1941), XXIV, 248.

116. Cameron to Thompson, October 16, 1860, Richard W. Thompson Papers.

117. *Complete Works of Abraham Lincoln*, VI, 62.

118. Milton, *The Eve of Conflict*, p. 496.

119. *Ibid.*, pp. 297 ff.

120. Moore (ed.), *The Works of James Buchanan*, XI, 2.

121. Springfield (Mass.) *Republican*, October 10, 1860; Indianapolis *Daily Journal*, October 12, 1860.

122. Seward, *Seward at Washington*, II, 472.

123. *The Wisconsin Magazine of History* (1921–1922), V, 100.

CHAPTER XIII

1. Sidney D. Brummer, *Political History of New York State During the Period of the Civil War*, p. 70.

2. *Complete Works of Abraham Lincoln*, VI, 52.

3. De Alva S. Alexander, *A Political History of the State of New York*, II, 305–323.

4. William E. Barton, *The Life of Abraham Lincoln*, 2-volume edition, I, 432; Edward E. Hale, Jr., *William H. Seward*, p. 259.

5. New York *Daily Tribune*, June 8, 1860.

6. New York *Herald*, August 23, 1860.

7. *Ibid.*, August 31, 1860.

8. Littlejohn to Sumner, September 18, 1860, Sumner Papers.

9. Brummer, *op. cit.*, pp. 70–71. For the "American" movement in New York, see Harry J. Carman and Reinhard H. Luthin, "The Seward-Fillmore Feud and the Disruption of the Whig Party," *New York History* (July, 1943), XXIV, 335–357.

10. Tracy, *Uncollected Letters of Abraham Lincoln,* p. 153.

11. Albany *Statesman,* quoted in New York *Herald,* May 24, 1860.

12. Buffalo *Commercial Advertiser,* quoted in New York *Daily Tribune,* May 21, 1860.

13. New York *Daily Tribune,* July 17, 1860.

14. Paul M. Angle, *New Letters and Papers of Lincoln,* p. 251.

15. New York *Herald,* June 26, 1860.

16. *Ibid.,* July 13, 14, 1860.

17. *Ibid.,* July 7, 1860.

18. Alexander, *op. cit.,* II, 271, 277–278, 298–303; *Speeches, Correspondence, etc., of the Late Daniel S. Dickinson, of New York,* II, 531–533; Stewart Mitchell, *Horatio Seymour of New York,* pp. 207–214.

19. Mitchell, *Seymour of New York,* pp. 207–214; Alexander, *op. cit.,* II, 303.

20. *Ibid.,* pp. 324–325.

21. Philip S. Foner, *Business and Slavery,* p. 1.

22. *Ibid.,* Chapters I–VIII.

23. Robert J. Murphy, "The Catholic Church in the United States During the Civil War Period, 1852–1866," *Records of the American Catholic Historical Society of Philadelphia* (December, 1928), XXXIX, 271–276; William G. Bean, "An Aspect of Know Nothingism—The Immigrant and Slavery," *South Atlantic Quarterly* (October, 1924), XXIII, 320 ff.; New York *Irish American,* May 12, June 2, October 26, 1860.

24. New York *Herald,* August 10, 1860.

25. *Ibid.,* July 19, 1860.

26. *Ibid.,* July 29, 1860.

27. *Ibid.,* July 23, 1860.

28. *Ibid.,* August 1, 1860.

29. *Ibid.,* July 17, 1860.

30. Hunt to Bell, May 24, 1860, in Louis M. Sears, "New York and the Fusion Movement of 1860," *Journal of the Illinois State Historical Society* (1923), XVI, 59.

31. *Loc. cit.*

32. Hunt to Bell, August 19, 1860, in Sears, "New York and the Fusion Movement of 1860," *op. cit.,* pp. 60–61.

33. Brummer, *op. cit.,* pp. 79–80.

34. *Ibid.,* pp. 80–81.

35. Belmont to Tilden, 1860 (no day), Samuel J. Tilden Papers, Box No. 20.

36. *Ibid.*

37. Belmont to Douglas, July 28, 1860, Douglas Papers.

38. *Ibid.*

39. New York *Herald,* September 9, 1860.

40. *Ibid.,* September 13, 1860, p. 4.

41. Brummer, *op. cit.,* pp. 83–86.

42. Sprague to Tilden, October 10, 1860, Tilden Papers, Box No. 20.

43. Brummer, *op. cit.,* p. 86.

44. Albany *Evening Journal,* August 28, 1860.

45. Brummer, *op. cit.*, pp. 89–90.
46. Albany *Evening Journal*, June 28, October 13, November 2, 3, 1860.
47. Thurlow Weed Barnes, *Memoir of Thurlow Weed*, p. 300.
48. Albany *Evening Journal*, November 5, 1860.
49. Alexander, *op. cit.*, II, 333.
50. Tilden to Robertson, January 18, 1861, Tilden Papers, Box No. 20.
51. William E. Baringer, "Campaign Technique in Illinois—1860," *Transactions of the Illinois State Historical Society*, 1932, p. 275.
52. *Ibid.*, p. 276.

CHAPTER XIV

1. Charles W. Ramsdell, "The Natural Limits of Slavery Expansion," *Mississippi Valley Historical Review* (September, 1929), XVI, 151–171. In 1855 there were only 192 slaves—less than 2½% of the population—in Kansas Territory. See *House Report* No. 200, 34th Cong., 1st sess., serial #869, p. 9. In some regions of the lower South it was felt that slavery was forever shut out of the existing territories of the United States. See P. L. Rainwater, "Economic Benefits of Secession: Opinions in Mississippi in the 1850's," *Journal of Southern History* (November, 1935), I, 459. In 1854 Stephen A. Douglas, in speaking of Kansas and Nebraska territories, told the Senate: "In that climate, with its production, it is worse than folly to think of its being a slave-holding country." See *Congressional Globe*, 33rd Cong., 1st sess., p. 279.
2. New York *Herald*, October 18, 1860.
3. *Complete Works of Abraham Lincoln*, VI, 8.
4. William Jayne to Lyman Trumbull, May 20, 1860, Trumbull Papers.
5. New York *Herald*, September 8, 1860.

Bibliography

PRIMARY SOURCES

MANUSCRIPTS

Nathaniel P. Banks Papers, Essex Institute, Salem, Massachusetts.
Nathaniel P. Banks Papers, Illinois State Historical Library, Springfield.
Edward Bates Papers, Missouri Historical Society, St. Louis.
Austin Blair Papers, Detroit Public Library.
Francis Preston Blair Papers, Library of Congress.
John Bigelow Diary MS., New York Public Library.
Sidney Breese Papers, Illinois State Historical Library, Springfield.
James O. Broadhead Papers, Missouri Historical Society, St. Louis.
Burton Historical Collection, Detroit Public Library.
Arthur B. Calif Papers, John Hay Library, Brown University.
Simon Cameron Papers, Library of Congress.
Henry C. Carey Papers, Historical Society of Pennsylvania, Philadelphia.
Salmon P. Chase Papers, Historical Society of Pennsylvania, Philadelphia.
Salmon P. Chase Papers, Library of Congress.
Chase-Hosea Papers, Widener Library, Harvard University.
Colfax-Orth Papers, Indiana State Library, Indianapolis.
Lewis Coryell Papers, Historical Society of Pennsylvania, Philadelphia.
John Covode Papers, Historical Society of Western Pennsylvania, Pittsburgh.
David Davis Papers, copies in possession of Professor Harry E. Pratt of Ball State Teachers College, Muncie, Indiana.
Henry L. Dawes Papers, Library of Congress.
James R. Doolittle Papers, New York Public Library.
Stephen A. Douglas Papers, Library of the University of Chicago.
Henry E. Dummer Papers (photostats), Chicago Historical Society.
William H. English Papers, William Henry Smith Memorial Library, Indianapolis.
Edward Everett Papers, Massachusetts Historical Society, Boston.
Jesse W. Fell Papers, copies in possession of Professor Harry E. Pratt of Ball State Teachers College, Muncie, Indiana.
Jesse W. Fell Papers (photostats), Illinois State Historical Survey, University of Illinois, Urbana.
Millard Fillmore Papers, Buffalo Historical Society, Buffalo, New York.
Hamilton Fish Papers, Library of Congress.
William Lloyd Garrison Papers, Boston Public Library.

Joshua R. Giddings Papers, Ohio Archaeological and Historical Society, Columbus.

Greeley-Colfax Papers, New York Public Library.

John H. Gundlach Collection, Missouri Historical Society, St. Louis.

Allen Hamilton Papers, Indiana State Library, Indianapolis.

Joseph R. Hawley Papers, Library of Congress.

George W. Julian Papers, Indiana State Library, Indianapolis.

Lincoln Collection, Chicago Historical Society.

Lincoln Collection, Illinois State Historical Library, Springfield.

Lincoln Collection, John Hay Library, Brown University.

Lincoln National Life Foundation Collection, Fort Wayne, Indiana.

Charles S. May Papers, Burton Historical Collection, Detroit Public Library.

John McLean Papers, Library of Congress.

Miscellaneous Papers, Indiana State Library, Indianapolis.

Justin S. Morrill Papers, Library of Congress.

George Peabody Papers, Essex Institute, Salem, Massachusetts.

Daniel D. Pratt Papers, Indiana State Library, Indianapolis.

Logan U. Reavis Papers, Chicago Historical Society.

Franklin P. Rice, "The Life of Eli Thayer," MS., Widener Library, Harvard University.

William Schouler Papers, Massachusetts Historical Society, Boston.

Carl Schurz Papers, Library of Congress.

William H. Seward Papers, in possession of Mr. W. H. Seward, Auburn, New York.

Reminiscences of Charles Perrin Smith, MS., New Jersey State Library, Trenton.

Sol Smith Papers, Missouri Historical Society, St. Louis.

John F. Snyder Papers, Missouri Historical Society, St. Louis.

Charles Sumner Papers, Widener Library, Harvard University.

Richard W. Thompson Papers, Lincoln National Life Foundation, Fort Wayne, Indiana.

Samuel J. Tilden Papers, New York Public Library.

Samuel Treat Papers, Missouri Historical Society, St. Louis.

Lyman Trumbull Papers, Library of Congress.

Benjamin F. Wade Papers, Library of Congress.

Elihu B. Washburne Papers, Library of Congress.

Thurlow Weed Papers, University of Rochester Library, Rochester, New York.

Gideon Welles Papers, Library of Congress.

Robert C. Winthrop Papers, Massachusetts Historical Society, Boston.

Richard Yates Papers, Illinois State Historical Library, Springfield.

PRINTED SOURCES

Ambler, Charles H. (ed.), *Correspondence of Robert M. T. Hunter, 1826–1876* (*Annual Report of the American Historical Association, 1916*, vol. II).

Angle, Paul M. (ed.), *New Letters and Papers of Abraham Lincoln* (New York, 1930).

Baker, George E. (ed.), *The Works of William H. Seward* (New York, 1884), vol. IV.

Bancroft, Frederick (ed.), *Speeches, Correspondence and Political Papers of Carl Schurz* (New York, 1913), vol. I.

Beale, Howard K. (ed.), *Diary of Edward Bates, 1859–1866 (Annual Report of the American Historical Association, 1930,* vol. IV).

Brainerd, Cephas, Broadsides. In possession of the Lincoln National Life Foundation, Fort Wayne, Indiana.

[Chase, Salmon P.] *Diary and Correspondence of Salmon P. Chase (Annual Report of the American Historical Association, 1902,* vol. II).

Clay, Cassius M., *Memoirs, Writings and Speeches* (Cincinnati, 1886), vol. I.

[Clay, Cassius M.] "The 1860 Presidential Campaign: Letters of Cassius M. Clay to Cephas Brainerd," *The Moorsfield Antiquarian,* vol. I (August, 1937).

[Cole, Cornelius] *Memoirs of Cornelius Cole* (New York, 1908).

Cullom, Shelby M., *Fifty Years of Public Service* (Chicago, 1911).

[Dickinson, Daniel S.] *Speeches, Correspondence, etc., of the Late Daniel S. Dickinson, of New York* (New York, 1867), vol. II.

Elliott, Richard S., *Notes Taken in Sixty Years* (St. Louis, 1883).

Hutchinson, John W. (ed.), *Hutchinson's Republican Songster for 1860* (New York, 1860).

Johnson, Charles W. (ed.), *Official Proceedings of the National Republican Conventions of 1856, 1860, and 1864* (Minneapolis, 1892).

Kasson, John A., "An Autobiography," *Annals of Iowa,* series III, vol. XII, pp. 346–358 (July, 1920).

Lambert, William H., "A Lincoln Correspondence," *Century Magazine,* February, 1909, pp. 622 ff.

McClure, Alexander K., *Abraham Lincoln and Men of War-Times* (second edition, Philadelphia, 1892).

McClure, Alexander K., *Old-Time Notes of Pennsylvania* (Philadelphia, 1905), vol. I.

McCormack, Thomas J. (ed.), *Memoirs of Gustave Koerner, 1809–1896* (Cedar Rapids, Iowa, 1909), 2 vols.

McKee, Thomas H., *The National Conventions and Platforms of All Political Parties* (Baltimore, 1900).

Moore, John Bassett (ed.), *The Works of James Buchanan* (Philadelphia and London, 1910), vol. X.

Newmark, Harris, *Sixty Years in Southern California, 1853–1913* (New York, 1916).

Nicolay, John G., and John Hay (eds.), *Complete Works of Abraham Lincoln* (New York, 1905–06), vols. V, VI.

Nunns, Annie A. (ed.), "Some Letters of Salmon P. Chase, 1848–1865," *American Historical Review,* XXXIV, 536–555 (April, 1929).

[Palmer, John M.] "Address of Gen. John M. Palmer, *"Transactions of the McLean County Historical Society,* III, 120–122 (1900).

Palmer, John M., *Personal Recollections* (Cincinnati, 1901).

Pease, Theodore C., and James G. Randall (eds.), *The Diary of Orville Hickman Browning, 1850–1864* (Springfield, Ill., 1925), vol. I.

Phillips, Ulrich B. (ed.), *The Correspondence of Robert Toombs, Alexander H. Stephens and Howell Cobb* (*Annual Report of the American Historical Association, 1911*, vol. II).

Pierce, Edward L., *Memoir and Letters of Charles Sumner* (Boston, 1893), vol. III.

Pike, James S., *First Blows of the Civil War* (New York, 1879).

Poore, Ben Perley, *Perley's Reminiscences of Sixty Years in the National Metropolis* (New York, 1886), vol. I.

Porter, Kirk H., *National Party Platforms* (New York, 1924).

Pryor, Mrs. Roger A., *Reminiscences of Peace and War* (New York, 1905).

Rankin, Henry B., *Personal Recollections of Abraham Lincoln* (New York and London, 1916).

Robinson, Mrs. W. S. (ed.), *Warrington's Pen-Portraits . . . from the Writings of William S. Robinson* (Boston, 1877).

Rowland, Dunbar (ed.), *Jefferson Davis, Constitutionalist: His Letters, Papers and Speeches* (Jackson, Miss., 1923), vol. IV.

Salter, William (ed.), "Letters of John McLean to John Teesdale," *Bibliotheca Sacra*, vol. LVI (October, 1899).

Schurz, Carl, *Reminiscences* (New York, 1907), vol. II.

Stanton, Henry B., *Random Recollections* (second edition, New York, 1886).

Seward, Frederick W., *Seward at Washington as Senator and Secretary of State* (New York, 1911), 2 vols.

Shuck, Oscar T. (ed.), *Masterpieces of E. D. Baker* (San Francisco, 1899).

Swisshelm, Jane Grey, *Half a Century* (Chicago, 1880).

Tracy, Gilbert A. (ed.), *Uncollected Letters of Abraham Lincoln* (New York, 1917).

Tribune Almanac, 1857 (New York, 1858).

Weed, Harriet A. (ed.), *Autobiography of Thurlow Weed* (Boston and New York, 1884).

GOVERNMENT DOCUMENTS

Congressional Globe.

"Covode Investigation," *House Report No. 648*, 36th Cong., 1st Sess., serial no. 1071.

Eighth Census of the United States: Population, 1860.

Richardson, James D., *Messages and Papers of the Presidents, 1789–1897* (Washington, 1897), vol. V.

NEWSPAPERS

Albany *Atlas and Argus.*
Albany *Evening Journal.*

Appleton (Wisconsin) *Crescent*.
Baltimore *Daily Clipper*.
Baltimore *Sun*.
Bangor *Daily Whig and Courier*.
Boston *Daily Advertiser*.
Bridgeport *Republican Farmer*.
Chicago *Press & Tribune*.
Cincinnati *Daily Gazette*.
Columbus *Ohio State Journal*.
Concord *New Hampshire Patriot*.
Detroit *Free Press*.
Detroit *Daily Tribune*.
Fort Wayne *Sentinel*.
Fort Wayne *Daily Times*.
Harrisburg *Telegraph*.
Hartford *Courant*.
Indianapolis *Daily Journal*.
Indianapolis *Old Line Guard*.
Indianapolis *Daily State Sentinel*.
Lexington (Ky.) *Observer & Reporter*.
Newark *Daily Advertiser*.
New Haven *Columbian Weekly Register*.
Newport *Advertiser*.
New York *Morning Courier & New York Enquirer*.
New York *Herald*.
New York *Irish-American*.
New York *Evening Post*.
New York *Daily Times*.
New York *Daily Tribune*.
Philadelphia *Evening Bulletin*.
Philadelphia *North American and United States Gazette*.
Philadelphia *Press*.
Philadelphia *Public Ledger*.
Philadelphia *Sunday Dispatch*.
Pittsburgh *Daily Commercial Journal*.
Pittsburgh *Gazette*.
Pontiac (Michigan) *Weekly Gazette*.
Portland *Oregon Weekly Times*.
Portland (Maine) *Transcript*.
Providence *Daily Journal*.
Providence *Daily Post*.
Rochester *Union and Advertiser*.
St. Louis *Daily Evening News*.
St. Louis *Daily Missouri Democrat*.
St. Louis *Daily Missouri Republican*.
San Francisco *Daily Evening Bulletin*.
Springfield *Daily Illinois State Journal*.
Springfield (Massachusetts) *Republican*.

Topeka *Kansas State Record.*
Trenton *State Gazette.*
Wilmington *Delaware Gazette.*
Wilmington *Delaware Republican.*
Winona (Minnesota) *Democrat.*

SECONDARY WORKS

Unprinted Doctoral Dissertations and Master's Theses

Bean, William G., "Party Transformation in Massachusetts with Special Reference to the Antecedents of the Republican Party, 1848–1860," MS., Ph.D. dissertation, Harvard University, 1932.

Brainerd, Ben R., "Public Opinion on Federal Land Policies in Minnesota, 1837–1862," MS., M.A. thesis, University of Minnesota, 1935.

Cavanagh, Helen M., "Antislavery Sentiment and Politics in the Northwest, 1844–1860," MS., Ph.D. dissertation, University of Chicago, 1938.

Franklin, Gladys, "The Know-Nothing Party in Connecticut," MS., M.A. thesis, Clark University, 1933.

Gates, Floy P., "Salmon P. Chase and the Independent Democrats," MS., M.A. thesis, University of Chicago, 1918.

Holbrook, Franklin F., "The Early Political Career of Ignatius Donnelly, 1857–1863," MS., M.A. thesis, University of Minnesota, 1916.

James, H. Preston, "Lincoln's Own State in the Election of 1860," MS., Ph.D. dissertation, University of Illinois, 1943.

Karstad, Ruby G., "Political Alignments in Minnesota, 1854–1860," MS., M.A. thesis, University of Minnesota, 1934.

Kuhn, Madison, "Economic Issues and the Rise of the Republican Party in the Northwest," MS., Ph.D. dissertation, University of Chicago, 1940.

McHugh, George J., "Political Nativism in St. Louis, 1840–1857," MS., M.A. thesis, St. Louis University, 1939.

McNeil, Floyd A., "Lincoln's Attorney General: Edward Bates," MS., Ph.D. dissertation, State University of Iowa, 1934.

Miller, Paul I., "Thomas Ewing, Last of the Whigs," MS., Ph.D. dissertation, The Ohio State University, 1933.

Myer, Walter E., "The Presidential Campaign of 1860 in Illinois," MS., M.A. thesis, University of Chicago, 1913.

O'Connell, Gertrude, "St. Louis in the 'Thirties and 'Forties," MS., M.A. thesis, St. Louis University, 1937.

Plunkett, Margaret L., "A History of the Liberty Party with Emphasis upon Its Activities in the Northeastern States," MS., Ph.D. dissertation, Cornell University, 1930.

Pratt, Harry E., "David Davis, 1815–1886," MS., Ph.D. dissertation, University of Illinois, 1930.

Rayback, Joseph G., "Land for the Landless: The Contemporary View," MS., M.A. thesis, Western Reserve University, 1936.

Ritchie, William, "The Public Career of Cassius M. Clay," MS., Ph.D. dissertation, George Peabody College for Teachers, 1934.

Robinson, Elwyn B., "The Public Press of Philadelphia during the Civil War," MS., Ph.D. dissertation, Western Reserve University, 1936.

Roseboom, Eugene H., "Ohio in the 1850's: A Study of Economic, Social and Political Life in a Transitional Period," MS., Ph.D. dissertation, Harvard University, 1932.

Smith, Earl O., "The Public Life of Austin Blair, War-Time Governor of Michigan, 1845–1863," MS., M.A. thesis, Wayne University, 1934.

Stoler, Mildred C., "Influence of the Democratic Element in the Republican Party of Illinois and Indiana, 1854–1860," MS., Ph.D. dissertation, Indiana University, 1938.

Strevey, Tracy E., "Joseph Medill and the *Chicago Tribune* During the Civil War Period," MS., Ph.D. dissertation, University of Chicago, 1934.

Tasher, Lucy L., "The *Missouri Democrat* and the Civil War," MS., Ph.D. dissertation, University of Chicago, 1934.

Wilson, Wilford L., "The Contest Between the North and South over the Building of the Pacific Railway," MS., M.A. thesis, Columbia University, 1926.

General Histories

Alexander, DeAlva S., *A Political History of the State of New York* (New York, 1906–1923), vol. II.

Ambler, Charles H., *West Virginia; stories and biographies* (New York, 1937).

Andrews, Matthew P., *History of Maryland: Province and State* (New York, 1929).

Angle, Paul M., *"Here I Have Lived": A History of Lincoln's Springfield, 1821–1865* (Springfield, Ill., 1935).

Bancroft, Hubert H., *History of California* (San Francisco, 1884–1890), vols. VI, VII.

Barker, Eugene C. (ed.), *A History of Texas and Texans by Frank W. Johnson* (New York and Chicago, 1916).

Bicknell, Thomas W., *The History of the State of Rhode Island and Providence Plantations* (New York, 1920), vol. II.

Buck, Solon J., *Illinois in 1818* (Springfield, Ill., 1917).

Cole, Arthur C., *The Era of the Civil War, 1848–1870* (vol. III of *The Centennial History of Illinois*, Springfield, Ill., 1919).

Conrad, Henry C., *History of Delaware* (Wilmington, Del., 1908), vol. I.

Crandall, Andrew W., *The Early History of the Republican Party, 1854–1856* (Boston, 1930).

Crockett, Walter H., *Vermont: The Green Mountain State* (New York, 1921), vol. III.

Eldredge, Zoeth S., *History of California* (New York, 1915), vol. IV.

Field, Edward, *State of Rhode Island and Providence Plantations at the End of the Century* (Boston and Syracuse, 1902).

Folwell, William W., *A History of Minnesota* (St. Paul, Minn., 1921–1930), vol. II.

Giddings, Joshua R., *History of the Rebellion: Its Authors and Causes* (New York, 1864).

Gue, Benjamin F., *History of Iowa* (New York, 1903), vol. IV.

Halstead, Murat, *Caucuses of 1860: A History of the National Conventions of the Current Presidential Campaigns* (Columbus, Ohio, 1860).

Hart, Albert Bushnell (ed.), *Commonwealth History of Massachusetts* (New York, 1930), vol. IV.

Hatch, Louis C., *Maine: A History* (New York, 1919), vol. II.

McClintock, John N., *History of New Hampshire* (Boston, 1889).

McMaster, John Bach, *A History of the People of the United States* (New York, 1913), vol. VIII.

Miller, Thomas C. and H. Maxwell, *West Virginia and Its People* (New York, 1913), 3 vols.

Pierce, Bessie Louise, *A History of Chicago* (New York, 1938), vol. II.

Powell, Walter A., *A History of Delaware* (Boston, 1928).

Rhodes, James Ford, *History of the United States from the Compromise of 1850* (New York, 1893), vol. II.

Scharf, J. Thomas, *History of Maryland* (Baltimore, 1879), vol. III.

Scharf, J. Thomas and Thompson Westcott, *History of Philadelphia, 1609–1884* (Philadelphia, 1884), vol. I.

Smalley, Eugene V., *A History of the Republican Party . . . to Which Is Added a Political History of Minnesota* (St. Paul, Minn., 1896).

Smith, Joseph P., *History of the Republican Party in Ohio* (Chicago, 1898), vol. I.

Stackpole, Everett S., *History of New Hampshire* (New York, 1916), vol. III.

Trumbull, J. Hammond, *The Memorial History of Hartford County, Connecticut, 1633–1884* (Boston, 1886), vol. I.

Turner, Frederick Jackson, *The United States, 1830–1850* (New York, 1935).

Tuthill, Franklin, *The History of California* (San Francisco, 1866).

Utley, Henry M. and Byron M. Cutcheon, *Michigan as a Province, Territory and State* (New York, 1906), vol. III.

Wilson, Henry, *History of the Rise and Fall of the Slave Power in America* (Boston, 1872–79), vol. II.

BIOGRAPHIES

Arnold, Isaac N., *The Life of Abraham Lincoln* (Chicago, 1885).

Bancroft, Frederic, *The Life of William H. Seward* (New York and London, 1900), vol. I.

Barnes, Thurlow W. (ed.), *Memoir of Thurlow Weed* (Boston and New York, 1884).

Barton, William E., *The Life of Abraham Lincoln* (Indianapolis, 1925), vol. I.

Barton, William E., *President Lincoln* (Indianapolis, 1933), vol. I.

Beveridge, Albert J., *Abraham Lincoln, 1809–1858* (Boston and New York, 1928), 2 vols.

Brigham, Johnson, *James Harlan* (Iowa City, Iowa, 1913).

Clark, Dan E., *Samuel Jordan Kirkwood* (Iowa City, Iowa, 1917).

Clark, George T., *Leland Stanford* (Stanford University, Cal., 1931).

Commager, Henry Steele, *Theodore Parker* (Boston, 1936).

Corning, Charles R., *Amos Tuck* (Exeter, N. H., 1902).

Craven, Avery, *Edmund Ruffin, Southerner: A Study in Secession* (New York and London, 1932).

Crippin, Lee F., *Simon Cameron: Antebellum Years* (Oxford, Ohio, 1942).

Curtis, George T., *Life of James Buchanan* (New York, 1883), vols. I, II.

Dubose, John W., *The Life and Times of William Lowndes Yancey* (1892).

Edwards, Arthur, *Sketch of the Life of Norman B. Judd* [n. d.].

Eggleston, Percy C., *Lincoln in New England* (New York, 1922).

Egle, William H., *Andrew Gregg Curtin* (Philadelphia, 1895).

Ehrmann, Bess V., *The Missing Chapter in the Life of Abraham Lincoln* (Chicago, 1938).

Fessenden, Francis, *Life and Public Services of William Pitt Fessenden* (Boston and New York, 1907), vol. I.

Flippin, Percy Scott, *Herschel V. Johnson of Georgia, State Rights Unionist* (Richmond, Va., 1931).

Frothingham, Paul R., *Edward Everett: Orator and Statesman* (Boston and New York, 1925).

Gresham, Matilda, *Life of Walter Quintin Gresham, 1832–1895* (Chicago, 1919).

Hale, Edward E., Jr., *William H. Seward* (Philadelphia, 1910).

Hamilton, Gail (Mary A. Dodge), *Biography of James G. Blaine* (Norwich, Conn., 1895).

Hamlin, Charles E., *The Life and Times of Hannibal Hamlin* (Cambridge, Mass., 1899).

Harlow, Ralph V., *Gerrit Smith: Philanthropist and Reformer* (New York, 1939).

Harris, Wilmer C., *Public Life of Zachariah Chandler, 1851–1875* (Chicago, 1917).

Hart, Albert Bushnell, *Salmon Portland Chase* (Boston and New York, 1899).

[Herndon, William H.], *Herndon's Life of Lincoln*, ed. by Paul M. Angle (New York, 1930).

Hertz, Emanuel, *Abraham Lincoln: A New Portrait* (New York, 1931), vol. II.

Hertz, Emanuel, *The Hidden Lincoln* (New York, 1938).

Holland, Josiah G., *The Life of Abraham Lincoln* (Springfield, Mass., 1866).

Hollister, O. J., *Life of Schuyler Colfax* (Chicago, 1887).

Hunt, Gaillard, *Israel, Elihu and Cadwallader Washburn* (New York, 1925).

Ingersoll, L. D., *The Life of Horace Greeley* (Chicago, 1873).

Johnson, Allen, *Stephen A. Douglas: A Study in American Politics* (New York, 1908).

Konkle, Burton A., *The Life and Speeches of Thomas Williams* (Philadelphia, 1905), vol. I.

Lamon, Ward H., *The Life of Abraham Lincoln* (Boston, 1872).

Lynch, Jeremiah, *A Senator of the Fifties: David C. Broderick of California* (San Francisco, 1911).

Malin, James C., *John Brown and the Legend of Fifty-Six* (Philadelphia, 1942).

Merriam, George S., *The Life and Times of Samuel Bowles* (New York, 1885), vol. I.

Milton, George Fort, *The Eve of Conflict: Stephen A. Douglas and the Needless War* (New York, 1934).

Mitchell, Stewart, *Horatio Seymour of New York* (Cambridge, Mass., 1938).

Morehouse, Frances M. I., *The Life of Jesse W. Fell* (Urbana, Ill., 1916).

Muzzey, David S., *James G. Blaine: A Political Idol of Other Days* (New York, 1934).

Nevins, Allan, *Abram S. Hewitt: With Some Account of Peter Cooper* (New York, 1935).

Nevins, Allan, *Frémont: Pathmarker of the West* (New York, 1939).

Nevins, Allan, *Frémont: The West's Greatest Adventurer* (New York and London, 1928), vol. II.

Nevins, Allan, *Hamilton Fish* (New York, 1936).

Newton, Joseph Fort, *Lincoln and Herndon* (Cedar Rapids, Iowa, 1910).

Nichols, Roy F., *Franklin Pierce: Young Hickory of the Granite Hills* (Philadelphia, 1931).

Parker, William B., *The Life and Public Services of Justin Smith Morrill* (Boston and New York, 1924).

Pearson, Henry G., *The Life of John A. Andrew* (Boston and New York, 1904), vol. I.

Phillips, Ulrich B., *The Life of Robert Toombs* (New York, 1913).

Putnam, George H., *Abraham Lincoln: The People's Leader in the Struggle for National Existence* (New York and London, 1909).

Ranck, James B., *Albert Gallatin Brown, Radical Southern Nationalist* (New York and London, 1937).

Roosevelt, Theodore, *Thomas Hart Benton* (Boston and New York, 1887).

Salter, William, *The Life of James W. Grimes* (New York, 1876).

Sandburg, Carl, *Abraham Lincoln; the War Years* (New York, 1939), 4 vols.

Schafer, Joseph, *Carl Schurz, Militant Liberal* (Evansville, Wis., 1930).

Schuckers, Jacob W., *The Life and Public Services of Salmon Portland Chase* (New York, 1874).

Sears, Louis M., *John Slidell* (Durham, N. C., 1925).

Seward, Frederick W., *Seward at Washington as Senator and Secretary of State* (New York, 1891), vol. II.

Smith, William E., *The Francis Preston Blair Family in Politics* (New York, 1933), vol. I.

Steiner, Bernard C., *Life of Henry Winter Davis* (Baltimore, 1916).

Tarbell, Ida M., *The Life of Abraham Lincoln* (New York, 1917), vol. II.

Villard, Oswald Garrison, *John Brown, 1800–1859: A Biography Fifty Years After* (Boston and New York, 1909).

Warden, Robert B., *An Account of the Private Life and Public Service of Salmon Portland Chase* (Cincinnati, 1874).

Weik, Jesse W., *The Real Lincoln* (Boston and New York, 1922).

Weisenburger, Francis P., *The Life of John McLean: A Politician on the United States Supreme Court* (Columbus, Ohio, 1937).

White, Laura A., *Robert Barnwell Rhett: Father of Secession* (New York, 1911).

Whitney, Henry C., *Lincoln the Citizen* (New York, 1908).

Special Works

Andrews, J. Cutler, *Pittsburgh's Post-Gazette* (Boston, 1936).

Angle, Paul M., *Lincoln, 1854–1861: Being the Day-by-Day Activities of Abraham Lincoln from January 1, 1854 to March 4, 1861* (Springfield, Ill., 1933).

Auchampaugh, Philip G., *James Buchanan and His Cabinet on the Eve of Secession* (Lancaster, Pa., 1926).

Baringer, William E., *Lincoln's Rise to Power* (Boston, 1937).

Bartlett, Ruhl J., *John C. Frémont and the Republican Party* (Columbus, Ohio, 1930).

Bassett, John Spencer, *Anti-Slavery Leaders of North Carolina* (Baltimore, 1898).

Bishop, Joseph B., *A Chronicle of One Hundred & Fifty Years: The Chamber of Commerce of the State of New York, 1768–1918* (New York, 1918).

Brennan, Brother Joseph, *Social Conditions in Industrial Rhode Island: 1820–1860* (Washington, 1940).

Briggs, Charles F., and Augustus Maverick, *The Story of the Telegraph and a History of the Great Atlantic Cable* (New York, 1858).

Brownson, Howard G., *History of the Illinois Central Railroad to 1870* (Urbana, Ill., 1915).

Brummer, Sidney D., *Political History of the State of New York during the Period of the Civil War* (New York, 1911).

Burk, Addison B., *Golden Jubilee of the Republican Party* (Philadelphia, 1906).

Carman, Harry J., and Reinhard H. Luthin, *Lincoln and the Patronage* (New York, 1943).

Carpenter, Jesse T., *The South as a Conscious Minority, 1789–1861* (New York, 1930).

Carroll, E. Malcolm, *Origins of the Whig Party* (Durham, N. C., 1925).

Caskey, Willie M., *Secession and Restoration of Louisiana* (University, La., 1938).

Cole, Arthur C., *The Whig Party in the South* (Washington, 1913).

Cooley, Henry S., *A Study of Slavery in New Jersey* (Baltimore, 1896).

Craven, Avery, *The Coming of the Civil War* (New York, 1942).

Curtis, Francis, *The Republican Party* (New York and London, 1904), vol. I.

Davis, Stanton L., *Pennsylvania Politics, 1860–1863* (Cleveland, 1935).

Davis, Winfield J., *History of Political Conventions in California, 1849–1892* (Sacramento, Cal., 1893).

Denman, Clarence P., *The Secession Movement in Alabama* (Montgomery, Ala., 1933).

Dixon, Mrs. Archibald, *The True Story of the Missouri Compromise and Its Repeal* (Cincinnati, 1898).

Dorman, Lewy, *Party Politics in Alabama from 1850 through 1860* (Wetumpka, Ala., 1935).

Dumond, Dwight L., *The Secession Movement, 1860–1861* (New York, 1931).

Eiselen, Malcolm R., *The Rise of Pennsylvania Protectionism* (Philadelphia, 1932).

Ellison, Joseph, *California and the Nation, 1850–1869* (Berkeley, Cal., 1927).

Ettinger, Amos A., *The Mission to Spain of Pierre Soulé* (New Haven, Conn., 1932).

Fahrney, Ralph R., *Horace Greeley and the Tribune in the Civil War* (Cedar Rapids, Iowa, 1936).

Field, Henry M., *The Story of the Atlantic Telegraph* (New York, 1903).

Fite, Emerson D., *The Presidential Campaign of 1860* (New York, 1911).

Foner, Philip S., *Business and Slavery* (Chapel Hill, N. C., 1941).

Garber, Paul N., *The Gadsden Treaty* (Philadelphia, 1923).

Gates, Paul W., *The Illinois Central Railroad and Its Colonization Work* (Cambridge, Mass., 1934).

Geary, Sister Theophane, *A History of Third Parties in Pennsylvania* (Washington, 1938).

Gresham, Otto, *The Greenbacks* (Chicago, 1927).

Hacker, Louis M., *The Triumph of American Capitalism* (New York, 1940).

Hafen, LeRoy R., *The Overland Mail, 1849–1869* (Cleveland, 1926).

Hamer, Philip M., *The Secession Movement in South Carolina, 1847–1852* (Allentown, Pa., 1918).

Harlow, Alvin F., *Old Wires and New Waves* (New York, 1936).

Harris, Alexander, *A Review of the Political Conflict in America* (New York, 1876).

Holst, Hermann von, *The Constitutional and Political History of the United States* (Chicago, 1892), vol. IV.

Hubbart, H. C., *The Older Middle West, 1840–1880* (1936).

Kennedy, Elijah R., *The Contest for California in 1861: How Colonel*

E. D. Baker Saved the Pacific States to the Union (Boston and New York, 1912).

Kinsley, Philip, *The Chicago Tribune: Its First Hundred Years* (New York, 1943), Vol. I.

Knapp, Charles M., *New Jersey Politics during the Period of the Civil War and Reconstruction* (Geneva, N. Y., 1924).

Lane, Brother J. Robert, *A Political History of Connecticut during the Civil War* (Washington, 1941).

Lunt, George, *The Origin of the Late War* (New York, 1866).

McClure, Clarence H., *Opposition in Missouri to Thomas Hart Benton* (Nashville, Tenn., 1927).

McConville, Sister Mary St. Patrick, *Political Nativism in the State of Maryland, 1830–1860* (Washington, D. C., 1928).

Meneely, A. Howard, *The War Department, 1861* (New York, 1928).

Mueller, Henry R., *The Whig Party in Pennsylvania* (New York, 1922).

Nichols, Roy F., *The Democratic Machine, 1850–1854* (New York, 1923).

Noonan, Carroll J., *Nativism in Connecticut, 1829–1860* (Washington, 1938).

Oldroyd, Osborn H., *Lincoln's Campaign; or the Political Revolution of 1860* (Chicago, 1896).

Perkins, H. C. (ed.), *Northern Editorials on Secession* (New York, 1942).

Porter, George H., *Ohio Politics during the Civil War Period* (New York, 1911).

Potter, David M., *Lincoln and His Party in the Secession Crisis* (New Haven, Conn., 1942).

Pratt, Harry E., *The Personal Finances of Abraham Lincoln* (Springfield, Ill., 1943).

Rainwater, Percy Lee, *Mississippi: Storm Center of Secession, 1856–1861* (Baton Rouge, La., 1938).

Randall, J. G., *The Civil War and Reconstruction* (Boston and New York, 1937).

Ray, P. Orman, *The Convention That Nominated Lincoln* (Chicago, 1916).

Ray, P. Orman, *The Repeal of the Missouri Compromise* (Cleveland, 1909).

Reid, James D., *The Telegraph in America* (New York, 1879).

Rice, Madeleine H., *American Catholic Opinion in the Slavery Controversy* (New York, 1944).

Rippy, J. Fred, *The United States and Mexico* (New York, 1926).

Russell, Robert R., *Economic Aspects of Southern Sectionalism, 1840–1861* (Urbana, Ill., 1924).

Rutter, Frank R., *South American Trade of Baltimore* (Baltimore, 1897).

Ryle, Walter H., *Missouri: Union or Secession* (Nashville, Tenn., 1931).

Schmeckebier, Laurence F., *History of the Know Nothing Party in Maryland* (Baltimore, 1899).

Scisco, Louis D., *Political Nativism in New York State* (New York, 1901).

Scrugham, Mary, *The Peaceable Americans of 1860–1861* (New York, 1921).

Shanks, Henry T., *The Secession Movement in Virginia, 1847–1861* (Richmond, Va., 1934).

Smith, Theodore Clarke, *The Liberty and Free Soil Parties in the North-west* (New York, 1897).

Stanwood, Edward, *American Tariff Controversies in the Nineteenth Century* (Boston and New York, 1903), vol. II.

Stephenson, George M., *The Political History of the Public Lands from 1840 to 1862* (Boston, 1917).

Streeter, Floyd B., *Political Parties in Michigan, 1837–1860* (Lansing, Mich., 1918).

Taussig, Frank W., *The Tariff History of the United States* (sixth edition, New York and London, 1914).

Taylor, Frank H., *Philadelphia in the Civil War, 1861–1865* (Philadelphia, 1913).

Thomas, Benjamin P., *Lincoln's New Salem* (Springfield, Ill., 1934).

Thomas, David Y., *Arkansas in War and Reconstruction* (Little Rock, Ark., 1926).

Thomas, Sister Evangeline, *Nativism in the Old Northwest, 1850–1860* (Washington, 1936).

Trexler, Harrison A., *Slavery in Missouri, 1804–1865* (Baltimore, 1914).

True, Alfred C., *A History of Agricultural Education in the United States, 1785–1925* (Washington, 1929).

Van Deusen, John G., *Economic Bases of Disunion in South Carolina* (New York, 1928).

Van Vleck, George W., *The Panic of 1857* (New York, 1943).

Wakefield, Sherman D., *How Lincoln Became President* (New York, 1936).

Wecter, Dixon, *The Saga of American Society; a Record of Social Aspiration, 1607–1937* (New York, 1937).

Welles, Gideon, *Lincoln and Seward* (New York, 1874).

Williams, T. Harry, *Lincoln and the Radicals* (Madison, Wis., 1941).

Wittke, Carl, *We Who Built America: The Saga of the Immigrant* (New York, 1939).

Woodward, Walter C., *The Rise and Early History of Political Parties in Oregon, 1843–1868* (Portland, Ore., 1913).

Zahler, Helene S., *Eastern Workingmen and National Land Policy, 1829–1862* (New York, 1941).

ARTICLES

Angle, Paul M., "Basic Lincolniana," *Bulletin of the Abraham Lincoln Association*, No. 43 (June, 1936); and No. 44 (September, 1936).

Angle, Paul M., "Lincoln's First Campaign for the Presidency," *Bulletin of the Abraham Lincoln Association*, No. 28 (September, 1932), pp. 8–9.

Auchampaugh, Philip G., "James Buchanan, the Court and the Dred Scott Case," *Tennessee Historical Magazine*, IX, 231–240 (January, 1926).

Auchampaugh, Philip G., "John W. Forney, Robert Tyler and James Buchanan," *Tyler's Historical Quarterly and Genealogical Magazine*, XV, 71–90 (October, 1933).

Auchampaugh, Philip G., "The Buchanan Douglas Feud," *Journal of the Illinois State Historical Society*, XXV, 5–48 (April, 1932).

Bacon, Walter R., "Fifty Years of California Politics," *Publications, Historical Society of Southern California*, V, 31–42 (1900–1901).

Bailey, Louis J., "Caleb B. Smith," *Indiana Magazine of History*, XXIX, 213–239 (September, 1933).

Baker, George E., "Seward, Weed, and Greeley," *The Republic* (Washington, 1873), I, 193–200.

Ballagh, James C., "Southern Economic History: The Tariff and Public Lands," *Annual Report, American Historical Association, 1898*, pp. 223–263.

Barbee, David R., "Hinton Rowan Helper," *Tyler's Quarterly Historical and Genealogical Magazine*, XV, 135–172 (January, 1934).

Baringer, William E., "Campaign Technique in Illinois—1860," *Transactions of the Illinois State Historical Society*, 1932, pp. 203–281.

Barnhart, John D., "The Southern Influence in the Formation of Illinois," *Journal of the Illinois State Historical Society*, XXXII, 358–378 (September, 1939).

Bean, William G., "An Aspect of Know-Nothingism—The Immigrant and Slavery," *South Atlantic Quarterly*, XXIII, 319–334 (October, 1924).

Beeler, Dale, "The Election of 1852," *Indiana Magazine of History*, XI, 314 ff. (1915–16).

Blegen, Theodore C., "Campaigning with Seward in 1860," *Minnesota History*, VIII, 150–171 (June, 1927).

Bonham, Milledge L., Jr., "New York and the Election of 1860," *New York History*, XV, 124–143 (April, 1934).

Boucher, Chauncey S., "*In re* That Aggressive Slavocracy," *Mississippi Valley Historical Review*, VIII, 13–79 (June–September, 1921).

Boughter, I. F., "Western Pennsylvania and the Morrill Tariff," *Western Pennsylvania Historical Magazine*, VI (January, 1923).

Bradley, Joseph P., "A Memorial of the Life and Character of William L. Dayton," *Proceedings, New Jersey Historical Society*, series II, vol. IV, pp. 71–118.

Brand, Carl F., "History of the Know-Nothing Party in Indiana," *Indiana Magazine of History*, XVIII (1922), 177–206.

Bruncken, Ernst, "German Political Refugees in the United States during the Period, 1815–1860," *Deutsch-Amerikanische Geschichtsblätter*, IV, 52 ff. (January, 1904).

Buck, Solon J., "Lincoln and Minnesota," *Minnesota History*, VI, 355–361 (December, 1925).

Caldwell, Joshua W., "John Bell of Tennessee," *American Historical Review*, IV, 652–664 (July, 1899).

Cale, Edgar B., "Editorial Sentiment in Pennsylvania in the Campaign of 1860," *Pennsylvania History*, IV, 219–234 (October, 1937).

Callahan, James M., "The Mexican Policy of the Southern Leaders under Buchanan's Administration," *Annual Report of the American Historical Association, 1910*, pp. 135–151.

Carman, Harry J., and Reinhard H. Luthin, "Some Aspects of the Know-Nothing Movement Reconsidered," *South Atlantic Quarterly*, XXXIX, 213–234 (April, 1940).

Carman, Harry J., and Reinhard H. Luthin, "The Seward-Fillmore Feud and the Crisis of 1850," *New York History*, XXIV, 163–184 (April, 1943).

Carman, Harry J., and Reinhard H. Luthin, "The Seward-Fillmore Feud and the Disruption of the Whig Party," *New York History*, XXIV, 335–357 (July, 1943).

Chatelain, Verne E., "The Federal Land Policy and Minnesota Politics, 1854–1860," *Minnesota History*, XXII, 227–248 (September, 1941).

Cleveland, H. I., "Booming the First Republican President: A Talk with Abraham Lincoln's Friend, the Late Joseph Medill," *Saturday Evening Post*, vol. 172, pp. 84–85.

Cole, Arthur C., "Abraham Lincoln and the South," *Lincoln Centennial Association Papers* (1928), pp. 47–78.

Cole, Arthur C., "President Lincoln and the Illinois Radical Republicans," *Mississippi Valley Historical Review*, IV, 417–436 (March, 1918).

Collier, T. Maxwell, "William H. Seward in the Campaign of 1860," *Michigan History Magazine*, XIX (1935), 91–106.

Conlin, Sister Frances L., "The Democratic Party in Pennsylvania from 1856 to 1865," *Records of the American Catholic Historical Society of Philadelphia*, XLVII, 132–183 (June, 1936).

Coulter, E. Merton, "The Downfall of the Whig Party in Kentucky," *Register, Kentucky State Historical Society*, XXIII (1925), 162 ff.

Cover, Joseph C., "Memoirs of a Pioneer County Editor," *Wisconsin Magazine of History*, XI, 247–268 (March, 1928).

Crenshaw, Ollinger, "The Speakership Contest of 1859–1860," *Mississippi Valley Historical Review*, XXIX, 323–338 (December, 1942).

Crenshaw, Ollinger, "Urban and Rural Voting in the Election of 1860," in Eric F. Goldman (ed.), *History and Urbanization: Essays in Honor of W. Stull Holt* (Baltimore, 1941), pp. 43–63.

Cucheval-Clarigny, "Les partis et l'élection présidentielle aux États-Unis," *Revue des Deux Mondes*, December 1, 1860, pp. 650–690.

Davis, J. M., "Origin of the Lincoln Rail," *The Century*, LX (1900), 271–275.

Dodd, Dorothy, "The Secession Movement in Florida, 1850–1860," *Florida Historical Society Quarterly*, XII, 45–66 (October, 1933).

Dodd, William E., "The Fight For the Northwest, 1860," *American Historical Review*, XVI, 774–788 (July, 1911).

Dubose, John W., "Yancey: A Study," *Gulf States Historical Magazine*, I, 241–245 (January, 1903).

Dudley, Thomas H., "The Inside Facts of Lincoln's Nomination," *The Century*, XL (1890), 477–479.

Eaton, Clement, "The Resistance of the South to Northern Radicalism," *New England Quarterly*, VIII, 215–231 (June, 1935).

Edwards, E. J., "The Time Lincoln Needed Cheering Up," St. Louis *Globe Democrat*, October 20, 1909.

Eriksson, Erik, "William Penn Clarke," *Iowa Journal of History and Politics*, XXV, 3–61 (January, 1927).

Ewing, Thomas, "Lincoln and the General Land Office, 1849," *Journal of the Illinois State Historical Society*, XXV, 139–153 (October, 1932).

Flom, George T., "The Scandinavian Factor in the American Population," *Iowa Journal of History and Politics*, III, 57–91 (January, 1905).

Gibson, Charles, "Edward Bates," *Collections, Missouri Historical Society*, II, 52–56 (January, 1900).

Gladden, Washington, "Samuel Galloway," *Ohio Archaeological and Historical Quarterly*, IV (1895), 263–278.

Greer, James K., "Louisiana Politics, 1846–1861," *Louisiana Historical Quarterly*, XII, 381 ff. (July, 1929).

Hafen, LeRoy R., "Butterfield's Overland Mail," *California Historical Society Quarterly*, II, 211–222 (October, 1923).

Hamer, Marguerite B., "The Presidential Election of 1860 in Tennessee," *East Tennessee Historical Society Publications*, III, 3–22 (January, 1931).

Hamlin, L. B. (ed.), "Selections from the Follett Papers," *Quarterly Publication of the Historical and Philosophical Society of Ohio*, XIII, 42–78 (April–June, 1918).

Harlow, Ralph V., "The Rise and Fall of the Kansas Aid Movement," *American Historical Review*, XLI, 1–25 (October, 1935).

Harrington, Fred H., "Nathaniel Prentiss Banks: A Study in Anti-Slavery Politics," *New England Quarterly*, IX, 626–654 (December, 1936).

Hennighausen, L. P., "Reminiscences of the Political Life of the German-Americans in Baltimore During 1850–1860," *Seventh Annual Report of the Society for the History of the Germans in Maryland* (1892–1893), pp. 53–59.

Herriott, F. I., "George W. Grimes versus the Southrons," *Annals of Iowa*, series III, vol. XV, pp. 403–432 (October, 1926).

Herriott, F. I., "The Germans of Davenport and the Chicago Convention of 1860," in Harry E. Downer, *History of Davenport and Scott County, Iowa* (Chicago, 1910), I, 839–846.

Herriott, F. I., "Iowa and the First Nomination of Abraham Lincoln," *Annals of Iowa*, series III, vol. VIII, pp. 81–115, 186–220.

Herriott, F. I., "Republican Presidential Preliminaries in Iowa—1859–1860," *Annals of Iowa*, series III, vol. IX, pp. 241–283.

Herriott, F. I., "The Conference in the Deutsches Haus, Chicago, May 14–15, 1860," *Transactions of the Illinois State Historical Society*, 1928, pp. 101–191.

Herriott, F. I., "The Germans of Chicago and Stephen A. Douglas in 1854," *Deutsch-Amerikanische Geschichtsblätter*, XII (1912), 381–404.

Herriott, F. I., "The Premises and Significance of Abraham Lincoln's Letter to Theodore Canisius," *Deutsch-Amerikanische Geschichtsblätter*, XV (1915), 181–254.

Hewitt, Warren F., "The Know-Nothing Party in Pennsylvania," *Pennsylvania History*, II, 69–85 (April, 1935).

Hodder, Frank H., "Some Phases of the Dred Scott Case," *Mississippi Valley Historical Review*, XVI, 3–22 (June, 1929).

Hofstadter, Richard, "The Tariff Issue on the Eve of the Civil War," *American Historical Review*, XLIV, 50–55 (October, 1938).

Holt, Edgar, "Party Politics in Ohio, 1840–1850," *Ohio Archaeological and Historical Quarterly*, XXXVIII (1929), 47–182, 260–402.

Hubbart, H. C., "Pro-Southern Influences in the Free West, 1840–1865," *Mississippi Valley Historical Review*, XX (1933), 45–62.

Johnson, Franklin, "Nominating Lincoln," *The Companion*, February 8, 1917.

Julian, George W., "The First Republican National Convention," *American Historical Review*, IV, 313–322 (January, 1899).

Karstad, Ruby G., "The 'New York Tribune' and the Minnesota Frontier," *Minnesota History*, XXVII, 411–420 (December, 1936).

Kettleborough, Charles, "Indiana on the Eve of Civil War," *Publications, Indiana Historical Society*, VI (1919), 137–189.

King, Charles, "Rufus King: Soldier, Editor and Statesman," *Wisconsin Magazine of History*, IV (1920–21), 371–381.

Knight, George W., "History and Management of Land Grants for Education in the Northwest Territory," *Papers of the American Historical Association*, I (1886), 3–175.

Krout, John A., "The Maine Law in New York Politics," *New York History*, XVII, 260–272 (July, 1936).

Latané, John H., "The Diplomacy of the United States in Regard to Cuba," *Annual Report of the American Historical Association, 1897*, pp. 210–277.

Laughlin, Sceva B., "Missouri Politics during the Civil War," *Missouri Historical Review*, XXIII, 400–426 (April, 1929).

Lefler, Hugh T., "Hinton Rowan Helper: Advocate of a 'White America,'" *Southern Sketches*, No. 1, pp. 5–25.

Levi, Kate E., "The Wisconsin Press and Slavery," *Wisconsin Magazine of History*, IX (1925–1926), 423–434.

Luthin, Reinhard H., "Abraham Lincoln and the Massachusetts Whigs in 1848," *New England Quarterly*, XIV, 619–632 (December, 1941).

Luthin, Reinhard H., "Abraham Lincoln and the Tariff," *American Historical Review*, XLIX, 609–629 (July, 1944).

Luthin, Reinhard H., "A Discordant Chapter in Lincoln's Administration: The Davis-Blair Controversy," *Maryland Historical Magazine*, XXXIX, 25–48 (March, 1944).

Luthin, Reinhard H., "Indiana and Lincoln's Rise to the Presidency,"

Indiana Magazine of History, XXXVIII, 385–405 (December, 1942).

Luthin, Reinhard H., "Organizing the Republican Party in the 'Border-Slave' Regions: Edward Bates's Presidential Candidacy in 1860," *Missouri Historical Review*, XXXVIII, 138–161 (January, 1944).

Luthin, Reinhard H., "Pennsylvania and Lincoln's Rise to the Presidency," *Pennsylvania Magazine of History and Biography*, LXVII, 61–82 (January, 1943).

Luthin, Reinhard H., "Salmon P. Chase's Political Career before the Civil War," *Mississippi Valley Historical Review*, XXIX, 517–540 (March, 1943).

Luthin, Reinhard H., "The Democratic Split during Buchanan's Administration," *Pennsylvania History*, XI, 13–35 (January, 1944).

Malin, James C., "The Proslavery Background of the Kansas Struggle," *Mississippi Valley Historical Review*, X, 285–305 (December, 1923).

Martin, Asa E., "The Temperance Movement in Pennsylvania Prior to the Civil War," *Pennsylvania Magazine of History and Biography*, XLIX, 195–230 (July, 1925).

McLure, Mary L., "The Elections of 1860 in Louisiana," *Louisiana Historical Quarterly*, IX, 644 ff. (October, 1926).

McMurtry, R. Gerald, "Disappointed Presidential Hopefuls in 1860," *Lincoln Herald*, XLV, 35–36 (October, 1943).

McMurtry, R. Gerald, "The Lincoln Migration from Kentucky to Indiana," *Indiana Magazine of History*, XXXIII, 385–421 (December, 1937).

Miller, Paul I., "Lincoln and the Governorship of Oregon," *Mississippi Valley Historical Review*, XXIII, 391–394 (December, 1936).

Monaghan, Jay, "Did Abraham Lincoln Receive the Illinois German Vote?" *Journal of the Illinois State Historical Society*, XXXV 133–139 (1942).

Monteiro, Margaret, "The Presidential Election of 1860 in Virginia," *Richmond College Historical Papers*, I, 222–258 (June, 1916).

Morrow, R. L., "The Liberty Party in Vermont," *New England Quarterly*, II, 234–248 (April, 1929).

Murphy, Charles B., "The Political Career of Jesse D. Bright," *Publications, Indiana Historical Society*, X (1931), 101–145.

Murphy, James L., "Alabama and the Charleston Convention of 1860," *Transactions of the Alabama Historical Society*, V (1904), 244 ff.

Murphy, Robert J., "The Catholic Church in the United States During the Civil War Period, 1852–1866," *Records of the American Catholic Historical Society of Philadelphia*, XXXIX, 271–346 (December, 1928).

Myers, C. Maxwell, "The Influence of Western Pennsylvania in the Campaign of 1860," *Western Pennsylvania Historical Magazine*, XXIV, 248 ff. (1941).

Nelson, E. C., "Presidential Influence on the Policy of Internal Improvements," *Iowa Journal of History and Politics*, IV, 3–69 (January, 1906).

Nettels, Curtis, "The Overland Mail Issue During the Fifties," *Missouri Historical Review*, XVIII, 521–532 (July, 1924).

Nichols, Roy F., "Some Problems of the First Republican Presidential Campaign," *American Historical Review*, XXVIII, 492–496 (April, 1923).

Nicolay, John G., "Abraham Lincoln," *Transactions of the McLean County* [Illinois] *Historical Society*, III (1900), 95–101.

Pearson, Henry G., "Massachusetts to the Front, 1860–1861," in Albert Bushnell Hart (ed.), *Commonwealth History of Massachusetts* (New York, 1930), IV, 499–515.

Pelzer, Louis, "The Disintegration and Organization of Political Parties in Iowa, 1852–1860," *Proceedings of the Mississippi Valley Historical Association*, V (1911–12), 158–166.

Pelzer, Louis, "The History of Political Parties in Iowa from 1857 to 1860," *Iowa Journal of History and Politics*, VII, 179–229 (April, 1909).

Phillips, Ulrich B., "The Central Theme of Southern History," *American Historical Review*, XXXIV, 30–43 (October, 1928).

Pitkin, Thomas M., "Western Republicans and the Tariff in 1860," *Mississippi Valley Historical Review*, XXVII, 401–420 (December, 1940).

Pratt, Harry E., "Abraham Lincoln in Bloomington, Illinois," *Journal of the Illinois State Historical Society*, XXIX, 42–69 (April, 1936).

Pratt, Harry E., "David Davis, 1815–1886," *Transactions of the Illinois State Historical Society*, 1930, pp. 157–183.

Price, Erwin H., "The Election of 1848 in Ohio," *Ohio Archaeological and Historical Quarterly*, XXXVI, 188–311 (April, 1927).

Rainwater, P. L., "Economic Benefits of Secession: Opinion in Mississippi in the 1850's," *Journal of Southern History*, I, 459–474 (November, 1935).

Ramsdell, Charles W., "The Natural Limits of Slavery Expansion," *Mississippi Valley Historical Review*, XVI, 151–171 (September, 1929).

Raleigh, Eldora M., "General Joseph Lane," *Indiana History Bulletin*, IV, Extra No. 1, pp. 71–82 (December, 1926).

Randall, J. G., "The Civil War Restudied," *Journal of Southern History*, VI (1940), 439–457.

Rathbun, Julius G., "The 'Wide Awakes': The Great Political Organization of 1860," *Connecticut Quarterly*, I, 327–335 (October, 1895).

Riddle, Albert G., "The Election of Salmon P. Chase to the Senate," *The Republic* (Washington, D. C.), IV, 179–183 (March, 1875).

Riddle, Albert G., "Rise of Anti-Slavery Sentiment on the Western Reserve," *Magazine of Western History*, VI (1887), 145–156.

Robertson, James R., "Sectionalism in Kentucky from 1855 to 1865," *Mississippi Valley Historical Review*, IV, 49–63 (June, 1917).

Roll, Charles, "Indiana's Part in the Nomination of Lincoln for President in 1860," *Indiana Magazine of History*, XXV, 1–12 (March, 1929).

Roseboom, Eugene H., "Salmon P. Chase and the Know-Nothings," *Mississippi Valley Historical Review*, XXV, 335–350 (December, 1938).

Russel, Robert R., "The Pacific Railway Issue in Politics Prior to the Civil War," *Mississippi Valley Historical Review*, XII, 187–201 (September, 1925).

Ryan, Daniel J., "Lincoln and Ohio," *Ohio Archaeological and Historical Quarterly*, XXXII (1923), 7–281.

Sanborn, John B., "Some Political Aspects of Homestead Legislation," *American Historical Review*, VI, 19–37 (October, 1900).

Sandbo, Anna I., "Beginning of the Secession Movement in Texas," *Southwestern Historical Quarterly*, XVIII, 41–73 (July, 1914).

Schafer, Joseph, "Carl Schurz, Immigrant Statesman," *Wisconsin Magazine of History*, XI, 373–394 (June, 1928).

Schafer, Joseph, "Prohibition in Early Wisconsin," *Wisconsin Magazine of History*, VIII (1924–25), 281–299.

Schafer, Joseph, "Who Elected Lincoln?" *American Historical Review*, XLVII, 51–63 (October, 1941).

Schneider, George, "Lincoln and the Anti-Know-Nothing Resolutions," *Transactions of the McLean County Historical Society*, III, 87–90 (1900).

Sears, Louis M., "New York and the Fusion Movement of 1860," *Journal of the Illinois State Historical Society* (1923), 58–62.

Sears, Louis M., "Slidell and Buchanan," *American Historical Review*, XXVII, 712–724 (July, 1922).

Sellers, James L., "James R. Doolittle," *Wisconsin Magazine of History*, XVII, 277–306 (March, 1934).

Sellers, James L., "Republicanism and States Rights in Wisconsin," *Mississippi Valley Historical Review*, XVII, 213–229 (September, 1930).

Sellers, James L., "The Make-Up of the Early Republican Party," *Transactions of the Illinois State Historical Society*, 1930, pp. 39–51.

Shutes, Milton H., "Colonel E. D. Baker," *California Historical Society Quarterly*, XVII, 303–324 (December, 1938).

Smith, Charles P., "The Nomination of Lincoln," *Beecher's Magazine*, V, 332ff. (June, 1872).

Smith, Donnal V., "Salmon P. Chase and the Election of 1860," *Ohio Archaeological and Historical Quarterly*, XXXIX (1930), 515–607.

Smith, Donnal V., "The Influence of the Foreign-Born of the Northwest in the Election of 1860," *Mississippi Valley Historical Review*, XIX, 192–204 (September, 1932).

Smith, Theodore Clarke, "The Free Soil Party in Wisconsin," *Proceedings of the State Historical Society of Wisconsin*, XLII (1894), 97–162.

Smith, Willard H., "Schuyler Colfax: Whig Editor, 1845–1855," *Indiana Magazine of History*, XXXIV, 262–282 (September, 1938).

Smithers, William T., "Memoir of Nathaniel B. Smithers," *Papers, Historical Society of Delaware*, XXIII (1899), 5–39.

Spaulding, Imogene, "The Attitude of California to the Civil War," *Publications, Historical Society of Southern California*, IX (1912–1913), 104–131.

Stenberg, Richard R., "An Unnoted Factor in the Buchanan-Douglas

Feud," *Journal of the Illinois State Historical Society*, XXV (1932–1933), 271–284.

Stickney, Charles, "Know-Nothingism in Rhode Island," *Publications of the Rhode Island Historical Society*, 1892–1894, pp. 243–257.

Street, Ida M., "The Simon Cameron Indian Commission of 1838," *Annals of Iowa*, VII, 115–139, 172–195 (July–October, 1905).

Strevey, Tracy E., "Joseph Medill and the *Chicago Tribune* in the Nomination and Election of Lincoln," in Paul M. Angle (ed.), *Papers in Illinois History* (1938), pp. 39–63.

Talbot, George F., "Lot M. Morrill," *Collections, Maine Historical Society*, series II, vol. V, pp. 225–275 (1894).

Tasher, Lucy L., "The *Missouri Democrat* and the Civil War," *Missouri Historical Review*, XXXI, 402–419 (July, 1937).

Tuska, Benjamin, "Know-Nothingism in Baltimore, 1854–1860," *Catholic Historical Review*, new series, V, 217–251 (July, 1925).

Van Deusen, Glyndon G., "Thurlow Weed: A Character Study," *American Historical Review*, XLIX, 427–440 (April, 1944).

Venable, Austin L., "The Conflict between the Douglas and Yancey Forces in the Charleston Convention," *Journal of Southern History*, VIII (1942), 226–241.

Warren, Louis A., "The Lone Whig from Illinois," *Lincoln Lore*, May 20, 1940.

Warren, Louis A., "Printing the Cooper Institute Address," *Lincoln Lore*, July 22, 1940.

Watson, Richard L., Jr., "Thurlow Weed, Political Boss," *New York History*, XXII, 411–425 (October, 1941).

Webb, Richard, "William Pitt Fessenden," *Collections, Maine Historical Society*, series II, vol. X, pp. 225–263 (1899).

Wessen, Ernest J., "Campaign Lives of Abraham Lincoln, 1860," in Paul M. Angle (ed.), *Papers in Illinois History* (1937), pp. 190 ff.

White, Horace, "Abraham Lincoln in 1854," *Transactions of the Illinois State Historical Society*, 1908, pp. 25–47.

White, Laura A., "The National Democrats of South Carolina, 1852–1860," *South Atlantic Quarterly*, XXVIII, 370–389 (October, 1929).

Wilson, Howard L., "President Buchanan's Proposed Intervention in Mexico," *American Historical Review*, V, 687–701 (July, 1900).

Wilson, Rufus Rockwell, "Learning about Lincoln," *Lincoln Herald*, XLV, 27–32 (October, 1943).

Workman, Charles H., "Tablet to Abraham Lincoln at Mansfield," *Ohio Archaeological and Historical Quarterly*, XXXIV, 505–521 (October, 1925).

Yonge, J. E. D., "The Conservative Party in Alabama, 1848–1860," *Transactions of the Alabama Historical Society*, V (1904), 509–515.

Zimmerman, Charles, "The Origin and Rise of the Republican Party in Indiana from 1854 to 1860," *Indiana Magazine of History*, XIII (1917), 349–412.

Index

"Abe's Boys," in Lincoln campaign, 197

Abolitionists, 3, 5, 70, 95; at Chicago convention, 137

Adams, John Quincy (6th Pres. of U. S.), comment on Judge McLean, 111

Adams, Stephen, senator from Mississippi, 8

Adams, Theodore, tours country for Cameron, 100

Adams House, Chicago, 138

Advertiser (Portland, Ore.), 195

African slave trade, its revival an issue, 130

"Ain't You Glad You Jined the Republicans?" sung when news of Lincoln's election came to Springfield, 219

"Alabama Platform," an answer to the Wilmot Proviso, 128; resurrected at Democratic convention in Montgomery, Ala., 129; in the Charleston convention, 130

"Albany Regency," in New York, supports Douglas, 212; 132, 213, 216–17

Allen, Cyrus M., 89

American Agriculture and Its Interest in the Protective Policy, a New York *Tribune* tract circulated in Northwest, 189

American party (Know-Nothing), splits on slavery issue, 3; nominates Millard Fillmore for President, 4; endorsed by Judge Bates, 52

"American-Republican" as a party name, 107

"American System" of Henry Clay, 69, 191

"Americanism" as a political issue, 25, 220

"Americans," in Pennsylvania, 30, 93; dissolve in separate party, 97; elect Gardner governor of Massachusetts, 107; espouse Republicanism, 108; sought for Lincoln support, 211; 27, 53–54, 56, 59, 61–62, 118, 168, 223

Andrew, John Albion, at Chicago convention, 143; candidate for governor of Massachusetts, 190; 108

Andrews, John W., 39

Anti-Catholic movement, in New York, 25; in Ohio, 41; an element of Know-Nothingism in Massachusetts, 107

"Anti-Masonic" party organized in New York, 23

Anti-Nebraska agitation, promoted by New York *Times* and *Tribune*, 25; convention at Saratoga to consider organizing a Republican party, 26; convention call for Ohio, 39–41; helps elect Pollock governor of Pennsylvania, 92; an element of Know-Nothingism, 107; 27, 70

Anti-slavery party, proposed by Theodore Parker, 26; as an issue, 93, 95, 106, 114, 150, 173, 221

"Appeal of Independent Democrats," manifesto against repeal of Missouri Compromise, 38

Arnold, Isaac Newton, at Decatur Republican convention, 91

Aspinwall, William Henry, mentioned, 215

Ashmun, George, at Chicago convention, 148, 161; letter from Lincoln on the spelling of his given name, 168

Astor House, New York, 171

Babcock, James F., 87

Bailey, Dr. Gamaliel, friend of Chase accused of conspiring against him, 50

Baker, Edward Dickenson, delivers funeral oration over Senator Broderick, 124–25; in Lincoln campaign, 193–94

Baker, Edward L., editor of the *Illinois State Journal*, 85; gets news of Lincoln's election, 219

Ballads in the Lincoln campaign, 175

Baltimore, one convention names Douglas for President, another nominates Breckinridge and Lane for President and Vice-President, 134–35

Banks, Nathaniel Prentiss, "dark horse" at Chicago convention, 106; goes to Congress and is elected Speaker of the House, 106–7; seeks nomination for President, 108–11, 118; his name in Chicago convention, 139; his boom collapses, 143; 223

Banners, inscribed, in Republican parade in Springfield, Ill., 183

Barney, Hiram, at Chicago convention, 139; 80

Barstow, William Augustus, elected governor of Wisconsin, 45

Bartlett, William O., 110

Bates, Judge Edward, his candidacy for presidential nomination promoted by Blair family, 49, 53, 55; his career, 51–52; hope of a coalition to help him, 56–57; endorsed by Jefferson City "Opposition" convention, 58; opposition to his candidacy among the Germans, 59–61, 64; gets support of Greeley and Colfax, 62; his diary quoted, 68; his name in Chicago convention,

140 ff.; lauds Lincoln, 168; 32, 54, 63, 65–67, 69, 77, 82, 86, 88–90, 171, 223

Beecher, Henry Ward, his Plymouth Church in Brooklyn, 79–80

Bell, John, senator from Tennessee, 65; attacked by Greeley on his record, 118–19; nominated for President by the Constitutional Union party, 119; his campaign, 138 ff.

"Bell-Everetters," branch of the Constitutional Union party, 174

"Bell-Ringers," supporters of the Bell-Everett ticket, 174

Belleviller Zeitung (Illinois), German newspaper, 185

Belmont, August, named National Chairman for the Douglas campaign, 172; his difficulty in raising funds, 215; 216

Bennett, James Gordon, editor of the New York *Herald*, puts forward Cameron for President, 98; supports Breckinridge in the campaign, 213; his analysis of Republican strategy, 222

Benton, Thomas Hart, proposed as Free Soil candidate for President, 26; defeated for governor of Missouri, 52; 24, 53

Bigler, William, Democratic candidate for governor of Pennsylvania, 93; opposes postponement of Morrill tariff bill, 207; 205

Birney, James Gillespie, and his Liberty party, 36

Bissell, William Harrison, governor of Illinois, 48

Blaine, James Gillespie, at Chicago convention, 144; in Lincoln campaign, 191

Blair, Austin, leader of Michigan Republicans, elected governor, 44; at Chicago convention, 138; seconds Seward's nomination, 162; 180

Blair, Francis Preston, Sr., joins Republicans, 27; delegate-at-large to Chicago convention, 67; 53, 66

Blair, Francis Preston, Jr., congressman from Missouri, attacks Mexican treaty, 17; his Free Democracy party becomes nucleus of Missouri Republican party, 54; promotes candidacy of Judge Bates for President, 55–58; at "Republican" state convention to select Bates delegates to Chicago convention, 59–60; at the convention, 138 ff.; nominates Bates, 162; 20, 53, 61–62, 65, 218

Blair, Montgomery, his letter on colonizing Negroes, 66; chairman of Republican state convention in Baltimore, 67; at Chicago convention, 161; 53

Blakey, George D., at Chicago convention, 136

Blatchford, Richard Milford, contributes to Lincoln campaign fund, 185; presides at Lincoln-Hamlin meeting at Cooper Institute, 211

"Bleeding" Kansas, 96, 221–22

Blickensderfer, Jacob, Whig politician, 39

Bolters from the Charleston convention hold conventions in Baltimore and Richmond, name Breckinridge and Joseph Lane for President and Vice-President, 134–35

Booth case, involving the Fugitive Slave Law, 149

Boutwell, George Sewall, at Chicago convention, 148

Bowles, Samuel, editor of the Springfield (Mass.) Republican, 110; campaigns for Banks, 111, 143

Brady, James Topham, nominated for governor of New York by Democratic "hard" faction, 213–14, 217

Breckinridge, John Cabell, Vice-President of the United States, defeats the homestead bill and Morrill's land-grant bill, 13–14; nominated for President at Baltimore and Richmond conventions, 135; his campaign, 172 ff.

Briggs, James A., raises protectionist issue in New Jersey for Chase, 47;

invites Lincoln to speak at Beecher's Plymouth Church in Brooklyn, 79; at Chicago convention, 139; 112

Bright, Jesse David, senator from Indiana, 63, 126; supports Breckinridge-Lane ticket, 173; feuds with Douglas, 199–200

Brinkerhoff, Jacob, named for Supreme Court in Ohio and elected, 181–82

British Parliament offers subsidy for trans-Atlantic telegraph cable, 6

Broadhead, James Overton, presides at "Opposition" convention in Jefferson City, 58

Broderick, David Colbreth, senator from California, critic of Buchanan, 11; reëlected, 123; unites with Douglas against Buchanan, 124; killed in duel with Terry, 124, 193–94; his killing laid to the Slave Power, 124–25

Brooks, Preston Smith, assaults Senator Sumner, 4

Brown, Aaron Venable, Postmaster General in Buchanan's Cabinet, his contracts for carrying overland mail denounced in the Senate, 11

Brown, Benjamin Gratz, editor of the St. Louis Democrat, 53; promotes candidacy of Judge Bates for President, 57–58; at "Republican" convention to select Bates delegates to Chicago, 59–60; 61, 65

Brown, John, his raid at Harpers Ferry, 19–20; as a political issue, 32, 57, 74–75, 80, 127, 149

Browning, Orville Hickman, supports Judge Bates for presidential nomination, 64; his interview with Lincoln, 65; at Chicago convention, 139, 144; 89

Bruncken, Dr. Ernest, 187

Bryant, William Cullen, at Chicago convention, 154; in Lincoln campaign, 210; 80, 84, 110

Buchanan, James (15th Pres. of U. S.), nominated by the Democrats, defeats

Frémont, 4, 29, 47, 73, 95, 120, 127, 143, 196; concern over Dred Scott case, 5; vetoes overland-mail, homestead, and land-grant bills, 11–14; the Ostend Manifesto, 15; plans to buy Cuba, 16; treaty with Mexico, 17; his administration denounced over the Chicago harbor situation, 83; allied with free-trade Democrats of the South, 92; break with Douglas, 121–26; 22, 30, 53, 57, 96–97, 132, 140, 173, 177

Buchanan-Douglas controversy disrupts Democratic party, 121–26, 128, 131, 172, 199, 203, 223

"Buchaneers" (Buchananites), defeated by Douglas in fight for the Senate, 122, 128; 194

Buckingham, William Alfred, elected governor of Connecticut, 82, 145

Bulletin (San Francisco), on Buchanan's veto of overland-mail measure, 12

Bullock, Alexander Hamilton, governor of Massachusetts, 22

Burlingame, Anson, at Chicago convention, 139; 110

Burnside, James, son-in-law of Cameron, 100

Bush, Asahel, Douglas's manager, 195

Butler, William, Illinois state treasurer, at Chicago convention, 139

Butterfield, John, obtains contract for carrying overland mail, 11

Caldwell, Alfred, at Chicago convention, 160

Calhoun, John Caldwell, 20, 36, 51–52, 149; his death, 127

California, its political battles, 123; in Lincoln campaign, 193–94

Cameron, Simon, senator from Pennsylvania, entertains Seward, 31; endorsed by the People's party for President, 33–34; Pennsylvania's "favorite son," 48; elected to Senate as protectionist Democrat, 92; candidate of the Know-Nothings for gov-ernor, 93; reëlected to Senate, 95; urges increased duties on coal and iron, 97; New York Herald suggests him for President, 98–99; begins active campaign for the nomination, 100 ff.; supports Lincoln, 168–69; his feud with Curtin, 202–3; 73, 80, 95, 223–24

"Cameron" and "corruption" as synonymous terms, 103

"Cameron and Lincoln Club," in Chicago, addressed by Judd, 79

Campbell, Lewis Davis, congressman from Ohio, 39

Campbell, Robert D., lieutenant governor of New York, renominated, 211

Canisius, Dr. Theodore, German editor in Springfield, Ill., asks Lincoln's views on Massachusetts' anti-alien law, 83–84

Carey, Henry Charles, called "Father of Pennsylvania Protectionism," 99–100; 30–31, 114

Cartoons in the Lincoln campaign, 175

Cartter, David Kellogg, nominates Chase at Chicago convention, 162; casts deciding votes for Lincoln, 166

Casey, Joseph, declares Cameron is not committed to Seward, 101; in Lincoln campaign, 202–3; 103, 105

Cass, Lewis, 183

Catron, Justice John, in Dred Scott case, 5

Chace, William M., treasurer of the Republican National Committee, 18

Chandler, Zachariah, senator from Michigan, in Lincoln campaign, 180; 8–9, 20

Charleston, S. C., meeting of the Democratic National Convention, 128–33; disrupted by bolters, 134–35

Chase, Salmon Portland, on Dred Scott case, 5; elected governor of Ohio, 27, 40–41, 43–44; incipient boom in New York for presidential nomination, 34; joins Liberty party, is elected to U. S. Senate, 36; leads

"Free Soil Democrats" on prohibition issue, 37; seeks to establish new party, 38–39; seeks presidential nomination, 42, 45–50, 106, 108, 112–16; his name in Chicago convention, 138 ff.; pledges support to Lincoln, 168; speaks in New York, 218; 24, 51, 61, 69, 73–74, 77, 80, 88–89, 168, 223–24

Chester County Times (Pa.), publishes autobiography of Lincoln, 76

Chicago, chosen for the 1860 Republican National Convention, 21, 78; story of the Republican success, 223

Chicago harbor, its improvement sought, 9–10; Buchanan administration denounced over its mishandling, 83

Cisco, John J., U. S. Subtreasurer, supports Breckinridge-Lane ticket, 213

Clark, Myron Holley, elected governor of New York, 26

Clay, Cassius Marcellus, promised War Secretary by the Blairs for support of Bates, 68; seeks nomination himself for President, 114; speaks at Cooper Institute in New York, 115; letters to Sumner, 115–16, 118; receives two votes at Chicago convention, 165–66; 18, 20, 197, 218

Clay, Clement Claiborne, senator from Alabama, 9

Clay, Henry, his "American System" admired by Lincoln, 69; his name in the Lincoln campaign, 183–84; 27, 51, 55, 72–73, 76, 114

Clinton, De Witt, 23

"Coalitionists" in Massachusetts, 106

Cobb, Howell, Secretary of the Treasury, his opinion of internal improvements, 9; criticized on Chicago harbor improvement, 10

Cole, Prof. Arthur Charles, 187

Colfax, Schuyler, congressman from Indiana, 8, 54–55; lends support to Judge Bates in his *St. Joseph Valley Register*, 62–63, 65; at Chicago convention, 141; 73, 83

Colgate Theological Seminary, 137

Collamer, Jacob, possible candidate for President, 118; "favorite son" at Chicago convention, 144; gets ten votes on first ballot, 163; 164, 223

Commercial (Cincinnati), 166

Commercial Advertiser (Buffalo), goes over to Lincoln, 213; 211

Compromise of 1850, 52, 130

Concord coaches to carry overland mail, 11

Conner, Alexander H., in Lincoln campaign, 198

"Conscience" Whigs, 106, 189

Constitutional Union National Convention, in Baltimore, 59; nominates John Bell and Everett for President and Vice-President, 119, 138, 157, 173, 190; convention in Indianapolis endorses ticket, 200

Cook, Burton Chauncey, at Chicago convention, 139; 91

Cooper Institute, in New York, Lincoln's address, 80, 82, 145, 224; Lincoln-Hamlin meeting, 210–11; 17, 20, 81, 115, 212, 217

Corcoran, William Wilson, banker, 120

Corwin, Thomas, congressman from Ohio, advocates higher tariff, 67; nominates Judge McLean at Chicago convention, 162; in Lincoln campaign, 197

Corwine, Richard M., delegate to Chicago convention, 88–89; 112

Cotterill, Prof. Robert Spencer, 125

"Cotton" Whigs, 106

Coulter, Dr. J. H., 39

County conventions in Illinois endorse Lincoln, 85

Courant (Hartford, Conn.), 146

Courier (Boston), Old-Line Whig organ, in financial difficulties, 190

Covode, John, congressman from Pennsylvania, 104, 125, 176

Covode Committee of Congress, 125, 175–76, 181

Crawford, Josiah, had rail cut by Lincoln, 169

Cuba, its annexation desired by southerners, 15; offer to purchase charged to Pierce, 15–16; as a political issue, 17, 221

Cummings, Alexander, prints New York *Herald* editorial in his *Evening Bulletin* suggesting Cameron for President, 98; prints similar articles from other papers, 99; launches campaign for Cameron, 100

Cummings, Amos Jay, sets type of Lincoln's Cooper Institute address, 81

Curtin, Andrew Gregg, feuds with Cameron, 103–4; nominated for governor of Pennsylvania by People's party, 104; at Chicago convention, 154–55, 157; in Lincoln campaign, 202–3; his campaign for governor, 205; elected, 208

Curtis, Justice Benjamin Robbins, dissents in Dred Scott case, 4–5

Cutts, Adele, married to Douglas, 186

Cutts, James Madison, father-in-law of Douglas, 173

Daenzer, Carl, editor of the St. Louis *Westliche Post*, his comment on Judge Bates, 60

Daily News (Philadelphia), 158

Davis, Judge David, devotes himself to the Lincoln cause, 85, 87, 89, 91; at Chicago convention, 136 ff.; in Lincoln campaign, 197, 202–3; 224

Davis, Henry Winter, Know-Nothing congressman from Maryland, 62; up for reëlection, 65; helps Republicans elect Pennington Speaker of the House, 66

Davis, Jefferson, senator from Mississippi, his attitude toward secession, 20; out to crush Douglas, 128; supports Breckinridge-Lane ticket, 172, 175; 134, 183

Dayton, William Lewis, candidate for Vice-President, as Frémont's running-mate, 95; seeking nomination for President, 48, 113–14, 118; his name in Chicago convention, 143 ff.; in Lincoln campaign, 171; 223–24

Debates of Lincoln and Douglas, 77, 89, 224

Defrees, John D., in Lincoln campaign, 198

Delahay, Mark W., seeks senatorship from Kansas, 87; 86

Delano, Columbus, seconds Lincoln's nomination at Chicago convention, 162

Delaware Republican (Wilmington), advocates Bates for President, 67

Democrat (St. Louis), 53, 55, 57–59, 63

Democratic convention in Montgomery, Ala., Yancey resurrects his "Alabama Platform," 129

Democratic National Convention of 1848, rejects the "Alabama Platform," 128

Democratic National Convention of 1856, Buchanan defeats Douglas for presidential nomination, 120

Democratic National Convention of 1860, in Charleston, 128–32; contests between two delegations from New York, 133; disrupted by bolters, 134

Democratic party, nominates Buchanan for President, 4; wide open split, 17; hostility to "free land" featured by Republicans, 18; split widening, 53; factionalism, 70; causes of the split, 120 ff.; shortsightedness helps Republicans, 221–22

Deutsches Haus, Chicago German fraternal center, 83, 156

Dickinson, Daniel Stevens, supports Breckinridge, 212–13; favors fusion, 217

Dickson, Mr., 46

Dixon, James, senator from Connecticut, declares Seward cannot win, 145; in Lincoln campaign, 190

Dodd, Prof. William Edward, 187

Dole, William P., 79

Donelson, Andrew Jackson, nominated for Vice-President by Know-Nothings and Whigs, 155

Doolittle, James Rood, senator from Wisconsin, 21; campaigns for Lincoln in New York, 218

Douglas, Stephen Arnold, senator from Illinois, seeks land bounty for Illinois Central Railroad, 10; on John Brown's raid, 20; introduces Kansas-Nebraska bill with repeal of Missouri Compromise, 24–25, 37–38, 45, 70; "squatter sovereignty" doctrine, 74; debates with Lincoln, 77; "popular sovereignty" doctrine, 115, 126, 130, 134; loses nomination for President to Buchanan, 120; denounces Lecompton constitution, 121; reëlected to Senate, defeating Lincoln, 122; "Freeport doctrine," 128; agrees to accept nomination for President if platform embodies principles of Compromise of 1850, 129–30; named for President by Baltimore remnant of Charleston convention, 134; his campaign for presidency, 171 ff.; married to Adele Cutts, is accused of conversion to Catholicism, 186; in Vermont election, 192; in California, 194; in New Jersey, 195–96; 22, 40, 69, 75, 86, 97, 133, 175, 220

Downey, John G., governor of California, in Douglas campaign, 193

Draper, Simeon, chairman of New York Republican State Central Committee, 211

Dred Scott decision, 4–5; Seward's tirade against it, 29; 32, 126, 221

Dubois, Jesse K., at Chicago convention, 139; on news of Lincoln's election, 219; 82, 89, 170

Dudley, Thomas H., at Chicago convention, 136, 151, 158–59; nominates Dayton, 162; 113–14

Dumond, Prof. Dwight Lowell, on the "Alabama Platform," 130

Eames, Benjamin Tucker, delegate to Chicago convention, 191

Endowments for agricultural-mechanical colleges as a political issue, 17

English, William Hayden, congressman from Indiana, his Kansas referendum bill rejected, 121

Errett, Russell, editor of the Pittsburgh *Gazette*, Cameron enthusiast, 103

Evarts, William Maxwell, at Chicago convention, 154; nominates Seward, 162

Evening Bulletin (Philadelphia), reprints editorial from New York *Herald* suggesting Cameron for President, 98; prints similar articles from other papers, 99; leaves Bell and supports Lincoln, 202; 100

Evening Journal (Albany, N. Y.), mouthpiece of Whig party, 23, 26

Evening Post (N. Y.), 84

Everett, Edward, nominated for Vice-President by Constitutional Union party, 19, 173, 190

Ewing, Thomas, last of the Whigs, speaks for Lincoln, 182

Examiner (Lancaster, Pa.), prints editorial suggesting Cameron for President and Lincoln for Vice-President, 102

Express (N. Y.), for Bell, 213

"Favorite son" at Democratic National Convention in Charleston, 131

Fell, Jesse W., sketches life of Lincoln for the *Chester County Times*, 75–76; at Chicago convention, 141, 161; 85

Fessenden, William Pitt, as a "dark horse" candidate for President, 117–18

Field, Cyrus West, obtains subsidy for trans-Atlantic telegraph cable, 6; it becomes a political issue, 17

Field, David Dudley, dropped as a delegate to Chicago convention, 33; at the convention, 139; 110

Fillmore, Millard, becomes 13th President of U. S., through the death of President Taylor, 24; nominated for President by the American party, 4, 52, 71, 95, 211; 51, 140, 156

Fish, Hamilton, senator from New York, 25, 29, 80

Fishback, William P., at Chicago convention, 142

Fitch, Graham Newell, in contest for the Senate, 199

Fitzpatrick, Benjamin, senator from Alabama, 14

Fogg, George Gilman, in Lincoln campaign, 171, 184

Forbes, Hugh, proposes a slave uprising, 19

Foreign-born in Massachusetts, 108-9

Forney, John Weiss, starts Philadelphia *Press*, his wife fails to obtain Cabinet post for him, and he attacks Buchanan, 96-97; rewarded by Republicans with clerkship of House of Representatives, 123; testifies against Buchanan before a House committee, 125; supports Douglas, 204

Forney, John Wien, editor of the Harrisburg *Telegraph*, 100

Foster, Henry Donnal, candidate for governor of Pennsylvania, 203-5; his campaign, 207; defeated, 208

Foy, Peter L., of the St. Louis *Democrat*, heads Bates men at Indianapolis "Mass" convention, 63

"Free Democracy," Frank Blair, Jr.'s party in Missouri, 54; nominates county ticket in St. Louis, 57

"Free harbors, free soil, free labor, and Frémont," Republican slogan, 8

"Free land" proposal, 12, 18; reformers called "homesteaders," 22; issue in Minnesota, 116; as a political issue, 150; attracts German vote to Lincoln, 186

"Freeport doctrine" of Douglas, 128

Free Soil Democrats, led by Chase, merge with Whigs in Ohio, 37-38,

40; in Michigan, merge with Whigs and prohibitionists to form a "Republican" party, 44; at Chicago convention, 137; urged to support Lincoln, 171; in New York, 210; 225

Free Soilers, nominate Van Buren for President, 36; candidates in Wisconsin temperance men, 45; 22, 29, 35, 70

Free Soil Whigs, at Chicago convention, 137

Free trade as a political issue, 6-7, 47, 208

Frémont, John Charles, nominated for President by the Republicans but defeated by Buchanan, 4, 29, 43, 47, 71, 73, 95, 107-8, 111, 127, 143, 150, 196; gets one vote in Chicago convention, 162-63; 8, 52-53, 74, 113-14, 123, 129, 145

Fugitive Slave Law, 24, 37, 59, 74, 94

Fusion ticket of state offices in Ohio wins, 39-40; organizes Republican party, elects Chase governor, 41

Gadsden treaty before Senate, 16

Galloway, Samuel, letter from Lincoln, 88; 87, 89

Gardner, Henry Joseph, elected governor of Massachusetts by the "Americans," 107-8

Garrison, William Lloyd, abolitionist, speaks to an audience of twenty-five in Harrisburg, 96; 18

Gazette (Cincinnati), Whig newspaper, 38-39

Gazette (Pittsburgh), 103, 205

General Land Office, commissionership sought by Lincoln, 69

George III mentioned, 28

German-Americans, as a political factor, support fusion ticket in Ohio, 39-41; their vote in Wisconsin, 45; in Missouri, 53-54; oppose Judge Bates's nomination for President, 59-61, 155; their activity in Illinois, 83; turn to support of Lincoln, 84; agitate for free land, 151; 3, 22, 109,

146–47, 152–53, 155–56, 179, 185–87, 198, 215, 217, 223

German-language newspapers supporting Lincoln, 187

German Turner Bund of the U. S., 84

Gibson, Charles, procures endorsement of Judge Bates for President by Whig convention, 58; at Indianapolis convention, 64

Giddings, Joshua Reed, congressman from Ohio, 38–39, 44; at "Mass" convention in Pittsburgh to organize a Republican party, 94; at Chicago convention, 136, 146, 165

Goodrich, John Zacheus, on foreigners voting, 109; 205

Granger, Julius N., brother-in-law of Douglas, 173

Greeley, Horace, editor of the New York *Tribune*, on Buchanan, 14; mouthpiece of Whig party, 23; takes up temperance movement, 24; opposes Kansas-Nebraska bill, 25; comes out in support of Judge Bates, 62, 64; attacks John Bell, 118; his name for the Constitutional party, 119; at Chicago convention representing Oregon, 137 ff.; on Lincoln campaign issues, 177; 31, 80, 111, 123, 176, 192–93, 210

Grimes, James Wilson, Iowa's first governor, 179

Grimshaw, Jackson, letter from Lincoln, 78; at Chicago convention, 139; 84–85

Griswold, John A., 89

Grow, Galusha Aaron, gets homestead bill through House, loses in Senate, 13; stumps Minnesota on issue and circulates the bill printed in German, 116–17

Gwin, William McKendree, elected to U. S. Senate with Broderick's help, then turns on him, 123–24, 193

Gwin-Broderick feud as an issue, 220–21

Hale, John Parker, senator from New Hampshire, 37

Hall, Benjamin Franklin, mayor of Auburn, N. Y., 32

Halstead, Murat, of the Cincinnati *Commercial*, reporting the Chicago convention, 159, 166

Hamlin, Hannibal, senator from Maine, 114; at Chicago convention, 144; chosen as Lincoln's running-mate, 166–67

Hanks, John, and the rails he and Lincoln split, 90

"Hard" and "soft" Democratic factions in New York, 212–14

Harlan, James, senator from Iowa, and his interest in the land question, 13

Harpers Ferry, raid by John Brown, 19–20; as a political issue, 32, 57, 127

Harrison, William Henry, 9th Pres. of the U. S., 112, 169, 183; his death, 88

Hart, Emanuel Bernard, Surveyor of the port of New York, supports Breckinridge-Lane, 213

Hassaurek, Frederick, in Lincoln campaign, 185; 46, 48–49

Hatch, Ozias M., Illinois Secretary of State, at Chicago convention, 139

Hay, C. D., 85

Helper, Hinton Rowan, his *The Impending Crisis of the South: How to Meet It* a campaign document, 18–19, 32

Hendricks, Thomas Andrews, candidate for governor of Indiana, 196, 199; defeated, 201

Henry, Joshua J., seeks fusion of Douglas and Breckinridge tickets in New York, 216

Herald (Dubuque, Iowa), on Buchanan's veto of the homestead bill, 179

Herald (N. Y.), on John Brown's raid, 19; editorials suggesting Cameron for President, 98–100; notice of dinner to Gov. Banks of Massachusetts, 110; on German help to Lincoln, 187; supports Breckinridge, 213; favors fusion, 217

Herndon, William Henry, Lincoln's law partner, 71–72, 79, 85; at Chicago convention, 142; 184, 208

Hielscher, Theodore, editor of the Indianapolis *Freie Presse*, opposes naming Bates delegates to the Chicago convention, 64; in Lincoln campaign, 185

"Higher law" doctrine of Seward, 32, 51

Homestead bill, passed by House, beaten in Senate, becomes an issue in 1860 campaign, 13, 17, 176, 179, 182, 187; 40

Homestead issue, in the West, 70, 83; in Minnesota, 116; in politics, 150–51; in Lincoln campaign, 177, 187; in Iowa, 178–79; in Northwest, 220

"Honest Abe of the West," song in the Lincoln campaign, 175

Hosea, Robert, 46

"House Divided" theory of Lincoln, 80

Houston, Samuel, runs for President on "Texas" Unionist ticket, 173

Hunt, Washington, ex-governor of New York, prepares to support Douglas, 213–14

Hunter, Robert Mercer Taliaferro, senator from Virginia, sponsors 1857 tariff, 7; postpones consideration of Morrill tariff bill, 207; 11, 16

Hutchinson's Republican Songster for 1860, 175

Illinois, its 1860 political campaign, 182, 186

Illinois Central Railroad, seeks land-grant, 10

Illinois State Journal (Springfield), prints Lincoln's Cooper Institute address, 81; publishes Lincoln's oration on Clay, 183; 85

Impending Crisis of the South: How to Meet It, The, a campaign document by Hinton Rowan Helper, 18, 32

Indiana, as a political prize, 62–63; in Lincoln campaign, 196–201

Internal improvements, old Whig program embraced by the Republican party, 8–9; demands by the West, 10; as a political issue, 17, 54; its importance in the Northwest, 188

Irish-Catholic immigrant, regarded as an enemy of American labor, 107

Iowa, homestead a live issue, 178–79

Irish vote in New York, 213–15, 217

"Irrepressible Conflict" address of Seward, 29, 32

Jackson, Andrew, 7th Pres. of the U. S., 23, 52–53, 127

Jayne, William, governor of Dakota Territory, comment on Lincoln workers, 224

Jefferson, Thomas (3d Pres. of U. S.), mentioned, 184

Jefferson City, convention of the "Opposition," endorses Judge Bates, 58; discord over sending delegates to Chicago convention, 59–60

Jessup, William, at Chicago convention, 148

Johnson, Franklin, student at Colgate Theological Seminary, at Chicago convention, representing Oregon, 137

Johnson, Herschel Vespasian, nominee for Vice-President on Douglas ticket, 172, 199–200

Jokes in the Lincoln campaign, 175

Jonas, Abraham, Jewish friend of Lincoln, 184

Journal (Indianapolis), favors either McLean or Lincoln, 89–90

Journal (Louisville), on Judge Bates as a candidate for presidential nomination, 61; 197

Juarez, Benito Pablo, President of Mexico, and his treaty with U. S., 17

Judd, Norman Buel, congressman from Illinois, 20–21, 64; seeks nomination for governor, 77–78; letter from Lincoln exonerating him of treachery, 78–79; letter to Trumbull, 79; at Chicago convention, 139–40, 154; nominates Lincoln, 162; 84–85, 87, 91

Kansas question, 4–5, 32, 121–22, 126; an issue in Lincoln campaign, 176
Kansas-Nebraska bill, introduced by Douglas, 24–25, 28, 37–39, 52, 70; responsible for fusion in Ohio, 40; effect on the Whigs, 114; 62, 92, 106, 118, 128, 220
Kasson, John Adam, at Chicago convention, 148, 152
Kelley, William, nominated by "soft" Democrats for governor of New York, 214
Kentucky, referred to by Lincoln as "my State," 72
King, Preston, his activity in forming the Republican party, 27; succeeds Fish in Senate, 29; at Chicago convention, 136, 167; in Lincoln campaign, 176
King, Rufus, owner of the Milwaukee *Sentinel*, 46–47; supports Lincoln, 180
Kirkwood, Samuel Jordan, governor of Iowa, on campaign issues, 179
Know-Nothingism, its revival in Massachusetts, anti-Catholicism one of its elements, 45, 107; in the border states, 52; in Illinois, 70; 108, 123, 222
Know-Nothings, nominate Fillmore for President, 4; oppose Seward in New York, 25; he protests combination with them, 27; help elect Chase governor of Ohio, 40–41; allied with Whigs in Pennsylvania, 92; 13, 22, 43, 70, 93, 95, 106, 142–43, 145, 152–53, 155–56, 189
Koerner, Gustave, former lieutenant governor of Illinois, 83; at Chicago

convention, 136, 139, 148, 151–52, 155–56; in Lincoln campaign, 185–86
Kreismann, Hermann, German Republican leader in Chicago, 109
Krekel, Arnold, German political leader, at "Opposition" convention in Jefferson City, 58; at Chicago convention, 155

Lamon, Ward Hill, Lincoln's one-time law partner, 78
"Land for the Landless," campaign leaflet, 13; Democratic party's hostility emphasized, 83; as an issue in Minnesota, 117, 178
Land-grants to railroads, 10
Lane, Henry Smith, nominee for governor of Indiana, at Chicago convention, 141, 154–55, 157, 159–60, 163; in Lincoln campaign, 196, 198–99; elected governor, 201
Lane, Gen. James Henry, 87
Lane, Joseph, senator from Oregon, nominated for Vice-President by conventions at Baltimore and Richmond, 135, 172–73, 194–95, 199–201
Lecompton, Kan., constitutional convention adopts a pro-slavery document, 121
Lecompton constitution, causes break between Buchanan and Douglas, 121; in California politics, 123–24; in Mississippi, 129; 97, 175, 222
Leib, Charles, Cameron lieutenant in Illinois, 101–2
Lewis, Joseph J., prints autobiography of Lincoln in the *Chester County Times*, 76
Liberty party, organized by James Birney, elects Chase to U. S. Senate, 36; in Vermont, 191
Lincoln, Abraham (16th Pres. of U.S.), on John Brown, 20, 80; Illinois' "favorite son" for presidency, 48; his early life, 69–70; defeated for U. S. Senate by Douglas, 71; attitude toward nomination for President, 72–73; his views on tariff,

74–75; letter on taking second place on ticket, 75; letter to Judd exonerating him of treachery, 78–79; speaks at Cooper Institute in New York, 80–81, 224; speaks in New England, 81; appeals to Trumbull to help governorship campaign in Connecticut, 82; is acceptable to Germans, 84; letter to Trumbull, 85–86; letter to Delahay, 86–87; letter to Trumbull in behalf of Delahay, 87; letter to Galloway, 88; acquires name of "Rail-Splitter," 90; cold to offer of second place, 101; status as candidate for presidential nomination, 106 ff.; name before Chicago convention, 139 ff.; nominated on third ballot, 166; letter on spelling of his given name, 168; his campaign, 169 ff.; elected, 218; goes home to tell his wife, 219; summary of his campaign, 225–27; 18, 21, 35, 61, 65, 224

Lincoln, Robert, elder son of the President, 81; dubbed the "Prince of Rails," 182

Lincoln-Douglas debates, 77, 89, 224

"Lincoln, the Pride of the Nation," song in Lincoln campaign, 175

Locofocos (Democrats), 67

Log cabin, popular symbol for Lincoln, 169

Logan, Stephen Trigg, Lincoln's onetime law partner, at Chicago convention, 139

Lopez, Narciso, Venezuelan "general," in filibustering expeditions against Cuba, 15

Lovejoy, Owen, congressman from Illinois, agitates for free land, 182–83, 186

Low, G., mentioned, 215

Lowell, James Russell, on Edward Everett, 190

Mail facilities, sectional aspects, 10; controversy over routes, 11; over-

land subsidy proposed, 11–12; measure vetoed by Buchanan, 12

Maine-lawism, an element of Know-Nothingism, 107–8

Marcy, William Learned, Secretary of State, and the Ostend Manifesto, 15

Mason, James Murray, senator from Virginia, opposes homestead bill, 13

"Mass" convention, at Indianapolis, avoids name "Republican," 63–64; at Pittsburgh, to organize a Republican party, 94

Massachusetts, its 1860 population, 108

McClure, Alexander Kelly, Republican state chairman of Pennsylvania, 34, 104; at Chicago convention, 154, 158; in Lincoln campaign, 202–3; in Pennsylvania governorship fight, 205; seeking funds for campaign, 206

McLane, Robert Milligan, minister to Mexico, negotiates treaty, 17

McLean, Justice John, dissents in Dred Scott decision, 4–5; sought presidential nomination in 1856 Republican convention, supported by Lincoln, 43, 71; put forward for the 1860 convention, 49, 85, 111–13, 118; his name in Chicago convention, 139 ff.; 86, 88–90, 95, 181, 223

McPike, Henry, describes scene in Springfield on news of Lincoln's election, 219

Medill, Joseph, letter on Lincoln, 73–74; comes out for Lincoln in editorial in his Chicago Press & Tribune, 76–77; publishes Lincoln's Cooper Institute address in pamphlet form, 81; undermining Seward in Illinois, 84; at Chicago convention, 139, 154, 160, 165–66; reprints editorial from Baltimore Turn-Zeitung, 157; biography quoted, 158; 82–83, 169

Mercury (Charleston, S. C.), 127–28

Mercury (Newark, N. J.), 196

Mexican War, 127

Mexico, its acquisition desired by southerners, 16; treaty with U. S., 17

Miller, Stephen, at Chicago convention, 151

"Minute Men," Bell supporters, 174

Mississippi, political trends, 129; turns against Douglas, 130

Missouri Compromise, declared unconstitutional, 4–5; its repeal included in Kansas-Nebraska bill, 24–25, 37–39, 70; its opponents, 40; 183, 212, 220, 222

Missouri Statesman, 58

Mitchell, Mr., 46, 48

Morgan, Christopher, in Lincoln campaign, 180

Morgan, Edwin Dennison, governor of New York, his leadership of the Republican party, 17–18; at Chicago convention, 148; in Lincoln campaign, 171; renominated for governor, 211; 20

Mormons mentioned, 196

Morrill, Justin Smith, sponsors tariff bill, 7, 189, 206–7; his land-grant bill beaten in Senate, 14; in Lincoln campaign, 191–92; in Pennsylvania governorship fight, 205

Morrill, Lot Myrick, at Chicago convention, 144

Morrill tariff bill, its effect in Pennsylvania, 206–8

Morton, Oliver Hazard Perry Throck, urges high tariff, 7–8

"Mozart Hall," Fernando Wood's party in New York City, elects him mayor, 132; merges with its foes in support of Douglas, 212; in contest over governorship, 214

Muench, Frederick, at Chicago convention, 155

National Democratic Committee, formed for the Breckinridge-Lane ticket, 172

"National Democratic Volunteers," 174

National Era (Washington), publishes "Appeal of Independent Democrats," 38

Native Americans movement in New York, 25; in Ohio, 41; supports Cameron for senator, 92; at Chicago convention, 137

Naturalization as a political issue, 152; in the Chicago platform, 153

Negro question disclaimed in Lincoln campaign, 188

Negroes, scheme for colonizing the emancipated, 53–54, 60–61, 66–67

New Jersey, in Lincoln campaign, 195–96

New York, as decisive factor in Lincoln campaign, 209–10

Nicholson, Thomas, "Union" candidate defeated for canal commissioner in Pennsylvania, 94

Nicolay, John George, 197

North American (Philadelphia), makes protectionism paramount issue in Pennsylvania, 206

Noyes, William Curtis, 80

Nye, James Warren, replaces Dudley Field as delegate to Chicago convention, 33

Oberkline, F., German leader in Cincinnati, 187

Oglesby, Richard James, introduces Lincoln to the Republican convention at Decatur, 90

Ohio, the October elections, 182

Ohio State Journal (Columbus), uses name "Republican" for state fusion candidates, 39

"Old Gentlemen's Party," Greeley's designation of the Constitutional Union party, 119

Old Line Guard, campaign newspaper, 199

Old-Line Whigs, in Wisconsin governorship election, 45; refuse to concede the Whig party was dead, 54; opposed to Douglas, 184; their organ the Boston *Courier* in financial difficulties, 190; 21–22, 55–59, 62, 95, 168, 183, 211, 225

Olden, Charles Smith, elected governor of New Jersey, 195

Opdyke, George, at Chicago convention, 139; member of New York State Central Committee, 211

"Opposition," groups opposed to the administration Democrats, 21, 54–56; endorse Judge Bates for President at Jefferson City convention, 58; New Jersey convention names Dayton as "favorite son," 114, 142–43; 195

Oregon, represented at Chicago convention by non-residents, 137; carried by Lincoln, 194–95

Ostend Manifesto, and the offer to purchase Cuba, 15–16

Ottendorfer, Oswald, German Douglas leader, 214

Otto, Judge William Tod, at Chicago convention, 142, 148

Overland mail, private company to be granted subsidy, 10–11; conflict over routes, 11–12; measure vetoed by Buchanan, made an issue in presidential campaign, 12; as a political issue, 17, 152, 220; in Lincoln campaign, 188–89

Pacific railroad, controversy over routes, 10; as a political issue, 17, 22, 54, 150, 152, 220; California's principal concern, 123; in Lincoln campaign, 176, 180, 188

Padelford, Seth, defeated for governor of Rhode Island, 82

Paine, Robert F., 112

Palmer, John McAuley, at Chicago convention, 139, 143

Panic of 1857, laid to low tariff, 7

Parker, Theodore, proposes formation of anti-slavery party, 26

Parrott, Marcus Junius, 88

Patriot (Baltimore), supports Bates for presidential nomination, 66

Pennington, William, elected Speaker of the House of Representatives, 66

Pennsylvania, as political battleground,

114; in Lincoln campaign, 201–3; governorship fight, 205–8

Pennsylvanian (Philadelphia), Buchanan organ, 206

People's party, opposition to Democrats in Pennsylvania, 21; victorious, 29–30; endorses Cameron for presidential nomination, 33–34, 100, 104; party organized in Delaware, holds convention in Dover, and sends Bates delegates to Chicago convention, 67; merges "Americans" and Republicans, 97; convention in Harrisburg, 103–4; in Lincoln campaign, 202; 123

Phillips, David L., 85

Phillips, Wendell, 18

Pierce, Franklin (14th Pres. of U. S.), signs subsidy bill for trans-Atlantic telegraph cable, 6; the Ostend Manifesto, and the offer to purchase Cuba, 15–16; defeats Gen. Scott for the presidency, 24; removes Gov. Reeder of Kansas Territory, 96; 22, 42

Pinner, Moritz, Jewish editor of a Kansas City German-language newspaper, opposes the candidacy of Judge Bates, 60

Platform of the Chicago convention, 148 ff., 224

Plymouth Church, Brooklyn, 79

Polk, James Knox, 11th Pres. of U. S.), 6

Pollock, James, elected governor of Pennsylvania, 92

Pony Express, established by private parties, 12

"Popular sovereignty" of Douglas, 115, 126, 130, 134

Pratt, Daniel Darwin, delegate to Chicago convention, 102

Press & Tribune (Chicago), preaches protection, 8; attacks Secretary of the Treasury Cobb, 9; offers Lincoln-Cameron ticket, 102; injects religious issue into Lincoln campaign, 185–86; 73, 77, 82, 84, 139, 160

Protection, as a political issue, 6–7, 17; adopted to cater to Pennsylvania, 8, 30; dominant concern, 96; endorsed by People's party, 104, 123; Philadelphia *North American* makes it paramount issue in Pennsylvania, 206

"Protestantism, Temperance, and Liberty," policy of Know-Nothings, 107

Pugh, George Ellis, senator from Ohio, 8

Putnam, James Osborne, leader of "Americans," supports Lincoln, 211–12

Quakers, preaching against slavery, 95–96

"Rail Maulers," in Lincoln campaign, 197

"Rail-Splitter," how Lincoln acquired the name, 90; popular symbol in his campaign, 169

Rail-Splitter, The, campaign sheet for Lincoln, 169

Railway building, federal aid sought, 10

Ramsey, Alexander, seeking nomination for President, 116–18; elected governor of Minnesota, 117; 178

Ray, Charles H., of the *Chicago Press & Tribune,* at Chicago convention, 139, 158

Raymond, Henry Jarvis, opposes Kansas-Nebraska bill in his New York *Times,* 25; at Pittsburgh meeting of the Republican party, 28; accuses Greeley of blocking Seward's nomination, 210

Read, Judge John Meredith, seeking nomination for President, 114, 118; gets one vote at Chicago convention, 163; 73

Reeder, Andrew Horatio, removed from governorship of Kansas Territory by President Pierce, 96; nominates Cameron at Chicago convention, 162

Religious issue, injected into Lincoln campaign, 185–86; in New York governorship fight, 213

"Republican" as a party name, 107

Republican (Springfield, Mass.), on the formation of the Republican party, 108; 111, 143

Republican Association of Washington, coöperating with the Republican National Committee, 18

Republican convention in Decatur, Ill., endorses Lincoln as "favorite son," 85, 90; originated rail-splitter background for Lincoln, 169

Republican convention in Syracuse declares for Seward for President, 33; later convention buries hatchet for duration of Lincoln campaign, 211

Republican National Convention of 1856, in Philadelphia, nominates Frémont for President, 4, 29, 43

Republican National Convention of 1860, in Chicago, 59, 66, 68, 135; its proceedings, 136 ff.; nominations begin, 162; balloting, 162–65; Lincoln nominated on third ballot, 166

Republican party, its appearance on the stage with an anti-slavery program, and make-up of its leaders, 3, 25; nominates Frémont for President, 4; platform demands internal improvements, 8; overland mail an issue in 1860 campaign, 12; leaders accused of instigating John Brown's raid, 19–20; elect Chase governor of Ohio, he seeks presidential nomination, 41–43; groups composing party in Wisconsin, 45; becomes strong through Democratic dissensions, 120; organized in California, 123; regarded as a sectional body by the South, 128–29; national convention of 1860 meets in Chicago,

136 ff.; nominates Lincoln and Hamlin, 166–67

Republican state convention in Baltimore, called by the Blairs, 66–67

Rhett, Robert Barnwell, editor of the Charleston *Mercury*, states' rights leader in South Carolina, 127–28

Richardson, William Alexander, friend of Douglas, 120–21

Richmond, Dean, chief of the "Albany Regency" in New York, opposes Fernando Wood's delegation at Charleston convention, 132–33; in coalition with Wood and Tammany in support of Douglas, 212, 215

Richmond, convention nominates Breckinridge and Joseph Lane for President and Vice-President, 134–35

Richmond House, Chicago, 138

Riggs, George Washington, supports Breckinridge-Lane ticket, 173

Rivers-and-harbors, appropriations favored by Republicans, 8; as a political issue, 150, 152; in Lincoln campaign, 176, 180

Rivers and Harbors convention in Chicago, 51

Roman Catholics, their political affiliations in Lincoln campaign, 185–87

"Rome, Rum, and Robbery," in Know-Nothing warfare, 107

St. *Joseph Valley Register* (South Bend, Ind.), supports Judge Bates's candidacy, 62

Sanderson, John Philip, of the Philadelphia *Daily News*, at Chicago convention, 158

Schafer, Dr. Joseph, 187

Schell, Augustus, supports Breckinridge-Lane ticket, 173, 213

Schneider, George, editor of the Chicago *Staats-Zeitung*, 156, 185

Schouler, William, editor of the Cincinnati *Gazette*, 39

Schurz, Carl, attracts German voters in Wisconsin, 45; delegate to Chicago convention, 47; in Chicago municipal campaign, 83; his attitude on candidates, 112; in Minnesota campaign on homestead issue, 117; at Chicago convention, 136, 148–49; seconds Seward's nomination, 162; in Lincoln campaign, 171, 198; in Pennsylvania governorship fight, 205; 20, 46, 152, 179–80, 185

Scott, Gen. Winfield, defeated for the presidency by Pierce, 24, 37, 220; blow to the Whigs, 45; 70

Secession, its early manifestations, 20, 128–29

Sentinel (Milwaukee), 47; supports Lincoln, 180

Seward, William Henry, attacks Supreme Court on Dred Scott decision, 5; accuses Pierce of offering to purchase Cuba from Spain, 15–16; elected governor of New York, 23; goes to U. S. Senate, 24; joins Republican party, 26–27; fails of presidential nomination in 1856 convention, 28; his "Irrepressible Conflict" address, 29; is acclaimed "the next President" on his return from Europe, 31; accused of complicity in John Brown's raid, 32; seeking nomination for President in 1860 convention, 33 *passim;* his name in Chicago convention, 138 ff.; announces himself for Lincoln, 168; in the campaign, 181 ff.; in contest to win New York, 210; 18–19, 25, 30

Seward-Fillmore feud, 220

"Seward, Weed & Greeley" as a political firm, 62, 210

Seymour, Horatio, possible Democratic standard-bearer, 212

Sherman, James T., at Chicago convention, 159; 113–14

Sherman, John, in contest for Speaker of the House of Representatives, 19;

in Pennsylvania governorship fight, 205; 218

Sibley, Hiram, obtains subsidy for transcontinental telegraph, 10

Simmons, James Fowler, senator from Rhode Island, at Chicago convention, 145–46

Slavery question, 4–5, 51, 126; a campaign issue, 18, 21, 39, 41, 43, 96, 108, 131, 150, 222; in the Chicago platform, 153; in Lincoln campaign, 187–88, 195–96; in Pennsylvania, 206; in Northwest, 220

Slaves, protection demanded for them as property, 134

Slidell, John, senator from Louisiana, 14; offers appropriation bill for purchase of Cuba, 16; dispenser of patronage in Buchanan administration, 120; out to crush Douglas, 128; at the Charleston convention, 130–31

Smith, Caleb Blood, at Chicago convention, 136, 141–42; seconds nomination of Lincoln, 162; 163, 197, 224

Smith, Prof. Donnal Vore, 187

Smith, Erasmus Peshine, opposed to "Americans," 30

Smith, Gerrit, abolitionist, 18–19; runs for President on anti-slavery and temperance platform, 173, 191

"Soft" and "hard" Democratic factions in New York, 212–14

Soulé, Pierre, senator from Louisiana, appointed minister to Spain, 15; at the Charleston convention, 130

"Southern rights" issue, 126–27; party headed by Yancey in Alabama, 128–29, 223; in Mississippi, 129; in other slave states, 130; at the Charleston convention, 131, 133–34

Spaulding, Elbridge Gerry, congressman from New York, 34

"Squatter sovereignty" of Douglas, 74, 128

Staats-Zeitung (Chicago), 156, 185

State Journal (Columbus, O.), supports Lincoln, 182

State Sentinel (Indianapolis), opposes Lincoln, 197–98

Statesman (Albany, N. Y.), 211

States' rights issue, 127

Stevens, Thaddeus, congressman from Pennsylvania, at Chicago convention, 139, 155

Stout, Lansing, congressman from Oregon, in Douglas campaign, 195

Stowe, Harriet Beecher, her Uncle Tom's Cabin appeal, 18

Sub-National Committee of the Republican National Committee conducts Lincoln campaign, 171, 184

Subsidies for rivers and harbors favored by Republicans, 8

Sumner, Charles, senator from Massachusetts, assaulted by Congressman Brooks, 4, 221–22; letters from Cassius M. Clay, 115–16; gets one vote in Chicago convention, 163; in Lincoln campaign, 171; 24, 37–38, 43–44, 61, 108–9

Swan, Judge Joseph Rockwell, of Ohio, 39

Swett, Leonard, candidate for governor of Illinois, 78; at Chicago convention, 139, 158; in Lincoln campaign, 202–3

Swift, W. H., 91

Switzler, Col. William Franklin, "American" leader and editor of the Missouri Statesman, at "Opposition" convention in Jefferson City, 58; opposed to Judge Bates's candidacy, 61

Tammany Hall, contests Fernando Wood's delegation at Charleston convention, 132; in coalition with Wood and Dean Richmond in support of Douglas, 212; contest over New York governorship, 214

Taney, Roger Brooke, Chief Justice, decision in Dred Scott case and Missouri Compromise, 5

Tariff of 1857, 7; tariff for revenue, 47; tariff as a political issue, 150,

176, 182, 220; in Chicago platform, 189; Morrill tariff bill in Congress, and its effect in Pennsylvania, 206–8

Taylor, Hawkins, delegate to Chicago convention, 87

Taylor, Zachary (12th Pres. of U. S.), 69, 112, 118; his death, 24, 88

Telegraph (Harrisburg), denounces anti-slavery extremists, 95; reprints New York *Herald* editorial on Cameron for President, 98; prints similar articles from other papers, 99; editorial "Cameron for President," 100

Telegraph facilities, sectional aspects, subsidy granted, 10

Temperance, as a political issue, 24–25, 37; dominates Wisconsin election for governor, 45

Terry, David Smith, kills Senator Broderick in duel, 124, 194

Thayer, Eli, congressman from Massachusetts, represents Oregon at Chicago convention, 137

Thompson, Richard Wigginton, in Lincoln campaign, 200–1

Tilden, Samuel Jones, his analysis of Lincoln's victory, 218

Times (N. Y.), opposes Kansas-Nebraska bill, 25; 28, 210

Toombs, Robert, senator from Georgia, opposes subsidy by Congress for trans-Atlantic telegraph cable, 6; his scheme for Mexican policy, 16; at the Charleston convention, 133

Torches in Lincoln campaign, 174

Trans-Atlantic telegraph cable, subsidy granted by Congress, 6; as a political issue, 17

Transcontinental telegraph, subsidy granted by Congress, 10; as a political issue, 17

Treat, Samuel, friend of Douglas, 120

Tremont House, Chicago, 87, 91, 138, 148–49, 157

Tribune (Detroit), supports Lincoln, 180

Tribune (N. Y.), mouthpiece of the Whig party, 23; takes up temperance movement, 24; opposes Kansas-Nebraska bill, 25; supports Judge Bates for presidential nomination, 62, 64; gets original manuscript of Lincoln's Cooper Institute address, 81; tract *American Agriculture and Its Interest in the Protective Policy*, 189; announces Republican triumph, 218; 14, 31, 137, 176–78, 192, 210

Trumbull, Lyman, senator from Illinois, appealed to by Lincoln to aid governorship campaign in Connecticut, 82; gets news of Lincoln's election, 219; 9–11, 69, 71–72, 77, 83, 85, 87, 89, 188

Turn-Zeitung (Baltimore), declares for Lincoln, 84; editorial on Lincoln as a final recourse, 157

"Two Year Amendment" in Massachusetts, 45, 48, 59, 108–9, 153, 156, 198

Uncle Tom's Cabin, by Harriet Beecher Stowe, its appeal, 18, 222

Union (Washington), Buchanan organ, 122

"Union Sentinels," Bell supporters, 174

"Unionism" as an issue, 220

Usher, John Palmer, Secretary of the Interior, 89

Van Buren, Martin (8th Pres. of U. S.), nominated for President on "Free Soil" ticket, 36

Vermont, in Lincoln campaign, 191–92

Wade, Benjamin Franklin, senator from Ohio, 9; "favorite son" for presidential nomination, 49, 111–13, 118; his name in the Chicago convention, 146 ff.; 24, 37, 168, 181

Wadsworth, James Samuel, mentioned for vice-presidential nomination, 112

"Walker" tariff act, 6–7

Wallace, Dr. Edward, sounds Lincoln on tariff views, 74

War between the states, interpretation of causes, 29

Webster, Daniel, mentioned, 27

Warren, Dr. Louis Austin, 81

Weed, Thurlow, organizes the Anti-Masonic party in New York, 23; his "call to arms," 24; seeking the elusive Cameron, 34; leads Seward delegation to Chicago convention, 35, 138, 141, 154, 157, 164; in Lincoln campaign, 197–98, 203, 210, 217–18; 26–29, 31, 33, 50, 77, 98–99, 223

Welles, Gideon, leader of Connecticut Republicans, 114; at Chicago convention, 145; in Lincoln's Cabinet, 18

Wendell, Cornelius, testifies against Buchanan before a House committee, 125–26

Wentworth, "Long" John, congressman from Illinois, 8; as mayor of Chicago raids evil resorts and discovers convention delegates, 136; his paper declares for Seward, 138

Western lands in sectional conflict, 12–13

Western Reserve, as the home of isms, 112

Western Union Telegraph Co., 10

Westliche Post (St. Louis), 60

"Whig General Committee of New York," letter to, from Frank Blair, Jr., 55–56

Whig party, disappearing, 3, 26–27; its program of internal improvements adopted by Republican party, 8; efforts to resurrect party fail, 20; its newspaper mouthpieces in New York, 23; controlled New York legislature through Democratic split, 23–24; merges with Free Soilers, 37; end of the party in Wisconsin, 45; convention in Lexington, Mo., endorses Judge Bates for presidential nomination, 58; allied with Know-Nothings in Pennsylvania, 92; split on slavery issue, 106; destroyed by Kansas-Nebraska act, 114; 23, 25–26, 40, 61, 65, 70, 93, 129, 169

"White" campaign in Missouri, 53–54

"White Man's Party," claimed for Republicans by northwestern press, 188

"Wide-Awakes," Republican groups, 173–74, 181, 185, 190, 195, 197

"Wigwam," in Chicago, meeting-place of the Republican National Convention of 1860, 136, 148, 160–61, 166

Williams, Thomas, congressman from Pennsylvania, 21

Williamson, Passmore, elected canal commissioner of Pennsylvania, 94

Wilmot, David, senator from Pennsylvania, 80; calls state Republican convention to select delegates to Chicago convention, 95; at the convention, 136, 148–49, 157–58

Wilmot Proviso, 127–28

Wilson, Henry, in Lincoln campaign, 171; speaks in New York, 218; 108

Winnebago Indians, their claims adjusted by Cameron with depreciated notes, 103

Wisconsin, homestead issue a primary interest, 179

Wise, Henry Alexander, governor of Virginia, 19–20

Wiss, George E., German-American leader, delegate to the Chicago convention, 67

Wood, Fernando, mayor of New York City, his version of John Brown's raid, 19–20; elected by Tammany, is refused renomination, organizes his own party as "Mozart Hall," and is again elected, 132; his delegation to the Charleston convention shut out, 133; reconciled with his foes and supports Douglas, 212–13; 215

Yancey, William Lowndes, states' rights leader in Alabama, resigns his seat in Congress, 127; introduces the "Alabama Platform" at the Democratic National Convention of 1848, 128; bolts Charleston convention, 131, 133–34; 129, 223

Yates, Richard, candidate for governor of Illinois, 78; at Chicago convention, 139

"Young Men's Frémont and Dayton Central Union," 80

Young Men's Republican Club of New York, 171

"Young Men's Republican Union," sponsors Lincoln's address in New York, 79–80